Jack A. McManemin III, CFP, is the author of the charts on these two pages. For more information, see page 6.

USE THIS PAGE IF SPOUSE IS THE BENEFICIARY

Beneficiary	Minimum Required Distributions
C. **Spouse** [For extent, if any, to which a trust for the benefit of spouse can qualify for special spousal rules, see *"When is a trust for the spouse the same as the spouse?"* Chapter 6.]	1) **Term Certain (owner and spouse)** -Acc't balance 12/31 of previous year divided by joint life expectancy. Reduce life expectancy by one each year. 2) **Recalculate (owner and spouse)** - Acc't balance 12/31 of previous year divided by joint life expectancy. Check IRS table VI (App. A) each year for new joint life expectancy based on attained age of each spouse that year. If spouse dies, switch to (A)(2) in following year. 3) **Recalculate owner & Term Certain spouse (hybrid)** - Acc't balance 12/31 of previous year divided by "adjusted joint life expectancy." 4) **Term Certain owner & Recalculate spouse (hybrid)** - Acc't balance 12/31 of previous year divided by "adjusted joint life expectancy."

3. MDIB (Minimum Distribution Incidental Benefit) Rule limits the LE spread (between owner and beneficiary) to 10 years for calculating lifetime required minimum distributions. See Chapter 1.

4. For requirements of a "qualified" trust see Chapter 6.

D1254105

What's new in this edition........

As compared with the 1996 edition (and <u>1998 Supplement</u>):

<u>Completely NEW material:</u> All of Chapter 9 (Pre-Age 59½ Distributions). Distributions of employer stock (Chapter 2). The Koslow, Stoltz and Mandel case studies in Chapter 11. Trust review checklist, Appendix C. Charts inside front and back covers (see "Acknowledgments").

<u>Completely REVISED material:</u> Chapter 4 (Non-Citizen Spouse). Charitable contributions (Chapter 7). Lump sum distributions (Chapter 2). Retirement benefits payable to trusts (Chapter 6). Chapter 5 (Roth IRAs) is completely revised since *The 1998 Supplement* to reflect the 1998 Technical Corrections law and IRS regulations. Chapter 3: "The Spouse and § 401(a)(9)." Able and Fallon case studies, Chapter 11. Appendix A charts.

<u>Completely UPDATED:</u> Chapter 1, The Minimum Distribution Rules. Chapter 8, Disclaimers. Non-LSD parts of Chapter 2. Life Insurance (Chapter 10). Forms, App. B

<u>Cut back or eliminated altogether:</u> Old Chapter 5 on the 15% excise tax, and all other reference to this tax. The "Grandfathers" (old Chapter 7, now in Chapter 10). Cavalho, Dingell, Eaton, Heinrich, Levine and Valdez case studies, Chapter 11.

The following portions of this book, in the form of articles by the author, were previously published in the following journals:

Chapter 2: "Mysteries of IRD," <u>Tax Management Memorandum</u> Vol. 38, No. 20, page 235 (Tax Management Inc., Washington, D.C., 9/29/97).

Chapter 5: "Roth IRAs: 1998 Technical Corrections and New Proposed IRS Regulations," <u>Tax Practitioner's Journal</u>, Vol. 5, No. 3, p. 16 (NADP, Appleton WI, Fall 1998).

Life and Death Planning
for Retirement Benefits

The Essential Handbook for Estate Planners

**Third Edition, Completely Revised
1999**

Natalie B. Choate

Ataxplan Publications, Boston, Massachusetts

For future updates of this book, visit our website:

www.ataxplan.com

Life and Death Planning for Retirement Benefits

The Essential Handbook for Estate Planners
Third edition, completely revised

By Natalie B. Choate

Published by: Ataxplan Publications
                  Post Office Box 1093-K
                  Boston, Massachusetts 02103-1093

Copyright © 1999 by Natalie B. Choate
Printed in the United States of America

Publisher's Cataloging-in-Publication Data
Choate, Natalie B.
        Life and Death Planning for Retirement Benefits: The Essential Handbook for Estate Planners— 3rd ed. / Natalie B. Choate
        p.   cm.
Includes bibliographical references and index.

ISBN 0-9649440-3-0

        1. Estate planning - United States. 2. Tax planning - United States. 3. Retirement income - Taxation - United States. 4. Inheritance and transfer tax - United States. I. Choate, Natalie B. II. Title

IF 6585 .C43 1999

To my mother

Jhan English Choate

who has had to put up with a lot

Warning and Disclaimer

The rules applicable to qualified retirement plan benefits and IRAs are among the most complex in the tax code. I have read few works on this subject that were, in my view, completely accurate; in fact most that I have seen, including, unfortunately, earlier incarnations of this work, contain errors. Furthermore, even accurate information can become outdated quickly as IRS or Congressional policy shifts. Despite my best efforts, it is likely that this book, too, contains errors. Citations are provided so that estate planning practitioners can check any statements made in this book and reach their own conclusions regarding what the law is.

This book is intended to provide general information regarding the tax and other laws applicable to retirement benefits, and to provide suggestions regarding appropriate estate planning actions for different situations. It is not intended as a substitute for the practitioner's own research, or for the advice of a qualified estate planning specialist. The author and publisher shall have neither liability nor responsibility to any person or entity with respect to any loss or damage caused, or alleged to be caused, directly or indirectly by the information contained in this book.

If you do not wish to be bound by the above, you may return this book to the publisher for a full refund.

Summary of Contents

Table of Contents

CHAPTER 1 - MIN. DIST. RULES, CONT.

CHAPTER 3 - MARITAL MATTERS, CONT.

CHAPTER 4 - NON-CITIZEN SPOUSE, CONT.

CHAPTER 5 - ROTH IRAS, CONT.

CHAPTER 7 - CHARITABLE GIVING, CONT.

CHAPTER 9 - PRE-59½ DISTRIBUTIONS, CONT.

Introduction

A major goal of estate planning for retirement benefits is to preserve the option of continued income tax deferral for the client's retirement plans for the longest period possible. The potential for continued income tax deferral after the death of the surviving spouse, over the multi-decade life expectancy of their children, is a valuable asset to be preserved. The goal will be achieved only if estate planners and their clients understand, and use to advantage, the rules governing plan distributions. Those rules are the subject of this book.

Limitations of this Book

Many important aspects of planning for retirement distributions are *not* covered in this book, such as annuity payouts, and investment alternatives and "financial planning" considerations generally. This book also does not cover the following topics: § 457 plans; qualified domestic relations orders (QDROs); stock options and other non-qualified forms of deferred compensation; ESOPs; spousal consent requirements; pre-nuptial agreements; creditors' rights; state tax issues; and community property. Other sources for some of these topics are mentioned in the Bibliography.

This book is designed to explain estate planning and tax planning issues for the benefit of estate and financial planners who are counseling individuals (and their beneficiaries) who have assets in retirement plans. It does not cover plan distribution issues which are of concern to plan administrators, but which do not have a significant impact on planning decisions for the individual participant, such as income tax withholding, rollover technicalities and distribution notice requirements.

This book deals with the *federal* tax law applicable to

retirement benefits, but in a few instances state law has a bearing on the subject. When state law has a significant impact, this book will describe the applicable law of Massachusetts (my home state). Planners in other states will need to determine the law applicable to their clients.

Explanation of Terms Used

Section numbers refer to the Internal Revenue Code of 1986 unless otherwise specified.

As used in this book, the term "retirement plan" refers to corporate and self-employed ("Keogh") pension, profit sharing and stock bonus plans that are "qualified" under § 401(a), as well as simplified employee plans (SEPs) under § 408(k), individual retirement accounts (IRAs) under § 408(a), and tax-sheltered annuity (or mutual fund) arrangements established under § 403(b). The narrower term "qualified plans" or "**qualified retirement plans**" includes only 401(a) plans.

The "participant" is the person whose benefits we are dealing with: the employee who has benefits in a pension or profit sharing plan, or for whom a tax-sheltered annuity was purchased; or the account-holder in the case of an IRA. For ease of understanding, throughout this book, except in some specific examples and case studies, the "participant" (P) is male and the feminine pronoun refers to the participant's spouse. Of course any statement would apply equally to a female participant and her male spouse.

Technical terms whose definition can be found in the Glossary are put in **bold** type the first time used in each chapter or section.

Abbreviations Used in this Book
(And where to find definitions)

5YFA	Five Year Forward Averaging; p. 102.
10YFA	Ten Year Forward Averaging ; p. 107.
Code	Internal Revenue Code of 1986.
COLA	Cost-Of-Living Adjustment.
CRT	Charitable Remainder Trust; p. 523.
DB	Designated Beneficiary; p. 13.
DNI	Distributable Net Income; p. 69.
GST tax	Generation Skipping Transfer tax; p. 525.
IRA	Individual Retirement Account; p. 2.
IRD	Income in Respect of a Decedent; p. 66.
IRS	Internal Revenue Service.
IRT	Individual Retirement Trust; p. 163.
LE	Life Expectancy; p. 50.
LSD	Lump Sum Distribution; p. 84.
MDIB rule	Minimum distribution incidental benefit rule; p. 36.
MRD	Minimum Required Distribution; p. 51.
P	Participant; p. 2.
PLR	IRS private letter ruling.
Prop. Reg.	Proposed Treasury Regulation (§ 1.401(a)(9)-1, unless otherwise indicated); p. 10.
QDRO	Qualified Domestic Relations Order; p. 1.
QJSA	Qualified Joint and Survivor Annuity; p. 304.
QPSA	Qualified Pre-retirement Survivor Annuity; p. 303.
QRP	Qualified Retirement Plan; p. 527.
RBD	Required Beginning Date; p. 21.
REA	Retirement Equity Act of 1984 (P. L. 98-397); p. 303.
S	Spouse.
TAMRA '88	The Technical and Miscellaneous Revenue Act of 1988 (P. L. 100-647).
TAPRA '97	Taxpayer Relief Act of 1997 (P. L. 105-34).
TEFRA '82	The Tax Equity and Fiscal Responsibility Act of 1982 (P. L. 97-248).
TRA '84	The Tax Reform Act of 1984 (P. L. 98-369).
TRA '86	The Tax Reform Act of 1986 (P. L. 99-514).
UCA '92	Unemployment Compensation Amendments of 1992 (P. L. 102-318).

How to Use Cross References

The book is divided into chapters. Chapters are divided into *sections* (with boldface, centered, larger-font headings and capitalized initials; see the title above). Sections are divided into *subsections* (italicized headings starting at left margin).

Cross references to other parts of the book are liberally provided. However, until you have read Chapter 1, the rest of the book will not be usable. The minimum distribution rules terminology explained in Chapter 1 is so essential and pervasive that it is not cross referenced every time.

If the cross reference is to a chapter, the chapter number is given; the reference means that item is discussed generally in that chapter. If the reference is to a section or subsection, the title of the section or subsection is given, so you can look it up in the table of contents. So you know what you are looking for, if the cross referenced title is *italicized*, that means it is a subsection; otherwise it is a section.

So you will know *where* to look, if the referenced section or subsection is in another chapter, the reference will give the number. If no chapter number is given, the referenced section or subsection is in the same chapter, either "above" (earlier in the chapter) or "below" (later in the chapter).

Case studies in Chapter 11 illustrate the planning principles and real life issues created by the labyrinth of rules discussed in the earlier chapters. Throughout the book, the text contains cross references to related case studies in Chapter 11.

Appendix B provides beneficiary designation forms for some common situations, along with some related trust provisions and other miscellaneous forms suggested in the text. Whenever a drafting suggestion or planning idea in the text is illustrated by a form in Appendix B, that form is cross-referenced. If there is no form reference, you can assume no form is provided.

Other Hints for Using this Book

There are many "gray areas" in the tax treatment of retirement benefits—questions the regulations simply do not answer; points of law subject to different interpretations; or regulatory positions that seem contrary to law or for some other reason likely to be changed in the future. When a practitioner encounters one of these in practice, the response may differ depending on whether he is doing advance planning for a client, or is dealing with a *fait accompli*. For this reason, from time to time in this book, in suggesting ways to deal with an issue, I distinguish between "planning mode" and "cleanup mode."

"<u>Planning mode</u>" deals with advance planning, and suggests a "safe harbor" course of action—the steps that should produce a predictable result and offer peace of mind. "<u>Cleanup mode</u>" deals with the *fait accompli* situation: when it is too late for advance planning, usually because the participant has already died or passed his "required beginning date." In cleanup mode, a more aggressive position may be appropriate on the issue, since there is often nothing to lose. Here, we want to consider every possible argument which may enhance or preserve the value of the retirement benefits for the client and his family.

At the end of each chapter, there is a summary of the planning principles developed in that chapter. Bear in mind that most of these are general guidelines which do not apply to every case. The more detailed discussion in the chapter provides the basis for these principles, and points out limitations and exceptions.

Acknowledgments

The McManemin charts

While Chapter 1 explains the "minimum distribution rules" of § 401(a)(9) perfectly, many readers of the 1996 edition requested charts that would summarize that chapter in an easy reference format. I never got around to preparing those, so I was delighted when Jack McManemin III, CFP, sent me the neat 2-page summary chart he had prepared. I found Jack's charts eminently readable and concise—just what the doctor ordered.

With his permission, I have modified his charts (to fit into, and conform to the style of, *Life and Death Planning for Retirement Benefits*), and the modified versions appear inside the front (Lifetime Distributions) and back (Post-death Distributions) covers of this book. The originals are even better, with color and more information. Laminated, they make a nice handout to staff or clients. For license or purchase info, please contact Jack directly at 3760 Highland Dr., Suite 400, Salt Lake City, UT 84106, 801-273-3310.

Reviewers and contributors

I gratefully acknowledge, and thank, the estate and retirement planning professionals who contributed their comments, ideas and suggestions to make this a better book.

Above and beyond the help one could reasonably hope to receive from volunteer "peer reviewers," Guerdon T. Ely, MBA, CFP, of Silver Oak Advisory Group (fee-only financial advisors), Chico, California, and Michael Jones, CPA, of Monterey, California, re-ran number-intensive case studies and examples throughout the book, and thereby killed a number of bugs; and Ellen K. Harrison, Esq., of Morgan, Lewis & Bockius LLP, Washington, DC, made major contributions to Chapter 4.

I am very grateful to the lawyers and others who took the time to review parts of the 1999 or 1996 edition and give me their comments, most of which led directly to improvements in the work (although I retain responsibility for all deficiencies in the finished product): Virginia Coleman, Esq., Ropes & Gray, Boston; Paul Frimmer, Esq., Irell & Manella, Los Angeles; Randall J. Gingiss, Esq., Katten, Muchin & Zavis, Chicago; Zoe M. Hicks, Esq., Hicks & Montgomery, Atlanta; Jerold I. Horn, Esq., Peoria, IL; Larry Katzenstein, Esq., Thompson Coburn, St. Louis; James H. Landon, Esq., Jones, Day, Reavis & Pogue, Atlanta; my Bingham Dana LLP colleague George Mair, Esq.; Al Martin, Esq., Shook, Hardy & Bacon LLP, Overland Park, KS; Ronald T. Martin, Esq., University of Miami Law School; David W. Polstra, CFP, Polstra & Dardamon, LLC, Norcross, GA; Michael G. Riley, Esq., McDonald, Hopkins, Burke & Haber, Cleveland; Kathleen R. Sherby of Bryan Cave LLP, St. Louis; Lee Slavutin, M.D., C.P.C., Stern Slavutin 2, Inc., New York; and Mark W. Worthington, Esq., Worcester, MA.

Many thanks also to the sharp-eyed people who alerted me to things in the first edition that needed fixing: Steven M. Glovsky, Stephen Koster and Barry Picker.

In over twenty years of consciously or unknowingly gathering material for this book, and in the years since publication of the prior edition, I have talked with, listened to, or read the work of hundreds of estate planners, actuaries, accountants, lawyers, financial planners, retirees, trust officers, mutual fund personnel, plan administrators, IRS and DOL staffers, plan participants and writers who have studied the subject matter. Since almost everyone who spends time thinking about these issues or working with the actual problems of real life employers and employees has some interesting and new insight into the subject, I have learned from almost every encounter. I would like to mention everyone who added to my understanding of retirement plan issues, but am limited to those whose names and contributions I managed to note and remember (and to the rest I apologize). Thank you:

Since the 1996 edition: William O. Allen, Ed Brennan, Carl Brooks, David Foster, Nancy Nearing Go, Sy Goldberg, Al Golden, Wells Hall, Beth Kaufman, Bob Keebler, John Kimpel, John Newton, Wilson C. Piper, Brian Quinn, Richard Popper, Marvin Rotenberg, Pam Schneider, Ed Slott, David Snyder and Margaret Welch.

From the 1996 edition: Deborah Bailin, Ken Bergen, Carol Brown, Jeffrey M. Brown, Virginia Coleman, Steve Crispigna, George Cushing, James S. Davis, Andrew Fair, David Fine, Bob Freedman, Jack Green, Gabriel Heiser, Marcia Chadwick Holt, Arnold Hunnewell, Patricia Hurley, Russell Isaia, Judy Jarashow, Raymond E. Johnson, Bill Kirchick, Harry F. Lee, Dick Marcil, Colin Marshall, Ronald Martin, Tom McCord, Lou Mezzullo, Clint Monts de Oca, Guy Moss, Tim Nay, Jeffrey Pennell, Joan Politi, Charles Rosebrock, Mary Rowland, Donald O. Smith, Anne Q. Spaulding, Lawrence O. Spaulding, Jr., Bob Starr, Bruce J. Temkin, Harvey B. Wallace II, Mervin Wilf, Mark W. Worthington, John Yagjian and William P. Young.

I used to wonder why authors thanked their typists. Now having had first hand experience (twice!) with the fantastic dedication and skill of the principal "word processor" of this book, Maureen Cash, I know. I relied heavily on her problem-solving ability and perfectionism, as well as the skills, professionalism and hard work of the others who worked on the production of the manuscript: in chronological order, Jeri Arbo, Sheila Irvine, Pat Longo and Joan Breen.

Special thanks to a special person
my husband
Ian M. Starr

The Minimum Distribution Rules

The minimum distribution rules of § 401(a)(9) dictate how quickly (or slowly) benefits come out of retirement plans. Understanding these rules is the key to successful tax planning for retirement benefits.

Introduction

Meet § 401(a)(9)

Congress wants tax-favored retirement plans to be *retirement* plans—not estate-building, wealth transfer vehicles. To promote its favored result, Congress enacted § 401(a)(9), which compels certain annual minimum distributions from plans beginning generally at age 70½ or (if earlier) at death. Failure to distribute the required minimum results in a 50% excise tax on amounts that should have been distributed but were not. § 4974.

There are really two sets of "minimum distribution rules," dealing with two totally distinct situations: one set of rules applies when the plan participant (P) dies before his "required beginning date." See "Death Before the RBD: The Five Year Rule." The other set of rules deals with distributions required *during life, i.e.,* distribution of "retirement benefits," when P reaches his "required beginning date." See "The RBD: Required Lifetime Distributions."

From the estate planner's point of view, the minimum distribution rules generate two concerns. First, the planner must make sure that the participant or beneficiary complies with the minimum distribution rules by withdrawing each year at least the amount required by these rules, to avoid the 50% excise tax. Second, in addition to telling us how much the participant must take out of the plan each year, the minimum distribution rules contain substantial material dealing with designating a beneficiary for retirement plan death benefits. The designation of a beneficiary for death benefits must satisfy various rules if the client wants the option of postponing income taxation of the benefits for the longest possible time.

The proposed regulations

On July 27, 1987, the IRS issued proposed regulations § 1.401(a)(9)-1 & 2 and § 54.4974-2, interpreting and implementing the minimum distribution rules. These proposed regulations were amended in December 1997; see Chapter 6. Most of the proposed regulations are addressed to qualified plans. Under the congressional mandate that "similar rules" shall apply to IRAs and **403(b)** plans (§§ 408(a)(6), 403(b)(10)), the IRS has made the 401(a)(9) proposed regulations applicable to these other types of plans as well, with certain variations. See Prop. Reg. § 1.408-8, A-1 (IRAs) and § 1.403(b)-2 (403(b) plans). To date, final regulations have not been issued, so these proposed regulations are *the* source material for understanding the minimum distribution rules. *References in this chapter to "proposed regulations" refer to Prop. Reg. § 1.401(a)(9)-1 unless otherwise specified.*

Warning: while the following discussion of the minimum distribution rules applies to most qualified retirement plans and IRAs, there are grandfather rules and exceptions which exempt some individuals and plans from some or all of the requirements. See "The Minimum Distribution Rule Grandfathers" and "Pre-1987 403(b) Plan Balances," Chapter 10.

Legal status of proposed regulations

The primary purpose of this chapter is to assist planners who are looking for a "safe harbor" for clients' estate plans. Accordingly, most of this chapter is about how to comply with the IRS's pronouncements, especially the proposed regulations. If a taxpayer *complies* with the proposed regulations, he is protected against later negative changes, because the IRS has said that: "taxpayers may rely on these proposed regulations for guidance pending the issuance of final regulations. If, and to the extent, future guidance is more restrictive than the guidance in these proposed regulations, the future guidance will be applied without retroactive effect." Prop. Reg., preamble.

Furthermore, if the taxpayer's actions are later prohibited by final regulations, but (at the time taken) constituted "a reasonable interpretation of the statute and proposed regulations," the taxpayer is once again in the clear. See, *e.g.*, discussion in PLR 9506001 (9/28/94). And if a particular interpretation of the law has been explicitly adopted by the IRS in one or more letter rulings, it presumably is safe to conclude that that interpretation is "reasonable." See, *e.g.*, PLR 9311037 (12/22/92).

On the other hand, if the taxpayer's actions are clearly *not* in compliance with the proposed regulations, his status is less favorable. Proposed regulations theoretically have a rather lowly status. They "are not entitled to judicial deference," Natomas North America v. Comm'r, 90 T.C. 710 (1988) (endnote 11), and have been described as "carry[ing] no more weight than a position advanced on brief by the" IRS. F.W. Woolworth Co. v. Comm'r, 54 T.C. 1233 (1970).

However, when the IRS ultimately issues final regulations, these may be made effective retroactively. Final regulations pertaining to statutory provisions enacted on or after July 30, 1996, can be made effective retroactive to the date of issuance of the proposed regulations "to which they relate," or even earlier in some cases. § 7805(b)(1)(B). For statutes enacted before that date (including the minimum distribution rules), there is no statutory limit on the retroactive effectiveness of final regulations. Therefore, even if a taxpayer's actions are based on a "reasonable interpretation of the statute," that will be little consolation if his actions are clearly contrary to a proposed regulation, and the proposed regulation in question is ultimately adopted by the IRS as a final regulation with a retroactive effective date.

Comments on the proposed regulations may be sent to the IRS at its website, http://www.irs.ustreas.gov/prod/. For an excellent discussion of the taxpayer's right (or lack thereof) to rely on IRS pronouncements of all types, see 1999 CCH *Standard Federal Tax Reporter* ¶ 43,282.01.

Death before the RBD: The Five Year Rule

One part of the minimum distribution rules tells us what distributions are required if a participant (P) dies before his "required beginning date" (RBD). § 401(a)(9)(C). Generally, the RBD is April 1 following the year in which P reaches age 70½, but see "The Required Beginning Date: When It Is," below, for exceptions. These rules are sometimes said to apply when death occurs "before age 70½." Strictly speaking, this should be "before the RBD."

Note: this set of distribution rules applies to a *Roth IRA* regardless of when P dies, because a Roth IRA has no "RBD." See Chapter 5.

The five year rule and its exceptions

Upon the death of a participant before his RBD, the

general rule is that all benefits must be distributed from the plan within five years after the date of death (the "five year rule"). § 401(a)(9)(B)(ii). Although the Code says "within five years after the death" of P, the proposed regulations are a little more liberal, requiring that the distribution must occur by "December 31 of the calendar year which contains the fifth anniversary" of the date of P's death. Prop. Reg. § C-2.

An *exception* to this rule permits payments to be made in annual installments over a period not exceeding the life expectancy of P's "designated beneficiary" (DB), beginning no later than 12/31 of the year after the year in which P died. § 401(a)(9)(B)(iii); Prop. Reg. § C-3(a). There are even more liberal exceptions to the five year rule if P's surviving spouse is the DB; these are discussed at "The Spouse and § 401(a)(9)," Chapter 3.

Importance of having a "designated beneficiary"

The option to defer income taxes can be extremely valuable. The financial effect on the family of being forced to take out all benefits *within five years after P's death*, versus being permitted to take them out gradually *over the life expectancy of a designated beneficiary*, can be dramatic.

Example: Lena and Tina. Two brothers died. Each brother left his entire estate, including a $500,000 IRA, to his daughter. Both daughters, Lena and Tina, were 38 years old. Each of the daughters, after taking a round-the-world cruise, buying a new house, and paying the estate taxes on her father's estate, was left with just one asset, the $500,000 IRA. Each daughter decided to regard the inherited IRA as her own retirement nest egg, and resolved to: withdraw from the IRA only the minimum amount required by law; invest the after-tax proceeds of the withdrawal; and accumulate the earnings (after taxes) as her retirement fund.

Each daughter kept her resolve, investing both in-plan

and out-of-plan assets in 8% bonds, and paying income taxes on all plan withdrawals and bond interest at the rate of 36%, but there was one difference: Tina's father had named Tina as his "designated beneficiary" (DB), so Tina was entitled to withdraw her father's IRA in installments over her 44.4 year life expectancy. Lena's father had named no beneficiary; he never got around to filling out a designation of beneficiary form. Under the terms of the account agreement governing his IRA, since he had not named any beneficiary, his "beneficiary" was his estate. In minimum distribution rule jargon, he "had no DB" (see "*Estate as beneficiary: death before the RBD*," below). Lena, the sole beneficiary of the estate, had to withdraw all money from her father's IRA within five years after his death.

After 30 years, Lena has a $1.5 million investment portfolio, all outside of any IRA. Tina has an investment portfolio of $1.4 million outside the IRA; and also has $1.5 million still *inside* the IRA she inherited from her father. Tina still has 14.4 years left in her "life expectancy" over which to withdraw the remaining IRA balance. After 30 years, the daughter who used the "installments over life expectancy" payout method has almost twice as much money as the daughter who withdrew benefits under the "five year rule."

Clearly, it is vital for the planner to understand how to go about naming a "DB." If P has a DB, then, on P's death, the DB will have the luxury of choosing to spread out the distributions from the plan over his life expectancy.

Remember, these distributions are just the *minimum* the beneficiary must take. The beneficiary can always take out more than the minimum—in fact the IRS would be delighted to have him do so. But if there "is no DB," then the recipient who inherits the benefits will have no choice: benefits must be distributed, and taxed, within five years after P's death.

DB is a term of art; it does not mean whatever

beneficiary P happens to have named. A DB must be an individual or a group of individuals. Prop. Reg. § D-2A. [If some tricky rules are complied with, P can name a trust as recipient of his death benefits and the *beneficiaries of the trust* will be treated as the DB; this topic is covered in Chapter 6.]

The DB can be one or more individuals designated as beneficiary by P on forms provided for that purpose by the plan, or may be designated by the plan itself. Prop. Reg. § D-1.

If the beneficiary is "my spouse," or "my children," or "my issue," or any other human being or group of human beings, everything is fine: P has a "DB," *i.e.,* an individual or group of individuals whose life expectancy(ies) can be used to determine the minimum required distribution ("MRD") period. If P's estate or a corporation is named as the beneficiary, or if a trust has been named but the technical requirements are not met (see Chapter 6), then for purposes of the minimum distribution rules, P is said to have "no DB" and therefore the benefits must be distributed by the end of the fifth year after his death.

Naming individual as beneficiary

This subsection deals with naming a non-spouse individual as beneficiary. If the beneficiary is P's spouse, see "The Spouse and § 401(a)(9)," Chapter 3.

If one individual (such as P's child) is the DB, then, under the exception to the five year rule, the beneficiary can withdraw the benefits "in accordance with regulations," beginning no later than the year after the year in which P dies, over a period of time that does not exceed the DB's life expectancy. § 401(a)(9)(B)(iii).

The proposed regulations provide that, to use this method, you first determine the beneficiary's life expectancy based on the beneficiary's age at his birthday in the year *following* the year of P's death. Prop. Reg. § E-2(a). Then, each year, the benefits remaining in the plan are valued, and the beneficiary must withdraw at least a certain fractional portion of those benefits. The first year, the fraction will be [one] divided by [the beneficiary's life expectancy]. In the second year, it will be [one] divided by [the beneficiary's original life expectancy reduced by one year], and so on. Prop. Reg. § F-1. (For full details on making these computations, see "How to Compute Life Expectancy and Installments" and "*P dies before RBD: Installments over DB's LE*," below.)

For example, if the beneficiary has a life expectancy of 27 years as of his birthday in the year after the year of P's death, he must withdraw 1/27th of the benefits in that year. In the second year, he must withdraw 1/26th and so forth. Each year, the benefits remaining in the plan are valued, and that year's new fraction is applied to the new plan value to determine that year's required *minimum* distribution. The beneficiary is, of course, free to withdraw more than the minimum in any year.

This fractional method of calculating minimum withdrawals tends to produce gradually increasing installments over the years, so long as the plan has a positive investment return. As long as the beneficiary's remaining life expectancy is greater than [100] divided by [the plan's annual growth rate], the plan balance will be growing faster than the beneficiary is withdrawing it. For example, if the plan is growing at 8% per year, and the beneficiary's life expectancy is 20 years, the required minimum distribution (1/20, or 5%) is less than the plan's earnings for the year (1/12.5, or 8%). Eventually the beneficiary's life expectancy is reduced to the point that he is withdrawing more than the year's investment return. If the plan is growing at 8% per year, this crossover point would be reached at 12.5 years before the end of the payout period. Even after this crossover point, however, the annual required minimum distributions tend to keep getting larger, even though the plan balance is now shrinking, because the fraction applied to them is greater.

Distributions must begin by year after death

  If the DB is taking out the benefits in installments over his life expectancy, the Code says such distributions *must* begin "no later than one year after the date" of death, "or such later date" as the IRS may prescribe by regulations. The proposed regulations require that the installments "commence on or before December 31 of the calendar year immediately following the calendar year in which" P died. Prop. Reg. § C-3(a).

  This feature of the installment method contrasts with the five year rule, under which there is no requirement that distributions be made annually, or that any money come out of the plan at all until the last day of the period. Prop. Reg. § C-2.

Naming more than one beneficiary: before RBD

  According to the proposed regulations, if there are multiple beneficiaries then:

  (a) All members of the group must be individuals in order for the exception to the five year rule to be available. If even $1 of the benefit is paid to a non-individual, P is deemed to have "no DB," and the five year rule applies. Prop. Reg. § E-5. The problems created by this rule when P wants to name both charitable and individual beneficiaries are discussed at *"Charity as one of several beneficiaries: before RBD,"* Chapter 7; and

  (b) If there are multiple beneficiaries, all of whom are individuals, the payout period is computed using the life expectancy of the beneficiary with the shortest life expectancy, *i.e.*, the oldest member of the group. Prop. Reg. § E-5(A)(1).

The proposed regulations provide that each of the beneficiaries may use his or her own life expectancy for his or her share of the benefits, *if* the retirement plan is divided into "separate accounts." Prop. Reg. § H-2(b). Thus, if P has four children, he could have four separate accounts, one payable to each of the children, within the IRA or retirement plan, and each "account" would have its minimum distribution calculated separately each year based on the life expectancy of the individual who was the beneficiary of that account. Similarly, if there are separate accounts and some are payable to individuals and some to non-individuals (an estate or charity for example), the individuals can use the life expectancy method for their separate accounts; the individuals' accounts are not "tainted" by the fact that other accounts are payable to non-individuals.

A "separate account" is "a portion of an employee's benefit determined by an acceptable separate accounting including allocating investment gains and losses, and contributions and forfeitures, on a pro rata basis in a reasonable and consistent manner between such portion and any other benefits." Prop. Reg. § H-2A(a).

Under the proposed regulations, these "separate accounts" must be established "as of" the date of P's death. Prop. Reg. § H-2(b). Many practitioners interpret "as of" the date of death to mean that a fractional division of the account that occurs *effective on* the date of death qualifies for "separate account" treatment, even if the accounts are not actually separated prior to the date of death. The Code supports this conclusion, since the Code says a payout over the life expectancy of the beneficiary is available for "the portion" of the account that is payable to that beneficiary. §401(a)(9)(B)(iii).

The IRS confirmed this conclusion in PLR 9809059 (12/4/97); however, in that ruling, the beneficiaries "physically" divided up the separate accounts by the end of the year in which P died and before any distributions were made. It is not clear to what extent the IRS considered this fact as a condition of the favorable ruling. See also "Taking Distributions from Multiple Plans," "*Notice 88-38*," below, and "MRD Potpourri," "*Who pays the penalty?*" below.

Estate as beneficiary: death before RBD

According to the proposed regulations, if benefits are payable to P's "estate," P has "no DB," and the five year rule applies, even if all beneficiaries of the estate are individuals. Prop. Reg. § H-7.

In this author's opinion, the IRS's position that the life expectancy method is not available if an "estate" is a beneficiary is incorrect. The Code provides that any portion of the employee's benefit payable "to (*or for the benefit of*)" a DB may be distributed over that beneficiary's life expectancy. § 401(a)(9)(B)(iii) (emphasis added). Benefits paid to an estate are paid "for the benefit of" the estate's beneficiaries, and if the beneficiaries of the estate are all individuals (or qualifying trusts; see Chapter 6), they should be recognized as "designated beneficiaries" and allowed to use the life expectancy method.

However, it is unquestionably the IRS's position that if any part of P's benefits is payable to P's "estate," there is a non-individual beneficiary, and P has "no DB." Accordingly, this book follows that rule. The author expects to publish further commentary on this issue, possibly in <u>Trusts and Estates</u> magazine, in the fall of 1999.

Cleanup strategies: death before RBD

When P dies before his RBD, and you discover that the beneficiary designation is not ideal, there are several strategies for correcting the situation and avoiding the five year rule.

1.   **Spousal rollover**. The IRS, in its rulings, has been liberal in permitting the spouse to roll over benefits even when S was not named directly as DB, so long as S had the absolute right (as beneficiary of an estate or trust) to receive the benefits. See *"Rollover when S inherits benefits through an estate or trust,"* Chapter 3. By rolling over the benefits to her own IRA, S can comply with the "five year rule" but still defer income taxes on the benefits.

2.   **Disclaimers**. If S is not directly or indirectly named as beneficiary, consider whether disclaimers can be used to shift the benefits to S. See *"Salvaging spousal rollover,"* Chapter 8.

3.   **IRS Ruling**. Perhaps you believe there is a "designated beneficiary" (DB) entitled to use the life expectancy (LE) method, but the proposed regulations indicate otherwise. For example, perhaps P's beneficiary designation form said "pay $10,000 of my benefits to the Red Cross and the balance to my child." You reasonably believe that, under Code § 401(a)(9), child is entitled to take his share of the benefits over his LE, but § E-5 of the proposed regulations indicates that, since one of the named beneficiaries is not an individual, there "is no DB" and the five year rule applies. Consider applying for a ruling. The IRS ruling staff have issued rulings which in some cases appear contrary to the regulations. See, *e.g.*, PLR 9037048 (6/20/90), in which the beneficiary of a testamentary trust was treated as a "DB" despite the fact that the trust was clearly not irrevocable on the RBD as was then required by the proposed regulations.

4.   **Wait and see**. If the client does not want to seek a private letter ruling, use a "wait and see" approach. Begin distributions based on the assumption that there is a DB, and that the installments-over-life-expectancy method is available. This means making annual installment distributions, beginning

by the end of the year after the year of death, based on the LE of the person you believe is the DB. Once four years have elapsed, review the situation again. By then there may be final regulations, cases or other legal guidance providing a definitive answer one way or the other, or the client may have decided that it is worth seeking a ruling. If the question has been answered unfavorably to your client, or if it still is ambiguous and your client still does not want to get a ruling, you can comply with the five year rule and distribute all benefits by December 31 of the year which contains the fifth anniversary of P's death.

5.   **Beg for mercy**. If all else fails, the 50% penalty tax can be waived by the IRS if the distribution shortfall is due to "reasonable error." § 4974(d).

The Required Beginning Date: When It Is

The preceding discussion dealt with the minimum distribution rules applicable when P dies before his RBD. Once the RBD is reached, a new set of rules comes into play; those rules are described in "The RBD: Required Lifetime Distributions" and succeeding sections, below. *This* section tells how to determine what the RBD is.

Definition of "required beginning date"

P's "required beginning date" may be different for different plans:

For Roth IRAs: There is NO "required beginning date." See Chapter 5.

For all other ("traditional") IRAs: The required beginning date is April 1 of the calendar year following the year in which

P reaches age 70½. § 401(a)(9)(C)(ii)(II).

For 403(b) arrangements: Effective for 1997 and later years, the required beginning date is April 1 of the calendar year following the *later of* the year in which P reaches age 70½ or the year in which P retires. § 401(a)(9)(C)(i); see also special rules in "Pre-1987 403(b) Plan Balances," Chapter 10.

For 401(a) ("qualified") plans: If P is a 5-percent owner (see *"Definition of 5% owner,"* below), the required beginning date is April 1 of the calendar year following the year in which P reaches age 70½. § 401(a)(9)(C)(ii)(I).

If P is not a 5-percent owner, the required beginning date, effective in 1997 and later years, is April 1 of the calendar year following the *later of* the year in which P reaches age 70½ or the year in which P retires. § 401(a)(9)(C)(i). See also special rules in "Minimum Distribution Rule Grandfathers," Chapter 10, for employees born before 1917 and employees who filed "TEFRA 242(b) designations."

Prior to 1997, the RBD was April 1 of the calendar year following the year in which P reached age 70½ for all types of plans and participants, except for the "grandfathered" individuals discussed in Chapter 10. TAPRA '97 changed the definition to read as above for non-5% owners who participate in 403(b) plans and 401(a) plans.

The ability to postpone the RBD until actual retirement is of no interest to workers who want to retire before age 70½; or to the business owner who owns more than 5% of his company and thus is not eligible. Thus, the most immediately apparent beneficiaries of the 1997 expansion of the definition of RBD are high-income executives and service professionals who work for large firms; and own either no interest or just a small interest—less than 5%—in the sponsoring employer; and want to keep working past age 70½.

Definition of 5% owner

The ability to postpone the RBD until actual retirement is not available for "an employee who is a 5-percent owner (as defined in section 416) with respect to the plan year ending in the calendar year in which the employee attains age 70½." § 401(a)(9)(C)(ii)(I). In determining ownership percentages under § 416, a modified version of the "constructive ownership" rules of § 318 applies. Under these very complicated rules, a participant could be deemed, for purposes of the 5% test, to own stock held by various family members, trusts, estates, partnerships or corporations; and stock options must be taken into account.

How little work is not "retirement"?

How many hours must P work, in what time frame, in order to be considered not "retired?" The author can find no definition of "retirement" in any IRS pronouncements issued under TAPRA '97 or under pre-1986 law (when, as now, "retirement" mattered as a trigger for required distributions). There will undoubtedly be close cases in which it is difficult to tell whether distributions are required to begin:

Example: Herbert "retires" as a 2% partner of the Olde Law Firm. He receives a distribution of his share of the firm's capital plus a gold watch. However, although he has given up his partnership position, he keeps working on a part time basis at his same desk, as a salaried employee. Has he "retired?" What if he works only a few hours per year? What if he takes a "leave of absence" for two or three years, before he officially "retires?"

One plan, different employers

Another problem that has surfaced with respect to the definition of "retirement" is whether a participant may be considered "retired" as to some assets in a plan but *not* retired as to some other assets in the very same plan.

Example: Elizabeth is working full time as a doctor at Tibias, Inc., and is a participant in the Tibias Pension Plan. Because she owns less than 5% of the sponsoring employer, her distributions from the plan do not have to begin until after she retires. However, in addition to the contributions by her current employer, this plan holds funds that were transferred to this plan from the plan of her *prior* employer, Femurs Corp., when her prior employer's practice was acquired by her current employer. Is the plan required to begin distributions from Elizabeth's account representing funds from the prior employer when Elizabeth reaches age 70½, since she is no longer working for the prior company (which no longer exists)?

There is a whole spectrum of variations on this theme. The IRS could decide that *all* funds held in a current employer's plan that represent accumulated contributions from a prior employer must begin distributing at age 70½, even if the change of "employer" was purely a change in the form of entity (*e.g.*, incorporation of a partnership). This approach would appear to be contrary to the intent of the new law, which is presumably to allow workers additional time to accumulate funds for retirement. Alternatively, the IRS could decide that all funds that are properly held by the current employer's plan (even if transferred from another employer's plan, or "rolled over" from another plan through an IRA) are eligible for the postponed RBD. Finally, the IRS could decide that *some* prior-employer funds held by the current plan sponsor (*e.g.*, where the current employer is a successor to the prior employer through a merger or other change of ownership form) are eligible for the postponed RBD, while some other types of prior-employer funds so held (*e.g.*, funds which were rolled into the plan from the plan of an unrelated former employer of P) are not.

Pending an IRS pronouncement on this issue, plan sponsors will have to determine what to do when holding plan funds that represent contributions for the same worker from different employers. Because compliance with the minimum distribution rules is a plan qualification issue, plans may tend to be conservative in interpreting the new law, and insist on making distributions from any prior-employer funds held for the employee, even if the employee is still working past age 70½.

Can a person "retire" more than once?

Example: Carmen retires from the Royal Cigar Company at 72 and starts receiving minimum required distributions. She is in the Palm View Senior Condo Development ... and hates it. She is bored and the Royal Cigar Company needs her back because business is booming. So at age 73 she goes back to work. Can her minimum required distributions be suspended until she retires *again*? The statute reads as though there is only one "retirement" per employee.

Effect of a second RBD

Example: Rachel works for the Red Cross. When she turned 70½ in 1995, she forgot to name a designated beneficiary. Since she had no designated beneficiary on her original RBD (April 1, 1996), she has been taking distributions over her own life expectancy only. But now she has named a beneficiary (her son), and she's still working. Normally, once the RBD is past, it's too late for a participant to name a "designated beneficiary" and change her minimum required distributions from single to joint life expectancy (see *"Changing DBs after the RBD,"* below). But under the 1997 change in the law it appears Rachel gets a brand new RBD, which will be April 1 following the year she retires. This should mean that after her new RBD the benefits can indeed come out over the joint life expectancy of herself and her new DB. In effect, employees who regret the way they set up the beneficiary designation on their original RBD get another bite of the apple under the new law—*if* they are still working.

The RBD:
Required Lifetime Distributions

Once a participant reaches his RBD, § 401(a)(9) forces him to start taking money out of his retirement plans.

What happens at the RBD

Money must start coming out of the retirement plan no later than the "required beginning date" (RBD). Although the date may differ for different people and different plans, as discussed in the preceding section, for most people in most plans the RBD is April 1 following the year in which P reaches age 70½ and the following discussion is based on that RBD.

The *slowest* rate the benefits can come out is, installments over P's life expectancy; or the joint life expectancy of P and his spouse; or the joint life expectancy of P and some other DB—who for this purpose will be deemed to be no more than 10 years younger than P, regardless of the beneficiary's actual age (see "Naming a Non-Spouse DB," below). A participant who has "no DB" as of his RBD must withdraw all plan benefits over only *one* life expectancy period—his own. At age 70½, the "life expectancy" under IRS tables is either 15.3 or 16 years (see "How to Compute Life Expectancy and

Installments," below).

Naming a DB at the RBD is similar to naming a DB for pre-RBD death benefits with several *extremely important* differences:

(a)   The existence or non-existence of a DB on the RBD, and the identity of the DB if there is one, freeze the payout period *permanently*. P can later change his DB, but can never do so in a way that lengthens the maximum payout period beyond what was established at the RBD. (The only "exception" to this rule is that, if P names his spouse as beneficiary, either before, at, or after his RBD, and she survives him, a spousal rollover can start a new payout period after P's death; see "Spousal Rollovers," Chapter 3. See also *Effect of a second RBD*," above.)

(b)   Trust beneficiaries can be used as the DB, *if* the trust rules are complied with. See Chapter 6.

(c)   P must make an irrevocable election whether or not to recalculate his (and his spouse's, if the spouse is the DB) life expectancy annually; see "Recalculating Life Expectancies: Participant and Spouse," below.

Traditionally, estate planners "planned" for only one event—death. Later, planners added disability planning to their repertoire. Now planners must add a third focus to their efforts: the RBD. When a participant names a beneficiary *prior* to the RBD, it is similar to writing a will—P can change his mind later and write a new will (or name another beneficiary). Estate planners are familiar with this mode and often do not realize that naming a beneficiary *on* the RBD has a quite different effect: the beneficiary designation on the RBD is not merely a will-like designation of who will receive the benefits after P's death (although it is that—and to that extent is changeable); it is *also* an election as to how P's minimum distributions will be calculated each year, and on this point it is irrevocable.

The RBD is the continental divide. Planning should begin early for this event. If a trust is to be named as beneficiary, EXTREME CARE must be taken to comply with the trust rules discussed in Chapter 6.

The good news is that most people have a "DB" whether they know it or not. A DB, for purposes of the rules, is simply "an individual who is entitled to a portion of an employee's benefit, contingent on the employee's death or another specified event." Prop. Reg. § D-2(a)(1). The DB can be named in the plan itself, or (if the plan permits) by P on a beneficiary designation form.

Under many employer-sponsored plans, if P does nothing, his spouse is automatically his DB. Under many IRA arrangements, if P has not designated a beneficiary all benefits are payable to P's estate, and thus he is deemed to have "no DB." A participant who "has no DB" on his RBD will be required to withdraw all his plan benefits over just his own life expectancy. § 401(a)(9)(A)(ii).

Naming the spouse as beneficiary

If the spouse is the DB, P can take his benefits out in installments over the joint life expectancy of P and the spouse—whatever it may be. Prop. Reg. § F-1; Prop. Reg. §§ 1.401(a)(9)-2, Q-7. If the spouses are close in age, this will probably not be the longest possible payout period; for example, the joint life expectancy of two individuals age 70 and 68 is only 21.5 years. However, naming S as DB offers other tax and estate planning advantages (see Chapter 3), and it is what most people want anyway.

Naming the spouse as DB will almost always lengthen

the payout period somewhat, compared to using just P's own life expectancy ("LE"), even if the spouse is the same age—or even if the spouse is older. The LE of an individual age 70 is 16 years; but the LE of two individuals both of whom are age 70 is 20.6 years. Even if the spouse is age 80 (*i.e.* 10 years older than P) adding her extends the payout period to 17.6 years.

Naming a non-spouse individual

Naming a child or other younger generation beneficiary often produces the longest possible payout period. See "Naming a Non-Spouse DB," below. Note: although the examples and discussion in this book usually speak of naming a child or grandchild as beneficiary, that is only because that is the most common situation. ANY individual—friend, relative or total stranger—can be a "DB."

Naming multiple beneficiaries: at the RBD

According to the proposed regulations, if there are multiple beneficiaries then:

(a)   All members of the group must be individuals in order for P to use the joint life expectancy payout method. If even $1 of the benefit is paid to a non-individual, P is deemed to have "no DB," and he will be limited to his own single life expectancy. Prop. Reg. § E-5; and

(b)   If there are multiple beneficiaries, all of whom are individuals, the payout period is computed using the life expectancy of the beneficiary with the shortest life expectancy, *i.e.*, the oldest member of the group. Prop. Reg. § E-5(A)(1).

Theoretically, this result can be avoided if the benefit is

divided into separate accounts payable to the different beneficiaries (in the same manner as before the RBD; see *"Naming more than one beneficiary: before the RBD,"* above). Prop. Reg. § H-2(b). A "separate account" is "a portion of an employee's benefit determined by an acceptable separate accounting including allocating investment gains and losses, and contributions and forfeitures, on a pro rata basis in a reasonable and consistent manner between such portion and any other benefits." Prop. Reg. § H-2A(a). However, in the case of lifetime distributions, these accounts would have to be established "as of" P's RBD. Prop. Reg. § H-2(b). This may be impossible to do within a single plan or IRA.

Estate as beneficiary at the RBD

The IRS's position that an "estate" cannot be a DB (even if all beneficiaries of the estate are individuals), while a trust can be (see *"Estate as beneficiary: death before RBD,"* above), can produce apparently arbitrary results. For example, if the beneficiary of Sylvia's IRA is a trust for the life benefit of Mickey, and the trust meets the requirements discussed in Chapter 6, Sylvia can withdraw from her IRA over the joint LE of herself and Mickey. But if the IRA is payable to her estate, of which the same trust is the sole beneficiary (or even of which Mickey himself is the sole beneficiary) there "is no DB" and the joint life expectancy method cannot be used. See, *e.g.*, PLR 9501044 (10/14/94).

Election to use single or joint LE

The wording of the Code suggests to some who read it that P must *elect*, on or before his RBD, to use either a joint or single life expectancy to determine his MRDs. § 401(a)(9)(A)(ii). However, P's "election" on this point has nothing to do with the determination of his MRDs.

As far as the Code is concerned, the MRDs are determined by whether or not P has a DB. If P has no DB then an "election" to use a joint life expectancy is irrelevant because P's minimum distributions will be based on his single life expectancy. Similarly, if P has a DB, "electing" to take benefits out over his own single life expectancy does not increase the MRDs: the MRDs are based on the joint LE of P and his DB, and if P chooses to calculate the distributions based solely on his own life expectancy he is simply taking larger distributions than he has to. He can revert to taking distributions based on the joint LE at any time (and his DB can take distributions over the balance of that LE after P's death). PLR 199915063 (1/21/99).

Example: Brenda names her husband Amnon as the DB of her IRA. When Brenda reaches her RBD she files a form with the IRA administrator, directing that the account be distributed to her over her LE only. However, she does have a DB: husband Amnon. As far as the minimum distribution rules are concerned, her MRDs are based on the joint LE of Brenda and Amnon, and she is simply choosing to take out larger distributions than she has to. She can switch any time to taking smaller distributions, based on the joint LE of herself and Amnon.

Special rule for determining DB for first MRD

There is an obscure rule for determining the amount of the first MRD. Generally, MRDs after age 70½ are based on the choice of designated beneficiary as in effect *on* the RBD (assuming there is no change of beneficiary *after* the RBD; see "*Changing DBs after the RBD*," below). However, for the *first* MRD (the one that must be made on or before the RBD) "designated beneficiary" has a special definition: It can mean any person who was named as the beneficiary at any time from

January 1 to April 1 of the year of the RBD. Prop. Reg. § 1.401(a)(9)-1, D-3(b). So, if you have a client who has changed his DB between December 31 of the year he turned 70½ and the RBD, his first MRD can be based on whichever beneficiary named during that period produces the most favorable MRD.

Recalculating Life Expectancies: Participant and Spouse

A major question facing a participant who names his spouse as DB is whether to exercise the option to "recalculate annually" the life expectancy of P, of the spouse ("S"), or of both. § 401(a)(9)(D).

How recalculation works

Absent "recalculation," the life expectancy period over which benefits must be paid out is established as a fixed number of years (or "term certain" or "period certain") on the RBD. Then each year the minimum distribution is calculated by multiplying the current account balance by a fraction: one divided by the remaining number of years in the term certain (see "How to Compute Life Expectancy and Installments," below). Prop. Reg. § F-1(d).

When life expectancy is being recalculated annually, on the other hand, you go back to the actuarial table each year, and determine an entirely new life expectancy based on P's (and/or spouse's) new age. Prop. Reg. § E-8. Under this method, life expectancy does not go down by one full year each year; it goes down by something less than a full year. For example, the life expectancy of a 70-year-old is 16 years, while the life expectancy of a 71-year-old is 15.3 years. Reg. § 1.72-9, table V. Thus, for a participant who is using only his own life expectancy to calculate minimum distributions, the second year's fraction will be 1/15.3 if he is redetermining his life expectancy annually, compared to 1/15 if he is using a "term certain." Redetermining life expectancy stretches out the distribution of benefits during P's lifetime.

The advantage of annual recalculation is that the participant or couple will never "outlive" the retirement benefits, if they take out only the MRD each year (and assuming the benefits do not disappear due to poor investment results). The IRS tables provide a life expectancy of more than one year all the way up to age 110. The disadvantage is that, in the calendar year following the death of a person whose life expectancy is being recalculated annually, that life expectancy is reduced to zero. If P's spouse dies, and her life expectancy was being recalculated, for example, P's remaining benefits will have to be paid out to him over only his own life expectancy. If both spouses' life expectancies are being recalculated, and both spouses die prematurely, the children (or whoever is the next succeeding beneficiary) will not get the benefit of a longer payout period—all remaining benefits will have to be distributed by the end of the year following the year of the surviving spouse's death.

In contrast, if life expectancies are NOT recalculated, the death of P or spouse makes no difference to the payout. See *"Effect of P's death after the RBD,"* below. Whoever inherits the benefits at that point simply continues to withdraw over the balance of the term certain.

Which method is best?

There is no simple or universally "right" answer to the question of whether it is desirable to recalculate annually. For a married couple whose principal goal is to enhance their own retirement security and maximize their tax deferred income from this plan, and whose health and genetic background indicate that they have an above-average life expectancy, recalculation of both life expectancies annually will *probably* provide the most extended payout term. But if one or both spouses die prematurely, "recalculate both" would result in an acceleration of distributions on the first death, and distribution of the entire balance by the end of the year after the year in which the second death occurs.

If the couple appear to have below-average life expectancies, then recalculation annually would probably not be advisable, and use of their fixed joint life expectancy period, determined as of the RBD, will probably produce a longer payout period and more tax deferral. (If both spouses clearly have shortened life expectancies, consider naming a child or grandchild as DB instead of S, to gain greater income tax deferral, if this would not jeopardize the surviving spouse's financial security; see "Naming a Non-Spouse DB," below.)

Under any method, if P dies first, the benefits can be paid to S and rolled over by her to her own IRA, where she can start the process all over again by naming a new DB and choosing a payout period based on the joint life expectancy of, say, herself and the children. See "Spousal Rollovers," Chapter 3.

A compromise position is to have P's life expectancy recalculated annually, but not S's. Prop. Reg. § E-7 permits P to recalculate the life expectancy of either spouse, neither, or both. This hedges the bets. If S dies first, then P will at least have assured that the minimum payout period over which the benefits can be distributed is S's original life expectancy. Thus there is a guaranteed minimum payout period, and no sudden acceleration of benefits if both spouses die prematurely. The payout period may be even more extended if P lives beyond his life expectancy.

This "split" or "hybrid" method has three drawbacks. First, calculating the annual distribution is more complicated (see "How to Compute Life Expectancy and Installments," below), although software can easily solve that problem (see Appendix D). Second, it tends to produce slightly *larger* required distributions than either of the other two methods (recalculate both, recalculate neither) in the early years, due to the IRS's prescribed formula which requires some rounding upwards of S's age. Third, on P's death, it creates greater time pressure for S to complete the rollover, due to the acceleration of required distributions that occurs in the year after P's death. See "Spousal Rollovers," Chapter 3.

Another "hedging the bets" approach is for P to have several plans and elect a different method for each. See "Taking Distributions from Multiple Plans," below.

Mechanics of making this election

The recalculation issue is benign if the spouses are aware of it and make a knowledgeable election. Unfortunately, that does not always happen. The proposed regulations permit a plan to allow participants to elect one way or another, but also permit plans to allow no choice—and some plans and IRA agreements require annual recalculation for both spouses. Furthermore, the proposed regulations say that if the plan (or IRA agreement) is silent on this subject recalculation is mandatory! Prop. Reg. § E-7.

The election to recalculate or not must be made *irrevocably* as of the date of the first required distribution (Prop. Reg. § E-7(c)) (even though the election has no effect on the amount of the distribution until the *second* required distribution).

Strangely, despite the importance of this election, many plans and IRAs do not have any particular form for making the election (and the IRS does not have any form on which participants can tell the IRS what election they have made). If the plan or IRA sponsor's forms do not cover this question, notify the administrator by (for example) a letter attached to the beneficiary designation form. See form 6.1 in Appendix B. Be sure to get an acknowledgment of receipt from the administrator, and to save the receipted copy "forever"; it will be needed, potentially, for several decades as evidence that minimum distributions are being calculated correctly.

Naming a Non-Spouse DB: The MDIB Rule

When a participant names someone other than his spouse as his DB, a special rule comes into play when determining the "joint life expectancy" of P and the DB. The so-called "Minimum Distribution Incidental Benefit" (MDIB) rule is designed to prevent a participant from unduly postponing distribution of his retirement benefits. This rule is not contained in the Code, although it is cryptically referred to in § 401(a)(9)(G), § 408(a)(6) and elsewhere. For details, see Prop. Reg. § 1.401(a)(9)-2, which this section summarizes.

Application during participant's life

Under the MDIB rule, P's minimum required distribution ("MRD") for each year is, as usual, determined by applying a fraction or "divisor" to the prior year-end value of the account. However, when the MDIB rule applies, the fraction P is required to use is whichever of the following produces a *larger* MRD: the actual joint life expectancy of P and the DB; or the divisor specified in the "MDIB rule table."

For example, suppose P is age 71 in his "first distribution calendar year" and his non-spouse DB is age 47. The fraction determined using their actual initial joint LE is 1/36.5, but the fraction under the MDIB table is 1/25.3. The larger fraction, 1/25.3, must be used to determine the MRD for the first year.

The "MDIB rule table" is contained in the proposed regulations at § 1.401(a)(9)-2; and in IRS publication 590; and in Appendix A of this book. The MDIB rule table contains divisors based, in each year, on the joint LE of P and someone 10 years younger than P. *E.g.*, in the year P is 70, the MDIB rule divisor is 26.2, which is the joint LE of two people ages 70 and 60. When P is age 81, the MDIB rule divisor is 16.8, which happens to be the joint LE of two people ages 81 and 71. The effect of the MDIB rule, approximately, is to "deem" the DB to be only 10 years younger than P every year. If the DB is less than 10 years younger than P (or is the same age as, or older than, P), the MDIB rule has no effect because the real joint LE will always produce a larger fraction (smaller divisor) than the MDIB table.

Obviously, the MDIB rule forces distributions out of the plan at a faster rate than would occur with use of the actual joint life expectancy of P and his young DB. However, it still provides a means to stretch out payments substantially during P's lifetime. In effect it provides the advantages of recalculating life expectancies (P never "outlives" the benefits) without the drawbacks (because there is no acceleration at P's death).

The flip at participant's death

If P dies before all his benefits have been paid out, the MRD calculations after his death will be based on the *actual* original joint life expectancy period of P and DB. The MDIB rule simply does not apply to distributions after the date of death. Prop. Reg. § 1.401(a)(9)-2, Q-3. Thus, if P dies before all benefits have been paid out, the beneficiary can get an extremely long payout period for what remains in the plan at P's death.

This "flip" which occurs at P's death, from MRDs based on the MDIB table to MRDs based on the real joint LE of P and the DB, is extremely confusing because it is an exception to the normal rule that, once a participant dies, payments must continue to come out to the beneficiary "at least as rapidly" as they were before P died (see *"Effect of P's death after RBD,"* below). Under the MDIB rule, and the "flip" that occurs at P's death, payments dramatically slow down upon P's death.

Whether to recalculate: non-spouse DB

The Code does not permit annual recalculation of life expectancy for anyone other than P and P's spouse. Therefore, the only election that must be made when a *non-spouse* is the DB is whether to recalculate P's life expectancy. The non-spouse DB's life expectancy is fixed on the RBD and cannot be recalculated.

Should P's LE be recalculated when there is a non-spouse DB? There is no simple "one-size-fits-all" answer to this question. Remember, what happens each year with a non-spouse DB while P is living is that you must determine *two* possible MRDs: the MRD based on the *actual* joint LE of P and the DB, and the MRD based on the "MDIB divisor table." If the actual joint LE (such as "46 years") is a larger number than the MDIB divisor table number (such as "25.3") then you must use the smaller number (25.3) because that produces a larger MRD. Once P dies, you use the remaining *actual* LE, and no longer need to bother with comparing the actual LE number with the MDIB table number.

If you elect to recalculate P's LE, then, when P dies, his LE will go to zero, meaning you are left with only the remaining LE of the DB to measure payouts. If P's LE was not recalculated, on the other hand, his LE would not "disappear" at his death, so the remaining *joint* LE of *both* P and DB would be available to measure payouts after P's death. Since the joint LE of P and DB would necessarily be longer than the single LE of DB, using the fixed term method will produce a longer payout period (smaller MRDs) *after P dies.*

Does this mean a P who names a non-spouse DB should always elect the "fixed term" method? Yes – *if* the DB is *much* younger than P. However, if the DB is *not* very much younger than P, and P lives a long time, using the "recalculate" method may produce smaller MRDs while P is still living. For example, suppose P is 70 and DB is 57. In the first year of the payout, their true joint LE (28.4) is ignored because the MDIB rule divisor (26.2) produces a larger distribution. However, when P gets older, the MRD could be quite different depending on which method P elected:

		Divisor when P is:		
		Age 80	**Age 85**	**Age 90**
1.	MDIB rule	17.6	13.8	10.5
2.	Actual remaining joint LE, fixed term method	18.4	13.4	8.4
3.	Actual joint LE, recalculated method	19.5	15.6	12.1

In this example, once P reaches his mid-80's, if he elected the fixed term method, the "actual joint LE" starts producing larger MRDs than the MDIB rule. That would never happen during P's lifetime if he had elected to recalculate.

Conclusion: although the differences are not dramatic, here are some guidelines on this decision:

1.   If the DB is *substantially* younger than P (*e.g.*, a child or grandchild) it will probably make *no difference*, as long as P is living, whether P's LE is being recalculated or not. This is

because the MDIB rule will always "override" the actual joint LE, that is to say, the MDIB rule will always produce a larger MRD. After P's death, the fixed term method will produce *slightly* smaller MRDs than the recalculation method. Therefore, if the DB is much younger than P, P should probably elect "fixed term" because that will produce slightly better results after P's death and will make no difference during P's life.

2.   If the DB is not much more than 10 years younger than P (*e.g.*, DB is in his late 50's), then which method is "better" depends on when P dies. If P dies before the end of the original joint LE of P and the DB, the DB will be better off if the "term certain" method was used—because the DB can withdraw over the balance of that joint LE and will not be forced to withdraw over only his or her own LE. But if P lives a long time, recalculation produces a better result, because smaller MRDs will be required during P's later life.

What Happens After the RBD

Effect of P's death after the RBD

When P dies after his RBD, the Code simply says that distributions must continue to be made "as least as rapidly" as prior to P's death. § 401(a)(9)(B)(2). ERISA practitioners confidently refer to this as the "Atleastasrapidly Rule," as if this phrase answered any possible questions. Actually, the meaning of this rule is far from self evident and payments in some cases do *not* have to be made "at least as rapidly" as prior to P's death. What happens to the required distributions after P's death depends on: who was P's DB at the RBD; what elections P made at his RBD regarding method of determining life expectancy; and whether P changed his DB after his RBD (and if so who he named as his new DB). For a quick overview, see the chart inside the back cover of this book.

A more precise statement of the rule is: when P dies after his RBD, distributions must continue to be made, to the beneficiary, over the remaining time of the single or joint life expectancy payout period that P was required to use to measure his MRDs immediately prior to death, subject to the following variations and wrinkles:

1.   The MDIB rule ceases to apply; see "*The flip at participant's death*," above, and "*Participant and non-spouse DB: the MDIB rule*," below.

2.   If P changed his beneficiary after his RBD, see the next two subsections.

3.   If P's life expectancy was being redetermined annually, it goes to zero in the year following his death.

4.   If P's beneficiary is his surviving spouse, see "Spousal Rollovers," Chapter 3.

5.   For the effect of a disclaimer, see Chapter 8.

6.   For exact details on how to compute the post-death MRDs in various situations, see "How to Compute Life Expectancy and Installments," below.

Changing DB after the RBD

This subsection deals with P's *naming* a new beneficiary after the RBD, not the death of the original DB. The death of the original DB is *not* considered a change of beneficiary. Prop. Reg. § E-5(e)(2). If a change of DB affects the size of distributions, the change applies beginning with the year *after* the year of the change. Prop. Reg. § E-5(c)(3). The biggest problem with changing the DB after the RBD is often the fact that you cannot change the election regarding recalculation of life expectancy. See the *Fallon* case study, Chapter 11.

P can change his DB after his RBD. He can change his DB every day of the week as far as the IRS is concerned. However, changing the DB may have an effect on the subsequent computations of his MRDs. P cannot, by changing to a *younger* DB (or creating a DB) after the RBD, lengthen the maximum payout period, but changing to an *older* DB (or no DB) can shorten it. Here are the rules:

1.   If P "had no DB" on his RBD, nothing he does later will change that fact. P can name a new beneficiary to receive the benefits after his death, but that new beneficiary will not be a "DB" for purposes of calculating a joint life expectancy payout period if there was no DB on the RBD. (The only "escape hatch" in this situation is this: if P "had no DB" on his RBD, but later names S as beneficiary, and S survives him, S can then roll the benefits to a new IRA in her own name and properly name a DB for it. See Chapter 3.)

2.   If the new beneficiary has a longer life expectancy than the original "DB," the change has no effect on the minimum distributions. The payout continues to be measured by the joint LE of P and the original DB.

Example: Changing to a younger DB. If the DB on the RBD is P's six-years-younger sister, P can change and name his eight-years-younger brother as his new DB. However, because the RBD has already passed, this will not lengthen the maximum payout period, which will continue to be measured by the joint life expectancy of P and the original DB, his sister.

3. If the new beneficiary has a *shorter* life expectancy than the original DB; or if P changes, after his RBD, from "having a DB" to "having no DB" (for example, by changing his beneficiary designation from "pay all to my child" to "pay all to my estate"); then subsequent payouts will be measured by the new shorter joint life expectancy of P and the new DB (or by P's life expectancy only, if the change is from "having a DB" to "having no DB").

Example: Changing to an older DB. If the original DB (as of the RBD) is P's brother (eight years younger than P) P can change and name his sister (six years younger than P) as his new DB. This will shorten the joint life expectancy for purposes of calculating subsequent minimum distributions because the new DB has a shorter life expectancy than the original DB.

4. If the DB is a non-spouse individual, P can change the DB to P's spouse (S). The new maximum payout period will be the joint life expectancy of P and S, or the joint life expectancy of P and the prior DB, whichever is shorter.

If the payouts prior to the change of DB were being measured under the MDIB rule limitation, does this artificially shortened joint life expectancy continue if S is named as the new DB? Possibly not. If "a new designated beneficiary with a life expectancy shorter than the life expectancy of the designated beneficiary whose life expectancy is being used to determine the distribution period...replaces a designated beneficiary, the new designated beneficiary is treated as the designated beneficiary for purposes of determining the distribution period." Prop. Reg. § E-5(c)(1).

Thus, if P named his child as his DB, and is taking distributions over the joint life expectancy of himself and the child as limited by the MDIB rule, P can reduce the distributions payable during his life, even after his RBD, by marrying someone who is more than 10 years younger than he but older than the child and naming her as his new DB. (Or, if he is already married to someone more than 10 years younger than he but older than his child, by naming his spouse as his DB instead of his child.)

5. P can change his DB from any individual to a trust of which that individual or other individuals are the beneficiaries. See Chapter 6 for additional requirements which must be met if a trust is named as beneficiary. Of course, if the life expectancy of the oldest trust beneficiary is shorter than the life expectancy of the original DB, the change will shorten P's payout period.

6. <u>Changing away from recalculation</u>: If the original DB was S, and P elected to redetermine S's life expectancy annually, and P changes to a younger DB, the MRDs will continue to be measured by the joint LE of P and S, with S's LE redetermined annually; and when S actually dies her LE will go to zero. See PLR 9450040 (9/22/94). If (while S is still living) P changes from S to a new DB who is *older* than S (so distributions cease to be measured by S's LE), it appears the recalculation method disappears. Prop. Reg. § E-5(c)(1).

Changing contingent beneficiary after RBD

If P changes his *contingent* beneficiary after his RBD but while the primary beneficiary (i.e., the "DB") is still alive, that change has no effect on anything. Prop. Reg. § E-5(e)(1). Even if the original DB dies after P's RBD, and then, *after* the original DB dies, P changes the name of his original contingent beneficiary, who is now his primary beneficiary due to the death of the original DB, this has no effect: the original DB's LE is carved in stone as the measuring period if he or she dies while still "the DB." Prop. Reg. § E-5(e)(2).

Changing marital status after RBD

A stumper: on his RBD, Grandpa names Lolita, his 25-year-old "significant other," as his DB. Payouts begin to Grandpa based on the joint life expectancy of himself and Lolita, as limited by the MDIB rule. At age 73, Grandpa marries Lolita. Does the MDIB rule go away now that the DB has become the spouse? The answer to this is not clear.

The proposed regulations are very clear on what happens if (i) S is the DB on the RBD and (ii) S ceases to be the spouse due to divorce or death. In that case, the MDIB rule does *not* kick in. A change of status from "spouse" (on the RBD) to "no longer spouse" (sometime after the RBD) has no effect, and P can continue to withdraw over the joint life expectancy of P and S (unless, presumably, he actually changes to a different DB). Prop. Reg. § 1.401(a)(9)-2, Q-7(d). The regulations are silent on a change of status in the other direction—from non-spouse on the RBD to, later, spouse.

Changing after 70½ but before RBD

A final emphasis: the key date is the RBD. The wise participant begins planning early for this event, and may file a beneficiary designation and elections regarding the form of benefits well before his RBD. As far as the minimum distribution rules are concerned, these are completely amendable and changeable at any time prior to the RBD. This may work favorably or unfavorably. Also, the *plan* may limit the options for later change even when the *tax law* does not.

Example: In 1998 Louise turns 70½. She names her grandson Waldo as beneficiary of her IRA, and her husband Ralph as her contingent beneficiary. Unfortunately, in March 1999, Waldo dies in an accident, just before Louise's RBD. Because he died before Louise's RBD, he was not her DB "on" her RBD. Ralph, the former contingent beneficiary, ends up as the DB "on" the RBD and Louise must measure MRDs using the joint life expectancy of herself and Ralph, not herself and Waldo, for her distributions for 1999 and later years. For her first MRD, however (the one for 1998—the "age 70½ year"— which must be distributed by 4/1/99), she can use the joint life expectancy of herself and Waldo (as limited by the MDIB rule) because he was her DB *at some point* in the first three months of 1999 (see "*Special rule for determining DB for first MRD*," above).

Taking Distributions from Multiple Plans

IRS Notice 88-38

If the client participates in more than one "qualified" retirement plan, the MRD must be calculated separately for each plan, and each plan must distribute the MRD calculated for that plan. Thus if the client is a participant in two pension plans and a 401(k) plan, he will receive three separate MRDs, one from each of these plans.

A different rule applies for IRAs. The MRD must be calculated separately for each IRA, but P is not required to take each IRA's calculated amount from that IRA. He can total up the MRDs required from all of the IRAs, and then take the total amount all from one of the IRAs, or from any combination of them. Notice 88-38, 1988-1 C.B. 524.

This special rule applies also to 403(b) plans. The MRD must be calculated separately for each 403(b) arrangement, but P is not required to take each 403(b) account's calculated amount from that 403(b) account. He can total up the MRDs required from all of his 403(b) arrangements, and then take the total amount all from one of them, or from any combination of them. Notice 88-38, 1988-1 C.B. 524.

Since each IRA (or 403(b) plan) may have a different "DB," or different method of computing P's (or S's) life expectancy, the Notice offers great planning flexibility.

Example 1: Anthony establishes two equal IRAs at his RBD, naming his wife Bernice as DB of one and their son Stacey as DB of the other. Because Bernice and Stacey are different ages, the annual MRD for each IRA will be different. Anthony wants to keep the bequests to his wife and son equal. Anthony can (1) determine the MRD separately for each IRA, (2) determine the total MRD for the year (the sum of the MRDs from each IRA) and (3) take half of the total MRD from each IRA.

Example 2: At her RBD, Marcia established three equal IRAs, naming one of her three children as DB of each. Investment results differ in the three accounts, causing them to become unequal in value. Because Marcia wants each child to receive an equal amount, she decides to take each year's MRD from only the larger account(s).

Example 3: Jo Claire established two IRAs at her RBD. Her spouse is DB of both, but on one account she elected to recalculate both spouses' life expectancies annually, and on the other she elected the fixed term method. Now she regrets the election to recalculate and wishes she had elected only the fixed term method for both. By taking the MRD for both IRAs only from the "recalculate" IRA, she can gradually deplete that one and allow the "fixed term" IRA to grow.

Example 4: Burton, age 72, is the beneficiary of his late mother's IRA. In addition, he has an IRA of his own. Both generate MRDs each year. He can take the total MRD for each year from either account.

Example 5: Jeffrey dies, leaving two IRAs. One is payable to a marital deduction trust, the other to a credit shelter trust. The "trust rules" (Chapter 6) are complied with, so the beneficiaries of the respective trusts are treated as Jeffrey's DB, and the life expectancy of the oldest is used to measure the post-death MRDs. Assume the credit shelter trust permits accumulation of income. If the family's goal is to maximize income tax deferral and minimize estate taxes, can each year's MRD be taken entirely from the IRA payable to the marital trust? If so, the credit shelter trust would get the maximum available income tax deferral and what income taxes had to be paid would be paid by the marital trust, where at least they could reduce S's future taxable estate. However, Notice 88-38 does not specifically mention this situation. The Notice suggests that it is the *recipient who must take the distributions* who can combine the IRAs he must take distributions from (see Example 4), not that IRAs *inherited from the same participant* by multiple beneficiaries can be "pooled."

Notice 88-38 applies only to IRAs and 403(b) plans. MRDs from qualified plans cannot be combined with each other or with IRAs or 403(b) plans, and IRAs cannot be combined with 403(b) plans.

Transferring between IRAs after RBD

It is *not* possible to improve MRD results by moving assets from one IRA to another after the RBD! Not only does transferring assets between IRAs after the RBD not improve the MRD status, it creates a major accounting headache: If assets in one IRA are moved to another IRA with a younger DB (or a different method of determining life expectancy), the proposed regulations require the "new" and "old" assets in the transferee IRA to be accounted for separately, and the MRD to be computed separately for each "pool." Prop. Reg. § G-2(b).

Example 6: Lullie (who is past her RBD) has two IRAs, with her husband as DB of one ("Husband IRA") and her child as DB of the other ("Child IRA"). All life expectancies are being determined using the fixed term method. Having decided that her husband is well provided for by his own assets, Lullie decides to shift some assets from Husband IRA to Child IRA. In effect she has changed the beneficiary of the transferred funds from an older DB (husband) to a younger (child). *If* the transferred assets could then be distributed over the joint life expectancy of Lullie and her child, just like the rest of Child IRA, this would result in smaller MRDs and longer deferral.

However, although the assets can be transferred, it won't accomplish anything as far as the minimum distribution rules are concerned. Lullie will be required to account for the portion of Child IRA that represents money that was in there since her RBD (and the earnings thereon) *separately* from the portion that was transferred from Husband IRA (and the earnings thereon).

Note that if Lullie had transferred money from Child IRA to Husband IRA, this would be the same as changing from a younger to an older beneficiary, and MRDs for *all* the funds in the transferee IRA would be determined based on the joint life expectancy of Lullie and her husband. The problem of having to account separately for two separate "funds" within one IRA arises only when money is transferred from an account with an older DB to one with a younger DB (or from an account with no DB to one with any DB).

How to Compute Life Expectancy and Installments

How to use this section

This section explains exactly how to calculate minimum required distributions in most situations. These illustrations apply to an IRA or any other retirement plan for which the RBD is April 1 following the year P reaches age 70½. To do the calculations for a plan for which the RBD is April 1 following the year P retires (see "The Required Beginning Date: When It Is," above), substitute "the year P retires" for "the year P reaches age 70½" and adjust all calculations accordingly.

To do these calculations, you need Tables V (single life expectancy) and VI (joint life expectancy) of Reg. § 1.72-9. These tables are partially reproduced in IRS Publication 590 and in Appendix A of this book.

The IRS tables are "unisex," so life expectancy ("LE") for men and women is the same. These tables were promulgated in 1986; the IRS updated its actuarial tables used for estate and gift tax valuations in May 1999, as required by § 7520, but this change did not affect minimum distribution calculations.

Determining P's life expectancy ("LE")

Prop. Reg. § 1.401(a)(9)-1(E) tells how to determine P's "life expectancy" (LE) as of his RBD. First, you determine the calendar year in which P will attain age 70½. Second, you determine P's attained age as of his birthday which falls within that calendar year.

Finally, you find the LE in Table V. The column entitled "multiple" in Table V is the LE for the applicable attained age, and becomes the "divisor" for purposes of these calculations.

If the RBD is based on the year P turns age 70½, and P's

birthday falls in the first half of the calendar year, the attained age will be 70. If his birthday falls in the second half of the calendar year, then his attained age on the birthday which falls within the calendar year in which he attains age 70½ will be 71. For age 70 the multiple (or "divisor" or "life expectancy") is 16.0 years. For age 71 it is 15.3 years.

Installments over P's LE: term certain

Once you have determined the applicable LE, here is how you compute the required minimum annual distributions, according to Prop. Reg. § 1.401(a)(9)-1.

Assume Whit's 70th birthday was 8/1/95. He accordingly turns 70½ on 2/1/96, so his RBD for his IRA is April 1, 1997. Since his age on his 1996 birthday (8/1/96) will be 71, his LE in his "age 70½ year" is 15.3 years. He does not elect to redetermine his LE annually. Table 1.1 shows how much the plan must distribute to him, and when, to avoid a penalty.

Note that there are two distributions required in the first year (1997). Whit can avoid this doubling of required distributions by taking his first required distribution in the year he turns 70½, rather than waiting until April 1 of the next year.

Whit can always take out *more* than § 401(a)(9) requires; § 401(a)(9) simply dictates the minimum. Taking out more than the minimum in a particular year does not give Whit any "credit" that can be carried forward and applied to a later year's minimum distribution; each year stands on its own. So even if Whit withdraws 50% of his entire account balance in 1998 (way in excess of the 1/13.3 he is required to withdraw), he will still be required, in calendar 1999, to withdraw 1/12.3 of whatever the remaining account balance was as of 12/31/98. (Of course, a larger-than-required withdrawal

Table 1.1

No later than this date	Distribute at least this much of his plan balance	Valued as of the last plan valuation date in
4/1/97	1/15.3	1995
12/31/97	1/14.3	1996
12/31/98	1/13.3	1997
12/31/99	1/12.3	1998
12/31/2000	1/11.3	1999
12/31/2001	1/10.3	2000
12/31/2002	1/9.3	2001
12/31/2003	1/8.3	2002
12/31/2004	1/7.3	2003
12/31/2005	1/6.3	2004
12/31/2006	1/5.3	2005
12/31/2007	1/4.3	2006
12/31/2008	1/3.3	2007
12/31/2009	1/2.3	2008
12/31/2010	1/1.3	2009
12/31/2011	100%	

indirectly reduces the required distributions for later years, by reducing the year-end account balance on which the subsequent year's minimum is calculated.)

Installments over P's LE: recalculation method

If payments are being made over Whit's LE solely, and he has elected to recalculate his LE annually, then each year's distribution during his life and for the year of death is calculated using a fraction, the denominator of which is Whit's LE as of his attained age on his birthday in that year. Table 1.2 shows the required distributions under this method.

Under the recalculation method, distributions continue until 2035 when Whit is age 110 and must withdraw 100% of the plan balance as of 12/31/2034. If Whit dies before reaching age 110, his beneficiaries must withdraw 100% of the benefits by 12/31 of the year following his death. To illustrate, suppose that as of 12/31/95 Whit's IRA balance was $1 million, growing annually at 8%. Whit turned 70½ in 1996, and his RBD is 4/1/97. Each year he withdraws the required minimum on the last possible date. He dies in the year 2000 at age 75. Table 1.3 shows the required distributions.

Table 1.2

No later than this date	Participant's Attained Age	Distribute at least this much of his plan balance	Valued as of the last plan valuation date in
4/1/97	71	1/15.3	1995
12/31/97	72	1/14.6	1996
12/31/98	73	1/13.9	1997
12/31/99	74	1/13.2	1998
12/31/00	75	1/12.5	1999
...etc.			

Table 1.3

Date	Withdrawal	Plan Balance
12/31/95	0	1,000,000
12/31/96	0	1,080,000
4/1/97	65,359	N/A
12/31/97	73,973	1,021,839
12/31/98	73,514	1,030,072
12/31/99	78,036	1,034,442
12/31/00	82,755	1,034,442
12/31/01	1,034,442	0

What balance the fraction applies to

The account value "as of the last valuation date" in the preceding plan year must be increased by certain plan contributions. See Prop. Reg. § F-5. For IRAs, the applicable valuation date is December 31st of the preceding year.

If all or part of the MRD for the age 70½ year is postponed until January, February or March of the following year (*i.e.*, the "age 71½" year), then the MRD for the "age 71½ year" is calculated in a special way. The appropriate fraction for the "71½ year" is applied to an "adjusted" preceding-year-end balance. The preceding-year-end balance is reduced by [the MRD for the age 70½ year] minus [amounts actually distributed in the age 70½ year]. Prop. Reg. § F-5(c)(2).

Example: David was born 7/1/24 and reached age 70½ in 1995. His wife Lisa, who turned 74 in 1995, is named as his DB, and their joint LE is 18.6 years. David elects not to recalculate either LE. David has an IRA which had a value on 12/31/94 of

$300,000. The MRD for 1995 is 1/18.6 x $300,000, or $16,129. David withdraws $5,000 from the IRA in 1995. On 12/31/95, the IRA value is $325,500. In January of 1996, he withdraws the rest of the 1995 MRD ($11,129). The 1996 MRD will be 1/17.6 x ($325,500 - [$16,129-$5,000]), or $17,862.

Installments over LE of P and S: fixed term

To determine the joint LE of P and spouse (S), use Table VI, using their attained ages as of their birthdays in the year P turns 70½.

For example, assume P turns 70½ on 2/1/93. His age on his 1993 birthday (8/1/93) is 71. S's date of birth was 4/15/25, so she will be 68 on her 1993 birthday. Table VI tells us that the joint LE of two people ages 71 and 68 is 21.2 years.

If neither spouse's LE is recalculated, then P will take distributions over the following schedule: 1/21.2 the first year; 1/20.2 the second year, 1/19.2 the third year, and so on. If either one or both die before the 21 years are up, the surviving spouse (or the contingent beneficiary, if S does not survive P) will continue to take installments over the remainder of the 21 years.

P and S: both LEs recalculated annually

If both spouses' LEs are being redetermined annually, you start off the same as in the preceding example: the first year's (1993) installment would be (in the above example) 1/21.2 times the prior year end account balance, because 21.2 years is the joint and survivor LE of two people ages 71 and 68 under Table VI. Then in each subsequent year you look at the couple's joint LE under Table VI for their attained ages *in that year*; so the second year's (1994) required distribution would be 1/20.3 times applicable account balance, since 20.3 years is the joint LE of two people ages 72 and 69. This continues until one of them dies.

The distribution in the year one spouse dies will still be calculated based on their joint LE as of their birthdays in the year of death—but in the *following* year, the decedent's LE is zero, so you switch to Table V and calculate further distributions based solely on the LE of the survivor.

So in this example suppose S dies in the second distribution year, 1994. The 1994 distribution is not changed—it is still 1/20.3 as calculated above. But in the next year, 1995, we look solely at P's LE. He will attain age 73 in 1995. The LE of a 73-year-old under Table V is 13.9 years, so the minimum distribution will be 1/13.9—a substantial increase over the prior year's 1/20.3 distribution.

And of course when the surviving spouse dies, his or her LE also goes to zero in the year following the death, and 100% of the plan benefits must be distributed by December 31 of the year after the year of death of the surviving spouse. (Note: if *P* died first, S could roll over the benefits to her own IRA and start a new distribution schedule going.)

P and S: "split" or "hybrid" method

This is very tricky. To calculate the joint and survivor LE of two people, when one LE is being recalculated annually and the other is not, you must go through the following routine prescribed by the proposed regulations. Alternatively, you can use a software program to do the calculations; see Appendix D.

In the following example, assume P turned age 71 in 1993, his first required distribution year, and S turned 68. His LE is to be recalculated, hers is not. Say it is now the fourth distribution year, 1996. Prop. Reg. § E-8(b) says you still use the joint and survivor LE from Table VI but you use P's *real age*, and an "adjusted age" for S. P's real attained age in year four is 74. S's real age is 71, but her "adjusted age" is determined as follows:

(a)   Determine her real LE, separately, for the year in which P reached age 70½. Her attained age in that year was 68. Her LE at age 68 under Table V was 17.6 years.

(b)   Now reduce her LE as determined under (a) above by one year for each year since that year. It has been three years, so her "adjusted" LE in year four is 17.6 minus 3, or 14.6.

(c)   Now determine the age in Table V which corresponds to a 14.6 year LE. That would be age 72. (If it came out in between two ages you would round up to the higher age.) So her "adjusted age" is 72.

(d)   The joint and survivor LE of two individuals age 74 and 72 under Table VI is 18.2 years, so this year's required minimum is 1/18.2.

If S in this example died, future installments would nevertheless continue to be calculated as before based on the "adjusted age" of the DB (ignoring the fact that she died, since P did not elect to recalculate her LE) and P's *actual* age. If P dies before S, future MRDs to S will be calculated based on the number of years remaining in her original LE (17.6 years). (Alternatively, she may elect to roll over the benefits to her own IRA and start a new minimum distribution game going.)

P and non-spouse DB: the MDIB rule

If P elects to take installments over the joint LE of himself and a non-spouse DB, the calculation of the annual required distribution during their joint lives will essentially be the same as when the spouse is the DB, *except* for one additional step required to comply with the MDIB rule: each year, the actual joint LE must be compared with the "applicable divisor" shown in the MDIB table at Prop. Reg. § 1.401(a)(9)-2, Q & A 4(a) (reproduced in Appendix A). The LE (divisor) used must be the *smaller* of those two numbers.

If P's attained age in the year he turns 70½ is 70, the divisor in the first distribution year under the MDIB rule is 26.2. If it is 71, it will be 25.3 years.

Then, when P dies, the MDIB rule disappears, and the divisor now "flips" to being based on the true joint LE of the DB and P, because "the MDIB requirement does not apply to distributions after the employee's death." Prop. Reg. § 1.401(a)(9)-2, Q & A 3.

For example, suppose Mimi commences taking installments at her RBD (4/1/94) over the LE of herself and her daughter Grizelda. In 1993, Mimi turns 70½ (on November 1); her attained age on her 1993 birthday (5/1/93) is 70, and Grizelda's age on her 1993 birthday is 40. Their joint LE from Table VI is 42.9 years. But the maximum "applicable divisor" permitted for Mimi's first distribution year under the MDIB rule is 26.2. The distribution schedule during Mimi's life is shown in Table 1.4.

Table 1.4		
Latest Withdrawal Date	**This Fraction**	**Applied to Plan Balance on**
4/1/94	1/26.2	12/31/92
12/31/94	1/25.3	12/31/93
12/31/95	1/24.4	12/31/94
....etc.		

Now suppose Mimi dies at age 86 in 2009. In the following year, 2010, distributions will "flip" to being calculated on the *original* joint LE of Mimi and Grizelda, without regard to the MDIB rule. The joint LE of Mimi and Grizelda back in 1993 (ages 70 and 40) was 42.9 years. 17 years have passed since then, so the remaining period certain is 25.9 years (42.9 minus 17), so distributions will from now on be as shown in Table 1.5. (This assumes Mimi elected not to recalculate her LE annually.)

Table 1.5		
By This Date	**Take Out This Fraction:**	**Of Plan Balance on:**
12/31/10	1/25.9	12/31/09
12/31/11	1/24.9	12/31/10
... and so on until 2036		

P dies before RBD: installments over DB's LE

Upon the death of P before his RBD, if distributions are to be made over the LE of the DB, the required annual distributions to the DB are calculated as follows. If there is one DB, determine his LE from Table V based on his attained age as of his birthday in the year distributions are required to commence, *i.e.* (in the case of a non-spouse DB) the year after the year in which P died, Prop. Reg. § E-3 & 4. If the DB is S, see "The Spouse and § 401(a)(9)," Chapter 3.

If there are several DBs, determine which of them is the oldest. Distributions will be based on the oldest one's LE calculated as above, unless "separate accounts" were established for the DBs "as of" the date of death.

MRD Potpourri

Non-taxable distributions

There is nothing in the Code that says only taxable distributions fulfill the requirement of taking a MRD. Thus, an employee who has made non-deductible contributions to his retirement plan can, if he wishes, use distributions from that account to fulfill the MRD requirement rather than taking fully taxable distributions.

Who pays the penalty?

Suppose P dies after his RBD, but before taking the MRD for the year of death. His beneficiary also fails to take any distribution in that year. Who is liable for the penalty on the undistributed amount? § 4974 says that the penalty is imposed on "the payee," by which Congress presumably meant the person who is supposed to receive payment of the distribution. Reg. § 54.4974-1 adds no enlightenment. Surely the penalty cannot be imposed on P, since at the time he died he was not yet required to take the distribution (he had until the end of the year). But imposing the penalty on the beneficiary also seems unfair, especially if P waited until the very end of the year, so the beneficiary did not have enough time to act.

Also unclear: if three beneficiaries divide an inherited IRA after P's death, who is liable for how much of the penalty if one of the three fails to take out his or her share of the MRD (assuming the shares were not considered "separate accounts"; see *"Naming more than one beneficiary: before the RBD,"* above)?

Estate planning for the beneficiary who inherits an IRA

Example: Jerry Johnson dies at age 69, leaving his IRA to his daughter Pam Johnson Williams as "Designated Beneficiary." Pam turns age 49 in the year after Jerry's death, so (according to the IRS tables) Pam's life expectancy is 34 years. In the year following her father's death, she begins withdrawing from the IRA, as beneficiary, in installments over her life expectancy, pursuant to § 401(a)(9)(B)(iii)—1/34th the first year, 1/33rd the second year, 1/32d the third year and so on. At age 62 (13 years into the 34-year payout), Pam dies. At this point, two questions arise: WHEN must the balance of Jerry's IRA be distributed? And TO WHOM is it distributed?

WHEN: The Code provides that, if Jerry died before his required distributions began [he did], and if his benefits were payable to a DB [they were—Pam], and if the DB took the first required distribution in the year after Jerry's death [she did], then the benefits can be "distributed (in accordance with regulations) over the life of such designated beneficiary *(*or over a period not extending beyond the life expectancy of such beneficiary*)*." § 401(a)(9)(B)(ii), (iii).

The proposed regulations provide that a plan can allow the employee or beneficiary to elect among the permitted distribution methods, can provide a default provision in case of no election or can provide a mandatory form of distribution. If an election is allowed, it becomes irrevocable on December 31 of the year in which distributions are required to commence, "with respect to the beneficiary *(and all subsequent beneficiaries)* and must apply to all subsequent years." § C-4(c) (emphasis added).

"For purposes of calculating the distribution period described in section 401(a)(9)(B)(iii), the designated beneficiary will be determined as of the employee's date of death," § D-4, even if he or she dies "after the employee but before" his or her birthday in the year following the date of death. § E-2(c). In other words, once the original participant's death has occurred, and the DB is alive on that date of death (i.e., survives the participant), the life expectancy payout period is established; the DB's life expectancy is "the distribution period." § E-5(a)(1). "If the DB whose life expectancy is being used to calculate the distribution period dies on or after the applicable date, such beneficiary's remaining life expectancy will be used to determine the distribution period whether or not a beneficiary with a shorter life expectancy receives the benefits." § E-5(e)(2).

So, if the DB lives longer than his "life expectancy," that does not give him the right to extend the payout. Similarly, if he dies before the end of the "distribution period," his death does not accelerate the distributions. (There is an exception—if the beneficiary's life expectancy is being recalculated, then his or her death *does* accelerate the payout. But since only the participant's and his spouse's life expectancies can be recalculated, this rule has no bearing on a payout to a *non-spouse* beneficiary.)

So the answer is: Pam's death has *no effect* on the schedule of required distributions. Whoever is next entitled to ownership of the account can continue to withdraw the benefits over the balance of Pam's original 34-year life expectancy. But the next big question is...

WHO is entitled to ownership of the account after the death of the original beneficiary? The Code and proposed regulations provide no answer to this question, because the minimum distribution rules are unconcerned with the question of who is entitled to the benefits. The minimum distribution rules are concerned only with WHEN the benefits must be distributed. Sometimes the question of WHEN the benefits must be distributed depends on WHO is entitled to them, but the IRS doesn't purport to say WHO that is.

In contrast to Question 1, there is not necessarily an easy answer to Question 2. In fact this is a vast unexplored territory. Depending on applicable state law and/or the terms of the contract between the original IRA owner and the IRA provider, the deceased beneficiary's interest in the inherited IRAs would pass either to a named beneficiary or as part of the deceased original beneficiary's probate estate.

If the account becomes an asset of the beneficiary's estate, the IRA custodian should accept direction from the duly appointed personal representative of the estate regarding how the account is now to be registered. For example, if the deceased beneficiary's will contains a specific bequest of this inherited IRA to the beneficiary's surviving spouse, or if the account passes to the surviving spouse by intestacy, the IRA provider should recognize the spouse as the new "beneficiary-owner" when directed to do so by the personal representative. This does not in any way necessitate distributing the account in a lump sum either to the estate or to the new owner of the account.

Example, continued: After Jerry's death, the name on his account was changed from "Jerry Johnson IRA" to either "Pam Johnson Williams, as beneficiary of Jerry Johnson, deceased" or "Jerry Johnson (deceased) IRA, for the benefit of Pam Johnson Williams, beneficiary," and the Social Security number on the account was changed from Jerry's to Pam's. When Pam died without having designated any further beneficiary for this account, the IRA provider's policy is to treat the account as an asset of her probate estate. The Lackov Trust Company is appointed as Pam's executor. Pam's will leaves her entire estate to her husband Trevor Williams. The Lackov Trust Company instructs the IRA provider to change the name on the account to "Jerry Johnson (deceased) IRA, f/b/o Trevor Williams beneficiary," and to put Trevor's social security number on the account.

Summary of Planning Principles

1.   The opportunity for continued income tax deferral on earnings and investment income is the most valuable feature of qualified retirement plans and IRAs. Preserving the option of continued tax deferral is an important goal of estate planning for retirement benefits. The minimum distribution rules set the outer limits on deferral and establish the requirements for reaching those limits. Planning for retirement benefits therefore requires familiarity with these rules.

2.   Naming a beneficiary for retirement benefits does more than determine who will receive the benefits after P's death; it also determines the maximum period of income tax deferral that will be available for those benefits.

3.   Once P reaches his RBD, the maximum deferral period for his benefits, as dictated by his choice of beneficiary, becomes substantially irrevocable. He can later change his choice of beneficiary, but cannot extend the payout period.

4.   Naming P's "estate" as beneficiary, generally speaking, substantially reduces the opportunities for continued income tax deferral compared with naming an individual beneficiary.

5.   Naming a trust as beneficiary has the same effect as naming an estate, unless the "trust rules" are complied with; see Chapter 6.

6.   Naming a young beneficiary at the RBD will

produce the longest possible income tax deferral, both during P's life and after his death. Naming any DB will almost always produce more potential income tax deferral than having "no DB."

7.   If P is naming more than one beneficiary, consider dividing the benefits into separate "accounts" before the RBD, especially if the beneficiaries are substantially apart in age, to enable each individual beneficiary to use his/her own life expectancy to measure payouts after P's death.

8.   Do not mix charities and individuals in a beneficiary designation if you want the individuals to be able to use the life expectancy payout method, unless you comply with the "separate account" procedure; see Chapter 7.

9.   When P reaches his RBD, consider carefully not only the choice of "DB" but also the decision whether to recalculate life expectancies. Carefully document the identity of the DB, and the choices regarding "recalculation," at the RBD and save these records "forever."

10.   If P is not certain who to name as DB at his RBD, or how to determine life expectancies, consider establishing separate IRAs, with different beneficiaries, or different methods of determining life expectancy, for each.

Income Tax Issues

*The impact of income taxes on
estate planning for retirement
benefits.*

Introduction

This chapter examines three aspects of the income tax treatment of retirement benefits: how benefits are taxed (as "income in respect of a decedent" or "IRD") after the death of the participant ("P"); the special tax treatment given to certain lump sum distributions and distributions of employer stock; and deferring income taxes with "rollovers."

For treatment of IRD payable to a charity or charitable remainder trust, see Chapter 7.

Income in Respect of a Decedent

Overview; no stepped-up basis

Although generally property in a decedent's gross estate gets a new basis for income tax purposes, equal to its estate tax value, "property which constitutes a right to receive an item of income in respect of a decedent" (IRD) is an exception; IRD does not get a new basis at death. § 1014(c). IRD is not defined in the Code, but may be generally defined as "income earned by an individual that is not realized until after his death."

§ 691 governs the income tax treatment of IRD. Under § 691(a)(1), IRD is includible (when received) in the gross income of the person or entity who acquired, from the decedent, the right to receive such income. This could be the estate (if the right to receive the income passes to the estate as a result of decedent's death); or a person who is entitled to receive the income directly as decedent's beneficiary under a retirement plan or similar arrangement; or a beneficiary who is entitled to receive the IRD by virtue of a bequest under the decedent's will.

§ 691(a)(2), in addition, imposes a tax on the transfer of the right-to-receive IRD by the person or entity who received the right-to-receive the IRD from the decedent. However, there is an exception: the tax is *not* imposed on a transfer of the right-to-receive IRD to the person who is *entitled* to the IRD by reason of the decedent's death or as a result of a bequest from the decedent. So, § 691 makes a distinction between "IRD" and "the right-to-receive IRD." Generally, IRD is taxed to the recipient upon receipt; but if the right-to-receive the IRD is transferred, before the IRD is actually received, the transfer itself will trigger an income tax unless the exception applies.

Death benefits under qualified plans, 403(b) plans, and IRAs are IRD, and thus will be subject to income tax when distributed to the beneficiary. There are a few exceptions: the employee's after-tax contributions (or other "investment in the contract" or "basis"), and the pure death benefit portion of life insurance, are not subject to income tax. The recovery of the employee's "basis" or "investment in the contract" normally has little impact on planning decisions and so is not discussed in this book, except in connection with plan-held life insurance; this and all other aspects of plan-held life insurance are discussed in Chapter 10. See also "LSD Rewards Part 1: Net Unrealized Appreciation," below, for another variation in the imposition of income tax on IRD.

Thus, retirement benefits are generally subject to *both* estate taxes and income taxes. This creates numerous planning considerations, one of which is the desirability of deferring the imposition of income taxes as long as possible; how best to achieve that goal was the subject of Chapter 1.

Another planning consideration is, once distribution does occur, how to keep the income tax as low as possible. If an IRD item is paid out to the named beneficiary (for example, if a profit sharing benefit is paid directly to an individual who is the designated beneficiary), then that beneficiary pays income tax on that money as it is distributed to him or her. This creates an incentive to direct these benefits to beneficiaries in a low income tax bracket.

Drawback of making IRD payable to a trust

IRD paid to a trust is generally subject to trust income tax rates. (For an exception, see "LSD Rewards, Part 2: Special Averaging Methods," below.) A trust reaches the highest federal income tax bracket (39.6%) at $8,450 of taxable income (1999 rates). An individual taxpayer does not hit that bracket until he has more than $283,150 of taxable income. Thus, making retirement benefits payable to a marital, credit shelter or other trust may result in the benefits' being taxed more heavily than if the benefits were paid to individual family members.

Example: Grover dies, leaving his $200,000 401(k) plan to a trust for his wife, Ginger. The trust provides that the income of the trust is to be paid to Ginger; at her death the principal is paid to their children. Under the terms of the 401(k) plan, the only form of benefit permitted is a lump sum. Assume that "forward averaging" (see "LSD Rewards, Part 2" below) is not available, and that this $200,000 is the only taxable income of the trust. The result? The trust receives the $200,000 distribution and pays $78,236 of federal income tax on it (1999 rates).

Now assume the lump sum had instead been paid to Ginger outright, and that her other income exactly equaled her deductions and exemptions. Her tax on the distribution would have been only $60,266 or $18,000 less than the trust had to pay. Thus if the benefits had been paid to the spouse individually rather than to a trust she would have had more money available to invest, spend or give away.

Note that IRD distributed from a retirement plan to a trust is generally "principal" for trust accounting purposes. However, for *income tax purposes*, it is "income."

A not-very-useful rule: a trust generally gets an income tax deduction for distributing income to trust beneficiaries. The beneficiaries then have to include that income on their individual tax returns. The calculation of what items of taxable income get passed out to the beneficiaries is based on a concept called "distributable net income" or "DNI." Distributions of "DNI" transfer the income tax burden from the trust to the beneficiary. The income will then be taxed at the beneficiary's personal rate rather than the trust's rate. §§ 661, 662. This method of shifting the tax liability is not normally very useful because the purpose of paying benefits to a trust will generally be defeated if the benefits are immediately distributed to the beneficiary.

Example: Colin names his credit shelter trust as beneficiary of his $600,000 IRA. The goal is to keep the benefits out of the taxable estate of his wife Chandler. Colin dies. The trustee of the credit shelter trust withdraws the income of the IRA annually and also withdraws the $600,000 "principal" of the benefits in five annual installments of $120,000. Under the terms of Colin's credit shelter trust, all income is paid to Chandler, so the trustee distributes the IRA income to her and it is taxed at her personal income tax rate. The annual withdrawals of $120,000 of "principal," however, stay in the credit shelter trust and are taxed at trust rates.

If the terms of Colin's credit shelter trust permit the trustee to distribute principal to Chandler, the trustee *could* reduce the income taxes by distributing to Chandler all the principal he is withdrawing from the IRA each year. This would cause these distributions to be taxed at Chandler's rate rather than the trust's—but it would also defeat the entire purpose of the credit shelter trust, which is to keep this asset out of Chandler's estate. Once five years had passed since Colin's death, the trustee would have withdrawn all benefits from the IRA and distributed them to Chandler and the credit shelter trust would be left with nothing.

Note: this is an extremely simplified description of a complex subject, namely, the income tax treatment of retirement benefits paid to and from trusts, a more thorough explanation of which is outside the scope of this book. See the Bibliography for other sources.

Tax treatment of IRD paid to an estate

IRD items will be taxed to the estate if paid to the estate. However, if the estate, before actually receiving the income, distributes the *right* to receive the income, then:

(a)   the distributee will be taxable on the income, if he/she acquired it by specific bequest or as residuary legatee of the estate; Reg. §§ 1.691(a)-2(b), examples (1) and (2); 1.691(a)-4(b).

(b)   If the distribution is treated as a "sale," however, the estate is taxable (on the greater of the value of the right transferred, or the consideration—if any—received for the transfer). Reg. § 1.691(a)-4(a). See *"Planning pitfall: assignment of the right-to-receive IRD,"* below.

If the will "bequeaths" retirement benefits to a particular

beneficiary, but the benefits are paid to the estate before the estate gets a chance to assign the "right-to-receive" the benefits to the beneficiary, distributing the benefits to the beneficiary upon receipt should carry out DNI to the beneficiary. Although normally all items of income are pro-rated proportionately among beneficiaries who receive distributions, a different allocation specified in the governing instrument is respected. Reg. § 1.661(b)-1.

The following examples illustrate these rules.

Example 1: Larry names Liz as beneficiary of his IRA. Liz is taxable on IRA distributions she receives after Larry's death.

Example 2: Mike names his estate as beneficiary of his IRA. His will provides that any IRA benefits are specifically bequeathed to Liz. After Mike's death, the estate assigns the IRA to Liz. Liz pays the tax on the IRA distributions.

IRD payable to non-charitable trust

If the right-to-receive IRD is distributed as a specific "bequest" from a *trust*, rather than an *estate*, the same principles should apply: the beneficiary who is entitled to the item, and not the trust, bears the income tax. Reg. § 1.691(a)-(4)(b).

If the right-to-receive is distributed to the trust beneficiaries under a discretionary power to distribute principal, do the beneficiaries pay the income tax? Presumably the answer is yes, although the regulations provide only that if a trust *terminates* and distributes the right-to-receive to the beneficiaries, the beneficiaries pay the tax. Reg. § 1.691(a)-4(b)(3). Jeffrey Pennell points out that possibly a discretionary distribution of principal would be considered a "partial termination" of the trust and thus fit within the regulation cited.

Planning pitfall: assignment of the right-to-receive IRD

The major planning pitfall of IRD has to do with "assignments" of the right-to-receive such income, which trigger immediate tax under § 691(a)(2). The problem of assignment of the right-to-receive IRD does not exist when IRD assets are divided up to fulfill **fractional bequests**; see, *e.g.,* PLR 9537005 (6/13/95), Ruling 7. The pitfall comes when the right-to-receive IRD is used to satisfy a **pecuniary bequest**.

It is axiomatic among estate planners that a distribution of the right-to-receive IRD in fulfillment of a pecuniary bequest triggers immediate realization of income by the estate or other funding entity.[1] In view of the universality of this belief, it is

---

[1]See, *e.g.*, Alan S. Acker, Income in Respect of a Decedent, 862 Tax Mgmt. (BNA), at A-11; Jonathan G. Blattmachr, "Income in Respect of a Decedent," 12 Probate Notes 47 (1986), 50; Natalie B. Choate, Life and Death Planning for Retirement Benefits, 1st ed., (Foundation for Continuing Education, 1993); CCH 1997 Standard Federal Tax Reporter, ¶25,306.0112; M. Carr Ferguson, *et al.*, Federal Income Taxation of Estates, Trust and Beneficiaries (2d ed. 1997) at 3:27; E. James Gamble, "Planning for Distributions from Retirement Plans," N.Y.U. Proceedings of the Forty-Fifth Institute on Federal Taxation, Vol. 1, Ch. 27, § 27.04[5] last paragraph (1987, p. 27-15); Norman H. Lane and Howard M. Zaritzky, Federal Income Taxation of Estates and Trusts, 2d Ed., (Warren Gorham & Lamont, 1988-1997) ¶15.08, pp.15-54,55; Alson Martin, Esq., "Recent Developments/Estate Planning/Post Mortem Planning for QRPs and IRAs," in course materials for ALI-ABA seminar Professional Organizations, Qualified Plans, etc., 2/98, at p. 103; Louis A. Mezzullo, Estate and Gift Tax Issues for Employee Benefit Plans, 378 Tax Mgmt. (BNA) A-31; Michael D. Mulligan, "Planning for Income in

surprising to learn that this result is not specified in any Code section, Treasury regulation or Revenue Ruling, nor has any reported case ever so held.

However, this widely held belief does not spring out of thin air. It derives partly from the regulations under § 691(a)(2). The IRS, in its regulations, does not come right out and say that transferring the right-to-receive IRD in fulfilment of a pecuniary bequest is treated as a non-exempt transfer of the right-to-receive, but strongly implies it. Reg. § 1.691(a)-4(b)(2) says that, if the right-to-receive IRD is transferred to "a *specific* or *residuary* legatee" (emphasis added), only the legatee includes the IRD in income. The negative implication is that fulfilling a *pecuniary* bequest with the right-to-receive IRD does *not* carry out the income tax burden to the legatee. In other words, the regulation implies that satisfying a pecuniary bequest with the right-to-receive IRD should be treated as a "sale," just as (under Reg. § 1.661(a)-2(f)(1)) satisfying a pecuniary bequest with appreciated property is treated as a "sale."

Furthermore, the IRS has indicated in several private letter rulings that it considers the "sale" principle of §1.661(a)-2(f)(1) applicable to funding a pecuniary bequest with the right-to-receive IRD. PLRs 9123036 (3/12/91) (using an installment obligation to fund a pecuniary **credit shelter** gift would trigger realization of gain); 9315016 (1/15/93) and 9507008 (11/10/94) (satisfying pecuniary legacies with Series E or H bonds triggers realization by the funding entity of the untaxed interest accruals on the bonds, which were IRD).

IRD, however, is taxed under § 691, not §§ 661-663. It

Respect of a Decedent Can Minimize Effects of Double Taxation," 57 J. Tax'n 22, pp. 106-112 (1982); Willard B. Thompson, "How to Structure a Trust as Beneficiary of a Qualified Plan or IRA Death Benefits," Estate Planning, January/February 1988 at p. 10.

is taxed only when § 691 says it is taxed. § 691's standards for carrying out the income tax burden to the beneficiaries are not the same as the "DNI" rules of §§ 661-663. Thus, it is quite logical, under the Code, that a pecuniary bequest funded with *IRD* could carry the income tax burden to the beneficiary when funding the same bequest with *appreciated property* would not.

Example: Ron dies, leaving his $1 million IRA payable to his trust as beneficiary. The trust contains a pecuniary marital formula bequest, under which the marital trust is entitled to $400,000. The trust holds no other assets except the IRA. Ron's trustee transfers $400,000 of the IRA to the marital trust and keeps the rest for the residuary credit shelter trust. In this example, surely the IRA is transferred to the marital trust "by bequest from the decedent." The funding trust is not "selling" or "exchanging" the IRA—it is fulfilling the pecuniary marital bequest, and a transfer in fulfillment of a bequest is not taxable under § 691(a)(2). The trust has no choice regarding which asset to use to fund the marital trust—the IRA is the only asset available.

Most commentators assume that transferring IRD in fulfillment of a pecuniary bequest is exactly the same as fulfilling such a bequest with appreciated property in kind, but the rationale for taxing the transfer of appreciated property in fulfillment of a pecuniary bequest does not exist in the case of Ron's IRA. When a pecuniary bequest is fulfilled by a transfer of appreciated property in kind, the transaction is treated as a "sale" of that property because the residuary estate has, by this transaction, realized the benefit of the appreciation that has occurred between the date of death and the date of funding the bequest. The residuary estate has an asset which has grown in value, and uses this to satisfy a fixed dollar liability, thereby in effect "cashing in" that appreciation to satisfy its obligation. The recipient of the pecuniary bequest did *not* benefit from the appreciation, because he would have received the same dollar value either way, whether in cash or in property.

IRD, however, is different. The right-to-receive IRD is not "appreciated property." In fact a retirement plan such as an IRA, which is a common form of "right-to-receive IRD," could easily have *depreciated* in value between the date of death and the date of funding particular bequests. The residuary estate has not necessarily realized any "profit" by funding the pecuniary bequest with IRD, or, if it has realized a gain, it is only to the extent there has been appreciation after the date of death.

Although the precise question discussed here has never been decided, the principle that § 691 overrides the §§ 661-662 scheme is established in other contexts. It has been stated that "the general distribution rules of subchapter J...do not apply to distributions of rights to [IRD]...[the DNI] scheme is antagonistic to the rules of section 691...Section 691...prevails over the rules relating generally to distributions, and a transfer to a beneficiary of property representing [IRD] is treated as a neutral event." James J. Freeland, *et al.,* "Estate and Trust Distribution of Property in Kind After the Tax Reform Act of 1984," 38 Tax L. Rev. 449, 463 (1985).

On another, similar issue, the question of whether an estate can take a distributions deduction for distributing the right-to-receive IRD, the Tax Court (in holding that the estate can not take such a deduction despite the specific language of § 661(a), which appears to allow deduction) has stated that, "We hold as a general principle that section 691 overrides sections 661 and 662" (Edmund D. Rollert Residuary Trust, 85-1 USTC ¶ 9139 (C.A. 6); 752 F2d 112) and "...the transfer by an estate of section 691 property is treated as a neutral event, and is not subject to the distribution rules of section 661 and 662" (Estate of Jack Dean, 46 TCM 184 (1983)).

Letter rulings allow fulfilling pecuniary bequests with IRD

Letter rulings indicate that the IRS *may* have recognized that transferring retirement benefits in fulfillment of a pecuniary marital bequest is not a § 691(a)(2) transfer. In PLR 9524020 (3/21/95), an estate was allowed to transfer an IRA directly to a surviving spouse in fulfillment of a pecuniary spousal share under state statute.

PLR 9608036 (11/29/95) involved the transfer of an IRA by a pourover trust in fulfillment of a pecuniary formula marital gift. The ruling treated the IRA, for purposes of the spousal rollover rules, as acquired by the spouse "from the decedent," not "from the trust." If the IRA were deemed acquired "from the trust" (a "third party") rather than "from the decedent," it would not have been eligible for rollover under § 408, according to the ruling. This logic is similar to that of § 691(a)(2), under which a transfer of the right-to-receive IRD to one who is entitled to it by bequest *from the decedent* is not a taxable event, while a transfer to any other person *is* taxable.

In PLR 9623056 (3/12/96), the decedent's IRA was payable to a trust which was also the residuary beneficiary of his will. The trust created a marital trust by means of a pecuniary marital formula, and a residuary credit shelter trust. The IRA was not payable to either of these specific subtrusts. The IRS permitted a tax-free rollover by the spouse of the portion of the IRA allocated to the marital trust.

In PLR 9808043 (11/24/97), an IRA was payable to P's estate. The will left a "pecuniary formula marital bequest outright to" the spouse, and left "the remainder" to a "credit shelter trust." Because the surviving spouse, as executrix, was entitled to and did use the IRA to fund the pecuniary marital bequest, and the bequest was outright, the IRS ruled that the surviving spouse was entitled to roll over the IRA proceeds distributed to her via the pecuniary bequest.

In none of these four rulings did the IRS say that the transfer of the IRA generated current income to the funding entity. Although the IRS did not mention the subject of IRD or § 691(a)(2) in any of these rulings, in view of the emphasis on the fact that pecuniary bequests were involved it is hard to believe the IRS is overlooking the § 691(a)(2) issue time after time.

A possible explanation, which would make these rulings consistent with the otherwise apparently inconsistent letter rulings (holding that Reg. § 661(a)-2(f)(1) applies to funding a pecuniary bequest with the right-to-receive IRD), *may* be found in the statutory conflict between §§ 402 and 408, on the one hand, and § 691(a)(2) on the other. The Code provides that the income represented by qualified plans and IRAs is included in gross income only when it is "actually distributed" (§ 402(a)) or "paid or distributed" (§ 408(d)(1)). These provisions override other normal income tax rules such as the doctrine of constructive receipt. Perhaps they also override § 691(a)(2).

For more on this issue, see "Mysteries of IRD," by Natalie B. Choate, Tax Management Memorandum Vol. 38, No. 20, p. 235 (Tax Management Inc., Washington, D.C., 9/29/97). See also discussion at Acker, *supra*, at § VII(A)(1)(g),(h), p. A-27; and PLR 1999-25033 (3/25/99) in which the IRS ruled that a non-pro rata division of community property, in which a surviving spouse took the decedent's IRA as part of the surviving spouse's share of the community property, did not constitute a § 691(a)(2) "assignment."

Planning mode: Because of the IRS' apparent position that funding a pecuniary bequest with IRD is a taxable transfer, planners are strongly advised to avoid having retirement benefits pass through a pecuniary funding formula. If benefits must pass to a trust, make them payable to a trust that is not going to have to be divided up. Or, if the benefits are going to a trust which

will be divided among various shares (*e.g.*, a marital and a family
share), either specify clearly (in both the designation of
beneficiary form and in the trust instrument) which trust share
these retirement benefits go to (so that the benefits pass to the
chosen share directly, rather than through the funding formula),
or use a fractional formula (fulfillment of which does not trigger
immediate realization of IRD) rather than a pecuniary formula
(which may).

Cleanup mode: Although it is highly advisable to steer
clear of funding a pecuniary bequest with qualified plan or IRA
benefits, inevitably some participants will leave their benefits
payable to a trust which contains a pecuniary funding formula.
In these circumstances, first look into the possibility of using
disclaimers to get the benefits payable to the "right" beneficiary
(see Chapter 8). If that course is not available, and the
retirement benefit must pass through the pecuniary funding
formula, see if the benefits can be passed through the pecuniary
formula to the spouse for a spousal rollover (see letter rulings
cited above), and the other arguments cited above for why
funding the pecuniary gift with this asset should not trigger tax.

Deduction for Estate Taxes Paid on IRD

How the deduction is calculated

The federal estate tax paid on IRD is deductible for
federal income tax purposes. § 691(c). To determine the amount
of the deduction, first determine the estate tax on the entire
estate. Next, determine the net value of all items of IRD that
were includible in the estate. For definition of net value see §
691(c)(2)(B). The estate tax attributable to the IRD is the
difference between the actual federal estate tax due on the
estate, and the federal estate tax that would have been due had

all the IRD had been excluded from the estate.

Example: Harvey dies in 1999, leaving his $2 million taxable estate (including a $1 million pension plan) to his daughter Emma. The federal estate tax on a $2 million taxable estate, after deducting the unified credit and the maximum credit for state death taxes, is $469,900. If the $1 million IRA were excluded from the taxable estate, the taxable estate would be only $1 million, and the estate tax would be $101,300. Thus the amount of federal estate tax attributable to the IRA is $469,900 minus $101,300, or $368,600. Emma will be entitled to an income tax deduction of $368,600 and will pay income tax on only $631,400 of the $1 million pension distribution. Note that, even though the IRA constituted only 50% of the taxable estate, it accounted for 75% of the estate tax.

Note also the following:

(a)   The deductible portion of the estate tax is computed at the marginal rate, not the average rate; this is favorable to the taxpayer.

(b)   State estate taxes are *not* deductible; this is unfavorable.

(c)   The computations become more complex if a marital or charitable deduction is involved; this topic is beyond the scope of this book. See Westfall, David and Mair, George P., *Estate Planning Law and Taxation*, (3d ed., Warren, Gorham & Lamont, Boston 1998), ¶ 14.02.

Planning for client with short life expectancy

There are times when an estate planner is called upon to advise a client who, due to accident or illness, has a severely shortened life expectancy. One suggestion to consider is cashing out retirement plan benefits that will have to be cashed out anyway shortly after the client's demise (either because of minimum distribution requirements, or to pay estate taxes, or just because the beneficiaries will want the money).

When an IRA or other tax-deferred retirement plan will have to be cashed out shortly after P's death anyway, there can be as many as three reasons why it is better to cash out the account immediately *before* death rather than immediately after:

First, if the plan is cashed out before death, the income taxes on the benefits are thereby removed from the estate for estate tax purposes—in effect, both the federal *and* state income taxes on the benefits become 100% deductible for estate tax purposes. If the plan is cashed out *after* death, the recipient of the benefits gets a federal income tax deduction under § 691(c) for the *federal* estate taxes paid on the benefits—but *not* for the *state* estate taxes.

Second, the § 691(c) deduction is an itemized deduction, and as such may not be fully deductible; see "*§ 691(c) deduction on the income tax return,*" below. Finally, the recipient may not be able to take the § 691(c) deduction in determining his *state* income tax. For all these reasons, paying the income taxes "first" and the estate taxes "second" may produce a lower tax burden overall than doing it the other way round. Another way to get the same advantages is to convert to a Roth IRA if the client is eligible; see "*The deathbed conversion,*" Chapter 5.

On the other hand, if the death benefits will be paid to charity (so they will not be subject to income taxes—see Chapter 7), or will be paid to a designated beneficiary over a long life expectancy (so the income taxes can be deferred for a long time—see Chapter 1) this arbitrage advantage disappears. Similarly, if the beneficiary is in a lower income tax bracket than P, that may reduce the "arbitrage" advantage.

Who gets the deduction

The deduction goes to the person who receives the IRD, not the person who paid the estate tax. If there are several beneficiaries who receive the IRD, the deduction is apportioned among them in proportion to the amounts of IRD each received.

Example: Jack dies with an estate of $3 million. He leaves his $1 million IRA (which is entirely IRD) to his daughters Jill and Holly. He leaves his $2 million probate estate (which is not IRD) to his son Alex. Alex pays the federal estate tax of $897,500. The § 691(c) deduction ($427,600) goes equally to Jill and Holly because they received the IRD.

§ 691(c) deduction for installment and annuity payouts

Calculating the § 691(c) deduction is easy when the beneficiary receives a distribution of the entire benefit all at once. What if the retirement benefit is not distributed as a lump sum but rather in installments over the life expectancy of the beneficiary? Clearly the deduction will also be spread out; but how much of the deduction is allocated to each payment? How much of each distribution represents "IRD" that was included in the gross estate, and how much represents income earned by the retirement plan after the date of death?

When IRD is in the form of a joint and survivor *annuity*, the Code requires that the § 691(c) deduction be amortized over the surviving annuitant's life expectancy and apportioned equally to the annuity payments received by the survivor. § 691(d). However, the author is aware of no authority discussing the allocation of the deduction to non-annuity payouts, such as instalment payments.

For a catalogue of several possible alternative methods, see the excellent article "Inherited IRAs: When Deferring

Distributions Doesn't Make Sense," by Christopher R. Hoyt, Trusts & Estates, June 1998, p. 52. For possible future developments in this area, keep an eye on QDOT regulations and rulings, where deciding which retirement plan distributions constitute IRD and which constitute post-death earnings is critical to application of the deferred estate tax; see Chapter 4.

Meanwhile, the method used by many practitioners (based on an unscientific survey by the author) could be called the "IRD comes out first" method. All distributions from the retirement plan are assumed to be coming out of the IRD (rather than out of the post-death earnings of the plan) until the § 691(c) deduction has been entirely used up:

Example: In the Jack and Jill example above, the total § 691(c) deduction was $427,600, which is 42.76% of the total $1 million IRA. Suppose the IRA has grown to be worth $1.2 million by the time Jill and Holly, the beneficiaries, take their first withdrawal of $30,000 each. They assume the distributions come entirely from the $1 million original principal of the IRA (from the IRD, in other words) and none of it from the $200,000 post-death earnings, so each daughter takes a deduction equal to 42.76% of her $30,000 distribution, or $12,801. She keeps doing this until the daughters collectively have received $1 million of distributions from the IRA, at which point they have used up the entire $427,600 § 691(c) deduction.

§ 691(c) deduction on the income tax return

The § 691(c) deduction is reported as an "other miscellaneous deduction" on the beneficiary's income tax return. As such, it is not subject to the 2% "floor" applicable to "miscellaneous itemized deductions." § 67(b)(7); see line instructions to IRS form 1040, Schedule A. However, it is an "itemized deduction," and as such it is subject to the reduction of itemized deductions by up to 3% of AGI in excess of $114,700 (as of 1995), if paid to an *individual*. § 68.

Example: In 1995, Joyce receives a $500,000 distribution from her deceased mother's IRA. Assume the § 691(c) deduction allocable to this distribution is $200,000. Assume Joyce's other AGI is $114,700, she is single, and she has no other itemized deductions. Her $200,000 itemized deduction for the estate tax paid on the IRD she has received will be reduced by 3% of her "excess" AGI. Her excess AGI in this example is $500,000 so the itemized deduction is reduced by $15,000.

The impact of the 3% reduction rule will vary from beneficiary to beneficiary depending on the size of the distribution and the amount of the beneficiary's other income and deductions. In the case of a very high income taxpayer, with few itemized deductions, the benefit of the § 691(c) deduction could be substantially reduced by the § 68 adjustment:

Example: same facts as in the preceding example, except now Joyce has $2 million of other income in excess of $114,700 and no other itemized deductions. If she did not receive the $500,000 IRA distribution, her taxable income would be:

Taxable income: $2,114,700

With the distribution, her income is:

Gross:		$2,614,700
Less: itemized deduction	200,000	
Reduced by (3% x $2,500,000)	-75,000	
	125,000	-125,000
Taxable income		$2,489,700

The § 691(c) deduction is chopped from $200,000 to $125,000. The fact that the 3% reduction rule does not apply to trusts tends to offset somewhat the higher income tax bracket generally applicable to trusts.

Lump Sum Distributions (LSD): The Basic Requirements

Introduction

Through the years, the Code has provided a special gentle treatment for "lump sum distributions" (LSD) from qualified plans. A person who wishes to obtain this special treatment is confronted with some of the most convoluted requirements known to post-ERISA man.

Congress has changed the rules on LSD treatment so often that the IRS has been unable to keep pace with regulations. There are only assorted proposed and temporary regulations issued from 1975 through 1979 (under old Code § 402(c)), which became obsolete before they could be finalized. The instructions to IRS forms 4972 and 1099-R are often the most up-to-date indication of the IRS's interpretation of the LSD rules.

From 1992 through 1999, the definition of LSD was found in § 402(d); after 1999, it will go back to its pre-1992 home, § 402(e).

For years prior to 2000, a "lump sum distribution" (LSD) from a qualified plan, as defined in § 402(d), may be eligible for various special tax treatments, including "five year forward averaging" ("5YFA") (§ 402(d)(1)); "ten year forward averaging" ("10YFA"); "20% capital gain tax" for benefits attributable to pre-1974 participation; and the postponement of tax on the "net unrealized appreciation" of employer securities distributed as part of the LSD. As a result of changes made by the Small Business Jobs Protection Act of 1996, *one* of these special deals, 5YFA, will no longer be available for distributions after 1999.

To achieve the favorable tax treatment, the taxpayer must clear various requirement "hurdles," many of which are surrounded by hidden issue "landmines." The definition of LSD, under both pre-2000 and post-1999 law, is summarized in the next section. The succeeding sections discuss the rewards granted to LSDs—and the additional "hurdles" and "landmines" which must be cleared for a particular LSD to qualify for each of these prizes.

This chapter does not exhaust the intricacies of § 402(d). The following aspects of LSDs are not treated here: LSDs under QDROs; interplay with the § 691(c) deduction; an LSD paid to multiple recipients; and distribution of annuity contracts as part of an LSD.

First hurdle: type of plan

Only distributions from § 401(a) "qualified plans" (pension, profit sharing or stock bonus) can qualify as LSDs. Both corporate plans and self-employed ("**Keogh**") plans can give rise to LSDs, but a distribution from an IRA, SEP-IRA or 403(b) plan can never qualify for LSD treatment. § 402(d)(4)(A) [before 2000]; § 402(e)(4)(D)(i) [after 1999].

Second hurdle: "reason" for distribution

The distribution must be made either:

(i)   On account of the employee's death; or
(ii)   After the employee attains age 59½; or
(iii)   On account of the employee's "separation from service."

§ 402(d)(4)(A)(i-iii) [before 2000]; § 402(e)(4)(D)(i)(I-III) [after 1999].

Reason (iii) is not available to the self-employed person; a distribution to a self-employed person is eligible for LSD treatment only under reasons (i) or (ii), or if he is "disabled," which for this purpose means "unable to engage in any substantial gainful activity by reason of any medically determined physical or mental impairment which can be expected to result in death or to be of long continued and indefinite duration." § 402(d)(4)(A)(iv) [before 2000]; § 402(e)(4)(D)(i)(IV) [after 1999]; § 72(m)(7).

These LSD "triggering events" are of significance primarily for determining whether there has been a distribution of 100% of the balance to the credit of the employee (see *"Third hurdle"*).

(a)   Landmine: separation from service

A treatise could be written on the subject of what constitutes "separation from service." If the employee in question was fired, moved to another state and is now working for a competing company while engaged in bitter litigation with his former company, he has probably "separated from service." On the other hand, if the employer from which he "separated" sold all its assets to a new company, which rehired the employee the next day to do the same job at the same desk, you may need a ruling to determine whether there has been a "separation from service." See, *e.g.*, PLR 1999-27048 (4/16/99). Defining "separation from service" is beyond the scope of this book.

(b)   Landmine: "on account of"

Occasionally taxpayers have had problems asserting that a particular LSD was made "on account of" a LSD triggering event. For example, if an employee receives a distribution upon separation from service, but at the same time the plan is terminating and *everyone* is receiving a full distribution whether or not he separated from service, the IRS may say the distribution is "on account of" the plan termination (which is not an "LSD triggering event") and *not* "on account of" the separation from service.

Third hurdle: distribution of entire balance in one taxable year

The distribution, to qualify, must be a "distribution within one taxable year of the recipient of the balance to the credit of [the] employee... from the plan." § 402(d)(4)(A) [before 2000]; § 402(e)(4)(D)(i) [after 1999]. This hurdle is surrounded by landmines. The general guiding principle is that the employee's entire balance in all "aggregated plans," determined as of the most recent triggering event (see "*Second Hurdle*," above) must be distributed to him within one calendar year. For exceptions to this rule, see the next subsection, "*Exceptions to the all-in-one-year rule*."

Clearly, if an employee takes out, say, one-third of his plan balance in 1997 and leaves two-thirds in the plan, the distribution of the one-third portion in 1997 does not qualify for LSD treatment because it is not a distribution of the entire balance. Now suppose the employee takes out the remaining two-thirds of his balance in 1998. He has taken out 100% of his (remaining) plan balance in 1998. Is the 1998 distribution a LSD? It is a distribution of 100% of the balance to his credit in one calendar year *if* the "balance to his credit" simply means the entire balance as of the date of distribution.

However, the rule is that, in order to qualify for LSD treatment, there can be distributions in only one taxable year following the most recent triggering event (see "*Second hurdle*"). See Prop. Reg. §1.402(e)-2(d)(1)(ii); Rev. Rul. 69-

495, 1969-2 C.B. 100. The "balance to the credit" of the employee is determined as of the first distribution following the most recent triggering event. This is the balance that must be distributed "in one taxable year." Notice 89-25, 1989-1 C.B. 662, Q&A 6.

Example: After Elaine retired from Acme Widget in 1997 at age 64, she withdrew $60,000 from her $800,000 Acme Widget Profit Sharing Plan account in order to fulfill her lifelong dream of traveling around the world in a submarine. Returning to the U.S. in 1998, paler but wiser, she wants to cash in the rest of her profit sharing account. This final distribution would not qualify for LSD treatment because the entire balance that existed on the date of the most recent triggering event (separation from service) was not distributed all in one calendar year.

In contrast to this, suppose that Elaine, upon returning from her cruise, died on her way to the Acme benefits office. Now there is a new triggering event, the death of the employee. Her beneficiary can elect LSD treatment for her remaining plan balance even though Elaine, had she lived, could not have done so. Another alternative: suppose Elaine had withdrawn the $60,000 for her cruise *before* she retired. Then her later separation from service would have been a new triggering event, and the final distribution would qualify for LSD treatment.

The IRS instructions to form 4972 (1998) make no reference to this requirement. Prior distributions from the same plan are referred to only in connection with the rule that if any prior distribution from the same plan was rolled over, subsequent distributions cannot receive special averaging treatment (see "*Seventh hurdle*" below).

These instructions give the erroneous impression that the IRS regards the triggering events as obsolete. However, unless the IRS has had an unpublicized change of heart, Notice 89-25 is still in effect. The Code's definition of LSD still includes the requirement that the distribution be of the "balance to the credit" of the employee which becomes payable "after the employee attains age 59½," or "on account of" P's death, separation from service (non-owner employees) or disability (owner-employees).

Here are other landmines surrounding this hurdle:

(a)   Landmine: Post year-end vesting and other adjustments

If you THINK you have withdrawn 100% of your plan balance, but then after the end of the year you receive a little extra due to a previous bookkeeping error, you have probably lost your LSD eligibility. However, if the post-year-end increase comes about because the employee is rehired, and prior forfeited amounts are reinstated, then, for years prior to 2000, see the "*Tenth hurdle*," below.

Here is an example of how this requirement can unexpectedly pose a problem:

Example: Lewis terminated his Keogh plan and took a lump sum distribution of the entire balance in 1997. He diligently closed every account the plan had and distributed all the assets to himself before the end of the calendar year. Then in January 1998 he received a notice from a federal court: because of certain securities transactions that had occurred in his Keogh plan account in 1993, he (in his capacity as trustee of the plan) was a plaintiff in a class action suit against the Aging Bull Brokerage Firm. Enclosed with the notice is a check for $1.98, representing his share of the winnings in the now-settled class action suit. The check is payable to (and presumably constitutes an undistributed asset of) the Keogh plan. The balance of his plan, in other words, was NOT distributed all in one year.

To avoid this problem, when distributing all assets of an account (or when terminating the plan altogether), have the plan trustee sign a blanket assignment of all remaining assets, claims, etc., known and unknown, to the recipient (P or the beneficiary, as the case may be). Thus, the recipient, not the plan trustee, becomes the owner of the stray interest, dividends, and class action claims that seem inevitably to turn up after the plan is liquidated, and the newly-discovered dollars do not upset the LSD status of the terminating distribution.

(b)   Landmine: aggregation of plans

In determining whether the entire balance to the credit of an employee has been distributed, certain plans must be aggregated. Specifically all profit sharing plans of the same employer are considered to be one plan for this purpose; all pension plans of the employer are treated as one plan; and all stock bonus plans are treated as one. § 402(d)(4)(C) [before 2000]; § 402(e)(4)(D)(ii) [after 1999].

Unfortunately it is not always easy to determine what type a particular retirement plan is. The employee is entitled to a summary plan description for each plan; that should tell what type it is. If not, you could request the answer from the company benefits office; or request a copy of the most recent IRS annual report (form 5500 series) filed by the employer. This form requires the employer to check a box indicating whether the plan is a profit sharing, pension or stock bonus plan, and the employer is required to provide a copy of this form on request.

But finding out what type of plan a particular retirement plan is does not necessarily end the problems with this requirement. For one thing, it may be impossible to obtain distribution of 100% of all similar plans. For example, the employer may have two pension plans (a defined benefit and a money purchase), which must be aggregated for purposes of this requirement, but the employer may permit lump sum distributions from only one of them. Also, plans may have to be aggregated, even if they are *not* both of the same type, if they have interrelated benefit formulas.

If the employer maintains more than one plan, and it is proposed to have a LSD from only one of them, it may require a legal opinion of an ERISA lawyer, or the employer's counsel, to be sure that this requirement is met for the proposed distribution.

(c)   Landmine: employers under common control

When aggregating "plans of a similar type" of the "employer," who is the "employer"? Must we aggregate separate employers, too, if they are under common control? When two employers are under common control (*e.g.*, a proprietorship and a corporation owned by the same person), § 414 says the two entities will be treated as one "employer" for purposes of certain Code sections relating to retirement plans. § 414(b),(c). § 402 is not among the listed sections. This would seem to imply that employers are *not* aggregated for purposes of § 402. However, the author is not aware of any authority one way or the other on this question.

If your client is taking a LSD from an employer's plan, while he still has a balance in a plan of "similar type" maintained by a different employer that is under common control, this question must be further investigated.

(d)   One taxable year of the "recipient"

Here's a stumper: Richard wants to take a LSD of his $300,000 profit sharing plan in 1999. He withdraws $200,000 in May; but due to delays in selling some stock inside the plan, the rest of the distribution is delayed a bit. Richard dies in June and the remaining $100,000 is paid in July to Richard's estate, after the end of Richard's taxable year (which ended unexpectedly at his death). Clearly the estate's $100,000 payment qualifies as a LSD (because Richard's death was a new "triggering event"); but is there any way that the entire $300,000 can be aggregated and treated as a LSD?

Exceptions to the all-in-one-year rule

"Accumulated deductible employee contributions" can be ignored in determining whether the employee has received a distribution of his entire plan balance. §402(d)(4)(A) [before 2000]; §402(e)(4)(D)(i) [after 1999]. This type of contribution, which was permitted under § 72(o) only for the years 1982 to 1986, is rarely encountered.

Another exception: "Dividends to ESOP participants pursuant to section 404(k)(2)(B) of the Code are not treated as part of the balance to the credit of an employee for purposes of the lump sum distribution rules under section 402(e)(4)(A) of the Code. Thus, such distribution does not prevent a subsequent distribution of the balance to the credit of an employee from being a lump sum distribution." PLR 9024083 (3/22/90).

Query: Can distributions from the employee's *after-tax contribution* account in one year be ignored in determining whether the distribution of the *employer-contribution* account in a later year qualifies for LSD treatment?

***

If a distribution clears the three "hurdles" described above it is a "lump sum distribution." That doesn't mean much, however, unless it meets further tests necessary to qualify for particular favorable tax treatments. If the LSD includes employer stock, see the next section, "LSD Rewards, Part 1."

If it meets numerous *additional* tests, it can qualify for special averaging treatment; see "LSD Rewards, Part 2," below.

LSD Rewards, Part 1:
Net Unrealized Appreciation

This section describes the special favorable tax treatment available for "lump sum distributions" (and certain other distributions) of employer stock from a retirement plan.

NUA: Tax deferral and long-term capital gain

The Code gives special favorable treatment to distributions of "employer securities" from a qualified plan. Any growth in value of such securities which has occurred between the time the plan originally placed the securities in the employee's account and the time of the distribution is called "net unrealized appreciation" (NUA). Under certain circumstances, NUA is not taxed at the time of the distribution; rather, taxation is postponed until the stock is later sold. § 402(e)(4).

When the stock is later sold, the NUA is taxed as long term capital gain, regardless of how long the recipient (or the plan) actually held the stock. See Reg. § 1.402(a)-1(b)(1)(i) (sale of such stock shall be treated as sale of a capital asset "held for more than 6 months"). This regulation was written before the holding period for long-term capital gain was extended to, as of this writing, twelve months, but Notice 98-24, IRB 1998-17, 4/13/98, confirms that the actual holding period need not be calculated to qualify for long-term capital gain.

Example: Joe Thomas, age 61, retires from Baby Bell Corp. and receives a LSD of his 401(k) plan, consisting entirely of 10,000 shares of Baby Bell stock. The plan's cost basis for that stock is $10 per share; the stock is worth $100 a share at the time of the distribution. Joe will receive a 1099-R from Baby Bell, indicating a gross distribution of $1 million and a taxable amount of $100,000. The NUA is $900,000. If Joe sells the stock immediately for $1 million, he will have long term capital gain of $900,000. Suppose he instead waits two months and sells the stock for $125 a share. Now he has a short term capital gain of $250,000 ($25 appreciation between date of distribution and date of sale, times 10,000 shares) in addition to his long term capital gain of $900,000. If he holds the stock for 12 months after receiving the distribution, all gain on any subsequent sale will be long term capital gain.

The tax deferral/capital gain treatment is not available for all distributions of employer securities. It applies in only two situations:

1.   If the securities are distributed as part of a "lump sum distribution," *all* the NUA is non-taxable at the time of the distribution.

2.   If the distribution is *not* a LSD, then only the NUA attributable to the *employee's* contributions is excludable.

Determining the amount of NUA

The employer is supposed to determine how much of a distribution of employer securities constitutes NUA. The employer then reports this figure in form 1099-R, box 6. For tax planning purposes the employee will probably want to know how much of the distribution is NUA no later than the date he receives the distribution, so it is to be hoped that the employer can provide this information then, rather than making the employee wait until January of the next year, when the 1099-R is prepared.

Reg. § 1.402(a)-1(b) and Notice 89-25, 1989-1 C.B. 662, Q&A 1, tell the employer how to calculate the NUA. For example, if the employer contributed employer stock directly to the employee's account, then the NUA is the difference between the value of the stock when originally contributed to the employee's account and the value of the stock on the date of the distribution. These calculations can be complex in many cases—for example, if there have been prior distributions, or if there are both employer and employee contributions, or if the plan holds other investments besides employer securities, or if the plan has sold some of the employer securities along the way.

Distributions after the employee's death

The favorable tax treatment of NUA also applies when employer stock is distributed to the employee's beneficiaries. So, even if the employee dies before taking a distribution of the employer securities, the beneficiary can exclude the NUA from income—*if* the beneficiary takes a lump sum distribution of the employee's balance. (If the beneficiary takes distribution of the benefits in some form other than a LSD, then the beneficiary can exclude only the NUA attributable to stock purchased with the employee's contributions.)

The IRS has held that the NUA, like other post-death retirement distributions, constitutes "IRD" (see "Income in Respect of a Decedent," above). Rev. Rul. 69-297, 1969-1 C.B. 131. So, when P's beneficiaries sell the employer stock that is distributed to them from the plan in a qualifying distribution, they will pay long term capital gain on the NUA portion of the sale proceeds. They will get a § 691(c) deduction (see "Deduction for Estate Taxes Paid on IRD," above) for the estate taxes paid on the NUA; this deduction will reduce the capital gain.

Basis of stock distributed during life and held until death

When the employee receives a LSD of employer stock and the NUA is excluded from his income, his basis in the stock going forward is the value that *was* taxed upon distribution, *i.e.*, the plan's original cost basis of the stock. In other words, the employee has a "carryover basis" from the plan.

If the employee still holds the stock at his death, does it receive a new basis equal to its date of death value—the so-called "stepped-up basis" of § 1014? The IRS has ruled that such stock does *not* receive a stepped up basis, to the extent the employee benefitted from exclusion of NUA. In other words, according to the IRS, the NUA which the employee received upon distribution of the stock to him originally, and which was not taxed when distributed to him, retains its character as NUA even after the employee's death, and will constitute IRD to the employee's heirs when they eventually sell the stock. Only to the extent, if any, that the stock appreciated in value *after* it was distributed to the employee by the plan does it receive a stepped-up basis. Rev. Rul. 75-125, 1975-1 C.B. 254.

Election to include NUA in income

The recipient can elect *out* of the favorable tax treatment, *i.e.*, can elect to have the NUA taxed currently rather than deferring tax until the stock is sold. This option could be attractive if (i) the distribution qualifies for "five year forward averaging" (5YFA) or "10 year forward averaging" (10YFA) (see "LSD Rewards, Part 2: Special Averaging Methods," below) and (ii) the total distribution is small enough that the tax under the special averaging method is less than the capital gain tax that will otherwise eventually have to be paid. Of course this decision is based on some guesswork, since it involves comparing today's special averaging rate with tomorrow's capital gain rate.

Rollovers and NUA

For most retiring employees, rolling over any large lump sum distribution received from an employer plan is the best tax-saving and financial planning strategy. The opportunity for continued tax-deferred growth of retirement assets inside an IRA offers the greatest financial value for *most* retirees.

A LSD which includes appreciated employer securities often provides an exception to this rule of thumb. Since the NUA is not taxed currently anyway, rolling it over does not defer tax on the NUA. The NUA, even if not rolled over, will not be taxed until the stock is sold. Furthermore, rolling over NUA will convert this unrealized long term capital gain into ordinary income, since IRA distributions are taxed as ordinary income. Thus, if the employee is planning to hold onto the employer stock, the rule of thumb would be: do *not* roll over NUA. (Note that NUA, unlike other "tax free" distributions, *can* be rolled over. Reg. § 1.402(c)-2, Q & A 3(b).)

If the LSD contains both employer stock and cash, the employee can roll over the cash to an IRA (to continue to enjoy tax deferral on that portion of the distribution), while holding the employer stock *outside* any retirement plan (so as to benefit from the deferral of income until sale, and capital gain treatment upon sale, of the NUA). See, *e.g.*, PLR 9721036 (2/27/97). If he rolls over some but not all of the employer stock, a ruling should be obtained to determine proper allocation of the NUA between the rolled and the non-rolled stock.

Different requirements for NUA versus 5YFA

Another alternative, if the LSD also qualifies for a "special averaging" treatment (see "LSD Rewards, Part 2," below), is not to roll over any part of the distribution, and pay tax on the taxable portion using the special averaging method. See IRS instructions to Form 4972.

Note: The requirements that a LSD must meet to qualify for the favorable NUA treatment are more lenient than the requirements that must be met for a LSD to qualify for five year averaging (5YFA) treatment. Although it is a requirement of 5YFA (see "*Ninth hurdle: the election*," below) that no portion of the LSD be rolled over, and indeed that no other qualifying distribution received in the same year be rolled over, no such requirement applies to obtaining the exclusion from income of the NUA portion of a LSD.

Accordingly, if the employee receives a distribution that (i) meets the LSD requirements (see "Lump Sum Distributions: The Basic Requirements," above) and (ii) includes employer securities, the employee can exclude from his income the NUA inherent in the securities, while rolling over to an IRA the *rest* of the distribution, *i.e.*, the assets other than the employer securities, which otherwise would be included in gross income. PLR 9721036 (2/27/97).

Similarly, an employee does not have to be over age 59½ to qualify for the exclusion of NUA, as he does to qualify for 5YFA. However, the 10% penalty on premature distributions will apply to the taxable portion of a distribution of employer stock unless some exception applies; see Chapter 9.

If the employee wants to sell the stock

If the employee wants to sell the employer stock he is receiving, then more complex calculations are necessary. He can take his distribution of employer stock, not roll it over, and sell it; he will then pay tax at long-term capital gain rates, to the extent the sale proceeds consist of NUA

Or, the employee can roll the stock over to an IRA and

sell it inside the IRA and pay *no* current tax. This approach could be attractive if the taxation can be deferred, via the IRA, for a very long period of time. Even if the employee's ordinary income tax bracket at the time of ultimate future distribution will be higher than the capital gain tax he would have to pay today if he sells the stock outside the plan, the advantages of deferral may overcome the bracket differential.

Another approach that may be attractive if the employee wants to sell the stock is discussed in the next subsection.

Charitable giving with NUA

A retired employee who is holding stock with untaxed NUA has the same options that other individuals owning appreciated stock have when they wish to diversify their investments and/or increase the income from their portfolios: either sell the stock, pay the capital gain tax and reinvest the net proceeds; or, contribute the stock to a **charitable remainder trust** (see Chapter 7) reserving a life income, thus avoiding the capital gain tax and generating an income tax deduction besides. See PLR 1999-19039 (2/16/99).

Client with shortened life expectancy

A client faced with imminent death may want to know what steps can be taken to increase the financial protection of his family if the anticipated event occurs. If such a client is a participant in a plan which holds appreciated employer stock, one point to consider is whether distribution should be taken before death. As with any retirement plan, distribution before death may have certain tax advantages (see "*Planning for client with short life expectancy*," above), but distribution of a plan balance that includes appreciated employer securities, with a rollover of as much of the currently taxable portion as possible, may be attractive if it is desired to continue the tax deferral on retirement benefits after the client's death:

Example: Dagwood has six months to live. He is a participant in his company's retirement plan. One-third of the account represents employer stock which has substantially appreciated; the other two-thirds consists of mutual funds. He has made no contributions to the plan. His "designated beneficiaries" are his children. If they inherit the plan, they are faced with a disagreeable choice: either they take a LSD of the entire benefit (in order to take advantage of the favorable treatment of the NUA portion of the distribution), thus forfeiting all possibility of continued tax deferral on the non-NUA (mutual fund) portion of the benefit; or, they opt for continued tax deferral by taking out all the plan benefits in instalments over their life expectancy—and forfeit the favorable capital gain treatment of the NUA. They are faced with this choice because they do not have the option of rolling over the taxable portion.

If, on the other hand, Dagwood takes a lump sum distribution of the entire plan balance while he is still living, *he* can use the partial rollover strategy to get the best of both worlds. He rolls over the portion of the distribution that is not employer stock; and the children, when they inherit this rollover IRA, can benefit from continued tax deferral by gradually withdrawing the IRA over their life expectancy. He does *not* roll over the stock with its built-in NUA; when the children inherit this stock, they can sell it and pay only long term capital gains tax on the NUA portion of the proceeds.

LSD Rewards, Part 2:
Special Averaging Methods

Introduction

If a lump sum distribution (as defined above) meets numerous *additional* requirements, the LSD can receive certain tax breaks: it can be excluded altogether from the recipient's adjusted gross income and taxed separately, according to a "special averaging method"—either the "five year" (5YFA) or "10 year" (10YFA) averaging method, with or without some "20% capital gain" method thrown in. This section first describes these rewards in detail, then describes (see "Fourth" through "Tenth" hurdles, below) the additional requirements the LSD must meet to qualify for these tax breaks.

Exclusion from gross income

An LSD for which a proper election is made is excluded from the recipient's adjusted gross income (AGI). § 402(d)(3); § 62(a)(8). The fact that a LSD for which special averaging is elected is excluded from AGI can be beneficial, but it can also create additional problems.

On the good side, it means the distribution will not be included in AGI for purposes of : the income limit for obtaining a Roth IRA (Chapter 5); the threshold for deducting medical expenses (7.5% of AGI) (§ 213(a)); the threshold for reduction of itemized deductions by 3% of "excess" AGI (§ 68) ($126,600 in 1999); the threshold for reducing personal exemptions (§151(d)(3)) ($189,950 for a married couple in 1999); or determining how much of the recipient's Social Security benefits for that year will be subject to income tax under § 86. On the negative side, the exclusion of the LSD from AGI may reduce the client's ability to make large charitable gifts (which are limited to a certain percentage of AGI).

> Mike Jones, CPA extraordinaire, who has "dominion over palm and pine" (he practices in California and Minnesota), rattled off the following observations about the special averaging treatment of LSDs, when he reviewed this chapter prior to publication:
>
> 1.   Special averaging treatment for a LSD is the only occasion in the Code when a trust or estate gets to use the *individual* income tax rate schedule rather than trust rates.
>
> 2.   The exclusion from income means a client can receive (say) a $100,000 LSD, elect 5YFA, pay roughly $15,000 of income tax, donate the $100,000 to charity, and take a deduction of $100,000 from his *ordinary* income (which saves roughly $40,000 of income tax).
>
> 3.   On the negative side, if the LSD is subject to state income tax, it may generate a large deduction for state income tax, which in turn may make the taxpayer subject to the alternative minimum tax if the LSD is excluded from AGI.

Five year forward averaging

The special method for taxing LSDs popularly known as "five year forward averaging" (5YFA) (although these words do not appear in the Code) is slated for extinction December 31, 1999, as a result of the Small Business Jobs Protection Act of 1996. For as long as it lasts, however, 5YFA can produce a very favorable tax result for those who qualify for it. Under the 5YFA method, the LSD is taxed as follows under § 402(d)(I):

(i)   Take 20% of the distribution.
(ii)   Determine the tax on the amount so determined using the tax tables "Schedule X" (single individuals) for the year of the distribution (reproduced in form 4972 instructions).

(iii)　　Multiply the result by five.

Exceptions:

* There is a "minimum distribution allowance" which produces an even lower tax for distributions under $70,000.
* No tax is paid currently on the value of certain annuity contracts included in the distribution, though it is still counted as part of the LSD.
* The above method determines the tax on the "ordinary income" portion of the LSD. See "*20% capital gain rate,*" below, for possible capital gain treatment of part of the distribution.

Because the "single individual" tax rate hits 39.6% at $283,150 of taxable income (1999), 5YFA means that a LSD does not hit that marginal bracket until it exceeds $1,415,750 (five times $283,150). A LSD of $750,000 (for example) would pay income tax of only $211,333—less than 29%—regardless of the taxpayer's other income.

From 1987 to 1991, when the top income tax bracket was 28% (reached at $29,750 for single individuals) "income averaging" seemed obsolete. The 1993 tax law changes brought it back to life. For a taxpayer in the 39.6% bracket, a 29% tax can look very attractive. For smaller distributions, the bargain is even more irresistible; a LSD of $100,000, for example, would be taxed at only 15%. Unfortunately, now that 5YFA is once again attractive, it is being taken away; it will not be available for distributions after 1999.

The additional requirements (over and above the basic "LSD" requirements—hurdles one through three above) which must be met in order to use 5YFA are as follows:

Fourth hurdle: the five year requirement

This requirement applies only to distributions prior to the year 2000.

To use 5YFA, a living employee must have been a "participant" in the plan for at least five taxable years prior to the year of the distribution. § 402(d)(4)(F). To determine whether a client meets this requirement, we need to understand what it means to be a "participant" and what time period constitutes a "year" of participation. Prop. Reg. §1.402(e)-2(e)(3) adds no enlightenment, simply paraphrasing the statute.

In determining what constitutes "participation" for purposes of this five-year requirement, the IRS apparently will use the "active participation" definition of § 1.219-2(d)(1), *i.e.*, only a year in which a contribution is actually made (or required to be made) to the employee's account will count. See PLR 8749081 (9/14/87). In counting "years of participation," if the client seems to be coming up short, don't overlook the possibility of tacking on years of participation in a prior plan, if the benefits to be distributed include benefits that were (1) accumulated under that prior plan and (2) transferred or rolled over to this plan; this topic is beyond the scope of this book.

The five-years-of-participation requirement does not apply to death benefits; it applies only to distributions "to" the employee.

Fifth hurdle: participant must be age 59½ or older

This requirement applies only to distributions prior to the year 2000.

Only distributions received "on or after the date on which the employee has attained age 59½" qualify for 5YFA. § 402(d)(4)(B)(i). This requirement is *not* waived for death benefits. The beneficiaries of an employee who died before reaching age 59½ could not use the special averaging treatment. Cebula v. Comm'r, 101 T.C. No. 5 (7/21/93).

Note that it is the *employee's* age at death which matters, not the beneficiary's age. An under-age-59½ beneficiary is eligible for special averaging treatment as long as the deceased employee was over age 59½ at death.

Sixth hurdle: only one use per customer

This requirement applies only to distributions prior to the year 2000. 5YFA is available only once "with respect to an employee" after 1986. § 402(d)(4)(B). So if Reggie left General Motors at age 60 in 1987, elected 5YFA for his pension plan distribution, and went to work for Ford, he will not be able to use 5YFA again when he retires from Ford in 1998, nor would his survivors be able to use it for distributions of death benefits from the Ford plan.

Seventh hurdle: no prior rollovers

This requirement applies only to distributions prior to the year 2000.

This hurdle is especially tricky because it is not found (or even referred to) in § 402(d). § 402(c)(10), added by UCA '92, provides that, "If paragraph (1) [of § 402(c)] applies to any distribution paid to any employee," then 5YFA will not be available for any subsequent distribution from the same plan (or from any other plan required to be aggregated with the distributing plan).

The "paragraph (1)" referred to (§ 402(c)(1)) says that properly rolled over distributions will not be included in income. § 402(c)(10) therefore denies LSD treatment to subsequent distributions if a prior distribution from the same plan was rolled over and excluded from gross income.

Notice 92-48, 1992-2 C.B. 377, explains: "If you have previously rolled over a payment from the Plan (or certain other similar plans of the employer), you cannot use [5YFA] tax treatment for later payments from the Plan." See also the instructions to IRS form 4972 (1999), providing that a distribution is not eligible for averaging treatment if "the participant or his or her surviving spouse received an eligible rollover distribution from the same plan... and the proceeds of the previous distribution were rolled over..."

Eighth hurdle: type of recipient

Only individuals, estates and trusts can elect these special methods. A distribution to a partnership or corporation will not qualify. § 402(d)(4)(B).

Ninth hurdle: the election

If the distribution meets all the requirements described above, LSD treatment is not automatic; it is elected by filing form 4972.

Landmine: The election, to be valid, must be made for all distributions in the same year which qualify for LSD treatment.

Example: Thalia is a participant in both the Great Northern Skateboard Company Pension Plan (balance $200,000) and Profit Sharing Plan (balance $300,000). She is retiring in 1999 and wants to cash in her pension plan balance, and get 5YFA treatment for it, but roll over her profit sharing plan balance to an IRA. If she receives total distributions from both plans in one year, she must elect 5YFA for both or neither; she cannot elect 5YFA for one and roll over the other. § 402(d)(4)(B)(ii). This problem can be avoided either by taking the rollover distribution and the 5YFA distribution in separate taxable years; or by taking out the "rollover plan" balance over two years, so it does not qualify for 5YFA treatment.

Tenth hurdle: rehired employee: post year-end vesting

If the employee has terminated his service and withdrawn 100% of his plan balance, but then after the end of the year the employee is rehired, and prior forfeited amounts are reinstated, then technically the prior LSD is not "disqualified"; however, there is a recapture provision under which the benefits received from 5YFA treatment must be paid back to the IRS in the year the increased vesting occurs. § 402(d)(6) [before 2000]. If the post-year-end increased vesting did not occur because of a rehire, but rather due to a plan termination (which sometimes causes 100% vesting of everyone retroactively), the status of the prior special averaging treatment is unknown.

Ten year forward averaging

Ten year forward averaging (10YFA) is available only for individuals born before 1936. TRA '86 § 1122(h) as amended by TAMRA '88, § 1011A(b)(11), (13)-(15). 10YFA is the same as 5YFA, except that:

(i)   You determine the tax on 10% of the LSD and multiply it by 10 (rather than 20% multiplied by five).
(ii)   The tax is determined using 1986 rates (conveniently reproduced in the instructions to form 4972).

Top rates were higher in 1986 than now. 10YFA produces a lower tax than 5YFA only for distributions of less than $318,000; see Ed Slott Table in Appendix A.

Note: this special grandfather rule is not expiring at the end of 1999; thus, it will continue to be available indefinitely for the LSDs of benefits of employees born before 1936.

20% capital gain rate

If the employee was a participant in the plan prior to 1974, part of the LSD for which the "special averaging method" has been elected is eligible to be treated as a "capital gain" taxed at 20%. This 20% rate represents the tax rate that once upon a time applied to long term capital gain, and now again applies to long term capital gains, but for purposes of this particular grandfather rule the rate is simply 20% without regard to the actual tax rate on capital gain in any particular year.

Prop. Reg. § 1.402(e)-2(d) provides that the "capital gain" portion of the distribution is determined by deducting the "ordinary income portion" (OIP) from the "total taxable amount" (TTA). The OIP is determined by multiplying the TTA by the following fraction:

> Numerator: Calendar years of active participation after 1973.
> Denominator: Total calendar years of active participation.

In the case of pre-1974 years, the employee gets twelve months' credit for each calendar year or partial calendar year of participation. For post-1973 years a different rule applies: He gets one *month's* credit for each calendar month or part of a month in which he is an active participant.

It is possible, with smaller distributions, for the 20% "capital gain method" to produce a higher tax than would apply under 5YFA or 10YFA. In this case, P can elect to have his capital gain portion treated as ordinary income; or rather, technically, to "treat pre-1974 participation as post-1973 participation." See § 402(e)(4)(L) as it existed prior to repeal by TAMRA '88 § 1011A(b)(8)(G). If this election is made, the 20% treatment is waived and the entire distribution is taxed under 5YFA or 10YFA.

Note: this special grandfather rule is not expiring at the end of 1999; thus, it will continue to be available indefinitely for LSDs of benefits of employees born before 1936.

Capital gain: what is an "active participant?"

What is an "active participant" for purposes of the fraction described above? The regulations under § 219(g) (which limits the income tax deduction for IRA contributions by those who are "active participants" in various types of retirement plans) gives a very specific definition. Under Reg. § 1.219-2 a person is an "active participant" in a money purchase pension plan in a particular year *only* if some of the employer contribution was required to be allocated to his account for that year; or in a profit sharing plan *only* if any forfeiture or employer contribution was added to his account in that year. If this § 1.219-2 definition were applied for purposes of determining the capital gain portion of a LSD, the OIP/TTA fraction would become fixed, once and for all, when the plan discontinued contributions on behalf of the employee, since "active participation" (in the § 219 sense) ends then.

But the IRS apparently does not apply the §219 definition of "active participation" to §402 for this purpose. Although this is not 100% clear, it appears that the IRS uses, for purposes of determining the "capital gain" portion of a LSD, a definition which makes no distinction between "participation" and "active participation," thus rendering nugatory the word "active" in the Code's phrase *"active* participation." The IRS definition is in a 1975 proposed regulation, § 1.402(e)-2; and is repeated in the instructions to form 1099-R, which is the tax form used (by the employer) to report how much of each distribution is ordinary income and how much is capital gain. From the 1998 "Instructions for Form 1099-R, Box 3," p. 24: "Active participation begins with the first month in which the employee became a participant under the plan and ends with the earliest of –"

(i)   The month the employee receives the LSD.

(ii)   The month the employee dies.

(iii)   In the case of a common law employee, the month of separation from service.

(iv)   In the case of a self-employed person who receives the LSD on account of disability, the month in which he becomes disabled.

The effect of this definition is to gradually and inexorably reduce the capital gain portion of the distribution, even if the plan has been "frozen" since 1974, since the fraction keeps changing until events (i) - (iv) occur.

This definition appears arbitrary and capricious, first, because it ignores the word "active" in the Code, and second, because the IRS uses the § 219 definition intact for *another* part of the LSD determinations under § 402 (namely the "five years of participation" requirement) (see *"Fourth hurdle: the five year requirement,"* above) when to do so favors the Treasury.

Tax on OIP when there is a capital gain portion

Once you have determined how much of the total taxable amount (TTA) is the "ordinary income portion" (OIP) (to be taxed under 5YFA or 10YFA), and how much is capital gain (to be taxed at a flat 20%), how do you calculate the tax on the OIP? There are two possible methods:

(i)   Calculate the 5YFA (or 10YFA) tax on the TTA then multiply the result by the fraction OIP/TTA; or
(ii)   Calculate the 5YFA (or 10YFA) tax on the OIP only.

Method (i) was required by § 402(e)(1)(B) before it was repealed by TRA '86. However, the grandfather rule which continues 20% capital gain treatment for those born before 1936 appears to adopt method (ii): see § 1122(h)(3)(b) of TRA '86 as amended by TAMRA '88 § 1101A(b)(11), (13)-(15). IRS form 4972 for 1998 clearly uses method (ii) (see part III of form). Method (ii) produces a lower tax than method (i). Thus, the treatment of "grandfathered" individuals is more favorable than the treatment they would have received prior to the change in the law that they are being grandfathered from.

Rollovers

In general: what a rollover is

Under § 402, generally, retirement plan distributions are not taxed in the year received if they are "rolled over" to a different retirement plan or IRA. A "rollover" is a distribution from one plan or IRA to P, followed by a transfer of the distribution by P to another plan or IRA maintained for him.

Of course there are various requirements that must be met to obtain tax-free rollover treatment: restrictions on the number of rollovers that may be done in one year, time limit for completing the rollover, etc. The technical details of how to accomplish a valid rollover are beyond the scope of this book; this section deals with the planning considerations and limitations. Needless to say, the technical rules should be consulted before actually doing a rollover.

A rollover differs from a "trustee-to-trustee transfer," "custodian-to-custodian transfer" or "plan-to-plan transfer."

With these types of transfers, the money is never distributed to P—it goes straight from one IRA to another (or from one qualified retirement plan (QRP) to another). Over the years, participants and the IRS learned that many of the technical rules that apply to rollovers (such as the one-per-year limit) do not apply to these transfers.

What has made things vastly more confusing, however, is that (since the "Unemployment Compensation Amendments of 1992") (P.L. 102-318) ("UCA"), the direct transfer of a participant's benefits from a QRP to an IRA is called a "direct rollover" and it *is* considered a rollover at least in some respects; likewise (since TAPRA '97) the conversion of a traditional IRA to a Roth IRA (Chapter 5), even if it is done by custodian-to-custodian transfer, must meet some (not all) requirements of a true "rollover."

Until 1992, the requirements for a valid rollover were almost as difficult and perilous as the LSD rules, but UCA '92 (applicable to distributions after 1992) vastly liberalized the rules, and now rollovers are much easier. Now, ANY distribution from a qualified plan, IRA or 403(b) plan can be rolled over, with only the following exceptions:

(a)   A required distribution under § 401(a)(9) (see Chapter 1) cannot be rolled over (see *"No rollover of minimum required distributions,"* below).

(b)   "Any distribution which is one of a series of substantially equal periodic payments" made annually or more often (a) over the life or life expectancy of P, (b) over the joint life or life expectancy of P and a DB, or (c) over a "specified period of 10 years or more" may not be rolled over. § 402(c)(4)(A). Reg. § 1.402(c)-2, Q&A-5, explains how to determine whether a distribution is part of a series of "substantially equal installments" over 10 or more years.

(c)   Certain corrective or "deemed" distributions

cannot be rolled over (for example, the P.S. 58 cost of insurance in a plan (Chapter 10), or a plan loan that is foreclosed, or the return of an excess 401(k) contribution).

(d)   Non-taxable distributions (such as return of after-tax contributions, and the pure death benefit portion of life insurance proceeds—see Chapter 10) cannot be rolled over. § 402(c)(2); Reg. § 1.402(c)-2, Q & A 3.

Rollovers of inherited benefits

A surviving spouse who inherits benefits can roll them over to an IRA in her own name, or elect to treat the decedent's IRA as her own; see "Spousal Rollovers," Chapter 3. Death benefits cannot be rolled over by any beneficiary other than the spouse, nor can a non-spouse beneficiary elect to treat the decedent's IRA as his or her own, with one "grandfather"-type exception: the beneficiary (even a non-spouse) of an IRA owner who died *before 1984* could elect to treat the decedent's IRA as his or her own IRA. See Prop. Reg. § 1.408-8, A-4.

No rollover of minimum required distributions

The rule that a minimum required distribution (MRD) cannot be rolled over (§§ 402(c)(4)(B), 408(d)(3)(E)) can take participants by surprise.

For example, the first distribution received in any year for which a distribution is required will be considered part of the "required distribution" for that year and thus cannot be rolled over. Reg. § 1.402(c)-2, A-7. Furthermore, the first year for which a distribution is required is the year P reaches age 70½, even though the first MRD does not have to be taken until April 1 of the *following* year. Any distribution received on or after January 1 of the 70½ year will be considered part of the MRD for that year, and thus cannot be rolled over. This can create problems since the *amount* of the first year's MRD will not be known until the RBD:

Example: Leonard turns 70½ in 1996. On 1/1/96 he retires from his job at XYZ Corp. and asks the plan administrator of the retirement plan to distribute his benefits to his IRA in a "direct rollover." The administrator replies that it can roll over everything except the MRD for 1996. Leonard replies, fine, he will take the 1996 MRD as a taxable distribution and roll over the rest. Since he has named his 40-year-old wife Louise as his designated beneficiary (DB) (see Chapter 1), the MRD should be 1/42.9th of the account balance, based on their 42.9 year joint life expectancy. But the administrator says, "Louise is your wife and DB now, but the MRD is based on who is your DB during the period January 1-March 31 of the year of your RBD, which is 1997. Between now and 1/1/97, Louise could die, or you could get divorced, or you could simply change your mind and name your estate and therefore have no DB. So we will distribute to you the MRD calculated based solely on your own LE—which is 1/16th of the account, not 1/42.9th."

For similar problems facing: a surviving spouse, see Chapter 3; would-be Roth IRA converters, see Chapter 5. The "Rollover Checklist" in Appendix C lists issues to consider before rolling over retirement plan benefits.

Summary of Planning Principles

1.   In choosing among possible beneficiaries (including trusts) for retirement benefits, consider their respective income tax brackets along with other factors. Other things being equal, it is more tax-effective to leave retirement benefits (and other IRD assets) to lower-bracket beneficiaries, and non-IRD assets to higher bracket beneficiaries.

2. Do not use retirement benefits to fund a pecuniary bequest or arrange retirement benefits so that they will have to pass through a pecuniary formula in a will or trust.

3. As between the marital and the credit shelter share, it is generally better to use IRD to fund the marital share, so no part of the "credit shelter" is "wasted" paying income taxes. Income taxes paid out of the marital share will reduce the future taxable estate of the spouse. Exception: the advantages of long term income tax deferral that are available for certain "credit shelter" dispositions may outweigh the drawbacks of funding a credit shelter gift with IRD.

4. When determining what benefits each beneficiary will receive, consider the impact of the § 691(c) deduction for estate taxes paid on IRD. This deduction benefits the person who receives the IRD, not the person who pays the estate tax.

5. If the client's retirement plan holds stock of the employer which sponsors the plan, evaluate the alternatives for treatment of the "NUA" before any distributions are taken from the plan (or before selling that stock inside the plan).

6. Use the "Checklist for Meeting with Client" (Appendix C) to determine whether a client is eligible for "lump sum distribution" income tax treatment. Do not take steps (such as a rollover) which would eliminate eligibility for beneficial LSD treatment without carefully considering the alternatives.

3

Marital Matters

*Rules and planning concerns
when leaving retirement benefits
to the surviving spouse or a
marital trust.*

Introduction

This chapter first summarizes the incentives offered by the tax laws for naming the spouse as beneficiary of retirement benefits, then examines two of these incentives (rollovers and § 401(a)(9) provisions) in detail. Naming a marital trust is more complicated and less advantageous tax-wise than naming the spouse individually; why this is so is explained in "Marital Deduction for Benefits Payable to QTIP Trust" and "Income Tax Disadvantages When QTIP Trust is Beneficiary." The next sections look at two other topics involving husband, wife and retirement benefits: simultaneous death clauses and "REA" rights.

If the participant's spouse is not a U.S. citizen, see also Chapter 4.

Advantages of Leaving Benefits to the Surviving Spouse

The estate and income tax laws often favor naming the participant's spouse as the beneficiary of retirement benefits.

Estate tax

If there is a choice of assets, generally speaking it is preferable to make the retirement benefits payable to the spouse ("S") of the participant ("P"), and use other assets to fund the "credit shelter" amount. If retirement benefits are made payable to a **credit shelter trust**, the income taxes the trust must pay on those benefits (see "Income in Respect of a Decedent," Chapter 2) will come out of the credit shelter amount. In effect, some of the P's federal estate tax exemption is "wasted" paying income taxes.

If S is the beneficiary, she too will have to pay income taxes when the benefits are distributed to her, but at least the income taxes she pays will reduce her future taxable estate. P's exemption will not have been partially "wasted" paying income taxes. See the *Able* case study. The same *estate tax* benefit can be achieved by naming either S individually or a marital trust as beneficiary, but *income tax* considerations favor naming S individually rather than a marital trust; see "Income Tax Disadvantages When QTIP trust is Beneficiary," below, and the *Koslow* case study.

This is not a hard and fast rule. The income tax deferral advantages of making benefits payable directly to children or grandchildren, rather than to S, can outweigh the disadvantages of using such benefits to fund the credit shelter amount; see the *Stoltz* case study.

Income tax

Compared with other beneficiaries, S has more options for deferring income taxes on inherited retirement benefits. See "Spousal Rollovers" and "The Spouse and § 401(a)(9)," below.

Spousal Rollovers

Advantages of spousal rollover

The surviving spouse's ability to "roll over" (see "Rollovers," Chapter 2, for definition) inherited benefits to her own IRA gives her a powerful option to defer income taxes that is not available to other beneficiaries. By rolling over benefits to her own IRA, S becomes the "participant" with regard to those benefits under the minimum distribution rules. She can then name her own designated beneficiary (DB) for the account, and commence distributions at *her* required beginning date (RBD) over the joint life expectancy of herself and the new DB. Whatever minimum distribution requirements were in effect prior to P's death disappear once the benefits have been rolled over by S (although of course they remain in effect until then).

This does not mean that naming S as beneficiary is necessarily the way to achieve the longest income tax deferral on benefits; often it is not. Nevertheless, the spousal rollover is still an extremely valuable deferral tool for two reasons: first, most participants want to name their spouses as beneficiaries, despite the longer income tax deferral that may be available if children or grandchildren are named, so the rollover becomes a way to revive the option of longer deferral if S survives P; second, once P has died or passed his RBD, the rollover shines as a way to correct problems that may exist with P's beneficiary designation.

The spousal rollover is so valuable that it is frequently the object of *post mortem* planning efforts. See "Salvaging the Spousal Rollover," Chapter 8, for the use of qualified disclaimers to redirect to S retirement benefits that were left payable to the "wrong" beneficiary, so the spousal rollover can be used.

The Rollover Checklist, in Appendix C, should be

helpful in evaluating a proposed spousal rollover.

Drawbacks of spousal rollover

The principal drawback of a spousal rollover is its effect on the 10%, pre-age 59½, distribution penalty (Chapter 9). If the surviving spouse is younger than age 59½, she is entitled to withdraw benefits from the deceased spouse's plan or IRA without a penalty, because the penalty does not apply to death benefits. If she rolls over the benefits to her own IRA, however, they lose their character as penalty-exempt-death benefits and she will not be able to withdraw them until she herself reaches age 59½, unless she either pays the 10% penalty or qualifies for one of the exceptions from that tax.

Because of this situation, planners may advise young widows and widowers either not to roll over any benefits until after reaching age 59½; or to roll over only funds they are certain they will not need until after that age, and in the meantime to withdraw from the deceased spouse's plan as much as they need, without a penalty, to pay living expenses.

However, PLR 9608042 (12/1/95) cast doubt on the availability of this approach. In this ruling, P died while S was under age 59½. Although the ruling confirmed that S could withdraw death benefits from P's IRA with no 10% penalty, the ruling went on to say that, by withdrawing *any* benefits penalty-free before she herself attained age 59½, S would be making an "irrevocable election" not to treat P's IRA as her own IRA. The IRS here is apparently working backwards from Prop. Reg. § 1.408-8(A-4(b)) (which lists ways a surviving spouse can elect to treat the deceased spouse's IRA as her own) to the idea that there are actions S can take which constitute an election NOT to treat it as her own. This PLR suggests that, by taking even $1 as a penalty-free death benefit from the deceased spouse's IRA prior to attaining age 59½, the surviving spouse is forever precluded from rolling over the *rest* of the deceased spouse's IRA to her own IRA.

If this ruling really means there is an election involved, one wonders to what extent the converse is presumably also true: by rolling over *some* of the benefits to her own IRA, is S electing to treat *all* of the account as her own and giving up the right to take the rest of it as a penalty-free death benefit? See also *"How does S elect to treat P's IRA as her own?"* below.

The "widow's election" policy advanced in this ruling has not (to the author's knowledge) been either affirmed or "overruled" by later IRS pronouncements. If it is IRS policy, is a trap for the unwary. The only people hurt by this policy are poor young widows. Older widows (those over age 59½), and wealthy widows (those who do not need to take money from the deceased spouse's retirement account), do not have the problem. For another possible example of the IRS's get-tough policy regarding young (non-citizen) widows, see *"How income can become principal,"* in Chapter 4.

Requirements for spousal rollover: QRP distribution

§ 402(c)(a) allows the participant in a qualified retirement plan (QRP) to "roll over" certain plan distributions to another QRP, or to an individual retirement account (IRA), provided various requirements are met. See "Rollovers," Chapter 2. If death benefits are paid to P's surviving spouse, the rollover rules "apply to such distribution in the same manner as if the spouse were" the participant, with only one exception: the spouse may roll over only to an IRA, not to another QRP.

The tests for determining whether a distribution is an "eligible rollover distribution," and other rollover rules, are the same for the surviving spouse as they would have been for the decedent; see Chapter 2 for details.

Note the following:

1.   The spouse can roll benefits to a pre-existing IRA or to a new IRA established just to receive this rollover.

2.   If S is past her RBD, a new IRA should be established for the rollover. If the rollover is mingled with a pre-existing IRA, you will have the difficulty of tracking two separate minimum distribution computations in one account. See *"Transferring assets between IRAs after the RBD,"* Chapter 1.

Example: Gordon owns IRA #1, worth $100,000, on which his wife Gloria is named as DB (with neither life expectancy recalculated). Gloria owns Pension Plan A, worth $100,000, on which Gordon is named as DB (with neither life expectancy recalculated). Their son Hiram is named as contingent beneficiary on both. Both spouses are past their RBDs. Gloria dies. Gordon accordingly inherits Plan A as beneficiary. He wants to roll it over to an IRA in his own name and name Hiram as beneficiary. On Gordon's *existing* IRA (IRA #1), because Gloria was his DB on his RBD, his MRDs will continue to be based on the joint LE of Gordon and Gloria. On the *inherited* benefit, however, once he rolls it over, his MRDs will be based on the joint LE of himself and son Hiram (subject to the MDIB rule) (because, as to this rollover amount from Plan A inherited from his deceased spouse Gloria, *Hiram* will be Gordon's DB). Thus, the benefits inherited from Gloria should be rolled to a separate, new IRA (IRA #2) naming Hiram as beneficiary. If Gordon rolls the inherited plan into his existing IRA #1, he will be forced to use the procedure described in *"Transferring assets between IRAs after the RBD"* (Chapter 1) for tracking merged benefits with different DBs. Creating a new, separate, IRA for the inherited money would not only avoid that nightmare, it would also allow Gordon to take advantage of Notice 88-38 (see "Taking Distributions from Multiple Plans," Chapter 1), by taking all his MRDs (for both IRAs) from his pre-existing IRA #1 (which has an older DB, and thus a shorter payout period and larger MRDs both during his life and after his death), thus depleting that account and allowing the new IRA #2 (which has a young DB, and thus a longer payout period and smaller MRDs both during his life and after his death) to grow.

3.   The distribution does not have to be a distribution of the entire account balance. Partial distributions are eligible for rollover, unless they are MRDs or part of a series of substantially equal payments (see "Rollovers," Chapter 2).

4.   The IRS has permitted the spouse to roll over benefits from decedent's plan and IRA into another IRA *still in the name of the decedent*. PLRs 9418034 (2/10/94), 9842058 (7/21/98). This approach may be more attractive than a rollover to an IRA in S's own name when S wants to move the benefits to a different IRA provider, but wants the benefits to retain their status as "death benefits" exempt from the penalty on premature distributions (see "*Drawbacks of spousal rollover*," above).

A minimum required distribution may not be rolled over

        The spousal rollover is not available for any minimum required distribution (MRD). § 402(c)(4)(B). The prohibition against rolling over MRDs could theoretically have a harsh result in certain circumstances:

Example: Melvin and Minnie: On his RBD, Melvin had named a charity as beneficiary of his profit sharing plan, and commenced taking MRDs based on his life expectancy, recalculated annually. When a person whose life expectancy is being redetermined annually dies, his life expectancy becomes zero in the year following the death (Chapter 1). After his RBD, Melvin changed his beneficiary designation to his wife Minnie instead of the charity. However, it was too late for Minnie to become a "DB," so he still had to continue withdrawals over only his single life expectancy. Suppose Melvin's "age 70½ year" was 1995 and his life expectancy in that year was 16 years. Accordingly, he withdrew his MRD of 1/16 of the account for 1995. In 1996, he properly withdrew 1/15.3 of the account balance, then died.

Clearly, Minnie can roll over the balance of Melvin's profit sharing plan account by the end of 1996. Once December 31, 1996 has passed, a new calendar year begins for purposes of the minimum distribution rules applicable to Melvin's account. The MRD for 1997 will be 100% of the account, since Melvin's life expectancy is now zero. Accordingly, it would appear that Minnie cannot roll over any portion of the account that is distributed after 1996.

Despite the clear rule in § 402(c)(4)(B), however, the IRS has allowed a surviving spouse to roll over the entire account in this situation in at least one case. PLR 9005071 (11/13/89) involved exactly the "Melvin and Minnie" facts. The IRS ruled that the surviving spouse could receive and roll over, in the year following P's death, 100% of the plan balance, so long as the deceased participant had withdrawn, prior to his death, the MRD for the year of death.

Deadline for completing spousal rollover

There is no time deadline, as such, for making a spousal rollover. Of course, once any benefits are actually distributed to S, they must be rolled over within 60 days or not at all. § 402(c)(3). But there is no specific time limit based on P's death after which it becomes "too late" to roll over distributions. The Code provides simply that a QRP distribution of death benefits to S can be rolled over by S if the deceased P could have rolled it over had it been paid to him. § 402(c)(9).

However, there are other rules which, as a practical matter, do create "deadlines" for completing the spousal rollover and/or otherwise function as limitations on the spouse's ability to roll over:

1.   If S happens to die before completing the rollover, a rollover by S's executor will probably not be allowed; see "*What if S dies before rolling over?*," below.

2.   If P was already past his RBD when his death occurred, minimum distributions must continue until the rollover occurs; thus delay may waste deferral opportunities or even eliminate the possibility of a rollover. See "*A minimum distribution may not be rolled over,*" above.

3.   If P died before his RBD, S is deemed to be "the participant" as far as the minimum distribution rules are concerned; this may cause problems which can only be fixed by a rollover. See "*The problem if P dies before his RBD,*" below.

4.   See "*Drawbacks of a spousal rollover,*" above, for the IRS's suggestion that under-age-59½ surviving spouses, by accepting any distributions as "death benefits," may forfeit the right to roll over subsequent distributions.

5.   Finally, the question exists whether there is any *other* action S might take (similar to taking a penalty-free death benefit distribution prior to attaining age 59½) that the IRS might consider an "election" on S's part *not* to roll over any subsequent distributions. If there is, the author has not heard of it or thought of it. Since the Code specifically states that the surviving spouse does not have to start taking distributions from

the plan until (approximately) the time the deceased P would have had to (see "The Spouse and § 401(a)(9)," below), and that S as beneficiary can roll over a distribution to the same extent P could have if it had been paid to him (§ 402(c)(5)), and since P could roll over any distributions made to him prior to his RBD (subject to the few exceptions in § 402), as well as distributions after his RBD in excess of the MRD, S should be able to roll over all partial, total and multiple distributions made to her from P's plan that are not specifically excepted by § 402, whether made in one year or multiple years, and whether made before or after P's RBD.

Rollover (or spousal election) for inherited IRA

§ 408(d), in a backhanded way, permits a surviving spouse to treat an inherited IRA as if it were S's *own* IRA. The Code provides that distributions from an "inherited IRA" may not be treated as tax-free rollovers; but then goes on to say that an "inherited IRA" means an IRA acquired by reason of the death of another individual, if the person who inherited the account is not the spouse of the decedent. § 408(d)(3)(C).

Thus an IRA inherited by the spouse is not subject to the restrictions applicable to an "inherited IRA," and by negative implication S may roll over distributions to her from the deceased P's IRA as if it were S's own IRA. This option is not available for benefits paid to a marital trust. PLR 9321032 (2/24/93).

How does S elect to treat P's IRA as her own?

§ 408(a)(6) does not provide specific payout rules for IRAs. Rather, it simply provides that the minimum distribution rules for IRAs shall be similar to the § 401(a)(9) minimum distribution rules for qualified plans, but the actual rules shall be contained in future regulations to be issued by the IRS.

All we have by way of regulations at this time are the proposed regulations issued in 1987. Prop. Reg. § 1.408-8, Q and A-4(b) provides that S "may elect" to treat her interest in an IRA inherited from the deceased spouse as her own account, and "an election will be considered to have been made by S if either of the following occurs."

Then two "occurrences" are described. These two "occurrences" are not positive elections; rather they are simply events that are consistent with the idea that the IRA is now S's IRA, and inconsistent with the idea that the IRA still belongs to the decedent. The first "occurrence" is: an amount required to be distributed under the minimum distribution rules has not been distributed within the required time after the death of the first spouse. The second "occurrence" is: S makes a contribution to the account. "The result of such an election is that S shall then be considered the individual for whose benefit the [IRA] is maintained." Note that rolling over part of the account to her own IRA is not listed as an "occurrence" that is deemed to be an election to treat P's entire IRA as her own IRA.

The proposed regulation does not specify any other method of "converting" the deceased spouse's IRA into S's IRA. Presumably the two "occurrences" listed in the regulation are not meant to be the exclusive methods by which S can convert the decedent's IRA into her own IRA. The IRS has recognized in at least one private letter ruling that a direction to transfer funds from an IRA in the name of the decedent to an IRA in the name of the spouse "constitutes a sufficient election" to treat the decedent's IRA as the spouse's IRA; PLR 9534027 (6/1/95). However, a rollover "in and of itself need not constitute" such an election if the benefits are rolled into an IRA still in the name of the decedent. PLR 9418034 (2/10/94).

What if S dies before rolling over?

The IRS has not allowed the executor of S's estate to exercise S's "personal" right to treat the deceased P's IRA as S's own IRA. PLR 9237038 (6/16/92). Or, as one lawyer put it, "She can't roll over in her grave" (Colin S. Marshall, 1997). Contrast this with other decisions regarding actions by executors:

•   An executor may not make a $2,000 IRA contribution on a decedent's behalf. PLR 8439066.

•   Where a participant had received a distribution, but then died before rolling it over, his executor could roll over the distribution to an IRA in the decedent's name, provided the rollover was completed within 60 days after the distribution was received by P. *Gunther v. U.S.*, 573 F. Supp. 126, 127 (1982) (USDC MI, 51 AFTR 2d 83-1314). Temp. Reg. § 54.4981A-1T (d-5)(c).

Thus, if a rollover will be desirable, it normally should be done as soon as possible after P's death.

If S dies without having done a rollover, what happens next depends, first of all, on whether P died before or after his RBD. If P dies *before* his RBD, see *"The problem if P dies before his RBD,"* below. If P was already *past* his RBD when he died, see the *Fallon* case study in Chapter 11, form 4.1 in Appendix B, and "Simultaneous Death Clauses," below.

Rollover by S after age 70½

If S is already past her RBD on the date she rolls over an inherited benefit to her own IRA is it too late for her to name a new DB? The proposed regulations do not discuss what RBD applies to a surviving spouse who is already past 70½ when she creates an IRA with benefits inherited from the deceased spouse.

This issue was squarely presented in PLR 9311037 (12/22/92). A and B were married to each other. Both were past age 70½ when A died. B was the DB of A's IRA. B rolled over A's IRA to a new IRA in B's name, but B's RBD had already passed when B established this IRA. B named C and D as the primary beneficiaries to receive the balance in this new rollover IRA at B's death. B requested and received a ruling that C and D would be treated as B's "designated beneficiaries" for purposes of the minimum distribution rules applicable to B's IRA established by a rollover from A's IRA.

From the ruling: "While the proposed regulations do not specifically answer [this question], in the absence of final regulations, issues may be resolved by a reasonable interpretation of the proposed regulations and statutory provisions. Accordingly, it is a reasonable interpretation of the minimum distribution requirements... that [C and D] may be treated as [DBs] since they were designated before your first required distribution date."

PLR 9534027 (6/1/95), also involving spouses who were both past age 70½ when the first one died, reached the same conclusion. This ruling held that, if the spousal rollover occurred in 1995, the spouse's "required beginning date" for the newly created rollover IRA would be December 31 of the following year (1996), and the "DB" would be determined as of that date.

Rollover when S inherits benefits through an estate or trust

The IRS, in letter rulings, has permitted a spousal rollover where S was not named as the DB, but the benefits were payable to P's estate and S was the sole beneficiary of the estate. See, *e.g.*, PLRs 8911006 (12/12/88); 9402023 (10/18/93) (S was sole beneficiary and executrix).

In two other rulings, S was not the sole beneficiary, but was the residuary beneficiary and also was the executrix. As executrix, she distributed the right to receive P's retirement benefits (which were payable to the estate) to herself in partial fulfillment of the residuary bequest. The IRS allowed her to roll the benefits over. PLR 9351041 (9/30/93); 9545010 (8/14/95).

In still another ruling, S claimed a statutory share of the estate. Under applicable state law, a surviving spouse who elected the statutory share could also specify which assets would be used to fund that share. S exercised this right by directing the trustee of the decedent's QRP (which was payable to the estate) to transfer assets of the plan directly into an IRA in S's own name. This was held to be a valid "direct rollover." PLR 9524020 (3/21/95). Virginia Coleman points out that the ruling does not mention the REA rights the spouse must have had in this QRP (see "REA '84 and Spousal Consent," below) which may have affected the ruling result.

There have been letter rulings permitting a spousal rollover where benefits were payable to a trust under which S had an unlimited right to withdraw the principal. S exercised her power to withdraw the funds from the IRA into the trust, then out to herself and into her own IRA. PLRs 9302022 (10/19/92); 9426049 (4/12/94); 9427035 (4/29/94); 9836029 (6/9/98); PLR 1999-25033 (3/25/99).

PLR 9426049 may be the most extreme of these favorable rulings. P's benefits were payable to a trust that was to be divided into two subtrusts at his death. S and a bank were co-trustees, but S had the right to remove the bank, and become sole trustee, one year after P's death. After the one-year period, the trustees allocated the benefits to one of the subtrusts, and caused them to be distributed to S under a discretionary power to pay her principal "in her best interest." This was held to be a valid rollover because of the spouse's power to remove the co-trustee and distribute principal to herself, even though for the first year after P's death she had no such power (and even though she did not exercise this power).

Based on these rulings, it is clear that S is entitled to roll over not only benefits that are paid to her directly as beneficiary, but also benefits that are paid to her as an estate or trust beneficiary *provided* that she is *entitled* to the benefits. She is entitled to the benefits if either: she is the *sole* beneficiary of the estate or trust; or she is a *partial* beneficiary but the benefits must be paid to her for some reason (*e.g.*, there are no other assets available to fund her share); or (if there is discretion regarding which assets will be used to fund her share), she is the one who (as beneficiary or as fiduciary) holds the discretion.

These rulings can obviously be useful in cleanup mode. The approach could also be useful for planning purposes. A client who wants to divide benefits between the spouse and a credit shelter trust by a formula could leave the benefits to a trust, have the trustee apply the formula to determine how much the spouse is entitled to, and then have the trustee direct the plan administrator to pay the marital portion of the benefits directly to the spouse. See form 3.2 in Appendix B.

If payment of the benefits to S depends on the discretion of some third party, however, such as a trustee who is not S herself, the rollover will not be allowed. The rulings have denied rollovers for an IRA payable to a QTIP trust where S's power to withdraw principal was not immediate and unlimited. PLRs 9322005 (2/24/93) (S could receive principal only in discretion of a third party trustee); 9321032 (2/24/93); 9445029 (8/18/94).

The Spouse and § 401(a)(9)

Special minimum distribution rules when S is the DB

Chapter 1 explains the minimum distribution rules generally. Special minimum distribution rules (described here) apply when P's surviving spouse is named as beneficiary. See *"When is a trust for the spouse the same as the spouse?"* (Chapter 6) for how these rules apply to a marital trust.

While the spousal rollover (discussed above) is normally the most powerful and beneficial income tax deferral tool available to a surviving spouse, the special spousal provisions of § 401(a)(9) can be significant in particular situations. Unfortunately, although these rules are obviously intended to provide "advantages" when S is named as beneficiary, they sometimes work in a disadvantageous manner, as explained in the following subsections.

Special life expectancy rules when S is the DB

When P reaches his RBD, he must start taking out benefits over the joint life expectancy ("LE") of himself and his "designated beneficiary" (DB). If his DB is his spouse (S), he can use their *actual* joint LE to measure minimum required distributions ("MRDs"). If P's DB is someone *other than* his spouse, and the DB is more than ten years younger than P, P must use a special table to measure MRDs, which essentially treats the DB as being only 10 years younger than P (see "Naming a Non-Spouse DB: The MDIB Rule," Chapter 1).

The fact that the MDIB rule does not apply when S is the DB makes a difference only for couples in which S is more than 10 years younger than P—in other words, not many cases.

Another special rule: While the "fixed term method" must be used to determine the LE of all other beneficiaries, S's LE (like P's) can be redetermined annually (*or* can be determined using the fixed term method). § 401(a)(9)(D). This option is available both for lifetime distributions (if the joint LE of P and S is being used to measure P's MRDs) (see "Recalculating Life Expectancies: Participant and Spouse," Chapter 1), and after death, if S is P's DB. While it is nice that there are more choices for S, this "advantage" can backfire; see discussions in Chapter 1 and the *Fallon* case study.

When MRDs must start if P dies before his RBD

If P dies before his RBD, P's *non-spouse* beneficiaries must begin to withdraw benefits from the plan by the end of the year following the year of P's death (or else withdraw *all* benefits by the end of the fifth year after P's death). If S is the beneficiary, on the other hand, and P dies before his RBD, the Code says distributions to S shall not be required to begin earlier than the date P would have reached age 70½. § 401(a)(9)(B)(iv)(I).

The proposed regulations change this slightly to the following: If P dies before his RBD, S must begin withdrawing the benefits (over a period not exceeding S's life expectancy) by the *later* of: December 31 of the year after the year in which P died; or December 31 of the year in which P would have reached age 70½. Prop. Reg. § 1.401(a)(9)-1, B-5(a), C-3(b). This means also that S must make her election whether to recalculate her life expectancy by that date or else be stuck with the applicable default rule (the plan's or the IRS's, as the case may be) (see "*Mechanics of making this election*," Chapter 1).

The problem if P dies before his RBD

The final special rule is that, if P dies before his RBD, leaving S as his DB, and S dies before the later of (1) December 31 of the year after the year in which P died, or (2) December 31 of the year in which P would have reached age 70½, MRDs after her death will be measured under the five year rule and its exceptions, as if *she* were the "participant." However, if she has remarried, her surviving new spouse does not get treated as a surviving spouse for purposes of § 401(a)(9). §

401(a)(9)(B)(iv)(II); Prop. Reg. § 1.401(a)(9)-1, C-3, C-5, C-6.

Example: Homer was born 9/1/34. He dies in 1999 at age 65 (in other words, before his RBD), leaving his IRA to Marge. Homer would have reached age 70½ on 3/1/2005. Marge does not have to start withdrawing benefits until 12/31/2005, which is the later of December 31 of the year (2000) following the year of death (1999) or December 31 of the year Homer would have reached age 70½ (2005). Marge dies in 2004 (in other words, before she was required to start taking benefits from Homer's IRA). As a result of Marge's death, benefits will have to be distributed from the account by the end of the fifth year (2009) following Marge's death or (if payable to a DB), beginning by the end of the first year (2005) following Marge's death, over the LE of the DB.

This again is an "advantage" which sometimes creates problems. The problem is that, if S dies shortly after P, she may not have gotten around to naming a DB for this account. Or, if she intentionally left it in P's name (so as, for example, to avoid the 10% penalty; see *"Drawbacks of a spousal rollover,"* above), there may be no mechanism whereby the IRA provider allows her to name a successor beneficiary for her interest (even though this is specifically permitted by Prop. Reg. § E-5(f)).

If she hasn't managed to name a beneficiary somehow, many plans and IRAs would require that the benefits be paid to her estate if she dies before withdrawing them, and the five year rule will be triggered. See also *"Estate planning for the beneficiary who inherits an IRA,"* Chapter 1.

Marital Deduction for Benefits Payable to QTIP Trust

Non-tax reasons to name a QTIP trust

For any number of reasons P may prefer to leave money in trust for S, rather than outright to her, and this usually means naming a "qualified terminable interest property" (QTIP) trust (see definition at "*Income requirement: QTIP trusts*," below) as beneficiary. Unfortunately, in many cases, the price of protecting the benefits from whatever risks P is concerned about is higher income taxes, and substantial loss of income tax deferral, as compared with leaving the benefits to S outright.

The client who wants to make his benefits payable to a QTIP trust faces several hurdles: qualifying for the marital deduction (discussed in this chapter); complying with the proposed regulations' "trust rules" so S can be treated as a "designated beneficiary" for purposes of the minimum distribution rules (see Chapter 6); and avoiding using a **pecuniary formula**, which may trigger an income tax when funding the QTIP (see "*Planning pitfall: assignment of the right-to-receive IRD*," Chapter 2).

The IRS's test for determining whether S is the beneficiary for purposes of the spousal rollover is different from its test for determining whether S is the beneficiary for purposes of § 401(a)(9); which is in turn different from its test for determining whether the interest qualifies for the marital deduction.

Marital deduction; Rev. Rul. 89-89

Death benefits payable directly to S outright in a lump sum should qualify for the marital deduction, provided S is a U.S. citizen (see Chapter 4 if S is not a U.S. citizen) and S is entitled to withdraw all the benefits. See, *e.g.*, PLR 8843033 (8/2/88). If the benefits are payable to a marital trust, however, rather than directly to S, the situation becomes less clear.

If it were not for the rulings discussed below, many practitioners would conclude that they could simply name a QTIP trust as beneficiary of the client's IRA and leave it at that. "Obviously" the IRA would qualify for the marital deduction since the QTIP trustee could withdraw the benefits from the IRA at any time either for distribution to S as "income" or for reinvestment as "principal." S would be fully protected by her right to receive all income of the trust and her power to require the trustee to invest in income-producing property.

However, the IRS, in TAM 9220007 (1/30/91) took a different view. This TAM held that the IRA *itself* was to be considered "terminable interest property." The IRA agreement in question (which was quite standard) did not contain any statement about when benefits would be paid out, other than the statement required by the minimum distribution rules to the effect that "benefits must be distributed no later than, etc." The IRA agreement did not explicitly state that the account holder could withdraw all benefits from the IRA at any time.

The TAM writer looked, in the IRA agreement, for a provision that would require the QTIP trustee to withdraw all income annually from the IRA and found no such provision. The TAM then stated that the QTIP trustee's ability to opt for some "settlement option" that *would* pay out all the income annually was not sufficient; since the mandatory income provision was not included as of the date of death, some discretionary act of the QTIP trustee *post mortem* could not cure it.

Rev. Rul. 89-89, 1989-2 C.B. 231, discussed a designation of a marital trust as beneficiary for an IRA that did work. In this ruling, the IRA beneficiary designation form *itself* contained all the required marital deduction provisions. Rather than simply naming the QTIP trustee as the beneficiary of the

IRA, the beneficiary designation form also stated how benefits had to be withdrawn. Specifically, it required the QTIP trustee to withdraw all income from the IRA each year.

Thus the IRS has given us a road map of what will definitely work in order for an IRA (or other retirement plan death benefit) payable to a QTIP trust to qualify for the marital deduction: having the IRA custodian (or plan administrator) be required to pay out to the QTIP trust all the income earned on the benefit every year. This is an awkward requirement in the case of IRAs since most IRA custodians are not equipped to deal with, and do not charge for, fiduciary responsibilities such as determining what is "income" and what is "principal." Since few planners want to take the risk that the marital deduction will be disallowed, many planners choose to use the Rev. Rul. 89-89 language (as subsequently refined; see examples in forms 3.3, 3.4 and 3.5 in Appendix B).

This series of IRS rulings appears to be erroneous to the extent it implies that the only way an IRA or other retirement benefit payable to a marital trust can qualify for the marital deduction is if the plan document (or IRA agreement) contains language requiring annual distribution of all income. The following paragraphs analyze the question by reference to the IRS's own regulations.

Income requirement: general power trusts

Under § 2056(b)(5), a trust qualifies for the marital deduction if S (1) is entitled to all income of the trust for life, payable at least annually, and (2) has the power, exercisable by her alone and in all events, to appoint the principal to herself or her estate, with no power in any other person to appoint any of the property to someone other than S. This type of trust is sometimes called a "general power marital trust."

Although generally this type of marital trust must

provide that S is "entitled for life to all the income" of the trust, long-standing IRS regulations make it clear that this does not mean that income must actually be distributed to S every year; rather, there are several ways a trust can meet the "entitled to all the income" requirement. For example:

1.   A power in the trustee to hold unproductive property (*i.e.*, property that does not produce income) will not disqualify the trust if S has the right to require the trustee either to make any such property productive or to convert it to productive property within a reasonable time. § 20.2056(b)-5(f)(4).

2.   If the trust corpus consists substantially of non-income producing property, and S does not have the power to compel the trustee to make it income producing, the trust will still qualify for the marital deduction if S can "require that the trustee provide the required beneficial enjoyment, such as by payments to the Spouse out of other assets of the trust." - 5(f)(5).

3.   An interest qualifies if the income may be accumulated in the sole discretion of S. - 5(f)(7).

4.   An interest qualifies if S has "the right exercisable annually (or more frequently) to require distribution to herself of the trust income, and otherwise [*i.e.*, if she does not require such distribution in any year] the trust income [for such year] is to be accumulated." -5(f)(8).

Thus, contrary to the implication of Rev. Rul. 89-89, an IRA (for example) payable to a marital trust should qualify for the marital deduction so long as S has (for example) the power to *require* that the IRA income be distributed to her (no. 4 above), or to require the trustee to distribute other assets to her (no. 2 above) to make up for IRA income's being accumulated.

Income requirement: QTIP trusts

The regulation quoted above deals with "general power" marital trusts. There are other kinds of marital trusts. Under § 2056(b)(7), a trust qualifies for the estate tax marital deduction if S is entitled to all income for life, payable at least annually, and no person has the power to appoint any of the principal to someone other than S during her lifetime, provided the executor files a special election with the estate tax return. This type of trust is called a "qualified terminable interest property" ("QTIP") marital trust.

The IRS's QTIP regulations specify that the same principles apply to "qualified terminable interest property" (in trust or otherwise) as apply to general power marital trusts in determining whether S is "entitled for life to all of the income." Reg. § 20.2056(b)-7(d)(2). Thus, the same alternative methods for meeting the "entitled to all income" requirement are available for QTIP trusts as for general power trusts.

Practitioner response to Rev. Rul. 89-89

To summarize, if you want retirement benefits paid to any marital trust to qualify for the marital deduction, the safest (and therefore the recommended) approach is to include language such as that used in Rev. Rul. 89-89 in the IRA beneficiary designation *(and* in the trust instrument; see further discussion, below, in this subsection). Also, although not required, it may make the trustee's duties clearer if you also include language requiring the trustee to withdraw enough from the IRA to comply with the minimum distribution rules, which Rev. Rul. 89-89 ignored. This approach is apparently being adopted by many practitioners. See, *e.g.*, PLRs 9321035

(2/24/93); 9321059 (2/26/93); 9418026 (2/7/94); 9348025 (9/2/93).

Although the forms in this book use the "safe harbor" approach of Rev. Rul. 89-89, the preceding discussion shows that there are several other methods that estate planning lawyers *should* be able to use to qualify retirement benefits payable to a marital trust for the marital deduction.

Note: The Rev. Rul. 89-89 language requires only that the income earned by the retirement plan be distributed to the spouse annually. Although the plan (or IRA) must distribute to the QTIP trustee the *greater* of the net income or the MRD for the year, the QTIP trustee is *not* required to distribute the greater of these two amounts to S. The QTIP trustee is required to distribute to S only the "income" of the trust.

Generally, what is "income" of a QTIP trust is determined by the applicable state law governing trust accounting. If a retirement plan's MRD for the year is greater than the income earned inside the plan for that year, the excess should be considered, for trust accounting (and marital deduction) purposes, "corpus" of the QTIP trust. The Code does not require that "corpus" be distributed to S as a condition of obtaining the marital deduction.

Even though it is not a marital deduction requirement that the QTIP trustee withdraw and distribute to the spouse the greater of the MRD or the income, it is sometimes appropriate to draft the trust this way. See "*The MRD Conduit Trust*," Chapter 6.

If relying on Rev. Rul. 89-89, it is also advisable to have, as a backup, matching language in the QTIP trust itself requiring the trustee to withdraw the income from the IRA or plan every year. This provides some protection in case the client, having dutifully signed the designation of beneficiary forms his lawyer so carefully prepared, with all the Rev. Rul. 89-89 language, later signs some new substituted form that might be given to him when (for example) he transfers to a different investment, or when the plan sponsor simply issues new forms periodically. See forms 3.5 and 7.4 in Appendix B.

Finally, when retirement benefits are payable to a QTIP trust, the executor needs to elect QTIP treatment for the benefits themselves as well as for the trust, according to PLR 9442032 (7/27/94).

Another alternative to avoid this issue, in the case of an IRA, is to structure the IRA *itself* as a QTIP: use a "trust IRA" rather than a "custodial IRA," include all required and desirable marital trust provisions, and have the IRA trustee pay the annual income directly to S. The drawback of this approach is that eventually the minimum distribution rules will start requiring distributions of principal as well as income. If S lives to her life expectancy, all the principal will eventually be paid out to S and it will not be "protected" for the children (as it would be if it were payable to a QTIP trust). Thus this alternative is normally attractive only to someone whose only goal in "QTIPing" the benefits is to protect S from mishandling a lump sum, rather than someone whose goal is (*e.g.*) to preserve principal for children of a first marriage.

Other marital deduction issues

There is another lurking marital deduction issue with retirement benefits.

Example: Jerry leaves his IRA outright to his wife Carol. However, Jerry's beneficiary designation form (or the account agreement governing the IRA) names his son Hanson as "successor beneficiary" [as recommended in Appendix B of this book] to take the (remaining) benefits if Carol dies after Jerry but before she has withdrawn the benefits. Since that successor beneficiary is someone other than Carol's own estate, Jerry asks you whether his IRA will qualify for the marital deduction for his estate, or whether it has been transformed into a nondeductible "terminable interest." He points out that it appears that an interest in the IRA (*i.e.*, the amount remaining in the account at Carol's death) will pass to someone other than Carol or her estate *(i.e.,* Hanson) upon the occurrence of an event or contingency (*i.e.*, Carol's failure to withdraw the benefits during her lifetime), which is the definition of a nondeductible terminable interest under § 2056(b)(1).

The author believes that this scenario does *not* create a nondeductible interest. For one thing, it meets the description of a deductible interest in § 2056(b)(5), which provides that an interest is deemed to pass to the spouse and only the spouse (and therefore is not a nondeductible terminable interest) if the spouse is entitled to all the income for life, at annual or more frequent intervals, and has the right (exercisable by her alone and in all events) to appoint the principal to herself with no person having the power to appoint it to someone other than her. The spouse has these rights with respect to an IRA left outright to her, assuming there is nothing in the beneficiary designation or account agreement that limits her right to withdraw the income or principal of the account.

The fact that the interest will pass to a successor beneficiary *if S chooses not to withdraw the benefits* does not transform this into a terminable interest. The situation is analogous to property left by husband to wife and child as joint tenants. After husband's death, wife can seek partition and take her share of the inherited joint property whenever she wishes, but *if she chooses not to withdraw her share*, it will automatically pass to child by right of survivorship on wife's death. This gift qualifies for the marital deduction. Treas. Reg. § 20.2056(b)-5(g)(2).

Furthermore, IRAs and other retirement plans are

considered "annuities" for estate tax purposes and are taxed under § 2039; see, *e.g.*, Treas. Reg. § 20.2039-5. § 2056(b)(7)(C) treats a surviving spouse's interest in a survivor annuity automatically as QTIP property, unless the decedent's executor elects otherwise, if the spouse is the sole beneficiary during her lifetime. Therefore, even if it were determined (wrongly, in the author's view) that Jerry's IRA in the example above *was* a terminable interest, the interest would qualify for the automatic QTIP marital deduction.

However, the fact that the question has even been raised suggests a preventive-medicine approach. One cannot be too cautious when it comes to qualifying for the marital deduction, and it is generally preferable to have a four-square match with an explicit Code provision or regulation than to have "merely" a good sound legal argument. To sidestep the issue altogether, one could include additional language such as that in ¶ 3.07 of Forms 2.1 and 2.2 in Appendix B when (1) P is naming S outright as beneficiary and (2) either the plan document or the beneficiary designation form names a successor beneficiary (other than S's estate) who will be entitled to receive the benefits that S does not withdraw during her lifetime. This language explicitly recites that S has the right to withdraw all income and principal of the benefits, tracking the wording of § 2056(b)(5) and Treas. Reg. § § 20.2056(b)-5(f)(8).

Why go to all this trouble to name a successor beneficiary if the surviving spouse fails to withdraw the benefits? Because of the difficulties under the minimum distribution rules if P and S both die before P's RBD and the benefits pass to S's estate. See "*The problem if P dies before his RBD*," above.

Income Tax Disadvantages When QTIP Trust is Beneficiary

Mandatory income distributions

The language used in Rev. Rul. 89-89 *may* involve a significant loss of potential income tax deferral. Depending on the rate of income earned by the plan investments, the minimum distribution rules might require S, as P's DB, to withdraw *less* than the income every year until the later years of the "life expectancy" payout period. This potential loss of deferral is not a concern, of course, if it is expected that S will want to withdraw all income of the benefits in any case, for her living needs. Furthermore, in the late 1990's, many trusts have the opposite problem—investment returns in the form of "income" are too low, not too high.

If the mandatory income-payout rule is a concern, here are two possible ways to deal with it:

1.   **Pay benefits to credit shelter share.** If the client's retirement benefits total less than $600,000, and the client is determined not to leave any assets outright to S, consider making the retirement benefits payable to the credit shelter trust, and using other assets to fund the QTIP trust. Although this is contrary to the usual rule of thumb ("don't waste your credit shelter paying income taxes"), it may increase the potential income tax deferral, because the credit shelter trust is not subject to the mandatory income payout requirement. If S is not a beneficiary of the credit shelter gift, only the children are, the income tax deferral may be further enhanced, assuming the children are younger than S, because the payout will be spread out over a longer life expectancy period.

2.   Rollover of excess income distributions. It may be that, with careful planning and proper timing, the annual income distribution problem can be mitigated by spousal rollovers. The trustee of the marital trust could withdraw the retirement plan's "income" once a year, as Rev. Rul. 89-89 apparently requires, and then immediately distribute it to S. S could then roll over to her own IRA the excess of the total distribution over that year's MRD. (The minimum distribution is not eligible for rollover. § 408(d)(3)(E).)

If S is relatively young, this technique of rolling over the "excess" income distribution every year can provide substantial additional tax deferral. As long as her rollover occurred within 60 days after the income was distributed from P's plan to the marital trust, and provided she received and rolled over no more than one distribution in any 12 month period, this may qualify as a proper spousal rollover. The IRS has ruled (albeit only in private letter rulings) that a plan distribution that passes through a marital trust on its way to S is eligible for a spousal rollover, provided that S had an absolute right to receive it, *i.e.*, the distribution of the retirement benefit to her from the marital trust was not subject to a third party's discretion. See "Spousal Rollovers," above.

No spousal rollover

Regardless of whether mandatory income distributions are causing accelerated distributions, it will still be true in many cases that making retirement benefits payable to a marital trust will result in much less income tax deferral than would be available if the benefits were payable to S personally and she rolled over the entire benefit to her own IRA, for three reasons:

First, with the rollover IRA, S can defer distributions altogether until she reaches age 70½. When she is receiving the benefits as beneficiary of a marital trust, in contrast, the minimum distribution rules may require annual non-rollable distributions to the trust beginning the year after P's death. For further discussion, see *"When is a trust for the spouse the same as the spouse?"* Chapter 6.

Second, with the rollover IRA, S can name the children as beneficiaries, and then withdraw over the joint life expectancy of herself and the oldest child (subject to the MDIB rule). When the benefits are paid to a marital trust, in contrast, minimum distributions will be based on the life expectancy of S solely (if she is the oldest trust beneficiary, and the other requirements for naming a trust as beneficiary are met; see Chapter 6).

Finally, with a rollover IRA, there can be a long period of deferral (over the children's life expectancies) for any benefits remaining in the IRA at S's death. When the benefits are paid to a marital trust, the minimum distribution rules will continue to operate after her death based solely on *S*'s life expectancy.

Making benefits payable to a marital trust, as opposed to S individually, thus often results in sacrificing decades of potential additional income tax deferral—all benefits will have to be distributed by the time S reaches the end of her IRS-defined life expectancy (age 86, approximately), whereas some deferral until the oldest child reaches that age is usually achievable when benefits are paid to S individually.

High trust tax rates

1993 tax law changes further battered retirement benefits payable to a QTIP trust (or to any other trust where the benefits are expected to be retained by the trust, rather than immediately distributed to the beneficiaries), by imposing high tax rates on trust income. See *"The drawback of making IRD payable to a trust,"* Chapter 2, and the *Koslow* case study.

Simultaneous Death Clauses

Uniform Simultaneous Death Law

If the participant (P) names his spouse (S) as his beneficiary, and they die simultaneously, it will be presumed under the Uniform Simultaneous Death Law that S predeceased. A presumption that S survives, if contained in P's will or pourover trust, will NOT govern retirement plan death benefits payable directly to S. Thus, in order to have a presumption that S survives in this situation, the presumption must be contained in the designation of beneficiary form itself. Such a presumption is often used, if S's estate is smaller than P's, to equalize the estates for estate tax purposes. What is the effect of such a survivorship presumption under the minimum distribution rules?

Note: Before attempting to create a presumption of spousal survival in a designation of beneficiary form, check the plan to make sure it does not create an irrebuttable presumption that P survives the beneficiary in case of simultaneous deaths.

Simultaneous deaths before P's RBD

If P and S die simultaneously before P's RBD, there would be no disadvantage (from the point of view of § 401(a)(9)) to presuming that S survives, if S is personally named as the "DB," *and* if the benefits pass to an individual DB after S's death. Unfortunately, this result may be difficult to achieve. See *"The problem if P dies before his RBD,"* above.

What if P designates, not S individually, but a QTIP trust as his primary beneficiary, and his children as contingent beneficiaries? Assume the "trust rules" (Chapter 6) are complied with. The beneficiary designation form and the QTIP trust both presume S survives P in case of simultaneous death. Assume the QTIP trust is to be distributed outright to the children on S's death, so the children get the benefits outright either as remainder beneficiaries of the QTIP trust or as contingent beneficiaries under P's beneficiary designation form. P and S both die, simultaneously, prior to P's RBD. There are three conceivable outcomes under § 401(a)(9):

(a)   One possibility is that Prop. Reg. § 1.401(a)(9)-1, C-5 applies, and the five year rule applies "as if" S were the participant. IRS rulings have been contradictory on this point. See *"When is a trust for the spouse the same as the spouse?,"* Chapter 6.

(b)   A second possibility is that the IRS would disregard the presumption of survivorship for purposes of § 401(a)(9) and would treat the children as P's "DB."

(c)   The third possibility is that the IRS would treat the benefits as paid to a non-spouse beneficiary, namely, a trust of which S was the oldest beneficiary, and benefits would have to be distributed to the trust over the LE of S determined as of what would have been S's birthday in the year after P's death.

If P dies after the RBD

Once the RBD has passed, the payout period of P's benefits is "carved in stone," and the only way it could be varied would be if S survived P and rolled over the benefits (or, in the case of an IRA, elected to treat P's IRA as her own). Therefore, presuming that S survives P in case of simultaneous deaths would *theoretically* enable S's executor to roll over the benefits or, in the case of an IRA, elect to treat the IRA as S's own IRA. Unfortunately it does not appear that the IRS will allow a surviving spouse's executor to take these actions. (See *"What if S dies before rolling over?"* above.)

Nevertheless, because of the tremendous potential value of these rights S has, it is worth trying to preserve those options in case of simultaneous death, especially if P's elections on the RBD now seem regrettable. One approach: Specify in the beneficiary designation form that S is presumed to survive in case of simultaneous death. Then have S elect in writing, *while P is still living*, to treat the IRA as her own (in the event she survives P), and name her own DB. Unfortunately, the IRS has not yet ruled one way or the other on this approach. See the *Fallon* case study and form 4.1 in Appendix B.

REA '84 and Spousal Consent

The Retirement Equity Act of 1984 ("REA"), Pub. L. No. 98-397, 98 Stat. 1426 (codified in scattered sections of 26 and 29 U.S.C.) gives certain rights to spouses of certain retirement plan participants. One part of REA, § 401(a)(11) of the Code, requires spousal consent in order for a participant to withdraw benefits from any pension plan (and certain profit sharing plans) in other than "qualified joint and survivor annuity" form. It also requires spousal consent for a participant to make all or part of a death benefit under a pension or profit sharing plan payable to a beneficiary other than the spouse. These requirements do not apply to IRAs.

Needless to say the spousal consent requirement creates serious obstacles when the spouses are separated, divorcing or otherwise hostile. It can also create very serious and sad problems when the spouse is mentally ill or disabled to such an extent that he or she is unable to consent.

Practitioners who have studied the spousal consent requirements are bedeviled by such problems as precisely when (relative to the distribution date) spousal consent must be obtained in order to be valid; whether a new spousal consent is required for every distribution if installments are being paid out prior to the RBD; whether the consent requirements limit the ability of a participant and spouse to change the form of benefits after the RBD; and whether a waiver contained in a prenuptial agreement can meet (or beat) the spousal waiver requirements.

This book does not cover these extensive problems. For other sources of information, see the Bibliography. See also discussion of spousal consent issues in connection with disclaimers in Chapter 8.

Summary of Planning Principles

1.   The tax laws generally, though not always, favor naming the spouse, personally, as DB of retirement benefits and using other, non-IRD, assets to fund a credit shelter trust.

2.   The IRS has issued rulings which provide clear instructions for qualifying retirement benefits payable to QTIP trusts for the estate tax marital deduction. Although the method specified in these rulings is not the only way to obtain the marital deduction for benefits payable to a QTIP trust, many practitioners are choosing to use it.

3.   Making benefits payable to a QTIP trust often results in a substantial loss of potential income tax deferral compared with leaving benefits to S outright.

4.   Review the issues discussed in the "Simultaneous Deaths" section of this chapter before inserting a "presumption of survivorship" clause in a beneficiary designation.

5.   Upon P's death it is extremely important for S to consider her options immediately, and to roll over the benefits if that is the chosen option, since her executor probably cannot exercise these options on her behalf.

Retirement Benefits
and the Non-Citizen Spouse

*If the participant's spouse is not
a U.S. citizen, the usual marital
deduction is not available. A
modified marital deduction is
available if certain requirements
are met. A long menu of
planning alternatives offers a
few practical solutions.*

This chapter explains the tax issues involved when the participant's spouse is not a U.S. citizen, then examines the most commonly used alternative methods for disposing of retirement benefits in this situation, and concludes with suggested investment and distribution strategies for QDOTs.

Modified Marital Deduction for Transfers
to a Non-Citizen Spouse

How the modified marital deduction works

For the estate of a decedent who dies after November 10, 1988, property passing to a surviving spouse (S) who is not a United States citizen will not qualify for the normal estate tax marital deduction. § 2056(d)(1). However, if the property is placed in a certain kind of trust, called a qualified domestic trust ("QDOT"), either by the decedent (D) himself or by S, it will qualify for a *modified* version of the marital deduction. § 2056(d)(2).

Under this modified marital deduction, the property is deducted on Schedule M of D's estate tax return (IRS form 706); but then, if principal is ever distributed to S from the QDOT, the principal distribution is subject to an estate tax at that time, computed at D's rate. If the estate tax is paid from the QDOT, the tax payment itself is treated as a further distribution subject to estate tax. Principal remaining in the QDOT at S's death is subject to the deferred estate tax at that time. § 2056A(b).

Under this modified form of marital deduction, the property is not deducted from D's estate and then added to S's estate, as normally occurs when the marital deduction is taken. Rather, the property remains permanently taxable as part of D's estate. The tax is merely deferred until (at the latest) S's death. The QDOT property will *also* be subject to U.S. estate tax as part of S's estate, under normal estate tax principles, although her estate will receive a credit for the deferred estate tax paid on the property by the QDOT. § 2056(d)(3). Under this scheme, if the non-citizen spouse dies a U.S. resident, the estate tax payable on the QDOT at S's death is essentially going to be at D's marginal rate, or at S's marginal rate, whichever is higher.

If S becomes a U.S. citizen, or is or becomes a non-U.S. resident

If S becomes a *U.S. citizen* prior to the filing of the estate tax return, *and* if S was a U.S. *resident* at all times after D's death and until she became a citizen, the normal marital deduction becomes available and it is not necessary to transfer property to a QDOT or worry about the deferred estate tax. § 2056(d)(4). This is often the simplest solution to the problem if S intends to remain permanently in the U.S. anyway. This approach should be explored at the planning stage if possible, otherwise as soon as possible after D's death, since becoming a citizen takes time and should not be left to the last minute.

Even if S becomes a U.S. citizen *after* the filing of the estate tax return, there is a favorable result: provided S was a U.S. *resident* at all times after D's death and until she became a citizen, all distributions to S thereafter from the QDOT (or from non-assignable property subject to an agreement with the IRS—see Alternative 4) are free of the deferred estate tax. The QDOT could terminate at that point and distribute its assets to S tax-free. § 2056A-10(a); Reg. § 20.2056A-10; see PLR 9848007 (7/27/98).

If the non-citizen spouse is or becomes a non-U.S. *resident*, different considerations may apply. This situation is beyond the scope of this book.

The rest of this chapter assumes S will remain a non-U.S. citizen.

Payment of deferred estate tax by QDOT

Once the property is in a QDOT (whether transferred there by D or by S), the QDOT can distribute *income* to S without triggering the deferred estate tax. In addition, the trust can reimburse S (out of *principal*) for certain income taxes without incurring the deferred estate tax (see "Interplay of Income Tax and Deferred Estate Tax"). Other principal distributions are subject to the deferred estate tax unless they qualify as hardship distributions (see "*Hardship exception*").

There are two other events, besides distributions, that cause the deferred estate tax to be due: If the trust ceases to qualify as a QDOT, the tax is imposed at that time; and in any case the tax is payable upon the death of S.

Overview of ways to qualify for the marital deduction

In summary, if the surviving spouse is not a U.S. citizen

(and will not become a U.S. citizen prior to filing the estate tax return), there are four possible ways to qualify for the modified marital deduction:

One is for D to have arranged his estate plan so that property for which the marital deduction is sought will pass, on his death, directly to a QDOT. See "Alternative 1."

If D's estate plan failed to do this, the modified marital deduction is still available if S *herself*, having inherited the property outright, transfers it to a QDOT prior to the filing of the estate tax return and no later than one year after the due date of the return. Reg. § 20.2056A-1(a)(iii). See "Alternative 2" and "Alternative 3."

Finally, "Alternative 4" describes two other methods that are available for "non-assignable property"—that is, property (such as a non-assignable annuity) which passes to S outright, but which cannot legally be transferred by S to a QDOT. S can get QDOT treatment for such "non-assignable property" by signing an agreement with the IRS that, when she actually receives the property, she will transfer it to a QDOT, or, alternatively, by signing an agreement that she will pay the deferred estate tax on the property when she receives it. The regulations permit S to elect to treat an individual retirement account (IRA) as non-assignable.

Distinguishing Features of a QDOT

The five requirements

The distinguishing characteristics of a qualified domestic trust are set forth in § 2056A(a):

(a)   At least one trustee of the QDOT must be an individual citizen of the United States or a United States domestic corporation.

(b)   The trust must be "maintained" under, and the administration of the trust must be governed by, the laws of a particular state or the District of Columbia. Reg. § 20.2056A-2(a).

(c)   No principal distribution may be made from the trust unless the U.S. trustee has the right to withhold from the distribution the deferred estate tax discussed above.

(d)   The trust must meet any additional requirements imposed by the Secretary of the Treasury by regulations to insure collection of the tax. The IRS has imposed some such additional requirements, such as bonding for non-bank trustees and limits on non-U.S. real estate investments. Reg. § 20.2056A-2.

(e)   Finally, there are various requirements for agreements and elections by the executor and surviving spouse.

Note that there is no requirement that all of the QDOT income be distributable annually to S, or even that S be the sole beneficiary of the QDOT. The *QDOT* requirements are concerned *only* with the identity of the trustee, necessary elections, and security for collection of the deferred estate tax.

In summary, in order to obtain the modified version of the marital deduction for property when S is not a U.S. citizen, the property must be placed (by D or by S) in a trust which meets the above requirements; and *in addition* the property must pass from D to S (or to a trust for S's benefit) in a way that qualifies for the marital deduction (aside from the QDOT requirements). The next two subsections look at the differences between a QDOT established by D (as part of his estate plan) and one established by S (after D's death).

Marital trust - QDOT created by decedent

Regardless of whether the surviving spouse is a U.S.

citizen, the marital deduction is not allowed for property passing from D to a trust for his spouse unless the trust meets certain requirements familiar to all estate planners: a "marital deduction trust" will be a nondeductible "terminable interest" unless it fits into one of the exceptions to the "terminable interest rule." This chapter assumes that any QDOT created by transfer from D will be either a "general power marital trust" or a "QTIP marital trust" (see Chapter 3),[2] meeting all the usual requirements of a marital trust, including, most significantly with regard to retirement benefits, the requirement that all income be distributed annually to S.

QDOT created by surviving spouse

If property passes from D to S *outright*, it qualifies for the marital deduction under § 2056(a). An outright bequest is not a "terminable interest," and accordingly does not have to comply with the marital deduction trust rules.

Therefore, when S receives an outright bequest, and transfers the inherited property into a QDOT *she* creates, there is no requirement that the terms of that QDOT be similar to those of a "normal" marital deduction trust (unless the trust also contains property transferred to it directly by D); only the QDOT requirements need be met. A "QTIP election" cannot be made for a QDOT established by S. Reg. § 20.2056A-4(d), example 5.

A QDOT created by S need not (and normally should not) be irrevocable. A QDOT created by S need not (but probably should) require annual distribution of all income to S.

---

[2] Two other categories of trust gift that qualify for the marital deduction, the rarely-used "estate trust," and the charitable remainder trust of which the spouse is the only non-charitable beneficiary, are not discussed in this chapter.

A QDOT created by S could (but probably should not) allow distributions to people other than S during her lifetime. For further suggestions regarding the terms of a QDOT created by S, see "Alternative 3," below.

Note: if the trust to which S transfers property *also* contains any property transferred directly to it by D then the *entire trust* must qualify for the marital deduction under § 2056. Reg. § 20.2056A-4(b)(1). In this chapter, a "QDOT funded by S" means a QDOT *exclusively* so funded.

Interplay of Income Tax and Deferred Estate Tax

Retirement benefits generally are subject both to income tax as "Income in Respect of a Decedent" ("IRD") (see Chapter 2) and estate tax. When the benefits are paid to a non-citizen spouse or a QDOT it is not always clear how the income tax and the deferred estate tax relate to each other.

Under the statute, it appears possible that S could be required to pay *both* income tax *and* deferred estate tax on the full amount of inherited retirement benefits, with neither tax deductible in determining the other. The regulations make it clear in a couple of situations that amounts used to pay income tax on IRD will not *also* be subject to the deferred estate tax; in other situations we are left to assume that this result is allowed, without specific authority.

If the client's retirement plan is an IRA, one way to avoid all the complications described in this section is to convert the IRA to a Roth IRA during life, so that distributions post-death will generally not be subject to income tax; see Chapter 5.

§ 691(c) deduction for deferred estate tax

Generally, as explained in Chapter 2, the beneficiary of

retirement benefits can deduct the federal estate taxes paid on the benefits in determining how much income tax the beneficiary must pay on those benefits, because § 691(c)(2)(A) allows an income tax deduction for estate taxes imposed on IRD "*under section 2001 or 2101*." Although the deferred estate tax is imposed by § *2056A*, the regulations provide that "The estate tax (net of any applicable credits) imposed under section 2056A(b)(1) constitutes an estate tax for purposes of section 691(c)(2)(A)." Reg. § 20.2056A-6(a).

While it is nice to know that the deferred estate tax qualifies for the 691(c) deduction, it is not clear how this will actually help the surviving spouse. Normally, estate taxes are paid when a decedent dies, then the beneficiary collects the benefits, and the beneficiary can deduct the estate taxes paid when computing his income tax on the benefits. In the case of the *deferred* estate tax, however, the surviving spouse (or the QDOT) normally collects the income-taxable benefits *first*, before the deferred estate tax has been "imposed" (at her death). On the other hand, since any federal income taxes S pays on the benefits are removed from the tax base for purposes of computing the deferred estate tax that will later be due (see the next three subsections), it makes sense that she does not also get a deduction in the other direction (i.e., deducting the estate tax for purposes of computing income tax).

In those situations (which planning will normally try to avoid) in which the deferred estate tax on retirement benefits has to be paid during S's life (*e.g.*, if the QDOT ceases to qualify as a QDOT) S will be able to take the § 691(c) deduction for the deferred estate tax with regard to subsequent distributions.

To the extent there are still some benefits inside the plan at S's death, the next succeeding beneficiary can take a § 691(c) deduction for the deferred estate tax (and/or for the first spouse's original estate tax and/or the surviving spouse's estate tax). The complications of computing the deduction in that situation are beyond the scope of this book.

Income tax paid by S on plan distributions

The Code exempts, from the deferred estate tax, distributions to S from a QDOT made to reimburse S for *federal* income taxes imposed on S on any item of income of the QDOT "to which the surviving spouse is not entitled under the terms of the trust." § 2056A(b)(15). The IRS in its regulations has interpreted this oddly worded Code provision in such a way as to alleviate the double taxation effect in some specific situations.

Under the regulations, if S receives a distribution from D's retirement plan and then "assigns" that distribution to the QDOT, the QDOT can reimburse S for the federal income tax on the distribution, free of deferred estate tax.

Example: The Acme Widget Profit Sharing Plan distributes $100,000 to S as a death benefit from D's account in the plan. S immediately takes the $100,000 check and deposits it in the QDOT. S then has to pay (say) $40,000 of federal income tax on the distribution. The QDOT can reimburse her for the $40,000 without having to pay deferred estate tax on the distribution.

This estate-tax-free reimbursement is available only for taxes imposed by subtitle A, *federal* income taxes. It is not permitted for state income taxes. The reimbursable tax is calculated at the marginal rate, *i.e.*, the difference between S's *actual* income tax for the year and what S's tax *would* have been if the distribution had not been included in her gross income.

Suppose that, when the profit sharing plan makes its distribution to S, the plan *withholds* $40,000 of income tax from the distribution. The withheld taxes are paid directly to the IRS. The wording of the regulation talks about "reimbursing" S for the taxes, as if S must still transmit the entire distribution to the QDOT, even the withheld portion she didn't actually receive, then get a check back from the QDOT for the federal income tax S owes on that distribution. Reg. § 20.2056A-5(c)(3)(iv). This is a rather awkward procedure, especially since S cannot compute the amount of reimbursable tax until she does her income tax return after the end of the taxable year.

Income taxes paid by the QDOT

Assume D left his retirement benefits to a QTIP-QDOT which provides "all income to S for life, remainder to my issue." Because S is only the income beneficiary, she is not treated as the "owner" of the trust principal for income tax purposes under § 678. Accordingly, income taxes on distributions of IRD to the trust are imposed directly on the trust.

In this situation, all income taxes on the benefits (both federal and state, apparently) are exempt from the deferred estate tax. "Payments to applicable governmental authorities for income tax or any other applicable tax imposed on the QDOT" (other than the deferred estate tax itself) are exempt from the deferred estate tax. Reg. § 20.2056-5(c)(3)(ii).

In contrast, when benefits are payable to S, and then transferred by S to the QDOT, only the *federal* income taxes S pays can be reimbursed by the QDOT free of deferred estate tax. § 2056A(b)(15); Reg. § 20.2056A05(c)(3)(iv). This slight discrepancy in treatment of state income taxes argues in favor of leaving the benefits to a QTIP-QDOT, rather than outright to S. The downside of leaving the benefits to a life income QTIP-QDOT is that the benefits will be taxed at trust rates, whereas income taxes might be lower if paid at S's personal rate.

QDOT income taxable to S under § 678; DNI taxable to S

As noted, the regulations provide that if retirement benefits are distributed to, and taxable to, a QDOT, the income taxes paid by the QDOT are not subject to the deferred estate tax. What if, under § 678, S, not the trust, is taxable on a plan distribution received by the trust, because she has the power to withdraw the distribution from the trust? The regulations do not explicitly give relief here. The regulations explicitly exempt from the deferred estate tax only income taxes "imposed on the QDOT," or paid by S on a plan distribution received by S and assigned to the QDOT.

However, the regulations do state that the non-taxable reimbursement of S for income tax is "not limited to" the specific situations mentioned. § 20.2056A-5(c)(3)(iv). Presumably, to be consistent, reimbursement of S by the QDOT for income tax paid by S on trust income she *is* entitled to receive would also be allowed free of deferred estate tax, despite the fact that the Code allows tax-free reimbursement of S only for taxes on trust income she is *not* entitled to.

The result should be the same when a distribution of IRD is made from the plan to the QDOT, and S is not deemed the owner of the QDOT principal under § 678, but the trustee distributes the principal to S under a discretionary power to distribute principal. The principal distribution carries out "distributable net income" (DNI) to S. Under §§ 661 and 662, a distribution of DNI is taxable to S rather than to the trust. The portion of such a principal distribution which S is required to pay to the IRS as income taxes should not be subject to the deferred estate tax, but there is as yet no official confirmation on this.

***

With this background on the requirements for a QDOT,

and the income tax treatment of benefits payable to or transferred to a QDOT, we next look at the pros and cons of specific alternatives for disposing of retirement benefits in the estate plan when the surviving spouse is not a U.S. citizen.

Alternative 1: D Makes Benefits Payable to a Marital Trust-QDOT

At the planning stage, the safest course is for the client to make his retirement benefits payable to a marital trust which will also qualify as a QDOT.

Mandatory income distributions

As discussed in Chapter 3 ("Marital Deduction for Benefits Payable to QTIP Trust"), it is the IRS's apparent position that benefits payable to a QTIP trust will not qualify for the marital deduction unless all income of *the plan* is required to be distributed annually out to the marital trust. This is not a drawback, in the case of a QDOT, because annual income distributions to S are recommended in any case even if they are not required as a condition of the marital deduction (see "QDOT Investment and Distribution Strategies," below).

High trust income tax rates

A disadvantage of making retirement benefits payable to a marital trust is that "principal" distributed from the retirement plan to the trust will be subject to income tax at trust income tax rates. This can be a major drawback. If the marital trust has more than $8,450 of taxable income (1999 rates), the excess over that amount will be taxed at 39.6%, the highest marginal rate. S, as an individual, does not reach the highest tax bracket until she has more than $283,150 of taxable income. Thus, in all but the wealthiest families, S will be in a lower income tax bracket than the trust. The § 691(c) deduction (see Chapter 2) will be available to reduce the income tax if estate tax was paid on the decedent's estate.

A marital trust for the benefit of a *citizen* spouse could minimize income taxes on a principal distribution from the retirement plan to the trust by passing some or all of the distribution out to the spouse-beneficiary, if the trust permitted this. This safety valve is not helpful in the case of a marital trust-QDOT, however, because non-hardship distributions of principal from the QDOT to S will attract the deferred estate tax.

This problem of a discrepancy between income tax brackets of S (low) and trust (high) is not a problem in a marital trust over which S has an unrestricted power to withdraw principal. Such a power would cause S to be treated as the owner of the trust under § 678, and thus to be personally taxable on the trust's income. She is unlikely to exercise the withdrawal power under a QDOT because exercise would trigger the deferred estate tax. The risk of using this approach in the case of a marital trust-QDOT, at the moment, is that, as yet, the regulations do not explicitly permit the QDOT to reimburse S for income tax she is required to pay on the trust's income under § 678, without paying the deferred estate tax on the reimbursement, although it appears *likely* that this is permitted; see "*QDOT income taxable to S under § 678; DNI taxable to S.*"

Loss of deferral after spouse's death

Another drawback of making benefits payable to a marital deduction trust is the loss of potential income tax deferral due to the operation of the minimum distribution rules. See "*No spousal rollover*" and "The Spouse and § 401(a)(9),"

Chapter 3.

Alternative 2: Spouse Rolls Over
Benefits to QDOT-IRT

As noted, if property passes outright to S, the modified marital deduction can still be obtained if S transfers the property to a QDOT. This option poses special problems in the case of retirement benefits that are paid to S individually.

Dilemma when benefits are paid directly to S

If S is named personally as the beneficiary of D's retirement plan, and she leaves the benefits in D's plan, the benefits will not qualify for the marital deduction because the retirement plan is not a QDOT. If she withdraws the benefits from D's plan, with the idea of transferring them to a QDOT, she will have to pay income tax on the benefits.

The combination QDOT-IRT

One way out of this dilemma is for S to take the benefits out of D's retirement plan and roll them over to a QDOT that is also an "individual retirement account" under § 408(a). This will not merely salvage the marital deduction; it generally will provide income tax deferral opportunities that are superior, both during S's life and after her death, to those available if D had made his benefits payable directly to a marital trust-QDOT.

There is no tax or legal obstacle in the way of combining an IRA and a QDOT. An individual retirement account can be in the legal form of a trust (§ 408(a)) or a custodial account (§ 408(h)), though most IRAs are in the form of custodial accounts. The term "individual retirement trust" (IRT) is used here to distinguish the individual retirement account in the form of a trust from the more common custodial form of IRA.

The practical difficulties of this approach include drafting the document and finding a U.S. bank willing to serve as trustee. Unfortunately, this difficulty may be substantial, especially in the case of a smaller retirement benefit. Larger banks' fee schedules make them good choices, usually, only for accounts worth $1 million or more. Smaller bank trust operations accept smaller trusts and IRAs, but in the author's experience smaller banks refuse to accept an *IRA* in the form of a trust because their IRAs are administered by an outside provider which furnishes all the forms and monitors compliance. A bank that does not have true in-house IRA capability will probably not be willing to take on something as unique as a QDOT-IRT.

If the amount involved is large enough to justify a professional trustee's fee, there is no reason why the neighborhood bank should not be willing to serve as trustee. It is probably already serving as trustee of a few QDOTs, and as custodian of numerous IRAs, and should have no problem combining both responsibilities for one entity for its customary fee.

No requirement income be distributed annually

The requirement that income be distributed at least annually to S as a condition of obtaining the marital deduction does not apply to a QDOT funded exclusively by transfers from S; see "*QDOT created by surviving spouse*," above. Therefore all S would have to withdraw from the QDOT-IRT each year would be the minimum required distributions (see Chapter 1). However, it may nevertheless be desirable for all income to be distributed to S annually from the QDOT-IRT, to minimize the eventual deferred estate tax; see "QDOT Investment and Distribution Strategies."

Possible further deferral after spouse's death

After S's death, if S has named a younger "designated beneficiary," the remaining plan benefits will be paid out over the life expectancy of the designated beneficiary, again resulting in substantial additional deferral compared to the marital trust-QDOT. See Chapter 1. Generally when retirement benefits are paid to a marital trust-QDOT, there can be no income tax deferral beyond the original life expectancy of S.

Deferred estate tax on principal distributions

There is a price to be paid for the greater income tax deferral that can be obtained with a QDOT-IRT. The price is paid when "principal" for which the marital deduction was taken in D's estate is distributed from the QDOT-IRT to S. At that time, the deferred estate tax, as well as income taxes, will have to be paid on the principal distribution.

Of course, deferred estate tax is due whenever principal is distributed to S from *any* QDOT. But with a normal QDOT, it is possible for the trust to exist for S's entire lifetime without ever distributing principal. With a combination QDOT-IRT, the minimum distribution rules require certain amounts to be distributed every year after age 70½. See Chapter 1. "Principal" will have to be distributed out to S when the minimum required distributions from the IRA exceed the "income" of the IRA.

If S has named a child or grandchild as designated beneficiary of her rollover QDOT-IRT, *and* (after age 70½) S is taking out only the required minimum distributions under the MDIB rule, *and* undistributed income inside the IRT retains its character as "income" for purposes of the deferred estate tax (see *"How income can become principal"*), then the distributions to S will not be coming out of principal until very late in S's life. The minimum required distributions will be less than the annual income so long as the MDIB rule divisor expressed as a percentage (i.e., one, divided by the remaining life expectancy) is less than the rate of income, so for many years after S's RBD the IRT will actually be accumulating some of its income.

Example: Suppose when S reaches her RBD, the first year's "MDIB rule divisor" (or "life expectancy") is 26.2. Expressed as a percentage, the minimum distribution for that year is 1/26.2, or 3.82%. If the QDOT-IRT earns more than 3.82% in income that year, the minimum required distribution will be less than the income. Even after the crossover point (where the current year's required distribution exceeds the current year's income), the excess distributions can be taken from accumulated income until that account is exhausted, before reaching the initial "principal" of the IRT. If D died when S was age 70, and the IRT consistently earns 8% annual income, and distributes only the minimum required each year, the first distribution that would necessarily include principal (and therefore be subject to deferred estate tax) would not occur until S was age 99. If S dies before age 99, the deferred estate tax will obviously be due at the time of her death—but that is true under any QDOT disposition.

The point of this discussion is that rolling benefits over to a QDOT-IRT can be effective, despite the minimum distribution rules of § 401(a)(9), to defer the deferred estate tax on the retirement benefits until S reaches a very advanced age.

However, this conclusion depends on treating income accumulated inside the QDOT-IRT as "income" for purposes of the deferred estate tax. If the IRS decides that "principal" for this purpose includes accumulated income (see *"How income can become principal,"* below), however, the crossover point (when minimum required distributions must necessarily include principal and therefore trigger deferred estate tax) will be reached much sooner. Accordingly, until further clarification of the IRS's position, accumulating income inside a QDOT-IRT is not recommended without obtaining a ruling on the status of undistributed income under § 2056A. In the absence of such a ruling, S should (1) withdraw all income of the QDOT-IRT annually and (2) in any year in which the income exceeds the MRD, roll over the excess to her non-QDOT-IRA.

No IRS ruling on QDOT-IRT qualification

"Receipt of a favorable opinion letter on an IRA ... is not required as a condition of receiving favorable tax treatment." Rev. Proc. 87-50, section 2.08. In fact, although it will issue opinion letters on prototype IRAs, "The Service will not issue rulings or determination letters to individuals with respect to the status of their" IRAs. *Id.*, § 4.03. There is unlikely to be any "approved prototype" IRA agreement that is also a QDOT in the foreseeable future.

Fortunately, the IRS has supplied a "Model Trust Account" form for an IRA, known as Form 5305. "Individuals who adopt the Model Trust ... Account will be treated as having an arrangement that meets the requirements of section 408(a)." *Id.*, § 5.01. By adopting form 5305, and adding to it the provisions required for a QDOT (and other provisions deemed desirable for proper trust administration), S has a QDOT-IRT.

Choice of trustee

As a practical matter, the trustee of a QDOT-IRT must be a U.S. bank or other financial institution; it is unlikely that an individual will be able to qualify.

In order for the trust to be an IRA, the trustee must be a bank or such "other person who demonstrates to the satisfaction" of the IRS that "such other person will administer" the IRA in the required manner. § 408(a)(2). The procedure for a non-bank to seek IRS approval to serve as trustee of IRAs involves a filing fee of several thousand dollars, as well as demonstrating institutional soundness and continuity to the IRS. It is generally undertaken only by a firm which has plans to serve as trustee for many customers. It is hard to see how an individual could demonstrate the required permanence. Therefore, even though an individual can serve as trustee of a QDOT, an individual will *not* be able to be trustee (or even co-trustee) of a QDOT-IRT.

Furthermore, in order to qualify as a QDOT, there must be at least one U.S. trustee. This leads to the conclusion that the trustee of a QDOT-IRT must be a U.S. bank.

Alternative 3:
Spouse Assigns IRA To A QDOT

Assignment of inherited IRA to a QDOT

Another approach is for S to assign ownership of an inherited IRA to a QDOT she creates. The QDOT becomes the "owner" (account holder) of the IRA. The Code does not prohibit the assignment of an IRA; see § 408.

The QDOT should be in the form of a revocable trust under which the grantor (the surviving non-citizen spouse) reserves the right to withdraw all principal and income (subject only to the trustee's right to withhold the deferred estate tax from principal distributions). This will cause the QDOT to be a "grantor trust" under § 676 as to both income and principal, meaning that the surviving spouse will be treated as the owner of all the trust's assets for income tax purposes. The assignment of an IRA to such a trust would not be a taxable event since the trust and grantor are effectively deemed one taxpayer.

Using a *revocable* trust also avoids gift tax problems; S's transfer of assets into a QDOT would be subject to gift tax if it put the property irrevocably beyond her control. Even if the initial transfer to the trust is structured so as not to trigger gift tax, distributions to someone other than S during her lifetime would constitute completed gifts, resulting in a gift tax payable by her. See Reg. § 20.2056A-4(d), ex. 5. Therefore typically a QDOT created by S would be for her own sole life benefit and fully revocable by her.

The regulations, by negative implication, recognize the assignment of an inherited IRA to a grantor trust-QDOT as acceptable. From the preamble to the regulations, § E: "In general, individual retirement accounts under section 408(a) are assignable . . . . However, if an [IRA] is assigned to a trust with respect to which [S] is *not* treated as the owner under section 671 *et seq*. ...then the entire account balance is treated as a distribution... includible in [S's] gross income" in the year of the assignment. (Emphasis added.)

The regulations also eliminate another possible problem with this approach, namely, the possible difference between irrevocably "assigning" an IRA to a QDOT and actually "transferring" the IRA property to the QDOT. Generally, property inherited outright by S must be actually transferred to a QDOT by a certain deadline to qualify for the modified marital deduction. The regulations provide that the assignment of an IRA to a QDOT (provided various technical details are complied with) "is treated as a transfer of such property to the QDOT, regardless of the method of payment actually elected." § 20.2056A-4(b)(7).

S can assign the inherited IRA to a QDOT *and* get the benefits of electing to treat the inherited IRA as her own (see "*Rollover (or spousal election) for inherited IRA*," Chapter 3), so that she can name a new designated beneficiary. She can then take her minimum distributions over the joint life expectancy of herself and the new beneficiary, starting at her RBD, rather than simply taking required distributions as the beneficiary of D.

Assignment of rollover IRA to a QDOT

The regulations mention the assignment approach only in connection with an IRA owned by D of which S is named beneficiary and which S then assigns to a QDOT she has created, with no rollover involved. The regulations do not specifically bless a rollover of D's benefits by S to her *own* IRA, followed by assignment of the *rollover* IRA to a QDOT. However, there should not be any difference in result. The modified marital deduction is available if S assigns to the QDOT *either* the asset(s) inherited from D *or* the "proceeds from the sale, exchange or conversion" of such asset(s). Reg. § 20.2056A-4(b)(3). If S receives a distribution from D's profit sharing plan (say), and rolls that distribution over to her own IRA, the rollover IRA presumably constitutes "proceeds" from the "conversion" of the inherited asset and thus is suitable for assignment to a QDOT.

Drawbacks and drafting issues when assigning IRA to QDOT

Despite the apparent simplicity of S's assigning an IRA to S's revocable living trust-QDOT, however, there are still a number of unanswered questions and cautious drafting is required. For instance, on the death of S, would the IRA be payable to the QDOT, or to some other beneficiary? If to the QDOT, then in order to preserve the option of income tax deferral as long as possible, the QDOT presumably must comply with the minimum distribution "trust rules" (Chapter 6).

If, on the death of the grantor-spouse, the IRA is distributable to some *other* beneficiary, not to the QDOT itself, the IRA agreement itself would presumably have to contain

QDOT language giving the QDOT trustee the right to withhold the deferred estate tax from the IRA before the assets pass out to the other beneficiaries. Essentially you would be right back in the situation of "Alternative 2" discussed above, drafting a hybrid QDOT-IRT.

Also, the ability of the QDOT to reimburse S for income taxes on the IRA distributions is not clear. See *"QDOT income taxable to S under § 678; DNI taxable to S,"* above.

Advantages of assigning IRA to QDOT

The "IRA assigned to a QDOT" has one advantage over the "combination QDOT-IRT," namely: principal distributions from the IRA at some point during S's life are unavoidable under the minimum distribution rules (Chapter 1) if she lives long enough; see *"Deferred estate tax on principal distributions,"* above. With an "IRA assigned to a QDOT," the inevitable principal distributions come out of the IRA but stay in the QDOT, and accordingly the deferred estate tax can continue to be deferred. In contrast, principal distributions from a QDOT-IRT to S individually will trigger deferred estate tax.

Alternative 4:
Non-Assignable Annuities, and IRAs
Treated as Non-Assignable Annuities

Two alternatives for treatment of non-assignable assets

The Code directs the IRS, by regulations, to permit the surviving non-citizen spouse to obtain QDOT treatment for assets, such as a life annuity, which S cannot legally transfer to a QDOT before the estate tax return is filed. § 2056A(e). The regulations provide a method of obtaining QDOT-type marital deduction treatment for such annuities, as well as for any "plan, annuity or other arrangement" that cannot be transferred to a QDOT (whether because of applicable federal, foreign or state law, or because of the terms of the "plan or arrangement"). Reg. § 20.2056A-4(c)(1). See also *Election to treat inherited IRA as non-assignable*," below.

All **qualified retirement plan** ("QRP") benefits are considered "non-assignable" because QRP benefits cannot be assigned as a matter of federal law. § 401(a)(13); Reg. § 20.2056A-4(c)(1). A QRP benefit, therefore, is automatically a non-assignable annuity for purposes of § 2056A, even if S has the option to take all the money out immediately.

For these and other "non-assignable" assets, S is given a choice of two methods in lieu of immediately transferring the asset to a QDOT:

1.   S can agree to pay, each year, the deferred estate tax on all non-hardship corpus distributions S receives from the arrangement in that year. This right is granted in Reg. § 20.2056A-4(c)(2) and accordingly such an agreement is referred to in this chapter as a "(c)(2) agreement."

2.   Alternatively, S can agree that she will transfer to a QDOT all non-hardship corpus distributions she receives from the arrangement, as she receives them. This type of agreement is described in Reg. § 20.2056A-4(c)(3) and is referred to in this chapter as a "(c)(3) agreement."

The advantage of the (c)(3) agreement compared with a (c)(2) agreement is that, under a (c)(3) agreement, S can continue to defer estate taxes until her death (or other triggering event), whereas under a (c)(2) agreement deferred estate taxes must be paid whenever principal is received. So why would anyone ever use a (c)(2) agreement? Its only advantage appears to be that it does not require drafting a QDOT. Perhaps the (c)(2) agreement would appear attractive if there is no QDOT already in existence created to receive other assets and either: the surviving spouse expects to become a U.S. citizen in the near future and eliminate the deferred estate tax that way (see, e.g., PLR 9713018 (12/27/96)); or the asset in question is of small value. In most other cases, presumably, the (c)(3) agreement would be preferable.

Upon S's death, the remaining value of the non-assignable asset is subject to the deferred estate tax. Reg. § 20.2056A-5(b)(2). Note that with other types of assets (that are actually assigned to a QDOT) the QDOT trustee is responsible for paying this tax. With a non-assignable asset it is not clear who is responsible to report the death and pay the tax if (as can happen under a (c)(2) agreement) there is no QDOT in existence, or if (under either form of agreement) the remaining value of the asset passes at S's death to beneficiaries other than the QDOT.

In PLR 199904023 (10/30/98), the spouse used some of each method in connection with a joint and survivor annuity inherited from decedent's pension plan: she paid the deferred estate tax on the corpus portion of annuity distributions she received prior to the completion of reformation proceedings designed to bring decedent's QDOT into conformity with final regulations, and agreed under (c)(3) to pay over to the QDOT any such payments she received after reformation was complete.

The (c)(2) and (c)(3) agreement scheme applies to a genuinely nonassignable benefit payable to S, which she does not (or can not) take out of the plan and roll over to an IRA; and *also* to an IRA established by D and inherited by S, which S *elects* to treat as a nonassignable benefit. Reg. § 20.2056A-4(c)(1).

How much of each annuity payment is "principal?"

Under either a (c)(2) or (c)(3) agreement, S is agreeing

that she will do something whenever she receives a "corpus" (principal) distribution from the non-assignable annuity. The regulations require use of the following formula to determine how much of each distribution from an annuity is "corpus":

$$PV/T = Corpus\ portion$$

Under the formula, "PV" is the "total present value of the annuity," i.e., "the present value of the nonassignable annuity ... as of the date of [D's] death, determined in accordance with interest rates and mortality data prescribed by section 7520." This should be same as the date of death value of S's interest in the annuity as reported on D's estate tax return, since the same method is used to value the annuity for estate tax purposes.

This "Present Value" is divided by the "expected annuity term" (T) to arrive at the "corpus amount" of the annual payment. The "expected annuity term" (T) is "the number of years that would be required for the scheduled payments to exhaust a hypothetical fund equal to the present value of the scheduled payments." To determine *this* figure, you need IRS Publication 1457, "Alpha Volume," which can be obtained from the Government Printing Office, and the § 7520 rate used to value the annuity as of the date of death; the IRS publishes the § 7520 rate monthly, and it can be found at www.tigertables.com (among other places). With Alpha Volume and the § 7520 rate in hand, the steps are as follows: Divide PV by the amount of the annual payment under the annuity. Take the resulting quotient and match it up with an "annuity factor" from column 1 of Table B for the applicable § 7520 rate, in Alpha Volume. If it falls between two factors, use the higher one (longer term). You now have "T."

Example 4 in Reg. § 20.2056A-4(d) illustrates the calculations. It has been pointed out that, in the IRS's Example 4, a 60-year old surviving spouse is required to recover all of the corpus portion of a life annuity within 16 years after D's death, even though her life expectancy is 24.2 years (according to IRS's Table V). Yet this author is unable to find anything in the regulation indicating that S can *stop* paying taxes on (or sending to the QDOT) the annuity payments once the "corpus" has been fully recovered under the above formula.

Determining "corpus" portion of individual account plan

The wording of Reg. § 20.2056A-4(c)(4) suggests that the above formula is the *only* method which may be used to determine the corpus portion of plan distributions subject to a (c)(2) or a (c)(3) agreement. However, several letter rulings have confirmed that the formula applies only when benefits are in fact taken in the form of an annuity. For determining the corpus portion of distributions from an individual account plan subject to a (c)(2) or (c)(3) agreement, the general (trust accounting) rules of Reg. § 20.2056A-5(c)(2) apply (see "*What is income?,*" below). See PLRs 9746049 (8/15/97), 9729040 (4/23/97) and 9713018 (12/27/96).

Election to treat inherited IRA as non-assignable

The final regulations issued in August 1995 contain a new permitted approach, not mentioned in the 1992 proposed regulations: the surviving non-citizen spouse may elect to treat an inherited IRA as a non-assignable annuity. § 20.2056A-4(c)(1).

Is the option to treat an IRA as non-assignable available for a *rollover* (as opposed to an inherited) IRA? The regulations say that "The Commissioner will prescribe by administrative guidance the extent, if any, to which" the election may be made for plan or IRA benefits which were distributed to S and rolled over by her after D's death. § 20.2056A-4(c)(1). Although no such formal administrative guidance has yet been issued, the IRS has allowed surviving spouses to make the election and enter into a (c)(2) or (c)(3) agreement regarding a rollover IRA. See PLR 9729040 (4/23/97), 9713018 (12/27/96).

Why would someone elect to treat an IRA as non-assignable, and enter into a (c)(3) agreement for it, when she could simply assign the IRA to a QDOT (Alternative 3) without the bother of a (c)(3) agreement? Perhaps because, in the case of non-assignable annuities (and IRAs treated as non-assignable annuities), the regulations allow the income taxes payable on the "corpus portion" (determined on a marginal basis) to be reimbursed to S out of the QDOT principal, so the income tax money escapes the deferred estate tax. Reg. § 20.2056A-5(c)(3)(iv). This clear and favorable treatment contrasts with the unclear and perhaps less favorable treatment afforded when an IRA is assigned to a QDOT (see "*QDOT income taxable to S under § 678; DNI taxable to S*," above).

However, this arrangement puts substantial responsibility on the surviving spouse. She must never make additional contributions to this particular IRA; she must be very careful that her withdrawals match the "income" of the account (or, to the extent withdrawals exceed income, she must carry out the terms of her agreement with the IRS). With the other IRA-type arrangements (QDOT-IRT, IRA assigned to a QDOT), there is a third party trustee interposed between S and the IRA who can monitor compliance with these points, but with an IRA S has elected to treat as non-assignable she is on her own. The spouse's ability to understand and comply with these requirements should be considered when adopting this approach.

Alternative 5:
Non-Marital Deduction
Disposition Alternatives

Non-marital deduction disposition

D could leave his retirement benefits to his children or other non-spouse beneficiary, or to a trust which does not qualify for the marital deduction. S could be a beneficiary of the trust or not, as the client prefers. The advantages of a "non-marital deduction" disposition would be: avoidance of the "distribute all income annually" requirement that arguably applies to a marital trust; and avoiding the problems of collecting deferred estate taxes on an income-taxable asset. The disadvantages are those that exist whenever retirement benefits are paid in a non-marital deduction disposition, *e.g.*, some of the unified credit is "wasted" paying income taxes.

Outright to spouse, not claiming marital deduction

Another alternative is to make the benefits payable to S but not claim the marital deduction, even if this means paying estate tax on the benefits. The complications of the QDOT are avoided; and S will get the benefit of the § 691(c) deduction for the estate taxes paid. This may be attractive if S will probably return to her country of origin. If S is likely to remain a U.S. resident, this approach would normally be unattractive because the benefits, already reduced by income taxes and by estate taxes at D's death, would be subject to estate tax again at S's death (although if S dies within 10 years after D the estate tax credit for tax on prior transfers would be available; § 2013).

QDOT Investment and Distribution Strategies

This section looks at various tax rules that have an effect on the administrative policies of a QDOT (including a QDOT-IRT), and the strategies suggested by these rules.

Hardship exception to imposition of the deferred estate tax

An important exception to the general rule that principal distributions to S from the QDOT are subject to the deferred estate tax is that distributions to S on account of *hardship* are not subject to that tax. Under Reg. § 20.2056A-5(c)(1), "A distribution of principal is treated as made on account of hardship if the distribution is made to the spouse from the QDOT in response to an immediate and substantial financial need relating to the spouse's health, maintenance, education, or support, or the health, maintenance, education, or support of any person that the surviving spouse is legally obligated to support. A distribution is not treated as made on account of hardship if the amount distributed may be obtained from other sources that are reasonably available to the surviving spouse; e.g., the sale by the surviving spouse of personally owned, publicly traded stock or the cashing in of a certificate of deposit owned by the surviving spouse. Assets such as closely held business interests, real estate and tangible personalty are not considered sources that are reasonably available to the surviving spouse."

This generous definition of hardship will make this exception a useful planning tool in many situations. The QDOT trustee should be on the lookout for possible hardship distribution opportunities. If the spouse keeps all her non-QDOT assets illiquid, more of her living expenses can be shifted to QDOT trust principal. If she needs money for living expenses, she should think of the QDOT trust as a resource first rather than (say) borrowing the money.

Investment disincentives of a QDOT: capital growth

The deferred estate tax problem can grow worse over the duration of the QDOT through capital growth and capital gains. The structure of the deferred estate tax encourages investing for income and discourages investing for "growth" or capital gain.

Of course, all assets held by S at her death (including QDOT income distributions she has accumulated) will be subject to estate tax if she is either a U.S. resident or a U.S. citizen at that time, so in many cases this distinction will make little difference. But if for any reason the estate tax rate on S's estate will be significantly lower than the deferred estate tax rate applicable to the QDOT (*e.g.*, because S ceases to be subject to U.S. estate tax), this factor becomes significant.

How income can become principal

All distributions of income from a QDOT are free of the deferred estate tax, whereas all non-hardship principal dollars will be subject to that tax. Therefore "income" is very valuable. Unfortunately, as the following examples illustrate, it appears that the IRS wants to herd as many dollars as possible into the "principal" corral, where they can be branded with the deferred estate tax, and make it difficult for "income" dollars to escape tax-free onto the open range.

For example, whatever was in the retirement plan at D's death *should* be considered the initial principal of the QDOT-IRT. However, the IRS apparently refused to rule its agreement with this simple statement in PLR 9729040 (4/23/97) (Ruling request 4). In another letter ruling, the initial principal of the

QDOT was defined as the amount rolled over to it, with no stated exception for post-death income that had accumulated in the retirement plan. Although possibly there *was* no post-death accumulated income (and maybe that's why the ruling doesn't discuss this subject), it's also possible that this ruling means that any accumulated income rolled to a QDOT must be added to principal for deferred estate tax purposes.

Second example: Reg. § 20.2056A-5(c)(2) states that "income does not include capital gains." This statement is unfortunate: If *income* is reinvested, and the reinvestment produces capital gain in the *income* account, that should be considered income for purposes of § 2056A, even if it is taxable as capital gain.

Third example: In PLR 9729040 (4/23/97), the surviving non-citizen spouse did not intend to take distributions from the rollover IRA until she reached age 59½. The agreement she signed with the IRS stipulated that all income accumulated in the IRA until she reached that age would be considered principal. Since it is hard to imagine that she would have suggested this stipulation, one wonders if the IRS gave her the following choice: take your "income" distributions now and avoid deferred estate tax on them (but pay income taxes now, plus 10% penalty—see Chapter 9); or defer income tax, and avoid the 10% penalty (but agree that the accumulated income becomes "principal" for purposes of the deferred estate tax). (This may be another example of the IRS's apparent "get tough" policy regarding young widows; see "*Drawbacks of spousal rollover,*" Chapter 3.)

Fourth example: On S's death, the deferred estate tax can no longer be deferred. The deferred estate tax is imposed on "the value of the property remaining in a qualified domestic trust on the date of death of the surviving spouse." § 2056(A)(b). It is not clear from this phrase that undistributed income would be excluded from the tax base. The *proposed* regulations issued in

1992, § 20.2056A-5, specified that "the amount subject to tax is the value of the trust *corpus* on the date of S's death" (emphasis added). However, the final regulations issued in August 1995 deleted this statement, retaining the ambiguity of the statute.

This situation leads to the following conclusions: the IRS intends to treat accumulated income as principal to the maximum extent possible. Therefore, the QDOT should distribute all income annually to S, so the IRS cannot impose deferred estate tax on it.

Rollover strategy for excess income distributions

If the income distributed to S in any particular year pursuant to above-suggested strategy from a QDOT-IRT, or from an inherited or rollover IRA assigned to a QDOT, is greater than would be required to be distributed to her under the minimum distribution rules, S could establish a separate IRA (not a QDOT-IRT, and not an IRA held by a QDOT) into which she rolls the excess distributions. Then, once she reaches age 70½, she can elect to satisfy the minimum distribution requirement each year, by using a combination of distributions from the various IRAs. See "Taking Distributions from Multiple Plans," Chapter 1. Withdrawals from the various IRAs should be structured so that the least-taxed dollars are distributed first in satisfaction of the minimum distribution requirements.

What is income?

The discussion above shows how certain traditional items of "income" (capital gains in the income account, and maybe all accumulated income) may be treated by the IRS as "principal." Assuming the trustee has decided to avoid that problem by promptly distributing all income, this subsection looks at the question of how the trustee (and the IRS) determine whether an item (or distribution) is allocated to "income" earned after D's death (not subject to the deferred estate tax), or "principal" (taxable)?

The regulations' pronouncements are all contained in Reg. § 20.2056A-5(c)(2). "Income" of the QDOT will mean income as it is defined in § 643(b), except that "income does not include capital gains....[or] any other item that would be allocated to corpus under applicable local law governing the administration of trusts irrespective of any specific trust provision to the contrary." § 643(b) defines "income" as "the amount of income of the estate or trust for the taxable year determined under the terms of the governing instrument and applicable local law." If local law has nothing to say on the subject, "the allocation...will be governed by general principles of law (including but not limited to any uniform state acts, such as the Uniform Principal and Income Act, or any Restatements of applicable law)."

Hopefully, "irrespective of any specific trust provision" means that the governing instrument's allocation will be respected, provided its method of determining principal and income is permitted under local law and provided it does not violate any specific QDOT rule. Or does it mean that income will be determined under local law, *without regard* to the specific provisions of the trust?

Regardless of what local law or the trust says, "income does not include items constituting" IRD unless otherwise provided in future administrative guidance. Thus, a trust provision defining all retirement plan distributions as "income" will not change the character of such distributions for purposes of the deferred estate tax. This is perfectly sensible. Also, the allocation of annuity payments between "corpus" and "income" by the method prescribed in the regulations (see "*How much of each annuity payment is principal?*") will be respected.

Summary of Planning Principles

As the discussion in this chapter indicates, there is no problem-free way to dispose of retirement benefits when the participant's spouse is not a U.S. citizen.

Benefits that can be rolled over

1.   If S inherits **qualified retirement plan** ("QRP") benefits outright, and wants to get both the income tax benefits of the spousal rollover and the estate tax benefits of the modified marital deduction: either S rolls over D's benefits to a combination QDOT-IRT (Alternative 2), or S rolls over the benefits to a non-QDOT IRA that S then "assigns" to a grantor-trust-type QDOT she establishes (Alternative 3). A third choice (for which a ruling should be obtained, since "administrative guidance" is yet to be issued on this choice) is to roll over the benefits to a (non-QDOT) IRA, elect to treat the rollover IRA as non-assignable, and then sign an agreement with the IRS, agreeing either that S will pay the deferred estate tax on the corpus portion of each payment as received or that S will assign such corpus portion to a QDOT (Alternative 4).

2.   If the inherited benefit is already in an IRA, things are a little easier: S has all the same choices as for inherited QRP benefits, but does not need a ruling to treat the inherited IRA as non-assignable.

3.   In the planning stage, while the client is still alive, the choice is even more complicated. The marital trust-QDOT (Alternative 1) will appeal to the client who wants to control the ultimate disposition of the asset, or who simply wants his estate plan to be self-executing, without requiring his spouse to undertake additional steps after his death. However, making

benefits payable directly to a QDOT eliminates the income tax benefits of a spousal rollover. Making benefits payable outright to S will appeal to the client who has no objection to giving his spouse control, desires maximum income tax deferral and is willing to adopt a plan which requires post-death action by his spouse in order to succeed.

4.   The client may be attracted to the income tax deferral possibilities of the rollover, but reluctant to leave qualifying for the marital deduction entirely up to *post mortem* action. What this client might want, ideally, would be a plan which would have all the elements in place to automatically qualify for the modified marital deduction, without foreclosing the option of the spousal rollover. One way to achieve this result (for an IRA) would be for D's IRA to be in the form of an IRT which will become a QDOT-IRT on his death (this is a variation of Alternative 2, not discussed in detail in this book). Another possibility is to leave the benefits to a marital trust-QDOT (Alternative 1), but name S as contingent beneficiary, so the trust can disclaim (see Chapter 8) the benefits and they will pass to S who can roll them over, on the assumption that the trust would disclaim unless S was disabled or for some other reason not able to carry out the rollover.

Benefits that cannot be rolled over

5.   If the benefits are non-assignable, and S cannot roll them over, the best alternative in most cases is probably for S to agree to deposit the benefits into a QDOT as they are paid to her ("(c)(3) agreement") rather than agreeing to pay the deferred estate tax on non-assignable benefits as they are received ("(c)(2) agreement"). However, agreeing to pay the deferred estate tax may be attractive for retirement benefits subject to income tax because the income tax can be deducted

from the amount that will be subject to the deferred estate tax.

Other comments

6.   If using the marital trust-QDOT option, consider giving S the unlimited right to withdraw principal, so that distributions of IRD from the retirement plan to the trust will be taxed at S's income tax rate, if that will be lower than the trust's income tax rate. Unless there has been further guidance from the IRS, however, it might be advisable to get a ruling confirming that principal distributions to S to reimburse her for income taxes imposed on her by virtue of § 678 on the distributions of IRD to the trust can be made free of the deferred estate tax before taking this route. Once the client has chosen to make the benefits payable either to S or to a marital trust, consider making them "disclaimable" to the other (trust or spouse) in case that option appears more attractive when death occurs.

7.   While the client is living, he should consider converting IRAs to Roth IRAs, if he is eligible to do so, to avoid many of these problems; see Chapter 5.

8.   In administering any QDOT, the trustee should take advantage of the hardship distribution exception whenever possible (to distribute principal to S free of the deferred estate tax); and should consider investing so as to minimize growth of the original "principal," while maximizing "income." All income (whether earned inside or outside a retirement plan) should be distributed to the surviving non-citizen spouse as soon as is practicable to avoid the risk that the IRS will say it has become "principal." If this income distribution includes retirement plan distributions in excess of the minimum required distribution, it may be that the excess can be rolled over by S to her own non-QDOT-IRA.

ROTH IRAS

*Roth IRAs offer an excellent
planning opportunity for a
limited number of people who
are eligible, and can afford, to
adopt them.*

Introduction

Meet the Roth IRA

§ 408A established a whole new kind of IRA, called a
"Roth IRA," beginning in 1998. The basic idea of the Roth IRA
is that contributions are non-deductible, but distributions are
tax-free; see "Tax Treatment of Distributions." In addition to
tax-free distributions, the Roth IRA offers other benefits: no
required distributions during life (see "Minimum Required
Distributions"); and no maximum age for making contributions.

The overriding rule is that "Roth IRAs are treated like
traditional IRAs except where the Internal Revenue Code
specifies different treatment." Reg. § 1.408A-1 (Q & A 1(b)).

There are two ways to create a Roth IRA. One is by
non-deductible contributions of up to $2,000 per year from
compensation income (the IRS calls these "regular
contributions"). Reg. § 1.408A-3 (Q & A 1). See "Regular
Contributions to a Roth IRA." The other is by rollover from an
existing "traditional" IRA (or by conversion of an existing
traditional IRA to a Roth IRA). See "Roth IRA Conversions."
The rollover (or conversion) of a traditional IRA to a Roth IRA
causes the full amount of the rollover to be currently taxed
although if the rollover occurred in 1998 the tax could be spread

over four years (see "1998 Conversions: The Four-Year Spread").

Each of the two methods has its own rules and eligibility requirements. The Roth IRA funded by annual contributions from earned income will be of interest exclusively to those who are still working. The rollover-funded Roth IRA will be of interest primarily but not exclusively to retired people. This chapter describes the legal characteristics and planning implications of Roth IRAs, emphasizing contrasts with traditional IRAs.

This book does not cover the reporting requirements (see Reg. § 1.408A-7, and instructions to forms 5498, 8606 and 1099-R) or withholding tax requirements (see Reg. § 1.408A-6, Q & A 12, 13) for Roth IRAs.

Roth IRA terminology

This chapter uses certain special terminology:

A "traditional" IRA refers to an individual retirement account or individual retirement trust established under § 408, which may contain deductible contributions, non-deductible contributions and/or rollovers from employer plans.

"Conversion" of a traditional to a Roth IRA includes a "rollover" from a traditional IRA to a Roth IRA. See *"How to convert to a Roth IRA."*

The "Five-Year Period" refers to the period of time after which distributions from a Roth IRA may be income tax-free. See *"Definition of the Five-Year Period."*

The "Ordering Rules" are the special rules which dictate which contribution (or earnings) a particular Roth IRA distribution is deemed to come from; see *"The Ordering Rules."*

For more special Roth IRA terminology, see *"Conversion/unconversion glossary."*

Where to find the law

§ 408A was added to the Code by TAPRA '97. Several technical corrections (some of which were actually substantive changes) to the Roth IRA rules were included in the IRS Restructuring and Reform Bill of 1998, signed into law July 22, 1998. In this chapter "Technical Corrections" refers to this July 1998 law. These changes were made retroactive to January 1, 1998, "as if included in" TAPRA '97 unless otherwise noted.

Proposed regulations were issued by the IRS on August 31, 1998, then modified by IRS Notice 98-50 (1998-44 I.R.B. 10). Final regulations were issued February 3, 1999, effective generally for taxable years beginning after December 31, 1997, except that to the extent they replace Notice 98-50 they are effective January 1, 2000.

At the invaluable website *www.rothira.com,* you can find the portions of TAPRA, legislative history and Technical Corrections dealing with Roth IRAs, as well as the regulations and articles about Roth IRAs, links to online software to compute the benefits of Roth IRAs, IRS pronouncements and other items of interest concerning Roth IRAs.

Tax Treatment of Distributions

Not all Roth IRA distributions are automatically tax-free; only "qualified distributions" from a Roth IRA are income tax-free. However, it is relatively easy to qualify for "qualified" distributions, and even non-qualified distributions get favorable treatment compared with distributions from traditional IRAs.

Definition of qualified distribution

"Qualified distributions" from a Roth IRA are not included in the recipient's gross income for federal income tax purposes, regardless of whether the recipient is the participant (P) or a beneficiary. § 408A(d)(1)(A). A qualified distribution is one made after the Five-Year Period (see *"Definition of Five-Year Period"*); and which *in addition* (§ 408A(d)(2)(A)):

1.　　　　Is made on or after the date on which P attains age 59½; or

2.　　　　Is made to a beneficiary (or to P's estate) after P's death; or

3.　　　　Is "attributable to" P's being totally disabled (as defined in § 72(m)(7)); or

4.　　　　Is a "qualified special purpose distribution." "Qualified special purpose distribution" is defined by cross reference to § 72(t)(2)(F), which is the exception to the 10% premature-distributions penalty for distributions of up to $10,000 for certain purchases of a "first home" (see Chapter 9). § 408A(d)(5).

In general these conditions for a qualified distribution from a Roth IRA resemble the requirements for avoiding the premature-distributions penalty of § 72(t) (Chapter 9), but are not identical; for example, withdrawals from a Roth IRA to pay "higher education expenses" are not qualified distributions, even though such withdrawals from a traditional IRA would be exempt from the 10% penalty. § 72(t)(2)(E).

Definition of "Five-Year Period"

The Five-Year Period (called in the statute the "nonexclusion period") for *all* of a participant's Roth IRAs begins on January 1 of the first year for which a contribution

was made to *any* Roth IRA maintained for the participant. §
408A(d)(2)(B); Reg. § 1.408A-6 (Q & A 2).

Example: Fred puts $2,000 into his Roth IRA for 1998.
His Five-Year Period starts January 1, 1998. The first year in
which he can possibly have a qualified distribution is 2003. If he
makes further contributions of any type to the same (or any
other) Roth IRA in later years, those contributions do not start
a new Five-Year Period running.

As originally enacted (in 1997), § 408A provided two
different methods for calculating the Five-Year Period, one to
be used for Roth IRAs which contained no conversion
contributions, and the other for Roth IRAs which *did* contain
money converted from a traditional IRA. The Technical
Corrections dropped this distinction. This change appears to
have made obsolete the recommendation originally made for
Roth IRA owners to establish separate Roth IRAs for "regular
contributions" and "rollover contributions," and to establish
separate Roth IRAs for rollover contributions made in separate
years; but see *"Determining net income attributable to
contribution."*

Tax treatment of non-qualified distributions

A non-qualified distribution is one made before the Five-
Year Period is up; or which is made after expiration of the Five-
Year Period but not for one of the specified reasons (age 59½,
disability, death, etc.). A non-qualified distribution is not *per se*
excludable from gross income. However, even if a distribution
is not "qualified" it receives favorable tax treatment compared
with distributions from a traditional IRA.

A Roth IRA contains two types of money. First, it
contains P's own regular contributions and/or conversion

contributions; since P has by definition already paid tax on these funds, there is no tax when these originally-contributed funds are distributed. This amount (plus any after-tax contributions contained in a traditional IRA that was converted to a Roth) constitutes P's basis or "investment in the contract." If the account has grown to be worth more than this basis, the rest of the account value (which represents the earnings and growth that have occurred since the original contribution(s)) has not yet been taxed (and may *never* be taxed if it is distributed in the form of a qualified distribution).

In a traditional IRA which contains non-deducted contributions, all distributions are deemed to come proportionately from the "basis" (non-taxable) portion of the account and the post-contribution earnings. §§ 408(d); 72(e)(2)(B), (e)(5)(A) and (D)(iii), and (e)(8). Thus, P's basis or investment in the contract is recovered only gradually, as he makes withdrawals from the account, and some part of every distribution is taxable.

In contrast to this unfavorable treatment, *all* distributions from a Roth IRA are deemed to come *first* out of P's contributions. Thus, if a Roth IRA participant needs to get money out of the Roth IRA, but the account has not been established long enough to generate qualified distributions, he can still take out money income tax-free, up to the amount he originally contributed. (See "1998 Conversions: the Four-Year Spread," and "10% Penalty for Premature Distributions," for situations in which the distribution of P's own contributions may nevertheless accelerate taxation or result in a penalty.)

The Ordering Rules

As originally enacted (in 1997), § 408A provided simply that Roth IRA distributions were deemed to come, first, out of contributions to the Roth IRA. Technical Corrections rewrote the provision and created new "ordering rules" for Roth IRA distributions. Any distribution from a Roth IRA (except a corrective distribution of an excess contribution; Reg. § 1.408A-6 (Q & A 9(e))) is deemed to come from the following sources, in the order indicated. § 408A(d)(4)(B); Reg. § 1.408A-6 (Q & A 9). These rules are referred to in this chapter as the "Ordering Rules."

• Any distribution is deemed to come, first, from *contributions* to the Roth IRA (to the extent that all previous distributions from the Roth IRA have not yet exceeded the contributions); and

• If P has made both "regular" and "rollover" (conversion) contributions, the distributions are deemed to come, first, from the regular contributions; then,

• Second, from rollover contributions, on a first-in, first-out, basis; and

• Once it is thus determined that the distribution is deemed to come from a particular rollover contribution, the dollars that were includible in gross income by virtue of that rollover are deemed distributed first, and non-taxable dollars last; and

• Finally, once all contributions have been distributed out, the balance of the distribution comes out of post-contribution earnings. Whew!

Fortunately, the Ordering Rules will never matter for most people. The Ordering Rules will have to be consulted only in certain situations, namely:

1.   The Ordering Rules matter most significantly for IRA owners who (A) convert a traditional IRA to a Roth in 1998 and (B) choose to spread the tax on the conversion over four years and (C) then take a distribution before 2001. See

"1998 Conversions: the Four-year Spread."

2.   The Ordering Rules may matter also for IRA owners who (A) convert a traditional IRA to a Roth in 1998 and (B) choose to spread the tax on the conversion over four years and (C) then die before 2002. See *How the Ordering Rules apply to a decedent's Roth IRA.*

3.   The Ordering Rules matter also for IRA owners who (A) convert a traditional IRA to a Roth before reaching age 59½, and then take a distribution (B) before reaching age 59½ and (C) within the five taxable years beginning with the year of the conversion. See "10% Penalty For Pre-Age 59½ Distributions."

4.   In general, the Ordering Rules matter for purposes of determining whether a non-qualified distribution is taxable; the Ordering Rules essentially mean that the distribution is NOT taxable until all contributions have been distributed out.

Aggregation of Roth IRAs

Under § 408(d)(2), all (traditional) IRAs are generally treated as one account (and all distributions in one year treated as one distribution) for purposes of determining what part of a particular year's distributions represents return of P's basis (*i.e.*, his non-deducted contributions). § 408A(d)(4)(A) provides that "section 408(d)(2) shall be applied separately with respect to Roth IRAs and other individual retirement plans." Under this provision, it is clear that the taxation of distributions from *traditional* IRAs will be computed without regard to the existence of, or distributions from, *Roth* IRAs in the same year.

The regulations flesh out the aggregation rules with considerably more detail. The regulations confirm that "[A]ll distributions from all an individual's *Roth* IRAs made during a taxable year are aggregated" for purposes of applying the Ordering Rules. Reg. § 1.408A-6 (Q & A 9(a)).

The regulations' aggregation of all Roth IRA distributions is undoubtedly the correct treatment even though certain statements in the statute (as amended by Technical Corrections) cast some doubt on the issue, particularly the Ordering Rules (which speak in terms of distributions from "the Roth IRA," rather than "the Roth IRAs" or "Roth IRAs"), and the provision for a surviving spouse to assume unpaid tax instalments (which speaks of "any Roth IRA to which" a particular 1998 rollover contribution is properly allocable, as if basis is allocated to particular accounts rather than "floating" among all Roth IRAs collectively).

Regular Contributions to a Roth IRA

For individuals who have "compensation income," there is now a greater (and more confusing) array of tax-favored individual retirement savings plans: traditional IRAs funded on a tax-deductible basis, traditional IRAs funded with non-deductible contributions and Roth IRAs. Not every working person will have a choice of all three modes, and indeed some will not be eligible to contribute to any type of IRA. Adding to the excitement, a person who has a choice of IRA types to contribute to, and exercises that choice by contributing to one or the other, can change his mind about which type he wants to contribute to and "recharacterize" his contribution, right up to the (extended) due date of his tax return for the year; see "Unconversions (Recharacterizations) and Corrective Distributions," below.

This section discusses the requirements for making a "regular" contribution to a Roth IRA, as contrasted with the rules governing traditional IRA contributions; summarizes the eligibility requirements for regular contributions to both types of IRAs; and discusses which type of contribution is best for those who have a choice.

How much may be contributed annually

One way to fund a Roth IRA is by making what the IRS calls "regular" (as opposed to "rollover") contributions. The maximum amount which may be contributed to a Roth IRA this way is defined in a convoluted manner, but may be summarized simply: it is (1) the lesser of $2,000 or the individual's "compensation" income for the year, minus (2) the amount contributed to any traditional IRA for that year. § 408A(c)(2).

Contributions to a "simplified employee pension" individual retirement account (SEP-IRA) (§ 408(k)) or a "simple retirement account" (SRA) (§ 408(p)) are *not* treated as "IRA contributions" for this purpose, so a person who is otherwise eligible to make a contribution to a Roth IRA in a particular year does not lose that eligibility just because $2,000 was contributed for him to a SEP-IRA or SRA. § 408A(f).

Whether an individual is entitled to make an IRA contribution, and if so to *which type* of IRA, depends on various eligibility factors, the first of which is the necessity of having "compensation" income for the year in question.

Definition of compensation

"Compensation" is partly defined in § 219(f)(1): it includes self-employment income (cross reference to § 401(c)(2)), and does *not* include pension, annuity or deferred compensation payments. It includes taxable alimony and separate maintenance payments (cross reference to § 71). And it includes "wages, commissions, professional fees, tips, and other amounts received for personal services." Reg. § 1.408A-3

(Q & A 4). Rev. Proc. 91-18, 1991-1 C.B. 522, provides further detail on the definition.

> Warning: The IRS's preamble to the proposed Roth IRA regulations issued in 1998 contained a reminder that compensation "does not include amounts transferred from one individual to another by gift (for example, a gift from a parent to a child)." If a parent decides to pay his toddler a salary for performing household chores, the IRS might maintain that the child has received a gift, not compensation, and that Roth IRA contributions based on this "compensation" are excess contributions subject to the 6% excise tax (§ 4973).

Who may contribute to a Roth IRA: income limits

Not just anyone who has compensation income can contribute to a Roth IRA. As with many tax breaks granted by TAPRA '97, there is an income limit.

The income limit for contributing the full $2,000 to a Roth IRA is: adjusted gross income (AGI) may not exceed $95,000 for a single taxpayer; $150,000 for a married taxpayer filing a joint return; or zero for a married taxpayer filing a separate return. The $2,000 contribution ceiling is phased out if income exceeds these levels to zero at AGI of $110,000 (single), $160,000 (married filing jointly), or $10,000 (married filing separately). § 408A(c)(3)(A), (C). For this purpose, "a married individual who has lived apart from his or her spouse for the entire taxable year and who files separately is treated as not married." Reg. § 1.408A-3 (Q & A 3(b)).

An individual who cannot make the total $2,000 contribution to a Roth because of these income limits can contribute his reduced maximum to the Roth and the balance of the overall $2,000 limit to a traditional IRA (assuming he otherwise meets the requirements for contributing to a traditional IRA). Reg. § 1.408A-3 (Q & A 3(d), example 4).

The definition of AGI for this purpose is the same as the definition used in applying the income limit for determining eligibility to make a conversion contribution to a Roth IRA; see *"Who may convert: income limit and filing status,"* below.

Who may contribute: other requirements

There is no maximum age limit for contributing to a Roth IRA, as there is for contributions to a traditional IRA; a taxpayer can contribute to a Roth IRA even after age 70½. § 408A(c)(4); compare §§ 408(o)(2)(B)(i), 219.

If an individual has earned income and is under age 70½, his contributions to a traditional IRA are tax-deductible if he is not a participant in an employer-sponsored plan. If he is a participant in an employer-sponsored plan, his contribution to a traditional IRA is deductible only if his income is below certain limits. § 219(g). In contrast, participation in an employer plan is *irrelevant* for purposes of determining whether (and how much) an individual may contribute to a Roth IRA.

Deadline for contributions, and other rules

As with traditional IRAs, only cash may be contributed. §§ 408A(a), 408(a)(1). The trustee or custodian must be a bank (or other entity that has gone through the IRS approval procedure for serving in this capacity). §§ 408A(a); 408(a)(2). The deadline for making a regular Roth IRA contribution for a particular year is the same as for a traditional IRA contribution, *i.e.*, the *unextended* due date of the tax return for that year (Reg. § 1.408A-3 (Q & A 2(b)); in other words, for most people, April 15 following the year in question.

Roth IRA Conversions

See "10% Penalty for Pre-Age 59½ Distributions" for interaction of Roth conversions and the 10% penalty.

How to convert to a Roth IRA

The second way to get money into a Roth IRA is to transfer it from a traditional IRA. The amount so transferred is included in P's gross income ("treated as a distribution from" the traditional IRA); thereafter the account will enjoy the favorable tax treatment afforded to Roth IRAs. § 408A(d)(3)(A), (B), (C).

Example: Manuel is 60 years old. He rolls $300,000 from his traditional IRA to a Roth IRA in 1999. The entire $300,000 is included in his gross income for 1999. He pays the income tax by selling off some of his municipal bond portfolio. When he retires at age 65, the Roth IRA has increased to $1.2 million. All subsequent distributions from the Roth IRA (whether made to Manuel or to his beneficiaries) will be income tax-free.

There are three ways to make this type of contribution to a Roth IRA (Reg. § 1.408A-4 (Q & A 1, (b)): A distribution from a traditional IRA can be contributed (rolled over) to a Roth IRA within the 60-day period described in section 408(d)(3)(A)(i); or money in a traditional IRA can be transferred in a trustee-to-trustee transfer from the trustee of the traditional IRA to the trustee of the Roth IRA; or all or part of a traditional IRA can simply be "redesignated" as a Roth IRA maintained by the same trustee. These three methods are generally referred to in this chapter interchangeably as "rollover" or "conversion" contributions. For tax purposes, all three are considered rollovers ("a distribution from the traditional IRA and a qualified rollover contribution to the Roth IRA"). Reg. § 1.408A-4 (Q & A 1(c)); see "Rollovers," Chapter 2.

The convenient term "conversion" (which is used in § 408A) distinguishes the "traditional-to-Roth" rollover (a "conversion," which is a taxable event) from a "normal" rollover (from one traditional IRA to another traditional IRA, or from one Roth IRA to another Roth IRA), which is non-taxable.

Both partial and total conversions are allowed. A person who converts part of his IRA to a Roth is free at any later time (in the same or a later year) to convert more of his IRA to a Roth. An individual may convert all, part or none of his IRA to a Roth; there is no limit on the number of times an individual may convert IRA funds to Roth IRA status (except in certain cases following an "unconversion"; see "Unconversions (Recharacterizations) and Corrective Distributions"); and no minimum dollar or percentage amount that must be converted to have a proper conversion.

What type of plan may be converted to a Roth IRA

An "individual retirement plan" may be converted to a Roth IRA. "Individual retirement plans" include individual retirement accounts (IRAs) and individual retirement trusts (IRTs) under § 408(a) and (h).

A "simplified employee pension" individual retirement account (SEP-IRA) (§ 408(k)) and a "simple retirement account" (SRA) (§ 408(p)) cannot themselves be "designated" as Roth IRAs (§ 408A(f)). However, these plans are "IRAs," and as such they can be rolled or converted into Roth IRAs, subject to one limit: a "SIMPLE IRA" distribution "is not eligible to be rolled over into" a Roth IRA "during the 2-year period...which begins on the date that the individual first participated in any SIMPLE IRA Plan maintained by the individual's employer." Reg. § 1.408A-4 (Q & A 4(b)) (cross reference to § 72(t)(6)). Once the conversion occurs, the account is not eligible to receive further contributions under the SEP or SIMPLE plan. Reg. § 1.408A-4 (Q & A 4(c)).

There is no way to transfer funds directly from a **qualified retirement plan** ("QRP") or **403(b)** plan to a Roth IRA, or to roll over a distribution from such a plan directly into a Roth IRA. § 408A(c)(6) says "No rollover contribution may be made to a Roth IRA unless it is a qualified rollover contribution"; and § 408A(e) defines a qualified rollover contribution as "a rollover contribution to a Roth IRA from another such account or from an individual retirement plan." Reg. § 1.408A-4 (Q & A 5). However, a participant in a QRP or 403(b) plan who receives from such plan a distribution eligible to be rolled to a traditional IRA can roll that distribution to a traditional IRA and then convert *that* to a Roth IRA.

The one-rollover-per-year limitation in § 408(d)(3)(B) does not apply to a conversion to a Roth, so such conversion may occur within 12 months of a tax-free rollover into a traditional IRA. Reg. § 1.408A-4 (Q & A 1(a)).

Education IRAs cannot be converted to Roth IRAs. Reg. § 1.408A-6 (Q & A 18).

Who may convert: income limit and filing status

No conversion is permitted if "the taxpayer's adjusted gross income for such taxable year exceeds $100,000." § 408A(c)(3)(B). In the case of a *married couple filing jointly*, the $100,000 limit applies to the AGI of the *couple*, not of each *spouse*. Reg. § 1.408A-4 (Q & A 2(b)).

Generally, no conversion is permitted if the taxpayer is *married filing a separate return* for the year. § 408A(c)(3)(B). However, if a "married individual has lived apart from his or her spouse for the entire taxable year, then such individual can treat himself or herself as not married for purposes of [the adjusted gross income test], file a separate return and be subject to the $100,000 limit on his or her separate modified AGI." Reg. § 1.408A-4 (Q & A 2(b)).

The year you look at for applying these rules, in the case of a Roth IRA conversion, is the year in which the distribution occurs (*i.e.*, the distribution that is rolled over), *not* the year that the contribution to the Roth occurs. In most cases, of course, the distribution from the traditional IRA and its recontribution to the Roth IRA occur simultaneously; but the rule provides guidance in case of a distribution from the traditional IRA that occurs in one taxable year, and is rolled over in the *next* taxable year (but still within 60 days of the distribution). Reg. § 1.408A-4 (Q & A 2).

Income limit: definition of adjusted gross income

The definition of AGI for purposes of the Roth IRA income limits starts with the definition of AGI used under § 219(g)(3) (income limits for making a deductible contribution to a traditional IRA when the individual is also a participant in an employer plan). The § 219(g)(3) definition of AGI includes the individual's taxable Social Security benefits (§ 86), and takes into account the disallowance of "passive activity losses" (§ 469) if applicable. § 408A(c)(3)(C). AGI as thus determined is further modified as follows for purposes of determining eligibility to contribute to a Roth IRA:

1.   AGI for this purpose does NOT include any amount included in gross income because of the conversion of a traditional IRA to a Roth IRA. § 408A(c)(3)(C)(i).

So, if, in the year being tested, the taxpayer does a conversion to a Roth IRA, resulting in the inclusion of some or all of the conversion amount in his gross income; and/or if the year being tested is 1999, 2000 or 2001 and gross income includes some income on account of a 1998 conversion for which the four-year spread was elected; the gross income resulting from the conversion is disregarded SOLELY FOR PURPOSE OF DETERMINING WHETHER THE TAXPAYER'S AGI IS LOW ENOUGH TO MAKE HIM ELIGIBLE TO CONTRIBUTE TO A ROTH IRA.

Thus, "adjusted gross income" (*including all interrelated computations*, such as how much of Social Security payments are taxable, and how much of passive activity loss is deductible) must be determined twice: first, for purposes of determining the taxpayer's *actual* tax owed, income resulting from conversions to a Roth is included in gross income (and all adjustments dependent on the taxpayer's "AGI"—such as taxability of Social Security—are determined based on this true AGI figure); then second, for purposes of determining the taxpayer's eligibility to contribute to a Roth, all gross income resulting from traditional-to-Roth conversions must be backed out (and all adjustments dependent on AGI redetermined accordingly). This second, fictional, AGI has *no relevance* to the taxpayer's actual tax burden—it is a pro forma number used solely to determine eligibility to contribute to a Roth. Reg. § 1.408A-4 (Q & A 9).

2.   The deduction under § 219 (IRA contributions) is not taken into account.

3.   For years after 2004 ONLY: AGI for this purpose will NOT include any amount that is included in adjusted gross income by reason of a required minimum distribution from an IRA. See *"Effect of required IRA distributions: after 2004,"* below.

Income limit: effect of minimum required distribution

What happens if P will be age 70½ or older by the end of the taxable year, and withdrawing his minimum required distribution (MRD) for the year would put his income over the $100,000 income limit?

Example: Jeanette is over age 70½. It is 1999 and she would like to convert her traditional IRA to a Roth IRA. Her adjusted gross income, before taking any IRA distributions, is $50,000, so based on this she meets the income limitation. But her MRD for 1999 from the traditional IRA is $75,000. If she has to take that much out of her IRA on a taxable basis she will be over the $100,000 income cap and cannot convert to a Roth IRA. Is there any way around this dilemma?

First question: Can the realization of deemed income that comes from converting to a Roth IRA count as fulfilling her minimum distribution requirement for 1999? After all, the point of the minimum distribution rules is simply to make you pay some income tax on your retirement plan, and she will have paid tax on 100% of the IRA value by converting it to a Roth. Unfortunately, there is no authority for the proposition that a Roth IRA conversion could be used, in place of an actual non-rolled-over cash distribution, to fulfill the minimum distribution requirement for the traditional IRA.

Second question: Since Jeanette is required to take an *actual* distribution in 1999, can she avoid the problem by first converting the IRA to a Roth, and THEN taking the distribution? The withdrawal from the brand-new Roth IRA is non-taxable because it is deemed to be a return of her basis—she has already paid tax on it by virtue of the conversion—and therefore the post-conversion distribution does not put her over the $100,000 income cap. Unfortunately, this maneuver is not possible either, because (1) MRDs may not be rolled over and (2) the first dollars distributed in any year are deemed to be part of the MRD for such year, until the MRD has been entirely distributed. See *"No rollover of minimum required distributions,"* Chapter 2.

Thus the Roth IRA provider cannot accept *any* rollover from Jeanette's traditional IRA without proof that she has actually withdrawn the MRD for the year. And of course once she actually withdraws the MRD of $75,000 her income will be over $100,000 and she cannot convert any part of the IRA to a Roth IRA. Reg. § 1.408A-4 (Q & A 6(b)). This result is not affected by the means through which the taxpayer effects the conversion, *i.e.*, whether by rollover or by trustee-to-trustee transfer, or by whether an amount greater than or equal to the year's MRD remains in the non-Roth IRA after the conversion.

If an amount is converted in violation of this principle, the amount is treated as a distribution to P, and (since it is not eligible for rollover) it would be treated as a regular contribution to the Roth IRA. Reg. § 1.408A-4 (Q & A 6(c)). As such it will attract a 6% excess contribution penalty if it is in excess of the applicable limits on a regular Roth IRA contribution for that person for that year. Reg. § 1.408A-3 (Q & A 7).

Trap for the unwary: conversions in the age 70½ year

The rule that required minimum distributions cannot be rolled over, and that the first dollars distributed in any year are deemed to come from the minimum required distribution until the minimum required distribution has been fully distributed, creates a trap for individuals in the year they turn age 70½.

Example: Jay, who is single, turns 70½ in 1999. His income (before taking any required distributions) is $80,000. He wants to convert his traditional IRA to a Roth IRA. His MRD from that IRA for 1999 is $45,000, but he does not have to take that distribution until April 1, 2000. Accordingly, he plans to defer that first distribution until January, 2000, so it will not count as part of his income for 1999 and therefore (he thinks) he is eligible to convert to a Roth in 1999 because his income is under $100,000. Unfortunately the no-conversion-until-after-taking-minimum-distribution rule applies to him just the same as it did to Jeanette in the preceding example. The $45,000 is a required distribution *for the year he turns 70½*, even though he is allowed to defer it until the next year.

So the rule really is: a participant does not have to take his minimum required IRA distribution for the year he reaches age 70½ until April 1 of the following year, *unless* he wants to convert to a Roth IRA. If he wants to convert to a Roth IRA in the year he reaches age 70½, he *cannot* defer that first year's distribution from his traditional IRA until the following April 1.

And the moral of the story is: A person who wants to convert his IRA to a Roth, and whose traditional IRA is large enough that minimum distributions could push him over the $100,000 limit, must act *before* the year he reaches age 70½. Note, however, that the rule apparently does not preclude postponing required distributions for the age 70½ year from *other* (non-IRA) kinds of retirement plans until April 1 of the following year, as a way of keeping income low enough to allow conversion of an IRA to a Roth.

Effect of required IRA distributions: after 2004

This problem goes away after 2004, at least as to MRDs from IRAs. MRDs (from IRAs only, according to the regulations) will be excluded for purposes of applying the

$100,000 AGI limit, but only after the year 2004. § 408A(c)(3)(C)(i)(II).

Example: In 2005, Lucy's MRD from her traditional IRA is $130,000. Her other income is $60,000. She will still be required to take, and pay tax on, the $130,000 distribution, and she can not roll that distribution over to a Roth IRA; but she will be able to convert the *rest* of her IRA to a Roth IRA in that year, because her AGI (not counting the MRD of $130,000, or the "deemed" income arising from the conversion) is only $60,000, and thus under the $100,000 limit.

Tax treatment of converting to a Roth—normally

The rollover from a traditional IRA to a Roth IRA is treated as a distribution from the traditional IRA. § 408A(d)(3)(A), (B), (C). Thus, the rollover amount is included in P's gross income, to the extent an actual distribution of the same amount from his traditional IRA would have been taxable.

The extent to which an IRA distribution (or conversion) is treated as a non-taxable return of basis (*i.e.*, the return of P's non-deductible contributions) is determined under § 408(d). Remember, under § 408(d)(2), all (traditional) IRAs are treated as one IRA, and all distributions in one taxable year are treated as one distribution, for purposes of determining how much of the year's distributions (and conversions) constitute non-taxable return of basis.

Although after-tax contributions to an employer plan cannot be rolled over to a traditional IRA, non-deducted contributions to a traditional IRA *are* eligible for conversion to a Roth. Reg. § 1.408A-4 (Q & A 7(a)).

1998 Conversions: The Four-Year Spread

See "When the Roth Owner Dies" for interaction of four-year spread and death of participant.

Four-year spread option for 1998 conversions

For rollovers in 1998 ONLY, the inclusion in gross income may be spread equally over the four taxable years 1998, 1999, 2000 and 2001. This treatment occurs unless the taxpayer elects *not* to have it apply. § 408A(d)(3)(A)(iii). The election not to use the four-year spread is made on Form 8606, and may not be made (or changed) after the due date of P's 1998 tax return (including extensions). Reg. § 1.408A-4 (Q & A 10).

The election out of the four-year spread, if made, must apply to all of the taxpayer's traditional IRA money transferred to a Roth IRA in 1998; there is no such thing as a partial election. Reg. § 1.408A-4 (Q & A 10).

To qualify as a 1998 conversion, the distribution from the traditional IRA must be made by December 31, 1998, and contributed to a Roth IRA within 60 days after the distribution

Accelerated inclusion for distributions before 2001

If an individual converted to a Roth IRA in 1998, and chose to spread the resulting taxable income over four years, but then takes a distribution from the conversion money during the first three years of the four-year spread period, he gets punished: he loses the benefit of further deferral of tax on the amount of the distribution.[3]

---

[3]The 10% penalty once proposed for such early withdrawals was not included in the final version of Technical Corrections.

§ 408A(d)(3)(E)(i) provides for an "acceleration of inclusion" in this situation. Specifically, taxable income for the year of the distribution "shall be increased by the aggregate distributions from Roth IRAs for such taxable year which are allocable under" the Ordering Rules (see *"The Ordering Rules,"* above) "to the portion of such [1998 conversion] required to be included in gross income."

However, there is an overriding limitation, to avoid double taxation: the amount required to be included in income in any of the four years may not exceed (A) the amount that would have been included in income in 1998 on account of the conversion, if the taxpayer had not chosen to do the four-year spread; minus (B) the amounts includible in all years prior to the current year on account of this conversion. Reg. § 1.408A-6 (Q & A 6). The effect of this overriding limit is to reduce the installments includible in the later years, in reverse order of date, to reflect the accelerated inclusion.

Minimum Required Distributions

Distributions from a Roth IRA do *not* count to fulfill a minimum distribution requirement arising from a traditional IRA. Reg. § 1.408A-6 (Q & A 15).

No MRDs during participant's life

There are no minimum required distributions (see Chapter 1) from a Roth IRA during the original Roth IRA owner's life. § 408A(c)(5) provides that § 401(a)(9)(A) (which contains the lifetime minimum distribution rules) and the "incidental death benefit requirement" do not apply to Roth IRAs. So a person who reaches age 70½ does not have to start taking distributions from his Roth IRA as he does from his traditional IRA.

After death, "death before RBD" rules apply

The Roth IRA is not exempted from any minimum distribution rules other than § 401(a)(9)(A) and the incidental death benefit rule, both of which apply only during P's life. Accordingly, the post-death minimum distribution rules (§ 401(a)(9)(B)) apply the same as to other IRAs.

Therefore, a participant who converts to a Roth before his required beginning date will never have a "required beginning date" (RBD) for his Roth IRA. Whenever he dies, even if he dies after reaching age 70½, the rules will be applied "as though the Roth IRA owner died before his or her required beginning date." Reg. § 1.408A-6 (Q & A 14(b)). See "Death Before the RBD: The FiveYear Rule," Chapter 1.

Designated beneficiary not determined until death

The Roth IRA participant will have the additional advantage of being able to change his "designated beneficiary" (DB) after age 70½, and having that change be effective for determining MRDs after his death; the new DB's life expectancy will be used for determining the amount of the required distributions. This makes planning much more flexible.

Example: Abelard names his spouse Heloise as the DB of both his traditional IRA and his Roth IRA. He names their child, Clothier, as contingent beneficiary on both accounts. Then he reaches, and passes, age 70½. When he is 75 years old, Heloise dies. Abelard dies the next year. If Heloise had *survived* Abelard, she could have rolled over each of the IRAs to new IRAs in her own name, naming son Clothier as her DB, thus (under IRS policy as evidenced by various private letter rulings) (see *"Rollover by S after age 70½,"* Chapter 3) assuring availability of long-term deferral for the funds remaining in the rollover IRAs at her death. But because she *predeceased* Abelard there will be no spousal rollover available.

Under the *traditional* IRA, because Abelard was past his RBD when he died, minimum distributions must continue to be made "at least as rapidly" as they were required to be made during Abelard's life. See *"Effect of P's death after the RBD,"* Chapter 1. Accordingly, Clothier, as Abelard's contingent beneficiary, must take out the balance of the IRA over no longer than the remaining joint life expectancy of Abelard and Heloise. With a traditional IRA, when the spouse is named as beneficiary at the RBD, and the spouse predeceases P, *there can be no deferral beyond the original joint life expectancy of P and his spouse as established at the RBD.*

Under Abelard's *Roth* IRA, however, Abelard is deemed to have died "before his RBD." Therefore, Clothier, even though he was originally only a contingent beneficiary, is Abelard's "DB" for the Roth IRA. So Clothier can withdraw Abelard's Roth IRA benefits over Clothier's life expectancy.

Thus, with a Roth IRA, P can name his spouse as beneficiary and still be confident of probably getting *some* long term deferral, regardless of which spouse dies first and when. If the spouse survives P, she can do a rollover and name the children as her beneficiaries. If the spouse predeceases P, *P* can now simply name the children as his new beneficiaries (or they will automatically become his beneficiaries, if they were already named as contingent beneficiaries), even if he is past his RBD. After his death, they can use the life expectancy of the oldest child as the measurement of required distributions.

Converting to a Roth IRA after the RBD

The holder of a Roth IRA is considered to die before his RBD with regard to his Roth IRA, *regardless* of whether the conversion to a Roth occurred before or after the RBD applicable to the predecessor traditional IRA. Reg. § 1.408A-6 (Q & A 14). Thus, converting a traditional IRA to a Roth IRA after age 70½ offers a golden opportunity to revise choices made for the traditional IRA at age 70½. A participant who at his RBD named the "wrong" (or no) beneficiary, or who regrets his choice of a method of determining life expectancy, can get a fresh start by converting to a Roth IRA, and naming the "right" beneficiary.

Clients Who May Profit From Roth IRA Conversion

Retiree with long life expectancy

Roth IRAs have appeal to those retirees who do not need to withdraw any funds from their IRAs during life, especially those who expect to live well beyond the average life expectancy due to their sex, genetic heritage and/or health. A traditional IRA participant approaching age 70½ faces the unwelcome prospect of forced distributions which will substantially diminish if not obliterate the account over a long life span. With a traditional IRA, the way to maximize tax deferral is to die prematurely (leaving benefits to a younger generation beneficiary).

By converting the traditional IRA to a Roth, this person can eliminate the forced lifetime distributions and reverse the usual rule of thumb. The way to maximize tax deferral with a *Roth* IRA is to live as long as humanly possible, deferring the commencement of ANY distributions until that way-later-than-normal death (and then leaving benefits to a young beneficiary).

The deathbed conversion

Converting to a Roth IRA just before death is the "move of choice" when benefits will otherwise have to be paid out just after death—for one thing, such conversion may permit the longer post-death deferral of distributions (see *"Converting to a Roth IRA after the RBD,"* above). It also may help reduce estate taxes (see *"Planning for client with short life expectancy,"* Chapter 2). But even if the traditional IRA is *already* set up so that it will be paid out after death over the life expectancy of a DB, it would be a great convenience to beneficiaries not to have to wrestle with the valuable but complicated IRD deduction every year as they do their income tax returns (see "Deduction for Estate Taxes Paid on IRD," Chapter 2).

Low-income parent with high-income children

Example: Rhonda is a widow, age 65, living happily on her Social Security payments plus $25,000 a year withdrawn from a substantial traditional IRA representing a rollover of her late husband's pension plan. For the last several years, she has withdrawn sufficient extra dollars from the IRA to use up the lower income tax brackets available to her. Even though she doesn't need this extra money for her living expenses, she knows that her children are all in the highest income tax bracket, and that some day those high brackets will apply to distributions the children take from the IRA they inherit at her death.

Now she has a new way to prepay the income taxes (at her low bracket) on the IRA benefits, so the children won't have to pay tax on them at their high rates: she can convert some of the traditional IRA to a Roth IRA, each year, to use the lower income tax brackets. This way she gets the same advantages she got by taking distributions—and the additional advantage of passing on to the children the tax-advantaged Roth IRA.

Funding a credit shelter trust

It is not uncommon for a married client to have enough assets to cause the couple's estate to be subject to estate taxes, but at the same time have no assets with which to fund a credit shelter trust other than his retirement plan benefits. Such a client has had, until now, only the following choices, none of which is very palatable: make a sufficient portion of the benefits payable to the credit shelter trust to fully use up the unified credit (drawbacks of this plan are discussed in the *Allen Able* case study); or, don't fund the credit shelter gift at all (drawback: wastes participant's unified credit, ultimately increasing estate taxes); or, withdraw enough from the plan during life to be able to fund the credit shelter trust at death with after-tax money (drawback: loss of further deferral on all the money withdrawn, and immediate loss of the money paid in income taxes on the distribution).

Now this individual has an additional choice (if he has an IRA, or can roll his plan benefits to an IRA, and if he meets the income requirement): converting to a Roth IRA, before death, enough of the traditional IRA to fund the credit shelter trust at death. Although this still involves the loss of the money used to pay the income taxes (a cost which could have been deferred for a while longer), it at least enables the individual to fund his credit shelter trust with a tax-deferred vehicle—without wasting any of the unified credit paying income taxes.

Funding a generation skipping gift

Many clients, as part of their estate plan, create a generation skipping trust designed to use up the federal **GST tax** exemption ($1 million plus COLA). By funding the generation skipping gift with Roth IRA death benefits (rather than traditional IRA death benefits), P still gives his beneficiaries the advantage of long-term tax deferral on investment growth; and this approach has the additional advantages of totally tax-free distributions and not "wasting" any of the GST exemption paying income taxes.

Funding a QTIP or QDOT trust

One drawback of funding a "qualified terminable interest property" ("QTIP") trust (§ 2056) with traditional IRA death benefits is that distributions of principal from the IRA to the trust are subject to income taxes (which may be at a higher rate than that paid by the surviving spouse on her individual income). Horrendous additional complications arise if the surviving spouse is not a U.S. citizen (see Chapter 4). Because many of these problems are caused by the fact that traditional IRA distributions are "income in respect of a decedent" (Chapter 2) the problems are diminished if the IRA is a Roth IRA.

Lifetime gifts of Roth IRAs

According to the regulations, assigning a Roth IRA during life as a gift "to another individual" (or presumably to a trust—with the possible exception of a trust which is a 100% **grantor trust** as to the Roth IRA owner) causes the Roth IRA to be "deemed" distributed to the owner-donor, and accordingly it ceases to be a Roth IRA. Reg. § 1.408A-6 (Q & A 19). Needless to say, this treatment completely eliminates the advantages of such a gift.

If any such gift was made prior to October 1, 1998, and "if the entire interest in the Roth IRA is reconveyed to the Roth IRA owner prior to January 1, 1999," the IRS "will treat the gift and reconveyance as never having occurred for estate tax, gift tax, and generation-skipping tax purposes and for purposes of this" paragraph of the regulations. Reg. § 1.408A-6 (Q & A 19).

Drawbacks and risks of Roth conversion

Most clients considering converting a traditional IRA to a Roth will evaluate the financial impact using computer projections of one brand or another. Computer projections of the benefits of converting an existing IRA to a Roth IRA are based on assumptions as to future tax rates, investment returns and withdrawal amounts.

Most of the published projections assume some constant rate of investment return continuing indefinitely into the future; that today's tax rates will last forever; and that participants and beneficiaries will withdraw from the account no more than required by today's minimum distribution rules. Other possible scenarios should be considered, such as a stock market decline; it would be a shame to pay income tax on today's stock values, only to find out later that this was the all time market high.

Also, there are some in Congress calling for repeal of the Internal Revenue Code and its replacement by a value added tax or a "flat tax" in the range of 20%. Needless to say, it would be disappointing to pay income tax on the entire value of one's IRA at today's rates and then discover one could have withdrawn the benefits at a much lower rate later.

Whether or not Congress radically changes income tax rates, Congress could decide to bring the minimum distribution rules back into line with the original purpose of tax-favored *retirement* plans, and require that all benefits be distributed within some much shorter period of time after the deaths of P and his spouse. Or, Congress could decide that the Roth IRA was too good a deal, and take away some of its favorable tax features on a prospective basis.

Converting to a Roth IRA is theoretically a very good

deal financially, especially (only?) for those who can pay the tax on the IRA conversion without taking the money out of the IRA itself. As retirement planning expert Marvin Rotenberg and others have pointed out, Congress is allowing you to increase the amount of money you have in a tax-sheltered investment account, by paying off the tax up front from other funds.

The client most certain to profit from converting to a Roth IRA is one who: has sufficient other wealth that he will never need to draw from the account during life; plans to leave the account to young generation beneficiaries, to be drawn down over their life expectancy after the client's death; and can afford to pay the income tax on the conversion, and the estate tax on the account's date of death value, from other assets, without sacrificing other goals such as his own financial security. Add steady to rising income tax rates, no negative tax law changes and positive investment returns and the conversion is a definite winner.

Many, perhaps most, of the clients who can afford to pay the taxes and take the risks will not qualify for the Roth conversion because of the $100,000 income limit. Most of the people who *are* eligible to convert simply cannot afford to write a check for the up-front tax on the conversion. Therefore, it may be that the Roth IRA conversion will mainly be of interest to: wealthy people who due to some fluke have income under $100,000 in a particular year; young people who face a long life expectancy and expect their tax bracket to rise; and, among "middle class" retirees age 60 and up, those who see benefits in the Roth IRA conversion besides just the ultimate numerical payout, such as improvements in their estate planning options.

10% Penalty For Pre-Age 59½ Distributions

Full details on this penalty are contained in Chapter 9. This section discusses the penalty as it applies to Roth IRAs, and assumes you have read Chapter 9.

Penalty does not apply to conversions

    The 10% penalty under § 72(t) (applicable to certain distributions before age 59½) does not apply to the "deemed" distribution that results from converting a traditional IRA to a Roth IRA. § 408A(d)(3)(A)(ii); Reg. § 1.408A-4 (Q & A 7(b)). Thus an (otherwise eligible) young person may convert his traditional IRA to a Roth IRA without penalty.

Penalty applies to certain distributions from the Roth IRA

    § 72(t) imposes a 10% penalty on any distribution from a "qualified retirement plan (as defined in section 4974(c))" made while P is under age 59½ (with various exceptions). The definition of "qualified retirement plan" in § 4974(c) includes traditional IRAs, but was not amended by TAPRA (or Technical Corrections) to specifically include Roth IRAs. Nevertheless the regulations confirm that the 10% penalty would apply to non-excepted premature distributions from Roth IRAs, the same as to traditional IRAs, under the rule that Roth IRAs are treated the same as traditional IRAs "for purposes of this title" unless § 408A provides otherwise. Reg. § 1.408A-6 (Q & A 5).

    The three situations in which a distribution *from* a Roth IRA may be subject to the 10% penalty are discussed in the next three subsections.

Conversion followed by distribution within five years

    A person who is under age 59½, although he can convert to a Roth without penalty, has to come up with the money to pay the income tax on the conversion from some source *other* than the Roth IRA (or a traditional IRA) because he will owe the penalty to the extent he taps his traditional IRA or his newly converted Roth IRA for this money.

If a P who is under age 59½ receives a distribution from a Roth IRA; and if "any portion" of that distribution is allocable under the Ordering Rules (see "*The Ordering Rules*," above) to funds rolled over to the Roth from a traditional IRA that were includible in gross income; and "the distribution is made within the 5-taxable-year period beginning with the first day of the individual's taxable year in which the conversion contribution was made"; then the § 72(t) penalty shall apply to the distribution. § 408A(d)(3)(F); Reg. § 1.408A-6 (Q & A 5(b)).

Note that this five-year period is *not the same* as the Five-Year Period for determining "qualified distributions" (see "*Definition of Five Year Period*," above). The latter begins in the first year *any* contribution is made to any Roth IRA; the former begins, as to any conversion of a traditional IRA to a Roth IRA, with the year of that *particular* conversion. Reg. § 1.408A-6 (Q & A 5(c)). Note also that this penalty applies regardless of whether the distribution is included in gross income in the year of the *distribution*.

Example: Rand, age 32, converts his $100,000 traditional IRA to a Roth IRA in 1999. He has no basis in the traditional IRA, so the entire $100,000 is includible in his gross income in 1999. He has no other Roth IRAs, and makes no other contributions to this one. In 2002, at age 35 (in other words, before the end of the five taxable years beginning with the year of the conversion, and while he is still under 59½) he takes $20,000 out of the Roth IRA to finance the purchase of a rare edition of *The Canterbury Tales*. Under the Ordering Rules, this distribution is deemed to come out of the portion of the 1999 conversion-contribution that was includible in gross income, and therefore it is subject to the 10% penalty.

"The exceptions under § 72(t) also apply to such a distribution," so there should be no penalty if the distribution is made after the death (or on account of the total disability) of P, for example. Reg. § 1.408A-6 (Q & A 5(b)). But see discussion of Reg. § 1.408A-6 (Q & A 11) under the topic *"How the Ordering Rules apply to a decedent's Roth IRA,"* below.

Taxable portion of non-qualified distributions

If there is a distribution from a Roth IRA before P reaches age 59½, but the distribution is *not* allocable under the Ordering Rules to money converted within the last five years from a traditional IRA, the penalty applies only to the portion of the distribution (if any) that is included in gross income. Reg. § 1.408A-6 (Q & A 5(a)).

Conversion while receiving series of payments

The 10% penalty does not apply to IRA distributions which are part of a "Series of Substantially Equal Periodic Payments" (see Chapter 9). The regulations prescribe what happens when an individual who is receiving such a series of payments from an IRA converts the IRA to a Roth. First, the conversion itself is "not treated as a distribution for purposes of determining whether a modification" of the series has occurred, so the conversion itself does not trigger the loss of the exempt status of the series. Reg. § 1.408A-4 (Q & A 12); see *"Modification of the series is prohibited,"* Chapter 9.

However, the conversion does not mean that the individual can stop taking his periodic payments. "If the original series...does not continue to be distributed in substantially equal periodic payments from the Roth IRA after the conversion, the series of payments will have been modified and, if this modification occurs within 5 years of the first payment or prior to the individual [sic] becoming disabled or attaining age 59½, the taxpayer will be subject to the recapture tax of § 72(t)(4)(A)." Reg. § 1.408A-4 (Q & A 12).

One aspect of this provision is mysterious: Why does he have to take them from the *Roth* IRA? Why can't he keep taking them from the (now-diminished) traditional IRA, at least until it runs out of money?

Unconversions (Recharacterizations) and Corrective Distributions

Corrective distributions

A taxpayer who is unhappy with the IRA contribution choices he made for a particular year, or who discovers that he was not eligible to make the contribution he made, has two ways to remedy the problem.

One is to distribute the contribution back to himself. If any Roth IRA contribution (together with its net income) is distributed before the due date (including extensions, if any) of the tax return for the year for which the contribution was made, then (a) the contribution is treated as never having been made and (b) the net income on the contribution is "includible in gross income for the taxable year in which the contribution is made." § 408(d)(4); Reg. § 1.408A-3 (Q & A 7), and - 6 (Q&A 1(d)). Query, if the net earnings were a loss, and the loss was realized inside the Roth IRA, is it treated as if it had been realized outside the Roth IRA, in other words, is it offset against capital gains for the year?

This solution can be useful for undoing *regular* Roth IRA contributions, but it is not much help for someone who has *converted* a traditional IRA to a Roth and then wishes he hadn't (or who discovers after the fact that he wasn't eligible). This person usually doesn't want to distribute the money out to himself, he just wants to restore the pre-conversion status quo. For this person, there is a second, method of fixing the problem: an "unconversion," or "recharacterization."

How to undo (recharacterize) a Roth IRA contribution

Any contribution made to any type of IRA during the taxable year may be transferred to any *other* type of IRA before the due date of the person's tax return for that year, and it will be treated as a contribution to the *transferee* IRA for tax purposes. § 408A(d)(6), (7). For example, if a person converts a traditional IRA to a Roth in 1998, and then discovers that his income for 1998 exceeds the $100,000 limit so he is ineligible to do that conversion, he can move the money back to a traditional IRA before the extended due date of his tax return for 1998 and it will be treated as a rollover contribution to the traditional IRA. For the purpose of recharacterizing 1998 conversions, "extended due date" means (for a calendar year taxpayer) October 15, 1999, regardless of whether the taxpayer actually filed for an extension. IRS Announcement 99-57 (5/26/99).

The regulations provide broad relief to taxpayers who wish to change the nature of an IRA contribution (and not only to correct Roth IRA conversions for which they were ineligible). See *e.g.* Reg. § 1.408A-5 (Q & A 10, Example 2).

Here are the most significant requirements for effecting a recharacterization:

1.   The transfer from the Roth back to the traditional IRA must be by trustee-to-trustee transfer (not by a rollover, which is a distribution to P followed by a recontribution to the other account). Reg. § 1.408A-5 (Q & A 1(a)).

2.   Not only the original contribution but "any net income allocable to such contribution" must be retransferred.

See *"Determining net income attributable to contribution."*

3.   Although the preamble to the proposed regulations stated that "Any portion or all" of the contribution may be recharacterized, both the proposed and final regulations themselves speak only in terms of recharacterizing "the contribution" (not "any portion or all of the contribution"), and the examples given deal only with total recharacterizations. Reg. § 1.408A-5.

4.   A recharacterization is "never treated as a rollover for purposes of the one-rollover-per-year limitation of § 408(d)(3)(B), even if the contribution would have been treated as a rollover contribution by the [transferee] IRA if it had been made directly to the" transferee IRA in the first place. Reg. § 1.408A-5 (Q & A 8).

5.   The election is made by providing notice and directions to the IRA trustee(s) involved. The election to recharacterize "cannot be revoked" after the transfer back to the traditional IRA has occurred. Reg. § 1.408A-5 (Q & A 6). But see *"Limit on the number of reconversions,"* below.

6.   A recharacterized contribution will be treated for Federal income tax purposes as having been contributed to the transferee IRA (rather than the transferor IRA) "on the same date and (in the case of a regular contribution) for the same taxable year that the contribution was made to the transferor IRA." Reg. § 1.408A-5 (Q & A 3).

"Conversions" vs. "recharacterizations"

While it is nice that taxpayers have been given a way to back out of Roth IRA conversions, so they need not be punished for (*e.g.*) making an incorrect prediction of their income, the addition of the recharacterization option is bound to create confusion among IRA owners and their advisors. Here are some points that will need to be constantly restated:

First, the ability to recharacterize up until the extended due date of the tax return for a particular year applies only to a contribution made to an IRA "during such taxable year." Thus the ability to recharacterize does *not* create a new extended right to do Roth IRA conversions up to the due date of the return.

An IRA or Roth IRA cannot, as such, be recharacterized as a different type of IRA; only a *contribution* to an IRA or Roth IRA can be recharacterized, and only a contribution that was contributed (either by a conversion to a Roth IRA, or by a regular contribution) in a timely manner for that particular taxable year, *i.e.*:

1.   A regular contribution to either a Roth or a traditional IRA for a particular year, that was made by the *unextended* due date of the return for that year, can be recharacterized by the *extended* due date of the return for that year.

2.   A conversion contribution to a Roth IRA that was made within 60 days after a distribution from a traditional IRA, where the traditional IRA distribution was made during the taxable year itself, may be recharacterized by the (extended) due date of the return for that year.

Second, not every type of contribution to a *traditional* IRA may be recharacterized—only regular contributions (the $2,000-per-year type). A tax-free rollover from an employer plan (or from another traditional IRA) to a traditional IRA may not be recharacterized as a Roth conversion or contribution, because "an amount contributed to an IRA in a tax-free transfer cannot be recharacterized." However, once the tax-free rollover to the traditional IRA from the employer plan (or from another traditional IRA) has taken place, if the IRA owner wants to have a Roth IRA, he can *convert* (not recharacterize) all or part of his traditional IRA to a Roth, *if* he meets all the tests for a conversion—including the deadline. Reg. § 1.408A-5 (Q & A 10, Example 4). (But he doesn't have to worry about the one-rollover-per-year rule, because Roth IRA conversions don't count for purposes of that rule.)

Similarly, employer contributions to a SEP or SIMPLE plan may not be recharacterized as contributions to a Roth IRA, because the employer could not have made direct contributions to a Roth IRA in the first place. Reg. § 1.408A-5 (Q & A 5).

Net income attributable to contribution

Not only the original contribution but "any net income attributable to such contribution" must be retransferred. Reg. § 1.408A-5 (Q & A 2(a)). This requirement may be met in one of two ways. Note that "net income" may be a negative amount—a loss, in other words.

Method 1: If the contribution in question was made to a separate IRA, *and* there have been no other contributions to or distributions from that separate IRA, *and* the entire contribution is being recharacterized, then simply transferring the entire account balance satisfies the requirement. Reg. § 1.408A-5 (Q & A 2(b)). This method being so much simpler than Method 2, there is an advantage to keeping each year's contributions to a Roth IRA separate from any pre-existing Roth IRA, until the period has expired for recharacterizing such contributions.

Method 2: If Method 1 is not available, "then the net

income attributable to the contribution is calculated in the manner prescribed by [regulation] § 1.408-4(c)(2)(ii)." Reg. § 1.408A-5 (Q & A 2(c)).

Limit on "reconversions" in 1998 and 1999: IRS Notice 98-50

In an attempt to limit market timers who would, if they could, unconvert and reconvert their Roth IRAs every time the market dipped, the IRS in Notice 98-50 (October 1998) amended its proposed Roth IRA regulations (issued September 1998). The rules in this Notice (which was incorporated into the final regulations at § 1.408A-5 (Q & A 9(b))) govern reconversions in 1998 and 1999; even stricter limits apply in 2000 and later years (discussed in the next subsection).

Specifically, for 1998 and 1999:

1.   The general rule is, a person may convert the same amount to a Roth IRA no more than twice in any one calendar year. That is to say, he may convert an IRA amount to a Roth (first conversion), then "unconvert" (recharacterize) it, then "reconvert" it (second conversion, or first "reconversion"). After that he can continue unconverting and reconverting as many times as he chooses; but any subsequent reconversions are considered "excess reconversions" and will *not* be used to determine the amount includible in gross income on account of the Roth conversion.

If the last step is a reconversion (so that when the music stops—on the extended due date of the person's tax return—the amount is in a Roth IRA, not a traditional IRA), gross income will still be based on the amount converted in the "first reconversion."

2.   However, reconversions prior to November 1, 1998 don't count toward the 1998 limit. So anyone who

converts to a Roth IRA at any time in 1998, and then unconverts at any time in 1998, may do one reconversion (or one *more* reconversion, as the case may be) between November 1 and December 31, 1998, regardless of how many reconversions (if any) he did prior to November 1, 1998.

3.   Anyone who converts to a Roth IRA at any time in 1998, and then unconverts at any time in 1998, may also do one (and *only* one) reconversion of the same amount in 1999.

4.   The limit in Rule 3 does *not* apply to a person who unconverted his 1998 conversion(s) because he was not *eligible* to convert, *i.e.*, whose 1998 conversion attempt(s) failed because his income turned out to be over $100,000. The Rule 3 limit applies only to a person who, though he was eligible to (and did) do a 1998 Roth conversion, "unconverted" that conversion and ended up with the amount in a traditional IRA at the end of calendar 1998.

5.   The limit in Rule 3 does not affect a person whose 1998 Roth conversion ultimately ended up 1998 in a Roth IRA, regardless of how many times he flipped it back and forth before the end of 1998. Since this person's 1998 Roth conversion ultimately stayed "converted," any 1999 conversion is a "new" conversion, not a reconversion of "the same amount." So this person gets a fresh start for 1999. It's all so easy once you know how!

Same-year reconversions outlawed: 2000 and later

In Reg. § 1.408A-5 (Q & A 9(a)), issued February 3, 1999, the IRS banned same-year reconversions, effective in 2000 and later years. Specifically, the new rule is that, once a recharacterization of a Roth IRA conversion occurs, the individual may not reconvert the amount to a Roth IRA until the taxable year following the taxable year of the original conversion, or until at least 30 days have elapsed since the recharacterization, *whichever is later*. If the individual defies this rule and attempts to reconvert before the prescribed time period ends, the result is a "failed conversion" (see next subsection).

Conversion/unconversion glossary

Failed conversion. Taxpayer converted all or part of his traditional IRA to a Roth IRA, but was not eligible to do so—either because his income exceeded the income limit, or because the conversion did not meet the requirements of a "qualified rollover," or because he was reconverting in the year 2000 (or later) too soon under the rule of Reg. § 1.408A-5 (Q & A 9(a)). This taxpayer must "unconvert" (recharacterize) his Roth IRA conversion, by transferring the amount converted (plus its earnings—or minus its losses, as the case may be) back to a traditional IRA on or before the (extended) due date of his tax return for the year in which the failed conversion occurred. If he does not recharacterize on a timely basis he will be liable for the penalty for an excess contribution to his Roth IRA.

Recharacterization. The IRS's term for undoing a Roth IRA conversion. A taxpayer who has converted all or part of a traditional IRA to a Roth IRA (whether by means of a "failed" conversion, a "reconversion," an "excess" reconversion or just a plain old "conversion") may undo (recharacterize) that conversion at any time up until the (extended) due date of his or her tax return for the year in which the conversion occurred. Until then, the door is always open for *un*conversions; there is no limit on the number of times a person may "recharacterize." (Only "*re*conversions" are limited.)

Reconversion. The conversion, from a traditional IRA to a Roth IRA, of an amount that was previously converted to a Roth IRA and then recharacterized (unconverted).

Excess reconversion. A reconversion to a Roth IRA occurring in 1998 or 1999 in excess of the limit imposed by Notice 98-50 (Reg. § 1.408A-5 (Q & A 9(b)). An "excess conversion" is a valid Roth contribution; the Roth IRA so established is recognized in all respects (assuming the person is otherwise eligible to convert to a Roth) and the contribution is not an excess contribution subject to penalty. However, the individual's taxable income resulting from the "excess reconversion" will be based on the value converted in the last "valid" (non-excess) reconversion to a Roth that occurred prior to the "excess" reconversion. In other words, a person making an excess reconversion will pay tax on the value of the converted amount as of the last preceding reconversion that was not an excess reconversion. And if the taxpayer doesn't like this result he can still undo all the conversions by recharacterizing back to a traditional IRA prior to the extended due date of his tax return. The term "excess reconversion" will have no application in 2000 and later years, when reconversions not in compliance with Reg. § 1.408A-5 (Q & A 9(a)) will simply be treated as failed conversions.

When the Roth IRA Owner Dies

This section collects rules that come into play upon death of the Roth IRA owner.

Five-Year Period: effect of the participant's death

The Five-Year Period does not start running over again just because the Roth IRA owner dies. The Five-Year Period applicable to distributions from an inherited Roth IRA is the Five-Year Period that applied to the account during the original owner's life. Reg. § 1.408A-6 (Q & A 7(a)). Also, the Five-Year Period requirement is not *waived* simply because the original owner dies—even though in most cases the minimum distribution rules (Chapter 1) require the beneficiaries to begin withdrawing from the account within one year after the date of death. Reg. § 1.408A-6 (Q & A 14(c)).

Example: Agatha, age 83, converted her traditional IRA to a Roth IRA in 1999, shortly before her death. She had made no prior Roth IRA contributions of any type. Her DB must begin taking required distributions in 2000. Because the Five-Year Period has not elapsed, the distribution is not a qualified distribution. However, so long as the distribution does not exceed the amount of Agatha's original rollover contribution it is still income-tax free (see "*Tax treatment of non-qualified distributions*," above). And beginning in 2004 all distributions will be tax-free as "qualified distributions."

Income in respect of a decedent problem

If P dies during the Five-Year Period, it will not be known at the time of his death whether post-death distributions from his Roth IRA will be "income in respect of a decedent" (IRD) (Chapter 2) or not. Any distribution made from the Roth IRA after the expiration of the Five-Year Period will not be IRD because it would be an income tax-free qualified distribution. But if beneficiaries withdraw from the account before the Five-Year Period expires, and the total withdrawals exceed P's contributions, the excess withdrawals will be taxable as IRD.

Recipients of IRD are entitled to an income tax deduction for federal estate taxes paid on IRD. The amount of the deduction depends on the amount of estate taxes paid on *all* of the IRD included in the estate and on what proportion of it each beneficiary received. § 691. Thus, in an estate which pays a federal estate tax, the existence of a Roth IRA for which the Five-Year Period had not expired at death may make it impossible for tax preparers to finalize beneficiaries' IRD deductions until expiration of the Five-Year Period (or earlier distribution of the entire Roth IRA).

Special rules for surviving spouses

A surviving spouse as beneficiary of a Roth IRA can roll the account over into a Roth IRA of her own, or elect to treat the deceased spouse's Roth IRA as her own Roth IRA. This treatment is elective, not mandatory. Reg. § 1.408A-2 (Q & A 4). The result of such rollover or election is that the minimum distribution rules and § 72(t) are then applied to the surviving spouse as owner, not on the basis of the deceased spouse as owner. Reg. § 1.408A-2 (Q & A 4).

The regulations provide a special favorable rule (not in the statute) for surviving spouses: if the beneficiary of a Roth IRA is the surviving spouse, and the "surviving spouse treats the Roth IRA as his or her own," and the surviving spouse also owns his or her own Roth IRA, "the 5-taxable-year period with respect to any of the surviving spouse's Roth IRAs" (including the inherited one that the surviving spouse has elected to treat as her own) ends "at the earlier of the end of either the 5-taxable-year period" for the deceased spouse's Roth IRA or that applicable to the surviving spouse's own Roth IRAs. Reg. § 1.408A-6 (Q & A 7(b)).

A distribution from a Roth IRA inherited by a surviving spouse that the spouse has rolled over to her own Roth IRA or elected to treat as her own Roth IRA is *not* "treated as made after the IRA owner's death." Reg. § 1.408A-6 (Q & A 3). Thus, even after expiration of the Five-Year Period, the spouse may not receive qualified distributions from the rollover account until she herself reaches age 59½ (unless another exception applies—see Chapter 9).

For more special rules for the surviving spouse, see *"1998 conversions: death during the four year period,"* below.

How the Ordering Rules apply to a decedent's Roth IRA

If a Roth IRA owner dies, leaving his Roth IRA(s) to more than one beneficiary, and his death occurs at a time when the Ordering Rules might matter (*i.e.*, before the end of the "Five-Year Period" necessary to have a qualified distribution), the various components of the decedent's Roth IRA(s) that matter for purposes of the Ordering Rules are carried over and allocated pro rata among the beneficiaries who inherit the Roth IRA(s). Reg. § 1.408A-6 (Q & A 11).

This section of the regulations indicates that such carryover and allocation also is necessary if the decedent died within five taxable years after doing a pre-age 59½ conversion, as if the 10% penalty could apply to distributions to the decedent's beneficiaries. However, distributions after death are excepted from the 10% penalty (§ 72(t)(2)(A)(ii)); and the regulations provide that the § 72(t) exceptions are available even for distributions within the five years following a conversion (Reg. § 1.408A-6 (Q & A 5(b)), so the author does not see how the 10% penalty could apply to such distributions.

Is this carryover and allocation in case of death within the five years following a pre-age 59½ conversion important for a surviving spouse who inherits a Roth IRA and elects to treat it as her own? Generally, the regulations provide that, when a surviving spouse elects to treat an inherited Roth IRA as his or her own, § 72(t) is applied as if the surviving spouse, *not* the decedent, were the owner of the account. Reg. § 1.408A-2 (Q & A 4). Does Reg. § 1.408A-6 (Q & A 11), suggest that, even though the surviving spouse is now treated as the owner for purposes of § 72(t), she still carries over the decedent's potential liability for the 10% penalty, if distributions occur within five years after the decedent's conversion? What if the surviving spouse is already over age 59½? Further clarification from the IRS is needed on this point.

Other rules for tax treatment of inherited Roth IRAs

Non-spouse beneficiaries cannot roll over an inherited Roth IRA (or convert an inherited traditional IRA to a Roth IRA), due to the prohibition on rolling over inherited IRAs. § 408(d)(3)(C).

Generally, if an individual (other than the surviving spouse—see above) inherits a Roth IRA, and also has a Roth IRA funded by his own contributions, the Five-Year Period runs separately ("is determined independently") for the two types. Reg. § 1.408A-6 (Q & A 7(b)). A beneficiary cannot aggregate an inherited Roth IRA with his own Roth IRA for purposes of the minimum distribution rules. Reg. § 1.408A-6 (Q & A 15).

1998 conversions: death during the four-year period

If a person who made a 1998 conversion dies before the end of the four-year spread period, all the deemed income for the rest of the four-year period is accelerated onto the decedent's final return. § 408A(d)(3)(E)(i).

However, if P's surviving spouse is the sole beneficiary of all of his Roth IRAs, the spouse "may elect to treat the remaining amounts [that have not yet been included in the decedent's return] as includible in the spouse's gross income in the taxable years of the spouse ending with or within the taxable years of such [decedent] in which such amounts would otherwise have been includible." This election is made on form

8606 or 1040, and may not be made (or changed) after the due date of the surviving spouse's tax return for the year of death. § 408A(d)(3)(E)(ii); Reg. § 1.408A-4 (Q & A 11).

If the election is made, the one-fourth instalment for the year of death is included on the decedent's final income tax return, and subsequent instalments are included on the surviving spouse's return. Reg. § 1.408A-4 (Q & A 11(b)). The surviving spouse also then becomes subject to the acceleration provision if she takes a distribution from the conversion amount prior to 2001. Reg. § 1.408A-6 (Q & A 6).

Presumably, the surviving spouse will make the election if (1) she is also the beneficiary of the rest of the estate and (2) accelerating the income onto the decedent's final return would cost her (as beneficiary of his estate) more than if she pays the taxes herself (as beneficiary of the Roth IRA) over the rest of the four-year spread period. Query, if she is *not* the beneficiary of the rest of the estate, does electing to assume the decedent's tax liability constitute a gift by the surviving spouse to the beneficiaries of the estate?

If the surviving spouse, having made the election, then herself dies before the end of the four year period, it appears that the remaining instalments are accelerated onto her return; see § 408A(d)(E)(ii)(I); although possibly if she has remarried and leaves the Roth IRA to the new spouse, he could again make the election to take over the payments.

Contributions, conversions and unconversions by the personal representative

"The election to recharacterize a contribution...may be made on behalf of a deceased IRA owner by his or her executor, administrator, or other person responsible for filing the final Federal income tax return of the decedent under section 6012(b)(1)." Reg. § 1.408A-5 (Q & A 6(c)).

The regulations do not address other issues; for rights of a personal representative regarding "traditional" IRAs, see *"What if S dies before rolling over?,"* Chapter 3.

Miscellaneous

State law problems: creditors and taxes and?

Many states' laws exempt IRAs from creditors' claims, but in many of these states the exemption refers to a specific Code section, namely § 408—which describes only traditional IRAs. Roth IRAs would presumably not be protected in such states without a legislative change. Similar problems can be expected with any state laws that deal specifically with IRAs by reference to § 408. For example, in states whose tax laws do not automatically follow federal Code changes, Roth IRAs may not receive favorable tax treatment without a legislative change.

Basis in property distributed from a Roth IRA

"The basis of property distributed from a Roth IRA is its fair market value as of the date of the distribution." Reg. § 1.408A-6 (Q & A 16).

Excess contributions: 6% penalty

There is an excise tax of 6% imposed on contributions to Roth IRAs in excess of the applicable limits, just as there is for excess contributions to traditional IRAs. § 4973; Reg. § 1.408A-3 (Q & A 7). This excise tax would apply, for example, to a person who converted an IRA to a Roth IRA in 1998 but was not eligible to do so—for example, because he had more than $100,000 of income. The "failed" conversion would be treated as a (taxable) distribution from the traditional IRA (and not eligible for the four-year spread, and subject to the 10% penalty under § 72(t) if the individual is under 59½), followed by an excess contribution to the Roth IRA. To avoid the penalty, the person would have to recharacterize the contribution. This excise is imposed *annually* on the excess contribution, until the excess contribution is distributed (together with the net income thereon).

Summary of Planning Principles

1.   Generally, it is easier to get money out of a Roth IRA tax-free than out of other retirement plans: P can withdraw his own contributions tax-free any time, and all distributions are tax-free after age 59½ once the account has been open five years. The only significant exceptions are that a person who converted to a Roth IRA in 1998 and elected the four-year spread will suffer some acceleration of the income tax if he withdraws from the account during the first three years, and a person who converts to a Roth while under age 59½ may have to pay a 10% penalty if he withdraws from the account within five years of the conversion.

2.   Funding a Roth IRA with annual contributions of up to $2,000 is an excellent tax shelter for individuals who have "compensation income" but are in a low income tax bracket; establishing such accounts for young family members may be a good way for parents and grandparents to make gifts.

3.   Converting a traditional IRA to a Roth IRA offers those who meet the income limit a chance to eliminate required lifetime distributions and (if they can pay the income tax on the conversion from other assets) a way to increase the tax-free portion of their investments.

4.   Consider converting traditional IRAs to Roth IRAs to accomplish some or all of the following goals, especially for an individual with a severely shortened life expectancy: simplifying income tax reporting for heirs; removing income taxes from the estate tax base; and (if the client is past his RBD) choosing a new DB with a long life expectancy.

5.   Other estate and tax planning reasons to consider converting a traditional IRA to a Roth IRA include: eliminating the drawbacks of naming the spouse as DB at the RBD; allowing the possibility of changing DBs (even after age 70½) to ever-younger family members, to capitalize on the tax-free build-up of the account over a long life expectancy; increasing the funding for a credit shelter or generation skipping trust; taking advantage of a low income tax bracket in the conversion year as compared to later years; taking advantage of a participant's low income tax bracket, as compared to that of the prospective beneficiary; and (after age 70½) correcting choices made at the RBD regarding beneficiary designation or method of determining life expectancy.

6.   A person under age 59½ can convert to a Roth, but must either pay the income tax on the conversion from other funds or pay a 10% penalty if he withdraws the needed money from the converted account (or from an unconverted IRA).

7.   The decision to convert is not irrevocable, since "recharacterization" (unconversion) offers a penalty-free way to back out of the conversion decision up until the extended due date of the tax return.

Retirement Benefits Payable to Trusts

> *A participant whose benefits are payable to a trust will not have a "designated beneficiary" unless the IRS's trust rules are complied with. The rules are not difficult to comply with if you plan for them, but are also easy to violate if you don't keep them in mind.*

The IRS's Minimum Distribution Trust Rules

In this chapter, "proposed regulation" refers to Prop. Reg. § 1.401(a)(9)-1 (as modified December 30, 1997). The "Trust Review Questionnaire" in App. C can be used to determine whether a particular trust complies with these rules.

IRS "trust rules" permit treating trust beneficiaries as DBs

Although the general rule is that a designated beneficiary (DB) must be an *individual*, the proposed regulations allow you to name a *trust* as beneficiary and still have a DB. These rules permit you to look through a trust instrument, and treat the *trust beneficiaries* as if they had been named directly as beneficiaries of the benefits, if the following four requirements are met:

1.   The trust must be valid under state law.
2.   The beneficiaries must be "identifiable from the trust instrument."

3.   "The trust is irrevocable or will, by its terms, become irrevocable upon the death of the" participant.

4.   Certain documentation must be provided to "the plan administrator."

If the participant (P) dies before the required beginning date (RBD), and the above four rules are satisfied, then, for purposes of § 401(a)(9), "distributions to the trust...will be treated as being paid to the appropriate beneficiary of the trust with respect to the trust's interest in the employee's benefit, and all beneficiaries of the trust with respect to the trust's interest in the employee's benefit will be treated as designated beneficiaries of the employee under the plan for purposes of determining the distribution period under" § 401(a)(9)(B)(iii) [distributions to non-spouse individual beneficiary] and (iv) [surviving spouse is the designated beneficiary]." Prop. Reg. § D-6.

Similarly, if the trust rules are satisfied as of the RBD, then, for purposes of distributions at and after the RBD, "distributions made to the trust will be treated as paid to the beneficiaries of the trust with respect to the trust's interest in the employee's benefit, and the beneficiaries of the trust will be treated as having been designated as beneficiaries of the employee under the plan." Prop. Reg. § D-5(a).

However, just complying with these four rules does not in and of itself ensure that the "life expectancy" method will be available. For one thing, treating the trust beneficiaries as if they had been named as beneficiaries directly does not get you very far if the trust beneficiaries themselves do not qualify as "designated beneficiaries." Accordingly, the "fifth rule" is that:

5.   All beneficiaries of the trust must be individuals.

Finally, there is another rule, not contained in the "trust" portion of the proposed regulations, but applicable to retirement benefits generally, which may affect the eligibility of a particular trust to use the life expectancy method:

6.   No person may have the power to change the beneficiary after the participant's death. Prop. Reg. § E-5(f).

The implications of this "sixth rule" are not yet fully established. See *"Sixth Rule,"* below.

The rules are not terribly difficult to comply with in most typical estate planning situations. The obstacles to success are, first, that most people are unaware of these rules and, second, that the application of the rules to several commonly used trust provisions is unclear at best and unfavorable at worst.

Effects of complying with (or flunking) the trust rules

If a trust is named as beneficiary of retirement benefits, and all these rules are complied with, the individual trust beneficiaries will be treated as P's DBs for purposes of § 401(a)(9), and the following favorable results ensue.

First, if P dies before his RBD, the "five year rule" will not be the only choice for distribution of benefits; benefits can be distributed to the trust (under the rule dealing with multiple designated beneficiaries) (see "Who Are the Beneficiaries of a Trust?" below) over the life expectancy of the oldest trust beneficiary. Prop. Reg. § E-5(A)(1). If the rules are *not* complied with, then the five year rule will apply and all of the benefits must be distributed to the trust by the end of the year that contains the fifth anniversary of P's death.

Second, if P reaches his RBD alive, he can compute his minimum required distributions (MRDs) using the joint life expectancy of himself and the oldest trust beneficiary. Prop. Reg. § E-5(A)(1). If the rules are not complied with, MRDs will be based on P's life expectancy only.

Finally, if P's spouse is the primary trust beneficiary, some of the special favorable rules for spouse-beneficiaries may be available; see *"When is a trust for the spouse the same as the spouse?"* below.

At what point compliance is tested

The rules apply slightly differently depending on whether P dies before his RBD or reaches his RBD alive; these differences will be noted with respect to each requirement.

In general, in the case of death *before* the RBD, the requirements must be met as of the date of death (except the documentation requirement, which must be met by the end of the ninth month after death; see *"Fourth Rule: documentation requirement: death before RBD,"* below).

In general, in the case of *lifetime* required distributions, the requirements must be met as of the RBD (or as of the date the trust is named as beneficiary, if later) and at all subsequent times (except the irrevocability requirement, which applies as of the date of death; see *"The new requirement as to irrevocability,"* below).

Let us next look at each of the requirements in turn.

Note: Some of the following discussion deals with what must be done or what must occur "as of the participant's required beginning date." In fact, the trust requirements applicable to lifetime required distributions apply at the RBD, or, *if later*, at the date the trust is named as beneficiary. Prop. Reg. § D-5(b). For the sake of brevity, in this chapter, "as of the RBD" means "as of the RBD (or as of the date the trust is named as beneficiary, if later than the RBD)."

First Rule: trust must be valid under state law

The first requirement is that "The trust is a valid trust under state law, or would be but for the fact that there is no corpus." Prop. Reg. § D-5(b)(1). This requirement presumably poses no obstacle in cases of death before the RBD.

If P does *not* die before the RBD, then the requirement must be met as of the RBD. Some practitioners are concerned that a testamentary trust is not a "valid trust under state law" as of the RBD if P is still alive, because the trust is not yet "in existence." This concern is misplaced. This rule does not (and is not intended to) prohibit the use of testamentary trusts as beneficiaries of retirement benefits.

If the testamentary trust will be a valid trust under state law after P's death (when it will be funded), then this requirement is satisfied. There is absolutely no requirement that the trust be "in existence" on the RBD. The clause "or would be [valid] but for the fact that there is no corpus" is clearly intended to *negate* the necessity of having a trust that is "in existence" on the RBD. The rule requires only that the trust, as it is written on the RBD, will be, once it receives the retirement benefits (*i.e.* once P has died), a legal trust that can be carried out in accordance with its terms under applicable state law.

The only trusts which would flunk this rule would be those which failed to meet some essential state law requirement of a valid trust—for example, a trust with no beneficiaries, or a trust which violated the rule against perpetuities.

Second Rule: beneficiaries must be identifiable

The requirement that the beneficiaries of the trust be "identifiable" means that it must be possible, at the applicable time, to determine who is the oldest person who could ever be a beneficiary of this trust. We need to ascertain who the oldest beneficiary is because it is the oldest beneficiary (or, as the IRS puts it, the "beneficiary with the shortest life expectancy") whose life expectancy is used as the measuring period under the minimum distribution rules.

A beneficiary "need not be specified by name" so long as he is "identifiable." Prop. Reg. § D-2. For example, a trust which provides that "all benefits will be distributed to my children" has "identifiable" beneficiaries; even though they are not named, the membership of the class of beneficiaries is fixed and determinable as of the date of P's death.

"The members of a class of beneficiaries capable of expansion or contraction will be treated as being identifiable if it is possible at the applicable time to identify the class member with the shortest life expectancy." Prop. Reg. § D-2(a)(1). Thus, if the trust beneficiaries are "all my issue living from time to time," the beneficiaries are "identifiable" even though the class is not closed as of the applicable date, since no person with a shorter life expectancy can be added later; the oldest member of the class can be determined with certainty on the applicable date.

Adoption of Adults

Actually, there is one potential problem with even this simple and typical provision: if people who are issue by virtue of legal adoption are to be included on the same basis as "natural" issue, there is a potential for violating the rule. After P's death, one of his issue could adopt someone who was born earlier than the person who was the oldest beneficiary of the trust at the time of P's death. It is not known whether the IRS would ever raise this "issue," but to avoid the problem, language can be included in the trust providing that older individuals cannot be later added to the class of trust beneficiaries by legal adoption; see Appendix B, form 7.3.

The rule that the beneficiaries must be "identifiable" is similar to the rule against perpetuities, in that the mere *possibility* that an older beneficiary could be added to the trust after the applicable date is enough to make the trust "flunk" this rule, regardless of whether any such older beneficiary ever is *actually* added.

Example: Kit leaves his IRA to a trust which is to pay income to his daughter Julia for her life, and after her death is to pay income to her widower (if any) for his life, with remainder to Kit's grandchildren. Kit dies before his RBD, survived by Julia (who is divorced) and several grandchildren. His trust flunks this Second Rule, because Julia, after Kit's death, *could* marry a new husband who was older than she. Thus an older beneficiary *could* be added to this trust after the applicable date.

Any trustee "**spray power**" or other "**power of appointment**" under which older beneficiaries *could* be added to the trust at a later date violates this rule. However, the possible later addition of "unidentifiable" beneficiaries (by means of a power of appointment or otherwise) can be ignored if it could occur, under the terms of the trust, only in case of the "premature" death of a prior beneficiary; see "*Disregarding certain contingent beneficiaries,*" below.

Third Rule: irrevocability requirement: the old rule

Under the proposed regulations issued in 1987, one of the "trust rules" was that a trust named as beneficiary of retirement benefits had to be irrevocable. This requirement applied as of the date of death, or, if earlier, as of P's RBD.

This rule was a trap for the unwary, since most estate plans use *revocable* trusts (either revocable "living" trusts or testamentary trusts). Even for the wary it posed many estate planning complications. Now the IRS has dropped this requirement.

The original reason for this rule, presumably, was the plan administrator's need for certainty as to the identity of the designated beneficiary. If the plan administrator made distributions to a participant based on the joint life expectancy of P and a beneficiary of a revocable trust, P could amend or revoke that trust without telling the plan administrator, and then the plan could be disqualified for failure to comply with the minimum distribution rules. The new proposed regulation (December 1997) solves this problem by making changes in the documentation requirements; essentially, the burden is on P to inform the plan administrator of any amendments to the trust. See *"Fourth Rule, continued: documentation requirement (at RBD),"* below.

The new requirement as to irrevocability

The new "third rule" is: "The trust is irrevocable or will, by its terms, become irrevocable upon the death of the employee." Prop. Reg. § D-5(b)(2).

The requirement that the trust will become irrevocable *"by its terms"* upon the death of P is causing concern to some practitioners, who fear that a testamentary trust does not become irrevocable "by its terms" on the testator's death—it becomes irrevocable *de facto* because the testator has died. Your author claims no special insight into the IRS's reason for this wording, but nevertheless is confident that any typical testamentary trust or revocable living trust meets the requirement, based on the following logic:

1.   The "terms" of a trust are not only those which are written in the instrument, but also include those which are automatically part of the trust by virtue of state law.

2.   A deceased person cannot revoke his will, nor can his personal representative revoke it on his behalf; therefore, "by its terms," a testamentary trust is "irrevocable" as of the testator's death.

3.   A deceased person cannot revoke an *inter vivos* trust he created, nor (unless the trust instrument expressly provides otherwise) can his personal representative revoke it. Therefore, a normal *inter vivos* trust created solely by P becomes irrevocable "by its terms" as of P's death.

Although, in planning mode, it wouldn't hurt to include in the trust a statement such as "This trust shall be irrevocable upon my death" (to appease possible future plan administrators and auditing IRS agents) this is certainly not necessary, since any testamentary trust or "living trust" automatically becomes irrevocable upon the testator's or donor's death, and therefore passes this test.

Unfortunately, it is not clear what the IRS is driving at with this rule; perhaps they are thinking of a situation where someone *other than* P has a power to "revoke" the trust after P's death. For example, a surviving spouse with a community property interest in the retirement benefits might have that power, or P might have left his benefits to a trust which is "revocable" by his spouse or someone else, and these trusts would fail this rule.

Fourth Rule: documentation requirement (death before RBD)

The former requirement that certain documentation be provided to "the plan" was substantially modified by the revisions to the proposed regulations issued in December 1997.

Under the new rule (Prop. Reg. § D-7), the *time limit* for supplying information about the trust to the plan administrator is "the end of the ninth month beginning after the death of" P (not "as of" the date of death, as under the 1987 version of the proposed regulations). The *person* who must fulfill the documentation requirement is "the trustee of the trust" [*i.e.*, the trust that is named as beneficiary]. And the documentation that must be supplied is *either* a copy of the trust instrument, *or* certain summary information about the trust beneficiaries (with an agreement to provide a full copy of the trust if requested). Under the prior version of the proposed regulations, providing a copy of the trust instrument was the only method of compliance allowed.

Supplying a copy of the trust would appear to be a simpler way of complying than providing a summary of who the beneficiaries are. However, some plans may decide to *require* the alternative method of compliance, since it relieves the plan administrator of the burden of reading the trust and determining whether it complies with all the technical requirements of the trust rules.

Here is an exact statement of the documentation that must be sent to the plan administrator in the case of a participant who dies before his RBD: "By the end of the ninth month beginning after the death of the employee, the trustee of the trust must either—

"(1) Provide the plan administrator with a final list of all of the beneficiaries of the trust (including contingent and remainderman beneficiaries with a description of the conditions on their entitlement) as of the date of death; certify that, to the best of the trustee's knowledge, this list is correct and complete and that the requirements of paragraph (b)(1), (2) and (3) of D-5A [*i.e.*, trust is valid under state law, trust will be irrevocable by its terms as of the date of P's death, beneficiaries are identifiable] are satisfied as of the date of death; and agree to provide a copy of the trust instrument to the plan administrator upon demand; or

"(2) Provide the plan administrator with a copy of the actual trust document for the trust that is named as a beneficiary of the employee under the plan as of the employee's date of death."

For sample forms to comply with this requirement, see Appendix B, Forms 8.1 and 8.2.

The documentation requirement: how to comply

Under the version of the proposed regulations that existed from July 1987 to December 1997, the documentation requirement was that "a copy of the trust instrument" had to be provided to "the plan," "as of the date of death." This wording made it sound as though "after" the date of death might be too late. Based on hints from the IRS, there was reason to believe that providing the documentation to the plan shortly after the date of death, before the first required distribution was made, was sufficient. However, not all plan administrators were willing to rely on such "hints."

Under the new revised documentation requirement, it is now clear that no documentation need be provided to the plan prior to the date of death. The deadline is now the end of the ninth month beginning after the date of death.

Planning mode: For the client who has not yet reached his RBD, and who wants to name a trust as beneficiary of his retirement benefits, filing a copy of the trust with the plan administrator is not required until after the date of death. Filing a copy of the trust pre-death does not help in any way, *if* the client actually dies before his RBD. The survivors get no "insurance protection" by filing a copy of the trust pre-death because it appears that, under the new rule, the trustee is required to file a "final" copy of the trust with the plan after the date of death *anyway*, so filing it in advance does not help.

On the other hand, there would still appear to be some advantage to filing a copy of the trust with the plan administrator along with the beneficiary designation form, namely: the client and planner have the comfort of knowing that if the client does *not* die before his RBD, the requirement of filing a copy of the trust with the plan administrator *by* the RBD has been complied with. Accordingly, planners may choose to file the trust with the plan if the client's RBD is "on the horizon"—say less than five years away.

Fourth Rule, continued: documentation requirement (at RBD)

A participant who reaches or has reached his RBD, and wants to name a trust as beneficiary of his plan benefits, and wants to determine his minimum required distributions using the joint life expectancy of himself and the oldest beneficiary of the trust, must provide certain documentation to the plan administrator, *before* (or on) the RBD (or on or before the date the trust is named as beneficiary, if that is later than the RBD). This participant has a choice: he can *either*:

(1) Provide to the plan administrator a copy of the trust instrument and [the rest of this sentence presumably applies only if the trust is *in fact* revocable or amendable] agree that if the trust instrument is amended at any time in the future, the participant will, within a reasonable time, provide to the plan administrator a copy of each such amendment; *or*

(2) Provide to the plan administrator a list of all the beneficiaries of the trust (including contingent and remainderman beneficiaries, with a description of the conditions on their entitlement); certify that, to the best of his knowledge,

this list is correct and complete and that the requirements of paragraphs (b)(1), (2) and (3) of D-5A [*i.e.*, trust is valid under state law, trust will be irrevocable by its terms as of the date of P's death, beneficiaries are identifiable] are satisfied; agree to provide corrected certifications to the extent that an amendment changes any information previously certified; and agree to provide a copy of the trust instrument to the plan administrator upon demand. Prop. Reg. § D-7(a).

Method 1 would appear to be a simpler way of complying than method 2. However, some plans may decide to require method 2, since it relieves the plan administrator of the burden of reading the trust and determining whether it complies with all the technical requirements of the trust rules. Also, some clients may prefer method 2 for privacy reasons.

Note that the person who must fulfill this requirement at the RBD is the *participant* (not the trustee, as is the case when P dies before the RBD). For sample forms to comply with this requirement, see Appendix B, Forms 8.3 and 8.4.

Effect on pre-1998 RBD participants

How does this change affect the person who was already past his RBD as of the date the new rules were issued (12/30/97), and who had named a trust as his beneficiary at or after his RBD, but who was out of compliance with the "irrevocable trust" requirement under the 1987 version of the proposed regulations?

Although that requirement no longer exists, this person is not automatically "saved" retroactively by the new rule unless, on or before his RBD (or on or before the date he named a revocable or testamentary trust as his beneficiary, if later than his RBD), he provided the plan administrator with a copy of his trust *and* agreed that if the trust instrument were amended, he would, within a reasonable time, send the plan administrator a copy of each such amendment. It hardly seems likely that anyone was so prescient. So the new proposed regulations unfortunately do not provide any "safe harbor" for individuals who were already past their RBD as of December 1997.

The IRS has not issued any guidance for these individuals. The IRS may take the view that, unless P has complied with *some* version of the proposed regulations, P cannot possibly have a DB if his benefits are payable to a trust, because the IRS may be of the opinion that allowing DB status to trust beneficiaries is a matter of grace on the IRS's part, so that the *only* way to get that result is to comply with whatever version of its proposed regulations is in effect at the applicable time. See also *"Legal status of proposed regulations,"* Chapter 1.

To whom is documentation provided?

The proposed regulations, although they apply to IRAs and 403(b) plans as well as "qualified" plans, are written in language that is designed for **qualified plans**. It is not clear, in the case of IRAs, who is the "plan administrator" who is to receive the documentation required under the Fourth Rule. IRAs do not have "plan administrators."

To date the only official pronouncement on this subject is the IRS's statement in the Preamble to the amended proposed regulations (December 1997) that the documentation must be provided to "the plan administrator *or IRA trustee, custodian or issuer*" (emphasis added). However, the proposed regulation itself says only "plan administrator"; and the Preamble is not even reproduced in most copies of the proposed regulations. There is no way the average planner (let alone retiree) could find this statement.

Arguably, if P himself had possession of the required

documentation (which he presumably would have in all cases—a copy of his own trust), this requirement is complied with. After all, P (and not the IRA custodian) is the one who is required to comply with the minimum distribution rules for his own IRA.

Conclusion: In *planning mode*, give the documentation to the IRA custodian or trustee and get a receipt. In *cleanup mode*, you must either take the position that P is the "plan administrator" of his own IRA, or capitulate and concede that P had no DB.

Fifth Rule: all trust beneficiaries must be individuals

As explained above (see *"IRS 'trust rules' permit treating trust beneficiaries as DBs"*), the result of compliance with the first four rules is that the *trust* beneficiaries will be treated as if P had named them *directly* as beneficiaries. The next step, therefore, is to make sure that these trust beneficiaries qualify as "designated beneficiaries," *i.e.*, that they are *individuals*. Prop. Reg. § D-2A, D-4(c), D-5(a) and E-5(a). This requirement is much trickier than it appears. First, some or all remainder beneficiaries count as beneficiaries for this purpose; see "Who Are the Beneficiaries of a Trust?" below.

Another major pitfall in this rule is that, according to the proposed regulations, an "estate" is not an individual and therefore an "estate" cannot be a DB. For comment on this IRS position, see *"Naming an estate as beneficiary: before the RBD,"* Chapter 1. Therefore, if any part of the trust's interest in the benefits will pass to an estate, P has "no DB" (unless the estate can be disregarded; see *"Disregarding certain contingent beneficiaries,"* below).

For problems this rule creates for a client who wants to benefit charity, see *"Benefits paid to a trust with charitable beneficiaries,"* Chapter 7.

Paying estate expenses, taxes, etc. from the trust

Some IRS letter rulings suggest that even *indirectly* allowing benefits to pass to P's estate (as through a trust provision which allows or directs the use of trust property to pay the deceased participant's debts or probate expenses) may be treated the same as naming the estate as a beneficiary and may result in having "no DB." See, *e.g.*, PLR 9809059 (12/4/97), in which part of an IRA was payable to "Trust K." In ruling that Trust K was entitled to use the "life expectancy method" for the IRA benefits payable to it, the IRS noted that "Trust K does *not* provide that trust assets shall be used to pay funeral costs," probate expenses or estate taxes (emphasis added). Although the ruling does not comment on the absence of such a provision, it merely recites the fact that the trust contained no such provision, one could conclude that the IRS ruled favorably on Trust K only because it did not contain the (forbidden?) clause.

What about estate taxes on the benefits themselves?

The language of PLR 9809059 suggests that even using trust property to pay estate taxes *attributable to the trust property* may be forbidden under the proposed regulations, but it is sincerely to be hoped that this is not actually the IRS's position. Since tax apportionment laws would give P's personal representative the right to recover such estate taxes from the trust property even if the trust instrument purports to prohibit such use, such a position on the part of the IRS would amount to saying that, despite the language of the proposed regulations permitting trust beneficiaries to be "designated beneficiaries," in fact such a result can only be obtained if either—

1.   The estate is too small to be subject to estate tax; or

2.   The deceased participant's will requires all estate taxes on the retirement benefits to be paid out of the probate estate *and* the probate estate is large enough to pay such taxes.

Furthermore, such an argument by the IRS would mean that even if P has named only one, individual, beneficiary (no trust involved) P will be deemed to have named *two* beneficiaries—the individual beneficiary and P's estate—unless (1) or (2) applies; and therefore P has "no DB."

What to do

Since the IRS is adamant that an "estate" is not an individual, it might be wise to include, in trusts which are to receive retirement benefits, a clause (such as Form 7.2, Appendix B) insulating such benefits from any trust provisions requiring or permitting the trustee to make payments to P's estate from trust property, and also insulating the benefits from any stray charitable bequests the trust may contain. This form will not help, however, if the retirement benefits are the only asset available to pay debts, expenses and estate taxes.

Sixth Rule: no changing beneficiaries after P's death

Prop. Reg. § E-5(f) provides that "If the plan provides (or allows the employee to specify) that, after the employee's death, any person or persons have the discretion to change the beneficiaries of the employee, then for purposes of determining the distribution period for both distributions before and after the employee's death, the employee will be treated as not having designated a beneficiary..." The intent and meaning of this provision are unclear. Might a **"spray" power** not limited by an ascertainable standard, or any other "**power of appointment**," be considered "the discretion to change the beneficiaries of the employee" after his death in violation of Prop. Reg. § E-5(f)?

Judging by recent letter rulings approving trusts which contained powers to appoint principal among the participant's issue (1999-03050, 1999-18065), the IRS apparently did not intend, by adopting § E-5(f), to prohibit this common estate planning device. Accordingly, it is commonly assumed that a power of appointment (or trustee spray power) that is *limited to a narrowly defined group* (such as P's "descendants," "children" or "issue") does not violate § E-5(f).

On the other hand, if the IRS intends to distinguish between these common estate planning devices (which are apparently permitted) and some broader category of "discretions" (which would be prohibited by § E-5(f)), the dividing line is not known. The IRS has never, to this author's knowledge, given any example of a beneficiary designation, plan provision or trust provision which would violate § E-5(f).

So, to err on the side of caution, until the IRS clarifies the boundaries, it would be wise to limit the potential appointees under a power of appointment to a narrow and clearly defined group, unless the power can be disregarded (see *"Disregarding certain contingent beneficiaries,"* in the next section).

Who Are the Beneficiaries of a Trust?

Introduction

For several purposes under the minimum distribution rules of § 401(a)(9) it is necessary to determine who are the "beneficiaries" of a trust:

1. Are the beneficiaries of the trust "identifiable" (see *"Second Rule,"* above)?

2. Are all beneficiaries of the trust individuals (see "*Fifth Rule*," above)?

3. Which trust beneficiary has the shortest life expectancy?

Despite the importance of the term "beneficiaries of the trust" for all of these questions, the proposed regulations never define that term.

Beneficiaries with respect to the trust's interest in the benefits

In determining who are the "beneficiaries," we need be concerned only with beneficiaries who are such "with respect to the trust's interest in the employee's benefit." Prop. Reg. §§ D-5(a), D-6(a).

Example 1: Calvin's IRA is payable to a trust. At his death the trust assets are divided between a marital trust and a credit shelter trust. However, Calvin's IRA is required to be paid to the marital trust (either because the plan beneficiary designation form names the marital trust directly as beneficiary, or because the trust requires that all retirement benefits are to be allocated to the marital trust). We need look only at the *beneficiaries of the marital trust* in applying the various tests and questions. However, if neither the beneficiary designation form nor the trust instrument required (as of the applicable date) that all benefits be paid to one share or the other, then we need to look at all beneficiaries of both shares.

Example 2: Katerina's 401(k) plan benefits are payable to her living trust as beneficiary. The trust provides for distributions to be made to her husband Lou, various relatives and assorted charities. However, the trust contains a provision prohibiting use of retirement benefits to pay charitable bequests. Accordingly, the charities should not be considered trust beneficiaries "with respect to the trust's interest in the employee benefit," and can be disregarded.

Note that this is not a "separate account" rule (see "*Naming more than one beneficiary*," Chapter 1); disregarding beneficiaries who are prohibited from sharing in the retirement benefit does not depend on the existence of "separate accounts" at the plan level or segregated "trust shares" in the usual tax or trust accounting sense. The conclusions in these examples are based on the proposed regulations' statement that "all beneficiaries of the trust *with respect to the trust's interest in the employee's benefit*" (emphasis added) will be treated as the beneficiaries of the employee. Prop. Reg. § D-6(a). *In the rest of this discussion, "beneficiaries of the trust" means "beneficiaries of the trust with respect to the trust's interest in the employee's benefit."*

Second, we must conclude that "all" trust beneficiaries ("current" beneficiaries, as well as those who have vested or contingent remainder interests) are considered "beneficiaries of the trust" for purposes of the proposed regulations—unless they can be excluded from consideration under Prop. Reg. § E-5.

What the proposed regulations say: § E-5

If the trust rules are complied with, then all "trust beneficiaries" are treated as having been named directly as beneficiaries by P. If the trust has more than one beneficiary, then: "In the case of payments to a trust having more than one beneficiary, see E-5 of this section for the rules for determining the designated beneficiary whose life expectancy will be used to determine the distribution period." For some unknown reason, in both the 1987 and 1997 versions of the proposed regulations, this cross reference is included only in Prop. Reg. § D-5(b) (trust named as beneficiary at and after the RBD) but presumably it applies equally to the interpretation of § D-6 (trust as beneficiary, death before the RBD).

Furthermore, for some other unknown reason, the cross-reference provides that § E-5 is to be referred to for "determining the designated beneficiary whose life expectancy will be used to determine the distribution period," with no mention of whether it can also be used for other needed purposes, such as determining whether all beneficiaries are individuals. Despite this omission, however, § E-5 is apparently supposed to be used for both purposes. See, *e.g.*, PLR 9809059.

Here is what § E-5 says: "If a beneficiary's entitlement to an employee's benefit is contingent on the death of a prior beneficiary, such contingent beneficiary will not be considered a beneficiary for purposes of determining who is the designated beneficiary with the shortest life expectancy...or whether a beneficiary who is not an individual is a beneficiary." Prop. Reg. § E-5(e)(1). "Except as provided in [Prop. Reg. § E-5(e)(1)] if a beneficiary's entitlement to an employee's benefit is contingent on an event other than the employee's death...such contingent beneficiary *is* considered to be a designated beneficiary for purposes of determining which designated beneficiary has the shortest life expectancy." Prop. Reg. § E-5(b) (emphasis added).

Are remaindermen beneficiaries?

Suppose a trust names the decedent's child as life beneficiary. The trust is to pay all income to child for life, and on child's death the principal goes to the Red Cross. In this example, the charity's interest is *postponed* until the death of the income beneficiary, but is not *contingent* on his death (unless you postulate that the income beneficiary may never die). Accordingly, the Red Cross, as remainder beneficiary, *is* counted as a beneficiary of the trust, and therefore this trust "flunks" the rule because not all beneficiaries are individuals. See PLR 9820021 (2/18/98) (a trust which provided income to spouse and remainder to charities; ruled, P had "no DB"); see also, *e.g.*, PLR 9322005 (2/24/93) (marital trust to a spouse for life, remainder to children; spouse *and children* regarded as beneficiaries).

Thus, if a trust with a vested charitable remainder is named as beneficiary of retirement plan death benefits, the participant "has no DB," and must accordingly, at his RBD, withdraw his benefits over a period not exceeding his own life expectancy; he cannot use the joint life expectancy of himself and the income beneficiary of the trust. Any benefits paid to a trust of this type would have to be paid out within five years after the date of death of a participant who died before his RBD.

Disregarding certain contingent beneficiaries

Remainder beneficiaries can be disregarded if *either*:

1.   The trust is treated as 100% owned by the life beneficiary under § 678; see "*The 100% Grantor Trust*," below; or

2.   Prop. Reg. § E-5 permits such remainder beneficiary to be disregarded. The rest of this subsection discusses the "disregard" test of § E-5.

Although holders of *vested* remainder interests are considered "beneficiaries," Prop. Reg. § E-5 says that some (not all) *contingent* beneficiaries can be disregarded. At this point we come to the hidden actuarial component of these proposed regulations. § E-5 says a beneficiary can be disregarded if his, her or its right to the benefits is contingent on the death of a "prior" beneficiary (other contingencies which might affect the distribution being disregarded). What this means is that a beneficiary can be disregarded if his, her or its rights are contingent on the *premature* death of a prior beneficiary, *i.e.*, the death of the prior beneficiary before the end of such prior beneficiary's IRS-defined life expectancy.

So, to test a trust on this point, project what will become of the benefits if all individual beneficiaries live to their full IRS-defined life expectancies. For this purpose, "individual beneficiaries" means beneficiaries who are living on the applicable date, and also includes later-born siblings of now-living individuals. If the benefits *must* be distributed to individual beneficiaries in that case, the trust passes this test.

Example 1: Hunter leaves his IRA to a trust which provides "income to my wife Anita for life, and on her death the principal shall pass to such of our three children, Peter, Paul and Mary, as are then living, or, if all of them are deceased, shall pass to The Massachusetts Audubon Society." Massachusetts Audubon Society is not an individual. However, since the Society's interest is contingent on Peter, Paul and Mary dying before their mother, its interest is contingent on the *premature* deaths of prior beneficiaries and therefore can be disregarded.

Example 2: Elana leaves her IRA to a trust for the benefit of her child Joshua, age 6. The trustee is given discretion to use income and principal for Joshua's support and education. The trust is to terminate, with all remaining assets being distributed to Joshua outright, when Joshua reaches age 30. If Joshua dies before age 30, the Cornell Ornithological Laboratory receives the trust property. In determining whether all trust beneficiaries are individuals, Cornell is disregarded, because its interest does not take effect unless the individual beneficiary (Joshua) dies before age 30, *i.e.*, well before the end of his life expectancy.

Example 3: This is like a combination of Examples 1 and 2: Pat leaves her IRA to a trust to pay income to her daughter Shannon for life. Upon Shannon's death, the principal is to be distributed to Shannon's children, with each child receiving his or her share outright at age 35. If all Shannon's children die without issue before Shannon's youngest child reaches age 35, the remaining trust assets will be distributed to charity. At Pat's RBD, Shannon has two children. Because all the benefits will be distributed to individuals if Shannon and her children (including later-born siblings of the now-living children) live to their life expectancy, the charity can be disregarded.

Examples 1, 2 and 3 are common "vanilla" estate planning examples which "pass" the requirement that all beneficiaries must be individuals, because, in these examples, the contingent charitable remainder beneficiaries can be disregarded under § E-5. Furthermore, whenever a remainder beneficiary can be disregarded under § E-5 because its interest is contingent on the death of a prior beneficiary, other normally "forbidden" clauses (such as a power to appoint to charity, or to older "unidentifiable" beneficiaries) that would apply to the benefits only upon such event can *also* be disregarded.

The following examples test the limits of E-5. While this author's reading of § E-5 would lead to certain answers, others may disagree with this interpretation.

Example 4: Consider Example 2 again but change the facts slightly: What if Elana's trust for Joshua is not to be distributed outright to Joshua until age 60 rather than age 30? Or what if the trust requires the trustee to determine Joshua's life expectancy as of Elana's date of death, and then to distribute the principal to Joshua one year prior to the end of that life expectancy period? If all E-5 requires is that the benefits will be paid to an existing individual if he lives to his IRS-defined life expectancy, these trust provisions would "pass" and the charity would be disregarded.

Example 5: Rhoda leaves her $1 million IRA to a **generation skipping** "dynasty" trust. The trust will pay all income to her issue living from time to time. The trust will terminate and be distributed to her then-living issue 90 years after her death; or, in default of issue, shall be distributed to charity. Rhoda has two living children and six grandchildren, the youngest of whom is age 10. This trust will extend beyond the IRS-defined life expectancy of the youngest now-living beneficiary. The charity will inherit the trust at the end of the 90 years, *if* by that time all of Rhoda's existing issue have died without issue. The charity's interest is contingent on something (a default of issue) other than strictly "death of a prior beneficiary before the end of his life expectancy," so this trust does not pass the strictest interpretation of Prop. Reg. § E-5, which apparently does not recognize any other contingency, no matter how remote.

Effect of powers of appointment

It appears that if a "countable" remainder interest is subject to a power of appointment upon the death of the life beneficiary, all potential appointees are considered "beneficiaries." Thus all such potential appointees must be (i) identifiable (ii) individuals who are (iii) younger than the beneficiary whose life expectancy is the one that the parties want to use to measure distributions, if you want the trust to "pass."

For example, "The trustee shall pay income to my spouse for life, and upon my spouse's death the principal shall be paid to such persons among the class consisting of our issue as my spouse shall appoint by her will" does not create a problem under this rule because the power is limited to a small, clearly-defined group (see *"Sixth Rule,"* above) of "identifiable" younger individuals. But "...upon my spouse's death the principal shall be paid to such members of the class consisting of our issue and any charity as my spouse shall appoint by her will" *does* create a problem: the benefits could pass under the power to a non-individual beneficiary, so this trust apparently flunks this rule.

(This does not mean that, so long as potential appointees are limited to younger individuals, a power of appointment is automatically "ok"; see *"Sixth Rule: no changing beneficiaries after P's death,"* above.)

Finally, if exercise of the power of appointment can affect the benefits only at a point where a contingent beneficiary could be ignored, the power can also be ignored. In other words, if you could disregard a contingent beneficiary, you can disregard a power of appointment that would determine the identity of that contingent beneficiary. See *"Disregarding certain contingent beneficiaries,"* above.

Example 6: Ned leaves his IRA to a trust which provides "income to my wife Jane for life, and on her death the principal shall pass to any individual or charity Jane designates in her will." The charity and "unidentifiable" beneficiaries Jane could appoint to are considered beneficiaries of the trust. This trust flunks rules 2 and 5 and possibly 6.

Example 7: Dudley leaves his IRA to a trust for the benefit of his child Haven, age 6. The trustee is given discretion to use income and principal for Haven's support and education. The trust is to terminate, with all remaining assets being distributed to Haven outright, when Haven reaches age 30. If Haven dies before age 30, the trust is distributed to any individual or charity Haven designates in his will. The charity and "unidentifiable" beneficiaries Haven could appoint to are disregarded, because no interest can pass to them unless the individual beneficiary

(Haven) dies before age 30, *i.e.*, well before the end of his life expectancy.

When is a trust for the spouse the same as the spouse?

Theoretically, if retirement benefits are payable to a trust, and the spouse ("S") is "the beneficiary" of that trust, and P dies before age 70½, § 401(a)(9) will apply as if S herself were the DB. Prop. Reg. § D-6(a). Under § 401(a)(9)(B)(iv), the trust would then have the right to defer commencement of distribution of the benefits until the year P would have reached age 70½; and if S also dies before that point is reached, she herself will be considered "the participant" for purposes of applying the five-year rule and its exceptions. See "The Spouse and § 401(a)(9)," Chapter 3. Also, P's lifetime distributions would not be subject to the MDIB rule.

Unfortunately, it is not clear what rights S must have under the trust in order to be considered the "beneficiary" of the trust for this purpose. Is it enough that she has the right to all of the income for life, and no principal can be distributed to anyone other than her (the requirements for the marital deduction)?

The proposed regulations suggest that, if S is not the *sole* beneficiary of the trust, then the trust is not entitled to the benefit of § 401(a)(9)(B)(iv), postponing distributions until P would have reached age 70½. Rather, the trust will be stuck with § 401(a)(9)(B)(iii), distributions commencing within one year after the date of P's death over the life expectancy of the oldest trust beneficiary. See Prop. Reg. § E-5(a)(1), last sentence, and H-2(b), second to last sentence.

The private letter rulings are not consistent. PLRs 9442032 (7/21/94) and 9623056 (3/12/96) ruled that a trust which provided income to the surviving spouse, remainder to children, *would* be entitled (under § 401(a)(9)(B)(iv)) to postpone distributions until the deceased spouse would have reached age 70½. Then PLR 9847022 (8/24/98) held exactly the opposite on apparently similar facts, saying § 401(a)(9)(B)(iv) treatment is available only if S is the "sole" beneficiary of the trust. But a still more recent ruling (1999-18065, 2/10/99) held once again that a trust of which S is merely the *oldest* (but not the sole) beneficiary (and which meets the various other trust requirements) *is* entitled to the postponement under § 401(a)(9)(B)(iv).

Pending further clarification from the IRS, and resolution of these contradictory rulings, there are still two types of trusts for the benefit of a surviving spouse which would *unquestionably* be entitled to postpone distributions in the same manner the surviving spouse herself could have done had she been the beneficiary of the benefits. These are a "conduit" trust of which S is the sole life beneficiary (see "*MRD Conduit Trust*," below); and a trust all of which is treated as owned by S under § 678 (see "*The 100% Grantor Trust,*" below).

Trusts That Are "Safe" under IRS Rules

Under the proposed regulations, there are three absolutely "safe" trust models to use when creating a trust to be named as beneficiary of retirement benefits.

The 100% Grantor Trust

Under § 678 (part of the so-called "**grantor trust** rules" of the Code), a beneficiary is treated for all purposes of the federal income tax as the "owner" of trust assets if such beneficiary has the sole unrestricted right to withdraw those assets from the trust. If an individual beneficiary is deemed the owner of all of the trust's assets under § 678, then the retirement benefits must be deemed paid "to" such individual beneficiary for purposes of the minimum distribution rules, and the "all beneficiaries must be individuals" test is met.

The IRS is required to recognize the life beneficiary as the sole DB, because § 678 says that "a person...shall be treated as the owner of any portion of a trust with respect to which such person has a power exercisable solely by himself to vest the corpus or the income therefrom in himself." See, *e.g.*, PLR 199903050 (10/28/98) ("Trust A").

This treatment has two significant results: first, income taxes on the trust's income will be imposed at the beneficiary's rate; and second, the identity of the remainder beneficiary becomes irrelevant. Thus an estate, older individuals or charities can be named as remainder beneficiaries (to succeed to whatever part of the trust is not distributed to or withdrawn by the primary beneficiary during his/her life) without loss of the use of the primary beneficiary's life expectancy as the measuring period for MRDs. Similarly, a power of appointment which affects the trust property only after the death of the primary beneficiary can be disregarded, if the primary beneficiary is deemed the "owner" under § 678.

Example 1: "The trustee shall pay all income of the trust to my spouse for life, plus such amounts of the principal (including all thereof) as my spouse shall request from time to time." The surviving spouse would be deemed the "owner" of the assets of this trust and therefore payout options would be the same for a retirement plan payable to this trust as if S had been named directly as beneficiary. It doesn't matter who are the remainder beneficiaries of this trust, or what power to appoint to whom S may have over the principal remaining at her death.

Example 2: "The trustee shall pay to my son such amounts of the income and principal of the trust as my son shall request at any time and from time to time, and such additional amounts as the trustee deems advisable. On my son's death, the remaining principal shall be paid to his widow." The son is treated as the owner of the principal and income of the trust under § 678; therefore, the fact that an older "unidentifiable" beneficiary (a new wife/widow) might be brought in later can be disregarded.

Example 3: "The trustee shall pay to my son such amounts of the income and principal of the trust as my son shall request at any time and from time to time, and such additional amounts as the trustee deems advisable. On my son's death, the remaining principal shall be paid to such charities as my son shall appoint by his last will." The son is treated as the owner of the principal and income of the trust under § 678; the fact that he has the power to appoint to charity is disregarded.

Under this model, the trust beneficiary is given the unlimited right to withdraw the benefits (and any "proceeds" thereof) from the trust at any time. Until the beneficiary chooses to exercise this right, the trustee exercises ownership rights and responsibilities on the beneficiary's behalf, for example, by investing the trust funds, choosing distribution options, and distributing income and/or principal to or for the benefit of the beneficiary.

This type of trust would be uncommon, since anyone wanting to give such broad rights to the beneficiary would presumably choose to leave the benefits outright to the beneficiary rather than in trust. However, there are two situations in which this model could be useful:

(a)   A marital deduction "qualified domestic trust" (QDOT) for the benefit of a non-citizen spouse (§ 2056A), where the only purpose of placing a trust between S and the retirement benefits is to qualify for the modified marital deduction available when the surviving spouse is not a U.S. citizen (see Chapter 4).

(b)   A trust to provide for a mentally handicapped beneficiary who can exercise the right of withdrawal only through a legal guardian. For this type of beneficiary, this type of trust provides the benefits of a discretionary trust without losing the benefits of the "life expectancy" method based on the life expectancy of the handicapped beneficiary.[4] This can be particularly helpful where the primary beneficiary does not have and is not likely to have issue, and the only likely remainder beneficiaries are the primary beneficiary's older siblings, the beneficiary's own estate or charities.

The MRD Conduit Trust

A "conduit trust" is not an official term, but is a nickname for a trust which serves as a conduit for minimum required distributions. The trustee is required to withdraw the minimum distributions from the retirement plan over the life expectancy of the trust beneficiary (or of the oldest member of a group of trust beneficiaries) and distribute the distributions out to that beneficiary (or the members of the group).

The trustee does not have the power to hold and retain inside the trust any plan distributions made during the lifetime of the beneficiary (or of the oldest beneficiary). If the (oldest) trust beneficiary lives to his or her full life expectancy, 100% of the benefits will have been distributed out to individuals. With a "conduit trust," the retirement benefits are deemed paid to the individual beneficiary for purposes of the minimum distribution rules, and the "all beneficiaries must be individuals" test is met;

---

[4]This type of trust may not be appropriate if preservation of the beneficiary's eligibility for means-tested government benefit programs is a concern. This type of planning is beyond the scope of this book.

remainder beneficiaries can be disregarded, because their entitlement to share in the benefits is contingent on the (premature) death of a prior beneficiary.

Example 4: "With respect to any IRA or other retirement plan or arrangement payable to the trust, the trustee shall withdraw from such plan, in each year, the minimum required distribution under § 401(a)(9) for such year computed based on the life expectancy of my oldest grandchild, and immediately distribute such amount in equal shares per capita to my grandchildren living at the time of such distribution. If all my grandchildren die before the trust has been entirely distributed, pay the balance of the principal to the Boston Foundation." The charitable remainder beneficiary can be disregarded, because it takes only if all the grandchildren die prior to the end of the life expectancy of the oldest grandchild.

Example 5: "With respect to any IRA or other retirement plan payable to the trust, the trustee shall withdraw from such plan, in each year, and distribute to my spouse, the greater of the income of such plan for such year, or the minimum required distribution for such plan for such year under § 401(a)(9) (computed based on the life expectancy of my spouse)." If S lives to her life expectancy she is guaranteed to receive all the retirement benefits, so you can disregard any remainder beneficiary, and any power of appointment which affects the remainder, under Prop. Reg. § E-5(e)(1).

Example 6: "The Trustee shall withdraw from the IRA, and distribute to my daughter, each year, the minimum required distribution for such year, based on my daughter's life expectancy. After my daughter's death, if she is survived by a husband, the trustee shall pay income of the trust to my daughter's surviving husband for life, remainder to my daughter's issue." If daughter lives to her full life expectancy she is guaranteed to receive all the retirement benefits, so the potential future older unidentifiable beneficiary can be disregarded.

The trustee could also be given discretion to withdraw and distribute to the life beneficiary *more* than the minimum in any year without upsetting this approach. The MRD Conduit Trust would be useful in the following situations:

(a)   Eli wants to leave his IRA to his wife Laura, but is concerned about her ability to handle a large sum of money. He is confident that she would handle wisely a stream of installment payments from the IRA. So he makes the IRA payable to a trust. The trustee will invest the IRA, and withdraw from the IRA and distribute to Laura each year the annual MRD based on Laura's life expectancy. (Note: this trust would not qualify for the marital deduction without additional provisions; see "Marital Deduction for Benefits Payable to QTIP Trust," Chapter 3; and this method would lose the benefits of the spousal rollover.)

(b)   Aunt Emily believes that leaving her IRA to her young nephews is a fine way to provide them with the start of a good retirement nest egg, but knows that, if she names them directly as beneficiaries, they will simply cash out the account immediately upon her death. So she leaves the IRA to an MRD Conduit Trust for them. The purpose of the trust is to make sure that the nephews take advantage of the "life expectancy method," whether they want to or not, and to provide professional management for the undistributed portion of the IRA. The trustee is instructed to withdraw from the IRA, each year, the MRD (based on the life expectancy of the oldest nephew) and distribute it equally to the surviving nephews.

Under this approach, again, the primary trust beneficiary is in the same position as if he or she had been named directly, individually, as beneficiary of the benefits, but with one difference from the "100% Grantor Trust" model. With the MRD Conduit Trust, it is as if P, instead of leaving it up to the beneficiary to decide when and how to take out the benefits, had specified a payout mode as well as a beneficiary. In this case, it is as if P had specified that distributions would be paid in instalments over the life expectancy of the DB. If the DB (or life beneficiary of the "MRD Conduit Trust") lives to his or her full life expectancy, he or she will have received 100% of the benefits and the remainder beneficiary will receive nothing. If the DB (or life beneficiary of the "MRD Conduit Trust") happens to die before the end of his or her life expectancy period, the remaining benefits will be paid to the remainder beneficiary of the trust (analogous to a contingent beneficiary).

With an MRD Conduit Trust, as with the 100% Grantor Trust, *the identity of the remainder beneficiary becomes irrelevant,* because a contingent beneficiary whose rights are contingent on the prior beneficiary's death *before the end of the prior beneficiary's life expectancy* can be disregarded. Prop. Reg. § E-5. Similarly, a power of appointment which affects the benefits only after the death of the "conduit" beneficiary can be ignored.

Life trust with remainder to individuals

As noted, the "100% Grantor Trust" and "MRD Conduit Trust" models solve the "trust rules" dilemma in a few limited situations. There are many other situations in which a trust is required, however, for which these two models are not suitable. For example:

(a)   Any case in which the purpose of holding the retirement benefits in trust is to keep this asset (or at least the "principal" portion of it) out of the gross estate of the life beneficiary—for example a "**credit shelter trust**" designed to benefit the surviving spouse for life but not be part of her taxable estate, or a "generation skipping trust" designed to benefit P's child for life without being included in the child's estate. Since all of the "100% Grantor Trust" model trust would be included in the life beneficiary's estate (under § 2041), and all of the "MRD Conduit Trust" property would be included in the life beneficiary's estate if he lived to his life expectancy (because it would all have been distributed to him at that point), these models are not suitable for these goals.

(b)   If the purpose of the trust is to assure that one beneficiary (*e.g.* a spouse) has the life use of the benefits, but that the principal will be preserved for the benefit of the remainder beneficiary (*e.g.* children), the first two models are not suitable because nothing may pass to the remainder beneficiary under those models.

(c)   There is a need to protect the trust principal from direct access by the beneficiary because the beneficiary is a spendthrift, or is too young, or is subject to creditors' claims—or any of the myriad reasons clients want to keep large sums of money out of beneficiaries' hands permanently or temporarily.

In all these cases, a "true" trust is called for—one that is *not* analogous to naming the beneficiary outright. From the point of view of the minimum distribution regulations, the key difference between this type of trust and the two models previously discussed is that, with this type, beneficiaries who come *after* the primary or life beneficiary will "count" as beneficiaries of the trust for purposes of determining whether all trust beneficiaries are individuals and who is the oldest beneficiary. This means that, under this model:

- All remainder beneficiaries (including contingent remainder beneficiaries and potential appointees under powers of appointment) must be individuals—no estates or charities.
- The oldest remainder beneficiary's life expectancy will determine MRDs even during the lifetime of the primary beneficiary if any remainder beneficiary is older than the life beneficiary.
- The trust should be tested to make sure that all benefits will be distributed outright to individuals at some time during the life expectancy of a living person (or of a later-born sibling of a now-living person).

Summary of Planning Principles

1.   If a trust is to be named as beneficiary of retirement benefits of a participant who has not yet reached his RBD, the trust must be drafted to comply with the rules explained in this chapter, or else benefits will have to be distributed under the Five Year Rule upon the client's death (the life expectancy payout method for a designated beneficiary will not be available).

2.   If a client dies prior to his RBD, leaving benefits payable to a trust, the trustee must file documentation with the plan administrator by the end of the ninth month following the date of death, or else all benefits will have to be paid out within five years after the date of death.

3.   In the case of a client who is approaching his

RBD, and who has named or who is going to name a trust as beneficiary of his retirement benefits, a copy of the trust (or other substitute documentation described in this chapter) must be filed with the plan administrator on or before the RBD, or the participant will be forced to use only his own life expectancy to measure required distributions.

4.   If a client who has passed his RBD proposes to name a trust as beneficiary of his benefits, a copy of the trust (or other substitute documentation described in this chapter) must be filed with the plan administrator simultaneously with the beneficiary designation, or else the participant will have "no DB."

5.   In general, because of the financial advantages of having a "designated beneficiary," and because of the stringency and specificity of the IRS's rules regarding naming a trust as beneficiary if "designated beneficiary" status is to be maintained, no estate planner should name a trust as beneficiary of retirement benefits without either mastering these rules or consulting with someone who has.

7

Charitable Giving with Retirement Benefits

*The pros, cons and pitfalls of
funding charitable gifts with
retirement benefits.*

Introduction

What this chapter covers

This chapter assumes the reader is familiar with the basic tax rules of charitable giving, and has read Chapter 1. For more explanation of the various charitable giving devices discussed, see the Glossary, and also sources listed in the Bibliography.

The planning principles discussed in this chapter generally do not apply to Roth IRAs (Chapter 5). Since Roth IRA distributions are generally not subject to federal income tax, there is no income tax advantage to leaving such benefits to charity. The best planning strategies for Roth IRAs therefore generally do not include leaving such plans to charity. This chapter deals only with traditional IRAs, **qualified retirement plans** ("QRPs") and **403(b)** arrangements.

Advantages of naming a charity as beneficiary

Because retirement plan death benefits are subject to income tax (see "Income in Respect of a Decedent," Chapter 2), it may be attractive to name a charity or **charitable remainder trust** ("CRT") as the beneficiary. Charities and CRTs are both generally exempt from income taxes, and thus can collect the entire death benefit without paying income taxes. §§ 501(a),

664(c). For the client who wants to leave some assets to charity at death, using the retirement benefits for that purpose is often the most tax-effective way to fund the gift.

Example: Helen wants to leave half of her $1.2 million estate to her favorite charity, the Boston Foundation, and half to her nephew Achilles. Her assets are: a $600,000 IRA and $600,000 of cash. Achilles is in the 40% income tax bracket. If Helen simply leaves half of each asset to Achilles and half to the charity, Table 7.1 shows what each receives.

Table 7.1	Charity	Nephew
½ cash	300,000	300,000
½ IRA	300,000	300,000
Gross bequest	600,000	600,000
Less: income tax on ½ IRA	- 0	-120,000
Net bequest	600,000	480,000

If, instead, she leaves the entire IRA to the charity and all the cash to nephew Achilles, her beneficiaries receive more, at the expense of the IRS, as shown in Table 7.2. This tax advantage of funding at-death charitable gifts with retirement benefits enables the client to leave more dollars to his favorite charity, or, viewed another way, to fund his charitable gifts at a lower "cost" to the family beneficiaries.

In addition to being a tax-efficient way to fund charitable bequests, leaving benefits to a CRT can also help the not-particularly-charitably-inclined client achieve dispositive goals. For example, when a participant is past his "required beginning date" (RBD), has no "designated beneficiary" (DB), has elected to recalculate his life expectancy annually for purposes of determining minimum distributions (see Chapter 1), and has no spouse who can roll over the benefits after his death (see

Table 7.2	Charity	Nephew
IRA	600,000	0
Cash	0	600,000
Gross bequest	600,000	600,000
Less: income tax on IRA	- 0	- 0
Net bequest	600,000	600,000

Chapter 3), the client's beneficiaries are faced with the potentially disastrous "one year rule" under the minimum distribution rules: all the benefits will have to be distributed by the end of the year after the year of the client's death. While leaving the benefits to a CRT can not change that fact, it can soften the blow by either eliminating the income taxes on the benefits, or deferring them in a manner that approximates a payout over the life expectancy of the family beneficiaries; see the *Fallon* case study, Chapter 11.

Despite the fact that it is generally desirable to use retirement benefits to fund at-death charitable gifts, however, it is not necessarily easy to integrate this planning idea into a particular client's estate plan; see the *Mandel* case study in Chapter 11, and the "pitfalls" discussed in the next section.

Pitfalls

Charity as one of several beneficiaries: before RBD

Naming a charity as one of *several* beneficiaries of retirement benefits presents a problem.

According to the IRS (Prop. Reg. § 1.401(a)(9)-1, § E-5(a)), ALL beneficiaries of a retirement plan death benefit must be individuals, if ANY of the benefits are to be paid out over the life expectancy of a beneficiary (see Chapter 1). Under this rule, it would appear that a $1 million IRA payable at death "$1,000 to Catholic Charities and the balance to my children" would have to be entirely distributed by the end of the fifth year after the death of a participant ("P") who died before his RBD. P would be deemed to have "no DB" because one of his beneficiaries is not an individual.

Is the IRS's position correct? The proposed regulation appears to be harsher than the Code, which says that "*if any portion* of the employee's interest is payable to (or for the benefit of) a designated beneficiary, *such portion*" may be distributed over the life expectancy of the designated beneficiary ("DB"). § 401(a)(9)(B)(iii) (emphasis added). Thus, the Code appears to permit a life expectancy payout to an individual DB of his portion, even if some *other* "portion" of the benefit is payable to a non-individual.

Even under the proposed regulations, it may be possible to have a life expectancy payout to an individual of part of the benefit, and distribute the rest of the benefit to a charity, if the respective shares of the individual and charity are defined as fractional or percentage shares, and P dies before his RBD. However, a **pecuniary gift** to charity followed by a "residuary" gift to family (or vice versa) might not qualify as establishing "separate accounts" as of the date of death. See "*Naming more than one beneficiary: before the RBD*," Chapter 1.

What to do: Unfortunately, the penalty for not complying with the minimum distribution rules is draconian (50% of the amount which should have been distributed; § 4975), and the value to the family of the life expectancy payout method can be enormous. Therefore the consequences of "being wrong" here are major. If the client wants to make part of his benefits payable to charity and part payable to an individual, and wants the individual beneficiary to be able to withdraw his share of the benefits over his life expectancy, the client has only the following choices:

Planning mode: client who has not reached RBD

Safest route: Divide the account into "separate accounts" during the client's life, and name the charity as beneficiary of one "account" and the individual as beneficiary of the other. For example, if the benefits are in an IRA, move the funds into two separate IRAs, with different account numbers, one payable to each beneficiary. This method clearly complies with the proposed regulations and will achieve the objective. However, if the benefits are in an employer plan rather than an IRA, it may be difficult or impossible to get the plan to create separate "accounts" for one employee's benefits.

Second safest: Name the individual and charity as beneficiaries based on a fractional or percentage method. This evidently works under the proposed regulations to establish "separate accounts" "as of" the date of death. It certainly *should* work, in view of the clear language of the Code permitting life expectancy payout of the "portion" payable to the individual beneficiary. On the other hand, since the one letter ruling clearly discussing the situation (PLR 9809059, 12/4/97) seems to require not only that the bequest be in fractional or percentage shares, but that such shares be separated after the date of death *before the end of the year in which the death occurred*, this approach could run into difficulties if the client dies late in the year so that division by year end is impossible.

These concerns do not arise when the benefit is payable partly to charity and partly to P's spouse, if P dies before his RBD and if the spouse in fact survives P, because the spouse does not need to take an installment payout of the benefits in order to defer income taxes; she can roll over her share of the benefits to her own IRA. See Chapter 3.

Client who dies before RBD: cleanup mode

If P has already died, and a retirement plan has been left to both charitable and individual beneficiaries, you need to be concerned that the IRS may challenge the individual beneficiary's right to take the benefits over his life expectancy. The recommended course of action is:

1.   Pay out the charitable share promptly.
2.   Begin distributing the individual beneficiary's share in instalments over the individual beneficiary's life expectancy. The first distribution MUST be made no later than the end of the year following the year of P's death.
3.   Then, no later than the year which contains the fifth anniversary of P's death, you examine the situation again:

(A)   If by that time it has become clear (through final regulations, cases or otherwise) that the individual beneficiary IS entitled to use the life expectancy method, continue to pay the instalments to him over his life expectancy.

(B)   If by that time it has become clear (through final regulations, cases or otherwise) that the individual beneficiary is NOT entitled to use the life expectancy method, the remaining benefits must be distributed to the beneficiary by the end of the year that contains the fifth anniversary of the date of death.

(C)   Finally, if the law is still unsettled as to whether the individual beneficiary is entitled to use the life expectancy method, the beneficiary must choose: either play it safe and withdraw all benefits by the end of year five; or take his chances and continue to use the life expectancy method, based on a "reasonable interpretation" of the statute and proposed regulations (see *"Legal status of proposed regulations,"* Chapter 1); or apply for his own ruling.

Charity as one of several beneficiaries: at or after RBD

Once P reaches the RBD, it does not appear possible to have multiple "designated beneficiaries," one or more of whom are not individuals, unless the plan or IRA is actually divided into "separate accounts," with separate accounting for each. See *"Naming multiple beneficiaries: at RBD,"* Chapter 1. So the recommended course of action would be to divide the (*e.g.*) IRA into two separate IRAs, one payable to the charity and one payable to individuals, *before* the RBD (or before naming the charity as a beneficiary, if that is to occur after the RBD).

Example: Edgar, age 70½ in 1998, has an IRA worth $600,000. He would like to leave $100,000 of IRA benefits to his favorite charity, the United Way, and the balance of the IRA to his grandchildren. You advise him to create two separate IRAs, prior to his RBD, one of $100,000 payable to the United Way and the other (initially worth $500,000) payable to the grandchildren. He does so in December 1998.

Minimum required distributions ("MRDs") from the "charity" IRA will be computed on the basis of his sole life expectancy. He elects to determine his life expectancy for this IRA by the "recalculate" method. This will minimize MRDs generated by this account during his life, with no downside in case of premature death, because (even though his life expectancy will go to zero on his death as a result of electing the recalculation method, so that all benefits from this account will have to be distributed within one year after his death), the benefits paid after his death will not be subject to income tax because they will be distributed to the charity.

MRDs from the "grandchildren IRA" will be based on the joint life expectancy of Edgar and his oldest grandchild, subject (during Edgar's life) to the MDIB rule (which artificially shortens the joint life expectancy so long as Edgar is living). For this account, it will make virtually no difference whether Edgar elects to recalculate his life expectancy or instead chooses the "fixed term method." See *"Whether to recalculate life expectancy: non-spouse DB,"* Chapter 1. So Edgar elects the fixed term method because it is simpler and easier to understand.

Benefits paid to a trust with charitable beneficiaries

Suppose a client wants to designate a trust as beneficiary of his retirement plan. His children are beneficiaries of the trust. He wants the plan benefits that pass to this trust to be paid out in installments over the life expectancy of his oldest child. Alternatively, if he is reaching his RBD, he wants to take his MRDs over the joint life expectancy of himself and the oldest child (subject to the MDIB rule).

To achieve the desired result, of course, the various "trust rules" must be complied with; see Chapter 6. One of these rules is that all trust beneficiaries must be individuals. This rule creates two problems in common estate planning situations involving charities.

First, *any* charitable gift payable from the trust at death, no matter how small, would apparently cause the trust to flunk this requirement, unless the trustee is forbidden to use the retirement benefits to fund the charitable bequest. Even the typical normally innocuous statement "this trust shall pay any bequests under my will, if my estate is not adequate to pay the same," could make the trust "flunk" if in fact the probate estate is not adequate, and the will in fact contains charitable bequests.

Thus, when drafting a trust which contains charitable gifts, or which may be used to fund charitable bequests under the will, it is extremely important to determine whether any retirement benefits may be payable to that trust, and if so to draft appropriate language to either:

(1)   Insulate the retirement benefits from the charitable gifts, if you want the benefits to be paid out over the life expectancy of individual trust beneficiaries. See Form 7.2, Appendix B.

(2)   Or, match the retirement benefits to the charitable gifts, if the goal is to have the benefits pass to the charity free of income taxes.

The second problem is that, generally, remainder beneficiaries are considered "beneficiaries" for this purpose. (There are some exceptions—see the "*The 100% Grantor Trust*" and "The MRD *Conduit Trust*," Chapter 6.) Thus, if at P's RBD, his beneficiary is a CRT, for example, P is deemed to have "no DB" and must use only his own life expectancy to measure required payouts. Even if the trust is not a qualified CRT, if any part of the remainder passes to charity (or could be appointed to charity under a power of appointment), the trust will flunk unless the charitable remainder beneficiary can be disregarded (see "*Disregarding certain contingent beneficiaries*," Chapter 6).

Naming a charity as beneficiary at RBD

Suppose your under-age-70½ client has named a charity or CRT as his beneficiary. What happens when this client reaches his RBD? On the RBD, the client must begin withdrawing his benefits over his life expectancy, or over the joint and survivor life expectancy of himself and a DB. If his beneficiary is a charity (or CRT), he will be limited to using only his own life expectancy, since a DB must be an individual and a charity is not an individual.

A solution sometimes suggested to this problem is for P to name his spouse as DB, so P can use the joint life expectancy of P and the spouse to calculate distributions during his lifetime, but name the charity or CRT as contingent beneficiary. The spouse can then disclaim the benefits (see Chapter 8) at P's death, allowing them to flow to the charity or into the CRT and be distributed free of income tax. This has been called the "reliable spouse" strategy[5], and can be appropriate if both spouses are committed to the same estate planning objectives.

However, relying on a primary beneficiary to disclaim is not very appealing to a client who definitely wants the benefits to go to charity at his death. A more straightforward way to achieve the objective is for the client simply to name the charity as beneficiary, and then start withdrawing the benefits over the client's single life expectancy, recalculated annually. This will provide a somewhat faster payout than if the client had named an individual DB. If the client is being forced by the minimum distribution rules to withdraw benefits from the plan more

---

[5] "Charitable Deduction Planning with Retirement Benefits and IRAs: What Can Be Done and How Do We Do It?," by Roger L. Shumaker, Esq. (with Michael G. Riley, Esq.), American Bar Association Section of Real Property, Probate and Trust Law meeting outline, Chicago, Illinois, August 1995.

quickly than he would like, he can donate these excess distributions to charity while he is still living

By recalculating life expectancy annually, the client assures there will always be something left in the plan at his death to pass to the charity income tax-free. The disadvantage of electing recalculation in this situation is that if the client later changes his mind and wants to name an individual beneficiary, he will still be stuck with the recalculation election.

Charitable pledges and other debts

If P names a creditor as beneficiary of his retirement benefits, so that the benefits will be used to satisfy P's debt to that creditor, the IRS might treat this as generating taxable income *to P's estate*. Although generally retirement benefits and other "income in respect of a decedent" ("IRD") items are taxed to the person who "receives" them (in this case the creditor) (see Chapter 2), the IRS could say that the estate "received" the IRD, because the estate's debt was canceled by the benefits' passing to the creditor.

Could this same result occur if benefits are made payable to a charity in fulfilment of a charitable pledge? A charitable pledge which remains unfulfilled at death may, depending on the facts and applicable state law, constitute a debt enforceable against the estate. See, *e.g., Robinson v. Nutt*, 185 Mass. 345, 70 N.E. 198 (1904) (unpaid written charitable subscription enforced as a debt against the estate due to charity's reliance), and discussion in *Congregation Kadimah Toras-Moshe v. DeLeo*, 405 Mass. 365 (1989), affirming the principle that a written pledge is enforceable if there is consideration or reliance, although holding that the oral pledge in that particular case was not enforceable.

In *John T. Harrington Estate*, 2 TCM 540, Dec. 13,405(M) (1943), the transfer of appreciated securities by an estate to a charity in fulfillment of pledges was treated as a "sale or exchange." The pledges had been deducted as debts on the estate tax return. This case (which has never been overruled, or explicitly repudiated by the IRS) would appear to support the conclusion that paying retirement benefits to charity in fulfilment of a pledge will indeed generate taxable income to the estate.

However, charitable giving expert Lawrence P. Katzenstein, Esq., points out that the *Harrington* case may no longer be a viable precedent in view of Rev. Rul. 55-410 (1955-1 C.B. 297). This ruling held that the assignment of property in fulfilment of a charitable pledge (by a living taxpayer in this case) would *not* be treated as a sale or exchange (the way payment of any other debt with appreciated property would be). Since the gift is deemed to occur when the property is actually transferred to the charity (not when the pledge is signed—no matter how binding that pledge may be), "it would be inconsistent to treat such payment or transfer as a 'contribution or gift' and at the same time as a satisfaction of a debt with the tax consequences which would ordinarily follow from the use of appreciated or depreciated property to pay a debt." Rev. Rul. 64-240 (1964-2 C.B. 172) confirmed that fulfilling a charitable pledge is treated as a "gift" not "payment of a debt" for income tax purposes.

The logic of these rulings would lead to the conclusion that making retirement benefits payable to a charity as beneficiary, in fulfilment of a charitable pledge, will not cause the estate to realize income when the charity collects the benefits, regardless of whether the pledge was enforceable as a debt against P's estate.

Various Ideas and Issues

Funding charitable gifts with plan benefits during life

How wonderful it would be if a participant could transfer his retirement plan to a CRT, reserving the CRT income for himself and his spouse for life, never paying income tax on the underlying benefits, and even getting an income tax deduction for the value of his remainder gift. The author has seen this strategy recommended in print more than once, but it seems unlikely to work. For one thing, true **qualified retirement plan** ("QRP") benefits are completely non-assignable (with limited exceptions for divorce and tax liens). § 401(a)(13). For another, the income tax deduction for a charitable gift of ordinary income property is limited to the donor's basis, which, in the case of an IRA, is generally either zero or a relatively small amount. § 170(e)(1)(A).

If the donor is willing to forego the income tax deduction part of the deal, can he assign an IRA to charity? An IRA is not *per se* non-assignable. One type of assignment is prohibited by the Code: if an IRA is pledged as security for a loan, it ceases to be an IRA and is treated as having been distributed to P. § 408(e)(4). The fact that one particular type of assignment is dealt with, and "punished," in § 408 implies that *other* assignments do *not* result in loss of IRA status.

However, the IRS has made clear in various regulations that, in its view, the assignment of an IRA, although effective to transfer the account, causes it to lose its special tax characteristics. Reg. § 20.2056A, preamble, § E, (dealing with the marital deduction for assets left to a non-citizen spouse) (see Chapter 4), states that the assignment of an IRA to any assignee other than a 100% "**grantor trust**" would cause the assignor to be taxed immediately on the full value of the IRA. Similarly, the assignment of a Roth IRA (Chapter 5) by gift would be treated as a distribution of the account to P and the account would cease to be any kind of IRA after the assignment. Reg. § 1.408A-6 (Q & A 19).

Looking to the future, the "Charitable Accord," a federation of charitable organizations, is seeking to get Congress to enact "The IRA Rollover Bill." This legislation would allow individuals to transfer their IRAs to a charity or CRT. While the donor would not be allowed an income tax deduction for the gift, he would also not have to recognize any income upon making the transfer. To find out the status of this effort, write to The Charitable Accord, P.O. Box 65061, Washington, DC 20035-5061, or call them at (202) 463-3957. For comment on this proposal, see "Why Not Allow Lifetime Charitable Assignments of Qualified Plans and IRAs?" by Frank M. Burke, Tax Notes 7/7/97, page 121.

Until that legislation is passed, however, the only choice for someone who wishes to give his retirement plan to charity is to take a distribution from the plan and then give the same amount to charity. *Theoretically*, the charitable deduction should offset the income, and there would be no net tax from the transaction; in real life, however, the percentage-of-income limits on the charitable deduction, the alternative minimum tax, state tax laws (which may not allow charitable deductions), and the limits on itemized deductions conspire to make it difficult in many cases to eliminate the income tax on the distribution.

Furthermore, someone under age 59½ must deal with the 10% penalty (Chapter 9) if he actually takes a distribution before making his charitable gift; and someone who uses a retirement plan distribution to fund a CRT to provide a lifetime income for himself and/or his spouse does not get an income tax deduction equal to the entire amount placed in the trust, since only part of it is a charitable gift. The Charitable Accord proposal would allow P (and P's spouse, if P so chooses) to receive a lifetime income (in the form of a unitrust or annuity trust payout) from the entire value of the IRA, not just the value of the IRA minus income taxes.

UBTI

A CRT is generally exempt from income tax if it meets all the requirements of § 664. However, a CRT is *not* income tax-exempt in any year that it has any "unrelated business taxable income" ("UBTI"). § 664(c). PLRs 9237010 (6/12/92) and 9253038 (10/5/92) involved CRTs that were to be named as beneficiary of QRP benefits and IRAs. The IRS ruled that the trusts in question qualified as "charitable remainder trusts," and thus were tax-exempt so long as they did not have any UBTI. Some practitioners take these rulings as implying that retirement plan distributions are *not* UBTI, although the rulings did not specifically say that.

Private foundation 2% excise tax

A private charitable foundation is subject to a 2% excise tax on its net investment income. § 4940. PLR 9633006 (5/9/96) ruled that a distribution from a Keogh plan to a foundation was subject to the 2% tax to the extent it represented investment accumulations in the plan, but not to the extent it represented plan contributions by the decedent or his employer. Timothy W. Mulcahy, CPA, criticized this ruling in "Is a Bequest of a Retirement Account to a Private Foundation Subject to Excise Tax?," Journal of Taxation, August 1996, page 108. Apparently the IRS agreed with his comments, and a later ruling, 9838028 (7/21/98) held that the § 4940 tax "is a limited excise tax that applies only to the specific types of income listed in that section. Amounts from retirement accounts are deferred compensation income," not part of "the gross investment income" of a foundation and therefore are *not* subject to the tax.

Gift of ESOP "qualified replacement property" to a CRT

The Code allows a business owner, if various requirements are met, to sell stock of his company to an "employee stock ownership plan" (ESOP), then reinvest the proceeds in marketable securities ("qualified replacement property"), without paying income tax on the sale. § 1042. The untaxed gain carries over to the qualified replacement property and the capital gain tax thus deferred will be paid when the qualified replacement property is sold or "disposed of."

A "gift" is not a disposition for this purpose, but since the Code doesn't define "gift," there is some question whether transferring qualified replacement property to a CRT (which is not totally a "gift" if the donor retains an income interest) is considered a gift for this purpose.

PLR 9732023 (5/12/97) answered this question favorably to the taxpayer involved in that ruling, concluding that "the contribution of the qualified replacement property to the charitable remainder unitrust will not cause a recapture of the gain deferred by the Taxpayers under section 1042(a) by operation of the provisions of section 1042(e)."

Unfortunately, even aside from the fact that a private letter ruling cannot be relied on as precedent, the language of the ruling is ambiguous and limited. It says: "In the present case, the transfer of the qualified replacement property to the charitable remainder unitrust constitutes a disposition of such property with the meaning of section 1042(e) of the Code. However under the facts of the present case, no gain is realized by the Taxpayers on the transfer...," with no indication of *why* no gain is realized. Presumably the rationale is that the transfer is a gift, and therefore excepted from the recognition of gain.

Assuming this ruling can be duplicated by other taxpayers, this approach represents a good way for some business owners to diversify their portfolios, and convert their closely held business into a lifetime income stream, without paying capital gain tax.

Net unrealized appreciation of employer securities

See "*Charitable giving with NUA*," Chapter 2.

Charitable lead trust

A charitable lead trust (CLT) is the mirror image of a CRT. With a CRT, a lead "unitrust" interest or annuity interest is paid to one or more individual beneficiaries for a term of years (or for life), and a remainder interest is paid to charity. § 664(d). With a CLT, a lead "unitrust" interest or annuity interest is paid to a *charity* for a term of years (or for the life of an individual), and a remainder interest is paid to individuals, such as the donor's children or grandchildren. § 170(f)(2)(B).

Leaving retirement benefits to a CLT appears generally to be a disadvantageous way to fund such a trust. Unlike a CRT, a CLT is not exempt from income tax. Thus it must pay tax on the retirement benefits when they are distributed from the retirement plan to the CLT. Generally, the planning advantage of a CLT funded at death is that, in addition to satisfying the donor's charitable intentions, it may allow funds to pass to the donor's issue free of estate taxes. This phenomenon occurs if the investment performance of the trust "beats" the IRS's § 7520 rate. When that occurs, the trust has more money than the IRS rates "predicted," so the excess passes free of transfer taxes to the family.

If the CLT is funded with retirement benefits, however, the CLT will generally start out at a disadvantage, since some of the principal that the IRS assumed the trust would have has in fact been used up paying income taxes. This makes it that much *less* likely that the trust will "beat" the IRS's § 7520 rate, because in effect the trust starts out with a loss. The client may well end up paying estate tax on *more* than the family beneficiaries eventually receive.

The exception to this rule is, if the distributions from the retirement plan can be matched to the lead-interest distributions to the charity, so the plan distributions are in fact income tax-free, the "starting-out-with-a-loss" effect may be avoided.

IRD payable to charity

A decedent's retirement benefit, until it is distributed, constitutes a "right to receive income in respect of a decedent" (IRD) (see Chapter 2). As such, if it is specifically "bequeathed" to a charity or CRT by P's will, or payable directly to the charity or CRT under a beneficiary designation form, § 691 would impose the income tax on the charity (or CRT). Since the recipient is income tax-exempt, there would be no income tax.

If the right-to-receive IRD is bequeathed to a charity or CRT, but the IRD is actually paid to the estate before the estate has a chance to distribute the "right-to-receive," the income tax treatment is trickier. There is no DNI deduction for distributions to a charitable beneficiary. § 663(a)(2). Therefore, the only way to "transfer" the income tax liability to the charity is by means of a charitable deduction under § 642. § 642(c)(1) allows the income tax charitable deduction to an estate or trust only for charitable gifts which are paid out of gross income pursuant to the governing instrument. A specific bequest of retirement benefits to charity would appear to meet this requirement.

§ 691(c) deduction and charitable remainder trusts

Suppose P leaves his $200,000 IRA payable to a charitable remainder annuity trust (CRUT). The CRUT holds no other assets and receives no other assets. The CRUT is to pay a 10% unitrust payment each year to P's child (C), and on P's death whatever is left in the CRUT is paid to the Red Cross. C is 48 years old at P's death. Assume the value of C's unitrust interest is $180,000 for estate tax purposes. Assume the federal estate tax attributable to this interest is $83,000.

The first year after P's death the unitrust earns 7% ($14,000) but pays out 10% ($20,000) to C. Clearly, $6,000 of the C's payment is coming from the "principal" of the unitrust, and just as clearly this payment is coming out of "IRD" that the CRUT received. If the IRD character of this distribution were recognized, C would get a § 691(c) deduction of $83,000/$180,000 X $6,000 = $2,766. However, there is no mechanism by which a CRT can pass out such a deduction.

A special "tiered" system of tax accounting applies to CRTs (see § 664). It appears that the 691(c) deduction would reduce the "taxable income" of the trust. Reg. § 1.664-1(d)(2). All the distributions to C would be deemed to come entirely out of the "net taxable income" of the CRT until it had all been used up. The income of the CRT that was sheltered by the 691(c) deduction would effectively become "principal" that could be distributed to C tax-free. However, the tax-free principal of the CRT is not deemed to be distributed to C until all net *taxable* income has been previously distributed. This point would never be reached in most CRTs, unless the unitrust payout rate substantially exceeds the anticipated income.

In this example, if the trust continues to earn 7%, the 10% unitrust payments will not be coming out of the non-taxable funds until approximately year 26. Thus, some part of the unitrust payments C receives after age 74 will be tax-free "return of principal" because of the § 691(c) deduction, but he gets no benefit from it for the first 26 years. The IRS has confirmed this explanation of how § 691(c) applies to a CRT in PLR 1999-01023 (10/8/98).

It is the experience of the author and others that (in view

of the treatment of the § 691(c) deduction when IRD is paid to a CRT) the long-term payout of retirement benefits to family beneficiaries over their life expectancy will produce more financial benefit to the family than would paying the benefit to a CRT in which the family members are life beneficiaries. This is not surprising since charitable gifts, however structured, are not designed to make a profit for the family. However, if the long term payout over life expectancy is not available, the family indeed may "make a profit" by having the benefits paid to a CRT, based on certain assumptions; see the *Fallon* case study.

Summary of Planning Principles

1.   For a client who wishes to make charitable gifts upon his death, there are tax advantages to using retirement benefits to fulfill those gifts.

2.   Despite the tax advantages of funding charitable bequests with retirement benefits, such gifts have some pitfalls and complications, particularly once the client reaches his required beginning date, or if the benefits flow through a trust, or if part of the benefits will pass to individual beneficiaries.

3.   Making benefits payable to a charitable remainder trust may maximize the value of the benefits to the family if the alternative is an immediate fully taxable distribution of the benefits at the client's death.

4.   The tax laws involved in charitable giving are just as complicated and technical as the rules dealing with retirement benefits, and when the two areas overlap the results are often unclear; if the position the client is looking for is not clear under the law, consider obtaining a ruling.

8

Disclaimers

Disclaimers have proven useful in post mortem planning for benefits. Nevertheless, questions remain regarding the use of qualified disclaimers of retirement benefits to solve estate planning problems.

Introduction

A disclaimer is the refusal to accept a gift or inheritance. Both state law and federal tax law recognize that a person cannot be forced to accept a gift or inheritance. State laws dealing with disclaimers generally regulate what actions will be recognized as disclaimers and to whom a gift or inheritance will pass if it is disclaimed by the original beneficiary.

A disclaimer is not a gift. Since the person making the disclaimer never accepted the property in the first place, the theory goes, he never owned it and therefore he could not have given it away. The disclaimed asset passes to the next beneficiary in line, usually as if the person making the disclaimer had predeceased the person from whom he inherited.

The tax code recognizes disclaimers if they meet certain requirements. If a disclaimer is "qualified," then it is not treated as a taxable gift. § 2518.

Example: Mary dies, leaving her $100,000 IRA to Maureen as primary beneficiary. Maureen is already wealthy, and does not need the money. Maureen disclaims the IRA by means of a qualified disclaimer meeting the requirements of § 2518 and applicable state law. As a result of the disclaimer, the IRA passes to the contingent beneficiary, Maureen's poor cousin Pat. Maureen has not made a taxable gift. By contrast, if Maureen had "accepted" the IRA (for example, by cashing it in and putting the proceeds in her bank account), and then written a check to Pat, she would have made a taxable gift.

The principal requirements for a "qualified" disclaimer under § 2518, stated in a necessarily oversimplified fashion, are:

1.   The disclaimer must be made within nine months after the disclaimed property was transferred by the original transferor (*i.e.*, the decedent or donor whose bequest or gift is being disclaimed).

2.   The disclaimant must not have accepted any benefits of the gift or inheritance disclaimed.

3.   The property must pass, as a result of the disclaimer, and without any direction on the part of the disclaimant, to someone other than the disclaimant. Exception: property can pass to the decedent's spouse as a result of the disclaimer, even if she is also the person making the disclaimer.

4.   Generally speaking the disclaimer must be effective under state law.

Disclaimers have proven their worth in *post mortem* planning for retirement benefits, as examples in the following section show. *Post mortem* planning flexibility can be increased if the possibility of disclaimers is planned for in the drafting stage, although excessive reliance on possible future disclaimers should be discouraged.

Disclaimers in Post Mortem Planning

Disclaimers have proven to be of great value in "cleaning up" beneficiary designations where the deceased participant named the "wrong" beneficiary. Disclaimers have been used to redirect benefits to the surviving spouse (so she can roll them over), and to create funding for a credit shelter trust which would otherwise have no assets. The following rulings illustrate the range of possibilities, and the creativity of *post mortem* planners, in using disclaimers to correct *pre mortem* mistakes:

Funding credit shelter trust

PLR 9442032 (7/27/94): the plan participant (P) named his spouse (S) as primary beneficiary and his trust as contingent beneficiary. The trust provided that all IRA benefits had to be allocated to the marital trust, over which S had a general power of appointment. No assets passed to the credit shelter trust. "To enable [the] estate to fully utilize the available unified credit," S, as beneficiary of the IRA, disclaimed her interest in the IRA, and then, as beneficiary of the marital trust, disclaimed her general powers over the marital trust. As a result of these disclaimers, the IRA was now payable to a trust of which she was merely the life income beneficiary, with no general power of appointment. Then, as executor, she made a fractional QTIP election for the IRA and the trust. The non-elected portion of the IRA and marital trust became in effect the credit shelter trust.

Salvaging spousal rollover

If P dies having named the "wrong" beneficiary (typically, in published rulings, a trust), it may be possible to get the benefits to the spouse (so she can roll them over) by having the trust (or other "wrong" beneficiary) disclaim the benefits.

This strategy works if, as a result of the disclaimer, the benefits pass outright to S either as contingent beneficiary, or (more typically) as the "default" beneficiary under the plan (i.e., the person who, according to the governing provisions of the plan or IRA agreement, takes the benefits if P fails to name a beneficiary). If P's "estate" is the default beneficiary under the plan, this strategy still works if (as a result of the disclaimer) the benefits will pass outright to S as residuary beneficiary under P's will or by intestacy. Unfortunately, there are some cases where the strategy doesn't work because the estate is the default beneficiary under the plan, and S will not get the benefits if they pass to the estate (for example, because the state intestacy law would cause the estate to pass to P's children).

In PLR 9045050 (8/15/90), P named a trust as his beneficiary. S was a trustee of the trust. Upon P's death, S, as trustee, made a qualified disclaimer of the benefits. As a result of the disclaimer, the benefits passed to S outright rather than to the trust, and she rolled them over. PLR 199913048 (1/5/99) was similar except that S was not named as trustee of P's trust, but the named trustee declined to serve and the probate court appointed S as "special trustee." Acting as special trustee, she disclaimed the benefits (with court approval) as did all other beneficiaries of P's trust, and the IRA passed to S as the default beneficiary under the plan. Note that the IRS in this ruling did not regard the other trustees' refusal to serve, or the court's appointment of S as special trustee, or the court's approval of the disclaimer by S as trustee (which presumably was required by local law to make the disclaimer effective) as constituting post mortem actions which made someone other than P the transferor of the benefits to S.

In PLR 9450041 (9/22/94), P's benefits were payable to a marital trust. Upon S's death, the marital trust was to pass to a family trust for P's children and their issue or (in default of issue) to nieces, nephews and a charity. S disclaimed all her interests under the marital trust, so the property passed to the family trust. Then every beneficiary of the family trust (the children and grandchildren, the nieces and nephews and the charity) disclaimed his, her or its interest. The benefits passed to S by intestacy and she rolled them over.

The most interesting aspect of this ruling was that S's disclaimer was not timely—it was made more than nine months after P's death. Therefore, for federal transfer tax purposes, S's disclaimer was not a qualified disclaimer. However, under applicable *state* law, a non-timely disclaimer was effective to transfer title to those who would have received the property if the disclaimer had been properly made. Since S's non-qualified disclaimer was legally effective as a transfer under state law, it was treated for tax purposes as a "new" transfer—essentially, as a gift by S to the beneficiaries of the family trust.

Because S's non-qualified disclaimer was treated as a new transfer, the disclaimers by all the beneficiaries of the family trust were timely (and "qualified") under § 2518 because they were made within nine months after the property was transferred to *them* by S's non-qualified disclaimer, even though made more than nine months after P's death.

Finally, since S's non-qualified disclaimer was a "new" transfer, it would normally have resulted in a taxable gift by her to the beneficiaries of the family trust. But since they all disclaimed this "gift," the property went to S by intestacy, and S's "transfer" was a transfer to herself, which is not taxable! This ruling shows creative *post mortem* planning and a bit of luck in the terms of the state disclaimer statute.

Planning in Anticipation Of Disclaimers

It is wise, at the estate planning stage, to anticipate the possibility of disclaimers. For example, a participant (P) may be trying to choose between naming his spouse (S) as beneficiary, to achieve deferral of income taxes via a spousal rollover, on the one hand, and naming a credit shelter trust as beneficiary, on the other hand, to take full advantage of his unified credit. Each choice has its merits and a clear "winner" may not be apparent during the planning phase.

P may decide to make the benefits payable to S as primary beneficiary, because his main goal is to provide for S's financial security (for example), but provide that, if S disclaims the benefits, the benefits will pass to the credit shelter trust. If funding the credit shelter trust appears to be the more attractive alternative at the time of P's death, S can activate the credit shelter plan by disclaiming the benefits, which will then pass to the credit shelter trust as contingent beneficiary. PLR 9320015 (2/17/93) contains an example of this type of planning. See also the *Allen Able* case study.

The apparent flexibility of disclaimers can tempt planners, in the author's view, to rely excessively on future disclaimers as a way of carrying out the estate plan. One justification for this approach is that it avoids the need to spend time analyzing the choices at the planning stage. Thus, professional fees are lower. The estate plan relies on the fiduciaries and beneficiaries to make the actual decisions later, when a more informed choice can be made.

For most clients, the "credit shelter trust" estate plan offers substantial estate tax savings. Before making these substantial savings (or other important estate planning goals) dependent on prospective disclaimers by beneficiaries or fiduciaries, the planner needs to weigh carefully the risks and drawbacks of relying on disclaimers. For example:

1.   Disclaimers by fiduciaries pose several issues. Although such disclaimers are clearly permitted under § 2518, there can be state law obstacles. Also, § 2518 requires that the

disclaimed property must pass either to the spouse or to someone other than the disclaimant, without any direction on the part of the disclaimant; the implications of these requirements are unclear where it is proposed to have property pass by disclaimer from one discretionary trust to a second discretionary trust with the same trustees or beneficiaries.

2.   Another requirement of a qualified disclaimer is that the disclaimant must not have accepted any benefits of the disclaimed property. Often a retired participant will have set up his retirement plan so that payments are made, automatically, every month or every quarter. Such payments may continue to flow in after P's death, and be received and deposited by the beneficiary, before the disclaimer subject is even broached, and this may constitute "acceptance" of the benefits, making a qualified disclaimer impossible.

3.   Disclaimers have an inexorable deadline of nine months after the date of death. Thus, an estate plan which depends on disclaimers is extremely dependent on rapid action *post mortem*, especially if an IRS ruling is required.

4.   No matter how cooperative and disclaimer-friendly the proposed disclaimant may have been during the planning stage, the emotional turmoil caused by P's death, or other factors, could cause him or her to have a change of heart and not sign a disclaimer when the time comes.

5.   If the surviving spouse is to disclaim, she cannot thereafter retain any discretionary distribution powers over the disclaimed benefits (unless limited by an ascertainable standard). For example, if S is disclaiming benefits which will then pass to a credit shelter trust for issue, she cannot be a trustee of that trust if the trustee has, say, discretionary power to "spray" the

trust among P's issue; nor can she have a power of appointment enabling her to, *e.g.*, decide which issue of P will receive the trust after her death. Thus, taking advantage of the flexibility of disclaimers may eliminate the use of other, even more flexible *post mortem* planning tools, such as a spousal power of appointment.

6.   Another factor which must be considered is, if estate taxes will be due on the disclaimed property, who will pay them? The decedent's will may contain a tax payment clause which may or may not operate correctly after the disclaimer.

The next three sections discuss other potential problems with the use of disclaimers: plan-level obstacles, spousal consent requirements and § 401(a)(9).

Disclaimers and the Plan Administrator

The plan administrator of a **qualified retirement plan** ("QRP") may refuse to recognize disclaimers. The plan administrator may take the position that the plan requires the benefits to be paid to the beneficiary named by P, and the plan has no authority to pay the benefits to someone else if the named beneficiary is in fact living; that ERISA requires the plan to be administered in accordance with its terms; and ERISA preempts state disclaimer laws.

In the author's view, this is not a correct interpretation of ERISA. QRP documents generally provide that the interpretation of the plan and administration of the trust are governed by state law to the extent not contrary to (or preempted by) ERISA. If the applicable state law permits disclaimers, the plan is required to give effect to them, in the author's view, unless the plan contains a specific provision to the contrary.

Most non-ERISA trust instruments say nothing one way or the other about disclaimers, but no one argues that trustees generally are entitled to ignore legally valid disclaimers. An ERISA trust is not different from any other trust except to the extent federal law requires it to be. In GCM 39858 (9/9/91), the IRS recognized that disclaimers do not violate ERISA (*i.e.*, a disclaimer is not an "assignment" of benefits).

In a similar vein, the IRS has recognized that a plan must conform to a state's "slayer" statute, and not pay benefits to the person who murdered the participant, even if that person is named as the beneficiary. See, *e.g.*, PLR 8908063 (11/30/88). There is no legal basis in ERISA or elsewhere for a plan administrator to disobey a state statute of general applicability.

On the other hand, plan administrators are justified in exercising caution when dealing with disclaimers. In GCM 39858, while the IRS strongly endorsed the validity of disclaimers of QRP benefits, the approval was limited to disclaimers that satisfy the requirements of § 2518 and of state law. Thus, the IRS has left open the possibility that a non-qualified disclaimer would be a prohibited "assignment" of benefits—which could, if allowed to occur, disqualify the plan. When confronted with a disclaimer, the administrator should consider obtaining an opinion of counsel that the disclaimer meets the requirements of applicable state law and § 2518.

But then again, despite the language of GCM 39858 limiting approval to qualified disclaimers, the IRS has approved a *non-qualified* disclaimer of QRP benefits at least once: PLR 9450041 (discussed at *"Salvaging spousal rollover,"* above) gave effect to a non-qualified disclaimer for purposes of § 402(c) (which determines who pays the income tax), and did not discuss the plan qualification issue or mention GCM 39858.

These issues are of less concern to IRA administrators, since IRAs are not subject to the prohibition against "assignment" of § 401(a)(13).

Effect of REA on Surviving Spouse's Ability to Disclaim

The nine months requirement for qualified disclaimers

One of the requirements for a disclaimer to be qualified under § 2518 is that the disclaimer must be made no later than "nine months after the ... date of the transfer creating the interest" being disclaimed.

The IRS's regulations under § 2518 provide that, generally speaking, the nine months are measured "with reference to the taxable transfer creating the interest in the disclaimant." A "taxable transfer" does not mean a transfer that was taxed, but simply a "completed" transfer for gift and estate tax purposes. "When there is a completed gift for federal gift tax purposes" (regardless of whether any gift tax is imposed), the nine months begin on the date of the completed gift, regardless of whether the gift is brought back into the estate for estate tax purposes. Reg. § 25.2518-2(c)(3).

Federal law gives married persons certain rights in each other's retirement benefits. If S acquired rights in P's benefits more than nine months before the date of death, is it too late for her to disclaim these benefits when P dies?

Spousal rights in pension plans under REA

As a result of The Retirement Equity Act of 1984 ("REA") (see "REA '84 and Spousal Consent," Chapter 3) federal law gives spouses certain rights in each other's retirement benefits. Specifically, REA requires all qualified pension plans to pay a "qualified pre-retirement survivor annuity" ("QPSA") to the surviving spouse of any participant who dies prior to commencement of withdrawal of his plan benefits, with limited exceptions. REA also requires pension plans to distribute benefits to most married participants only in the form of a "qualified joint and survivor annuity" ("QJSA") (which is a life annuity to P and a survivorship annuity to S) unless S consents to some other benefit form. A spouse cannot be involuntarily divested of her QPSA and QJSA rights except by divorce. § 401(a)(11)(B). Thus, under a qualified pension plan, S acquires vested rights in P's benefits at the same moment P does (or upon their marriage, if the marriage occurred when P was already in the plan).

REA applies differently to most profit sharing plans, and does not apply at all to IRAs; see separate discussion of profit sharing plans and IRAs at the end of this section. The rest of this section deals with disclaimers of REA-guaranteed rights under pension plans.

The question presented

If P's participation in a plan is deemed to create a "transfer" of the survivor annuity rights to S, then the question is whether it will be too late, at P's death, for S to disclaim the survivorship annuity if more than nine months have passed since P joined the plan.

Example: Bill goes to work for Acme Widget Co. and becomes a participant in the Acme Pension Plan. Under the plan, Bill's wife Isabelle is entitled to QJSA and QPSA benefits; in other words, whenever "accrued benefits" are credited to Bill under the plan, Isabelle automatically "accrues" some benefits at the same time.

If Bill's working for Acme Widget is deemed to constitute a "transfer" of some of his pension benefits to Isabelle, then it would be too late, upon his death, for her to disclaim any benefits that "accrued" more than nine months prior to Bill's death. Therefore a purported disclaimer by

Isabelle would be either completely ineffective or would be a taxable gift by her to the next beneficiaries.

Statute and G.C.M. 39858

§ 2503(f) provides that *certain* spousal waivers of retirement benefits are exempt from gift tax. Specifically, § 2503(f) says that, "If any individual waives, *before the death of a participant*, any survivor benefit, or right to such benefit, *under § 401(a)(11) or 417* [REA benefits, in other words], such waiver shall not be treated as a transfer of property by gift for purposes of this chapter" (emphasis added). Thus, the Code has a specific exemption from gift tax for *certain* spousal waivers, namely, waivers (1) of REA-guaranteed survivor benefits (2) that occur before the death of the participant. Does this mean that (1) waivers of *other* spousal plan benefits, or (2) waivers that occur *after* the participant's death, *are* taxable gifts?

1.   Many plans, for administrative reasons, give spouses more benefits than REA strictly requires. Although the statutory exemption is limited to REA-guaranteed benefits, presumably the IRS would not attempt, in the case of a spousal waiver, to assess gift tax on the "enhanced" value of any plan spousal benefits over the strict minimum guaranteed by REA. However, there is no authority on this question, yet, one way or the other.

2.   The IRS has answered the second question. The Service announced in GCM 39858 (9/9/91) that § 2503(f) does not imply Congressional intent to impose gift tax on spousal waivers that occur *after* P's death: "no inference should be drawn from § 2503(f) that a disclaimer of plan benefits *after* the participant's death should receive unfavorable tax treatment simply because Congress provided for favorable gift tax treatment if plan benefits are waived *before* the participant's death."

IRS position

GCM 39858 involved a spousal disclaimer of REA-guaranteed benefits. The IRS stated that: "There is no evidence that Congress intended to preclude a spouse from disclaiming or renouncing benefits under a qualified plan payable after the participant's death." In view of the IRS's strong policy statement in this GCM, it appears the IRS has answered, for now, any questions that might exist about the disclaimer of REA-guaranteed benefits: such benefits can be the object of a qualified disclaimer, according to GCM 39858.

Nevertheless, it should be noted that this language was mere "dictum," not essential to the "holding" of the GCM. The holding of the GCM was simply that a qualified disclaimer would not constitute a prohibited "assignment of benefits" under § 401(a)(13) and would be effective to shift income tax liability to the next beneficiary. The ruling involved a spouse's disclaimer of a QPSA, but the fact that this disclaimer was "qualified" was stipulated by the parties, so no-one ever asked the IRS to rule that the disclaimer was in fact qualified. Thus it is conceivable that the IRS could, in the future, decide that a spousal waiver of REA-guaranteed benefits, by disclaimer, after the participant's death, was not a "qualified disclaimer."

What to do: planning mode

REA permits a spouse to waive her QPSA rights if P is over age 35. The law contains elaborate requirements for such a waiver. Unless the QPSA is the only death benefit provided by the plan (which is the case in some defined benefit plans; but presumably there would be no reason to waive the QPSA in such a case), the effect of the waiver is to allow P to designate another beneficiary for the portion of the benefits represented by the QPSA, or to designate S as the beneficiary but change the form of benefits from a QPSA to something else.

If the plan permits S to give an unqualified waiver of her QPSA rights, and she does so, reserving no right whatsoever to veto P's future choice of beneficiary, and P names S as his beneficiary (but still has the right to designate someone else, without her consent), any possible questions about S's right to later disclaim should go away. Accordingly, such an unqualified waiver of QPSA rights would appear to be a recommended ingredient of an estate plan intended to be activated by means of a spousal disclaimer where there are REA - guaranteed benefits.

Another approach is, rather than making the benefits payable to S and "disclaimable" to the credit shelter trust, to make the benefits payable *to the trust* as primary beneficiary, and disclaimable to S (as secondary beneficiary), in addition to obtaining an unqualified spousal waiver of QPSA rights. This method works if the trust or applicable state law permits trustees to disclaim. This approach has been sanctioned in letter rulings 8838075 (7/1/88), 9045050 (8/15/90), and 9247026 (8/24/92) (trust disclaimed, benefit passed to S who rolled it over to an IRA). The nine months question is sidestepped.

IRAs and profit sharing plans

IRAs are not subject to REA at all. IRA beneficiary designations are normally completely revocable at will by the participant. Thus, even if S is named as beneficiary of P's IRA prior to P's death, there is no "transfer" to her until the actual date of death, so S has nine months from that date to execute the disclaimer. Reg. § 25.2518-2(c)(3). See, *e.g.*, PLRs 9037048 (6/20/90); 9320015 (2/17/93).

Under a profit sharing plan, REA generally requires that P's spouse be named as beneficiary of his death benefits unless she consents to naming another beneficiary. However, REA permits profit sharing benefits to be distributed to P (solely) during life without S's consent. There is generally no QJSA requirement for lifetime distributions from profit sharing plans as there is for pension plans. If P is free to withdraw his benefits during life without spousal consent, the transfer of the benefits to her clearly does not occur until P's death and the "when do the nine months begin?" problem does not exist.

Unfortunately, this general rule does not apply to all profit sharing plans. Some profit sharing plans are subject to the same REA rules as pension plans—for example, a profit sharing plan which was at one time a pension plan; or which contains assets resulting from a merger with or a transfer from a pension plan; or which offers certain annuity benefits.

Are Disclaimers Effective to Change the "Designated Beneficiary"?

Importance of having a "designated beneficiary"

§ 401(a)(9)(B) generally requires that retirement benefits payable on account of a P's death prior to age 70½ be entirely distributed within five years after the date of death. If the benefits are payable to a "designated beneficiary" (DB), however, the benefits may be distributed (beginning within one year after the death) in installments over the life expectancy of the DB. § 401(a)(9)(B)(iii). The IRS's proposed regulations provide detailed requirements for determining *whether* a participant has a DB and *who* that DB is. See Chapter 1.

Suppose child, C, is named as the primary beneficiary of parent's (P's) retirement benefits, and grandchild (GC) is the contingent beneficiary. P dies at age 65. At that time, C is age 42, so his life expectancy is 40.6 years and GC is age 17, so his life expectancy is 64.8 years. Reg. § 1.72-9, Table V. C disclaims all interests in the benefits by means of a qualified disclaimer under § 2518, so the benefits become payable to GC.

But whose life expectancy is used as the measuring period for the annual required distributions under: C's or GC's?

If C had *actually* predeceased P, then unquestionably GC would be entitled to withdraw the benefits over his 64.8 year life expectancy. Prop. Reg. § 1.401(a)(9)-1, E-5(a)(1) and (e)(1). Where C is merely "deemed," for gift tax purposes, to have predeceased P, but is actually still alive, will the change of identity of the DB be recognized under § 401(a)(9)?

The proposed regulations do not address this. They say only that (with certain exceptions not relevant) "the DB will be determined as of the employee's date of death." § D-4. The question is, whether a qualified disclaimer will be given the same effect under § 401(a)(9) as under § 2518, and treated as effective retroactive to the date of death.

Statute

§ 2518 recognizes qualified disclaimers "for purposes of this subtitle." § 2518 is part of Subtitle B of the Code, "Estate and Gift Taxes." The minimum distribution rules under § 401(a)(9) are part of Subtitle A, "Income Taxes." Therefore § 2518 does not govern the result under § 401(a)(9).

The income tax rules applicable to trusts, in Subtitle A, contain their own section dealing with disclaimers, § 678(d). § 678(d) provides that a beneficiary will not be treated as having held or released a power over a trust if the power "has been renounced or disclaimed within a reasonable time after the holder of the power first became aware of its existence." There is no statutory provision other than § 678(d) dealing with the effectiveness of disclaimers *for purposes of Subtitle A*.

Legislation passed by Congress in late 1995 (but vetoed by President Clinton) would have eliminated this problem by amending § 2518(a) to provide that qualified disclaimers are effective for purposes of "Subtitle A" (which contains §

401(a)(9) among other things) as well as for purposes of Subtitle B (estate and gift taxes). See H.R. 2419, 104th Cong., 1st Sess. § 14619(e) (1995). As written, this change would have been effective as to "transfers and disclaimers" occurring after the date of enactment.

Effect of GCM 39858

It is widely believed that, in GCM 39858 (9/9/91), the IRS "blessed" disclaimers of retirement benefits for all purposes, but this is not the case. In this GCM, the IRS Chief Counsel's office recognized the effectiveness of a qualified disclaimer of retirement benefits for *certain purposes*: to wit, that a disclaimer meeting all requirements of § 2518 *and* applicable state law will not be deemed an "assignment or alienation" of plan benefits in violation of ERISA's anti-alienation provisions (§ 401(a)(13)) and will be effective to shift the income tax on the benefits from the disclaimant to the person who actually receives the benefits. The GCM did *not* address other issues, such as the effect of a disclaimer for § 401(a)(9) purposes.

The IRS's recognition of qualified disclaimers for purposes of imposition of income tax is encouraging. Perhaps it means that the IRS will recognize qualified disclaimers for *all* subtitle A purposes, including § 401(a)(9); but it is not determinative on this question. The IRS was probably more or less forced to recognize qualified disclaimers as effective to shift the income tax burden to the "new" beneficiary by the unique income tax treatment of retirement benefits. Taxation of retirement benefits is generally governed by § 402, which taxes only "amounts actually distributed to any distributee." "Normal" income tax rules (such as the doctrine of constructive receipt) are suspended. When a disclaimer is clearly effective, under § 2518, to shift ownership of the benefit to a new beneficiary, the IRS would find it difficult to impose income tax on the disclaimant, since the income tax falls only on "amounts actually distributed" and nothing is "actually distributed" to the disclaimant.

This type of statutory restraint does not apply to § 401(a)(9), however. The IRS could ignore disclaimers for purposes of § 401(a)(9) without violating the letter or the spirit of § 2518, or § 401(a)(9), or GCM 39858.

Other rulings

There are as yet no revenue rulings or cases deciding this issue. Several private letter rulings, while not precisely determining the question, do not support the conclusion that a qualified disclaimer by a beneficiary is treated the same as the death of that beneficiary for purposes of determining who is the DB under § 401(a)(9).

In PLR 9320015 (2/17/93), the IRS refused to decide who were the "designated beneficiaries" for purposes of § 401(a)(9) in a disclaimer situation. The basis for its refusal was that the question was hypothetical (P had not died yet). In PLR 9037048 (6/20/90), P had reached age 70½ and elected to take benefits out of his IRA in installments over the joint life expectancy of himself and his spouse (S). When he later died, S disclaimed in favor of the contingent beneficiary, a trust for their child. The IRS ruled that, because the disclaimer met all the requirements of § 2518, the disclaimed interests in the decedent's IRA passed to (and were taxable to) the contingent beneficiary.

Nothing in this ruling, however, turned on the issue of whether the disclaimer changed the DB for § 401(a)(9) purposes. That aspect was moot because P was already past age 70½ when he died, so the question of whether he did or did not have a DB was settled at his "required beginning date." (See Chapter 1.) What prevailed at his later death was significant for

§ 401(a)(9) purposes only insofar as the IRS did not rule that the disclaimer constituted a *change* of beneficiary; the IRS stated simply that distributions after the decedent's death would have to continue at least as rapidly as under the method in effect prior to his death, *i.e.*, installments over the life expectancy of decedent and spouse.

In PLR 9450040 (9/22/94), the IRS specifically refused to treat a qualified disclaimer as a "death" for the purpose of determining the DB under the minimum distribution rules. In this ruling, P was past age 70½, and was withdrawing his IRA benefits over the joint life expectancy of himself and his wife, with both life expectancies recalculated annually. Husband died. Wife proposed to execute a qualified disclaimer so that the benefits would pass to their children. If the IRS had treated the qualified disclaimer as a "death" for purposes of § 401(a)(9), then all benefits would have had to be distributed within a year after husband's death. (Since both spouses' life expectancies were being redetermined annually, the deaths of both would have resulted in both life expectancies going to zero in the year following the year of death; see Chapter 1.)

Instead, the IRS said it would not be appropriate to treat the wife as dead, since she was not in fact dead, and therefore the children could continue to withdraw the benefits over the remaining life expectancy of the wife, recalculated annually, so long as she was actually alive. Although the ruling was favorable to these taxpayers, it may have negative implications for use of disclaimers to shift benefits from an older generation to a younger in hopes of getting an extended payout period.

The way of the future?

In PLR 9537005 (6/13/95), the IRS analyzed a disclaimer as if it were a change of beneficiary made by P at the moment of death. This ruling may point the way to the future;

it seems to adopt a sensible approach to integrating qualified disclaimers and § 401(a)(9). In this ruling, P was past his RBD and was taking minimum required distributions based on the joint life expectancy of P and his DB, S, recalculated annually. A revocable trust was named as P's contingent beneficiary. At P's death, S proposed to disclaim the benefits and allow them to pass to the trust, of which she was the life beneficiary.

The IRS made specific findings that the trust met the requirements of the "trust rules" of the proposed regulations, including the requirement (which has since been "repealed") that the trust be irrevocable as of the later of the required beginning date or the date the trust is named as beneficiary. Prop. Reg. § 1.401(a)(9)-1, D-5. The IRS considered the date of death to be the date the trust was named as beneficiary, because "as a result of the proposed disclaimer, the residuary trust will be the beneficiary of the IRA as of the date" of death. Since S was the DB both before (individually) and after (as trust beneficiary) the date of death and disclaimer, the IRS was able to conclude that payments would continue to be made "at least as rapidly" after P's death as before, and therefore payments could continue to be made over S's life expectancy.

It is to be hoped that the IRS will give effect to qualified disclaimers, retroactive to the date of death, for purposes of § 401(a)(9); treating a qualified disclaimer as a change of beneficiary by the participant, as of the moment of death, would be a sensible outcome. The point of this discussion is that the IRS has not yet announced that it will do so, and planners must deal with the possibility that the IRS may *not* do so.

What to do: planning mode

This issue is not a problem for a disclaimer from S to any trust of which she is the oldest beneficiary. Either way, her life expectancy can be used; there is no attempt to lengthen the §

401(a)(9) distribution period by means of the disclaimer.

On the other hand, if the goal is to permit shifting of the benefits, by disclaimer, from an older beneficiary (*e.g.* child) to younger (*e.g.* grandchild), so that, if it appears desirable at the time of P's death, the longer life expectancy of the younger beneficiary can be used, the only safe approach is to arrange the plan benefits so the disclaimers will go in the *other* direction, *i.e.*, from the younger to the older generation, so the younger beneficiaries, with their long life expectancies, are clearly the designated beneficiaries, and the parties can either do an installment payout to them over their life expectancy, or have the younger generation disclaim to the older. However, this choice may not be practical if the younger beneficiaries are minors, since a disclaimer by a minor usually requires court proceedings and the consent of a disinterested guardian.

Summary of Planning Principles

1.   Upon the death of a client, all plan and IRA beneficiary designations should be reviewed as soon as possible. No benefits should be distributed to any beneficiary until this review is completed. If any beneficiary designation appears undesirable, consider the use of qualified disclaimers to redirect benefits to the "right" beneficiary.

2.   When preparing beneficiary designations as part of the estate planning process, be sure to name a contingent as well as a primary beneficiary. Consider whether different contingent beneficiaries should be named in case of a disclaimer by, as opposed to the death of, the primary beneficiary.

3.   When choosing among competing considerations in naming a primary beneficiary, the client should make the choice based on the relative priorities the client assigns to the

choices (such as "financial security of spouse" versus "saving estate taxes for children"). To allow maximum flexibility after the client's death, name the second choice as contingent beneficiary.

4.   If a proposed disclaimer involves a spouse's disclaimer of REA-guaranteed benefits, or a shift of benefits to a contingent beneficiary who has a longer life expectancy, consider the issues discussed earlier in this chapter regarding whether the disclaimer will be effective to accomplish the goals.

5.   When a disclaimer is anticipated at the estate planning stage, take steps beforehand to facilitate that process, including: spousal waiver of REA rights, if needed; clear instructions to the beneficiaries regarding the choices that will be available to them and what considerations should be applied in making the choice; granting disclaimer authority to fiduciaries, along with guidelines for exercise of the power to disclaim; review the plan documents, § 2518 requirements, and state law to make sure these pose no obstacles to the proposed disclaimers; and make sure that there are no instructions for automatic benefit distributions which could cause the beneficiary to receive and be deemed to have "accepted" benefits after P's death, and thus lose the right to disclaim.

Distributions Before Age 59½

*What distributions the 10%
penalty under § 72(t) applies to
and how to avoid it*

Meet § 72(t)

An individual who is under age 59½ and wants to withdraw money from his retirement plan faces a special obstacle: the 10% penalty imposed by § 72(t) on retirement distributions prior to age 59½. This chapter describes various details of the penalty, then explains a highly useful and flexible exception to the penalty, the "series of substantially equal periodic payments." Finally, the chapter reviews the requirements of the other 11 exceptions to the penalty.

The application of § 72(t) to Roth IRAs is covered in Chapter 5, and to plan-held life insurance in Chapter 10. For inter-relation with the spousal rollover, see *"Drawbacks of spousal rollover,"* Chapter 3.

10% penalty for "early" or "premature" distributions

§ 72(t) generally imposes a 10% "additional tax" on retirement plan distributions made before the participant (P) attains age 59½. This additional tax is usually referred to as the "10% penalty" on "early" (or "premature") distributions. It is not intended as a punishment for wrongdoing, but rather as a disincentive for early distributions (to encourage saving not only *for* but *until* retirement). The idea is to remove some of the benefits of tax-free accumulation if the accumulated funds are not used for their intended purpose.

§ 72(t) was added to the Code by the Tax Reform Act of 1986. Prior to this Act, there was a comparable penalty for premature distributions from IRAs (only) under now-repealed §408(f). By July 1999 Congress had already amended §72(t) five times. The IRS has not issued regulations under §72(t), presumably because it has been unable to keep up with Congress's whims.

What types of plans the penalty applies to

§ 72(t)(1) says that the penalty applies to any distribution from a "qualified retirement plan (as defined in § 4974(c))." The plan in question does not have be "qualified" at the time of the distribution, as long as it was once a qualified plan. Powell v. Comm'r, 129 F.3d 321 (4th Cir. 1997). § 4974(c)'s definition of "qualified retirement plan" includes 401(a) plans (true "qualified" retirement plans) as well as **403(b)** arrangements and IRAs (both of which are not normally included in the term "qualified retirement plan"). [It also includes other types of plans not dealt with in this book.] Although § 72(t) includes all of these plans in the term "qualified retirement plan," *in this chapter the term "qualified retirement plan" ("QRP") refers only to plans qualified under § 401(a), as distinguished from 403(b) arrangements and IRAs.*

When does a person reach age 59½?

The author has not found an official IRS pronouncement on the subject of when a person reaches age 59½, but by analogy to Prop. Reg. §1.401(a)(9)-1, B-3 (decreeing when a person reaches age 70½), it would be on the date which is six months after his 59th birthday. The penalty applies to any distribution received before that date (*not*, as some people mistakenly believe, before January 1 of the year in which the person turns age 59½).

Penalty applies to portion included in income

The 10% penalty is calculated only with respect to "the portion of [the distribution] which is includible in gross income." § 72(t)(1); Notice 87-16 (Q & A D-9). To the extent the distribution is *income tax-free* because (for example) it represents the return of P's own after-tax contributions (§ 72(d),(e)), or because it is rolled over to another plan or IRA in a qualifying rollover (§ 402(c)), it is also *penalty-free*. See, *e.g.*, PLR 9253049 (10/6/92) (because a pre-age 59½ IRA distribution was excluded from the taxpayer's gross income by virtue of the U.S.-U.K. tax treaty, it was also not subject to the 10% penalty); PLR 9010007 (12/14/89) (tax-free rollover not subject to penalty).

Other than the fact that the penalty applies only to the portion of a distribution that is includible in gross income, the 10% penalty has nothing to do with the income tax treatment of the distribution. Nevertheless, the § 72(t) exceptions are a constant source of confusion to clients and practitioners, who sometimes wrongly conclude that distributions that are *penalty-free* under § 72(t) are also *income tax-free*.

Enforcement of the penalty

The IRS eagerly seeks to collect the penalty wherever it applies. People who take money from their retirement plans without being aware that the penalty exists are of course caught by the penalty. A more sympathetic case (though not to the IRS) is presented by people who did not know they had received a distribution, or who had reason to believe the distribution in question was tax-free, and then find out the hard way that not only have they received a taxable distribution but it is subject to a penalty.

This can happen to a person who takes a loan from a retirement plan but fails to meet the exact requirements of §72(p), so that the loan is treated as a distribution rather than a loan. IRS Notice 87-13, 1987-1 C.B. 432 (Q & A 20) confirms that the penalty applies to such "deemed" distributions. It happens to people whose attempts to roll over plan distributions are held for one reason or another not to constitute "qualified rollovers"; see, *e.g.*, <u>Rodoni v. Comm'r</u>, 105 T.C. 29 (1995) (husband's distribution improperly rolled over into IRA in the name of wife).

Adding to the fun, the penalty may itself generate *another* penalty, if its existence means the taxpayer underpaid his estimated taxes: According to Notice 87-13, Q & A 20, "the taxpayer may have estimated tax liability with respect to such additional income tax."

The Tax Court strictly enforces the penalty, expressing sympathy for the taxpayers in appropriate cases, but declining to modify the clear words of the statute. But see "*IRS levy on the account.*"

Overview of the exceptions to the penalty

There are 12 exceptions to the penalty. The exceptions are not the same for all types of retirement plans. For example, some exceptions that are available for QRPs and 403(b) arrangements are *not* available for IRA distributions. Other exceptions apply *only* to IRAs. Some exceptions are available for all types of plans but apply differently depending on the type of plan involved.

Most of the exceptions have limited usefulness for planning purposes because they are triggered only by particular hardships (such as death, disability, unemployment) (although there is no "hardship exception *per se* to this penalty), or depend on a particular use of the funds distributed (such as college tuition, health insurance premiums, "first time" home purchase). But one of the exceptions stands out as an extremely useful planning tool: the "series of substantially equal payments."

Series of Substantially Equal Payments

Part of a "SOSEPP"

The penalty does not apply to a distribution which is "part of a series of substantially equal periodic payments (not less frequently than annually) made for the life (or life expectancy) of the employee or the joint lives (or joint life expectancies) of such employee and his designated beneficiary" ("DB"). § 72(t)(2)(A)(iv). While at first this appears to be a rather narrow window, in fact it is a wide open door, because:

- Liberalized rollover rules introduced in 1992 (§ 402(c)) make it relatively easy to create an IRA of the desired size to support the series.
- The payments do not in fact have to continue for P's entire life or life expectancy period, but only until P reaches age 59½, or until five years have elapsed, whichever occurs later.
- The IRS allows numerous methods for determining the size of the "equal payments."

This is the most significant exception for planning purposes. Everyone who has an IRA (or who can get one via a rollover from some other type of plan) can use the SOSEPP exception. Participants in QRPs can also use this exception—*if* they have separated from service. § 72(t)(3)(B). (See also, for these participants, *"Distribution after separation from service after age 55,"* below.)

There is one significant limitation on this exception: if the series of payments is "modified" before the five years are up (or before P reaches age 59½, if he started the SOSEPP more than five years before reaching age 59½), *all* payments in the series lose the shelter of the exception, and the penalty applies, retroactively and with interest, to all pre-age 59½ distributions. § 72(t)(4)(A). See "*Modification of the series is prohibited*," below.

SOSEPP payments may not be rolled over to another plan or IRA. § 402(c)(4)(A)(i).

How this exception works

The SOSEPP exception starts from the premise that there is a fund of money (the retirement plan account) that will be gradually exhausted by a series of regular distributions over the applicable period of time, *i.e.*, the life expectancy of P (or the joint life expectancy of P and the DB). Thus, the SOSEPP must be designed so that, if it continued for that period of time, it would exactly exhaust the fund—even though the payments actually have to be made for only five years (or until P reaches age 59½, if later).

Note that § 72(t)(2)(A)(iv) *itself* does not say that the SOSEPP must be designed to *exhaust* the account over the applicable time period: It says only that the equal payments must be "made for" the applicable period of time. This wording clearly would preclude a series of equal payments that would exhaust the fund *before* the end of the applicable time period, but would not necessarily preclude a series of equal payments which would be too small to exhaust the fund. For example, if payments of $50,000 per year would exhaust the account over P's life expectancy, § 72(t)(2)(A)(iv)'s wording would *appear* to permit him to take any amount *up to* $50,000 per year, so long as the payments were equal every year and continued for the required period of time.

However, the IRS's view is that the SOSEPP must be designed to exactly exhaust the fund over the applicable time period. See Notice 89-25, at 666 (Q & A 12) and PLR 9805023 (10/31/97). P cannot take annual distributions that are too small to exhaust the account, even if they are equal, regular, payments designed to continue over the applicable time period. Fortunately, if P's benefits are in (or can be rolled to) an IRA, it is very easy to get around this problem; see *"Applying the exception to multiple IRAs,"* below.

How to determine the size of the payments

To determine the size of the required payments, you start with the current value of the fund (see further discussion of adjusting the size of the fund as a way of adjusting the size of the payments, under *"Applying the exception to multiple IRAs,"* below), then apply several variables.

The first variable is the life expectancy measuring period. You can use the single life expectancy of P, which is what you should use if you want the largest possible payments. If for some reason you want relatively smaller payments, you can use the joint life expectancy of P and his beneficiary, which may produce that result.

The next variable is how the life expectancy is to be determined: Which mortality table is used? Will a fixed life expectancy be used, or will life expectancy be redetermined annually?

The final variable is an interest rate assumption. The size of the payments required to exhaust a fund will vary substantially depending on whether the assumed rate of return for the fund is high (larger payments required) or low (a low interest rate assumption produces smaller payments).

Note that the whole idea of the "series of substantially

equal periodic payments" is fictional. In order for a SOSEPP to actually—and exactly—exhaust a fund of money over the applicable time period, the fund would have to grow steadily at the specified rate of return. In reality, an investment fund rarely grows steadily over any period of time. Investments may even shrink in value. Therefore, in reality, if the series continued for the entire specified time period, it is likely that either the fund would be exhausted before the end of the period, or the payments would not exhaust the fund.

The IRS in Notice 89-25, Q & A 12, sets forth three methods for calculating the periodic payments, saying that "Payments will be considered to be substantially equal periodic payments within the meaning of § 72(t)(2)(A)(iv) if they are made according to one of" these three methods.

First IRS method: minimum distribution

"Payments shall be treated as satisfying § 72(t)(2)(A)(iv) if the annual payment is determined using a method that would be acceptable for purposes of calculating the minimum distribution required under § 401(a)(9). For this purpose, the payment may be determined based on the life expectancy of the employee or the joint life and last survivor expectancy of the employee and beneficiary."

Under this method, each year's distribution is determined by dividing the fund balance as of the preceding year end by the applicable life expectancy. This method is equivalent to assuming, for purposes of computing each year's payment, that *no* interest will be earned by the fund in the future. Then, each year, the payments are in effect adjusted to reflect the actual investment growth or decline since the prior year's distribution. As is true for "minimum required distributions" under § 401(a)(9), the payments will grow larger each year if there is a positive investment return.

Presumably this method brings with it the benefits of minimum distribution calculations (such as the option to recalculate life expectancy), and the limitations (such as the MDIB rule, if the beneficiary is not P's spouse). See Chapter 1. One major difference, however, is that in the case of a SOSEPP under § 72(t)(2)(A)(iv), the resulting distribution amount is not merely the *minimum* distribution, it is also the *maximum* distribution.

Prop. Reg. § 1.401(a)(9)-1, Q & A E-3 & 4, dealing with required minimum distributions, requires "use of the expected return multiples [life expectancies] in Table V [single life] and VI [joint and survivor] of [Regulation] § 1.72-9." Because this first method exactly tracks the proposed minimum distribution regulations under § 401(a)(9), these life expectancy tables must be used for method one.

The author has found no ruling or case in which the taxpayer used the minimum distribution method. Why is this method unpopular? Perhaps because it produces smaller payments at the beginning of the program than the other methods. People embarking on a SOSEPP program, in the author's experience, assume that they need more money at the beginning of the program, to take care of some "one-time" expenses (new home, travel, etc.), and that they will need less going forward, so they look for the largest possible payment at the beginning, not the smallest. Also, this method does not produce the steady predictable flow of income which is apparently preferred.

Second IRS method: amortization

Under this method "the amount to be distributed annually is determined by amortizing the taxpayer's account balance over a number of years equal to the life expectancy of the account owner or the joint life and last survivor expectancy of the account owner and beneficiary (with *life expectancies determined in accordance with proposed section 1.401(a)(9)-1* of the regulations) at an *interest rate that does not exceed a reasonable interest rate* on the date payments commence. For example, a 50 year old individual with a life expectancy of 33.1, having an account balance of $100,000, and assuming an interest rate of 8 percent, could satisfy section 72(t)(2)(A)(iv) by distributing $8,679 annually, derived by amortizing $100,000 over 33.1 years at 8 percent interest." (Emphasis added.)

This second method creates a predictable stream of payments that will in fact be equal. See, *e.g.,* PLR 9830042 (4/29/98). The annual payment amount is determined at the beginning of the period in the same manner as the payments on a fixed-rate mortgage: a fixed dollar amount of principal (the retirement fund), plus a fixed rate of interest, are amortized over a fixed period of time (the life expectancy), with a series of level payments. The fixed payment so determined is paid out to P each year, regardless of the actual investment performance of the fund.

This method requires P to come up with a "reasonable interest rate" (see *"What is a reasonable interest rate?"* below), but (as in the case of the minimum distribution method) life expectancy must be determined using the IRS tables referenced in the proposed minimum distribution regulations; see *"First IRS method,"* above.

The amortization method is the popular favorite, judging by private letter rulings where it outnumbers the annuity method (discussed next) by five to one.

Third IRS method: annuity

Under this method, "the amount to be distributed annually is determined by dividing the taxpayer's account balance by an annuity factor (the present value of an annuity of

$1 per year beginning at the taxpayer's age attained in the first distribution year and continuing for the life of the taxpayer) with such annuity factor derived using a *reasonable mortality table* and using *an interest rate that does not exceed a reasonable interest rate* on the date payments commence. If substantially equal monthly payments are being determined, the taxpayer's account balance would be divided by an annuity factor equal to the present value of an annuity of $1 per month beginning at the taxpayer's age attained in the first distribution year and continuing for the life of the taxpayer. For example, if the annuity factor for a $1 per year annuity for an individual who is 50 years old is 11.109 (assuming an interest rate of 8 percent and using the UP-1984 Mortality Table), an individual with a $100,000 account balance would receive an annual distribution of $9,002 ($100,000/11.109= $9,002)." (Emphasis added.)

This method allows more actuarial creativity, since any "reasonable mortality table" (not only the IRS's tables) may be used. It also tends to produce the largest payments of any of the three methods, for reasons best known to actuaries. Also, despite the suggestion that the payments, once initially determined, must never vary in amount, the IRS has allowed taxpayers using this method to revalue their account balances and redetermine the interest factor annually. See *"Permitted variations in designing the SOSEPP,"* below.

Here are the questions that come up in designing and administering a SOSEPP:

What is a reasonable interest rate?

There is no IRS prescribed or safe-harbor interest rate.

Methods two and three allow any interest rate that "does not exceed" a reasonable rate, so presumably an interest rate from as low as zero to as high as a reasonable rate is acceptable; method one assumes a zero interest rate. Although sometimes the IRS states that it is opposed to use of an "unreasonably high" interest rate (which would produce excessive distributions) (see, *e.g.*, PLRs 9830042 (4/29/98), 9604026 (11/1/95) and 9601052 (10/12/95)), elsewhere the IRS says is it opposed to use of *any* "unreasonable interest rate" (see PLR 9747045 (8/28/97)).

Most letter rulings state the interest rate the taxpayer is using, but do not state the basis for choosing that particular rate. The IRS has approved rates from as low as 5.6% (PLR 9514026 (1/12/95)) to as high as 8.2445% (PLR 9830042 (4/29/98)). In seven rulings issued in 1995, the IRS approved programs based on interest rates of 5.6% (March), 5.95% (June), 6% (July), 7% (August), 8.8% (October), 6% (November) and "the Federal Mid-Term Applicable Rate" (May); this illustrates the variety of acceptable interest rates.

The § 72(t) private letter rulings which reveal the basis for selecting a particular interest rate used some variation of the applicable federal rate ("AFR") prescribed under § 1274(d). In PLR 9240042 (7/9/92), the long-term AFR was used. (Under § 1274(d) the long-term AFR is used for obligations with a term of over nine years.) The taxpayer in PLR 9531039 (5/10/95) used the mid-term AFR (applicable, under § 1274(d), to obligations with a term of three to nine years). In PLR 9747039 (8/26/97), the IRS approved use of "120% of the federal *mid*-term rate" for the last month of the year preceding the year the series commenced. Two days later, in PLR 9747045 (8/28/97), the IRS approved use of the then-current "*Long* Term 120% AFR." In PLR 9812038 (12/23/97), the IRS approved use of the long-term AFR.

These rulings suggest that any rate from the mid-term AFR up to 120% of the long-term AFR, and any other rate for which a valid justification can be presented, should be acceptable.

Which mortality table should be used?

Most people who obtain rulings for their SOSEPPs use the mortality tables explicitly blessed in Notice 89-25.

As required by the terms of method two, all rulings using method two use § 1.72-9's "Table V" for single life expectancy and "Table VI" for joint life expectancy. The life expectancies are determined based on attained age in the year distributions commence. Notice 89-25, Q&A 12. One daring taxpayer modified his Table V life expectancy to the extent of rounding it down to the next lowest whole number, with IRS approval. PLR 9747039 (8/26/97).

Method three (annuity) allows the use of any "reasonable mortality table." The one example of method three in Notice 89-25 uses the UP-1984 Mortality Table, and most of the rulings in which the annuity method was used also used this table. The exceptions were PLR 9021058 (2/28/90), which used the 1983 IAM Male Mortality Table, and PLR 9824047 (3/18/98), in which the IRS approved the use of Life Table 80 CNSMT.

Does the MDIB rule (Chapter 1) apply when a joint life expectancy with a non-spouse beneficiary is used? Clearly it is required under method one, since method one simply tracks the minimum distribution rules calculations. It is not clear whether use of the MDIB rule is required under the other two methods. In PLR 9824047 (3/18/98) the joint life expectancy of the taxpayer and her son-beneficiary was determined, under method three, using the MDIB rule, with IRS approval, but the ruling does not specify whether this was required or the taxpayer simply chose to do it that way. In PLR 9747045 (8/28/97), the taxpayer used the joint life expectancy of herself and her (apparently non-spouse) DB, based on Table VI of the § 72 regulations, for a method two series, and there is no mention of the MDIB rule.

What happens if P is using a joint life expectancy factor

but then changes his DB before the end of the no-modification period (see *"Modification of the series is prohibited,"* below)? Is he required to change the life expectancy factor to reflect the new beneficiary? Is he forbidden to do so? The author has found no source addressing this question.

Permitted variations in designing the SOSEPP

Although IRS Publication 590 ("Individual Retirement Arrangements (IRAs)"; edition for use in preparing 1997 returns) states at page 22 that you "must" use one of the three "IRS-approved distribution methods," in fact Notice 89-25 does not state that you are limited to these methods, and several rulings have approved variations of the IRS-approved models. For example, in PLR 9816028 (1/21/98), P's SOSEPP was based on the annuity method, but called for the payments to increase by 3% annually as a cost of living adjustment ("COLA"). PLRs 9747045 (8/28/97), 9723035 (3/10/97) and 9536031 (6/15/95) also approved the use of an annual 3% COLA.

In PLR 9531039 (5/10/95), the taxpayer received IRS approval for a SOSEPP under which he proposed to redetermine the life expectancy, interest rate and account balance each year, rather than setting these factors once and for all at the beginning of the SOSEPP as method three requires. In PLR 9021058 (2/28/90), also, the IRS approved a SOSEPP in which the taxpayer planned to redetermine the interest rate factor and account balance each year.

Applying the exception to multiple IRAs

Must all IRAs be treated as one IRA for purposes of computing the SOSEPP payments? Or can one IRA be isolated from other IRAs owned by the same participant and used separately as a basis for these distributions?

§ 408(d)(1), which governs IRAs, provides that IRA distributions are includible in gross income "in the manner provided under § 72." § 408(d)(2) then provides that: "For purposes of applying section 72 to any amount described in paragraph (1)—(A) all individual retirement plans shall be treated as 1 contract, [and] (B) all distributions during any taxable year shall be treated as 1 distribution..." Some practitioners have concluded based on this section that all IRAs must be aggregated for all purposes of § 72, including applying the SOSEPP exception.

However, § 408(d)(2) by its terms applies only for the purpose of determining how much of any distribution is *included in gross income* (the subject of § 408(d)). There is no requirement that IRAs be aggregated for purposes of *§ 72(t)*.

Similarly, the IRS, in Notice 89-25, at 665 (Q & A 7), states that "For purposes of determining the taxation of IRA distributions, all IRAs maintained for an individual must be aggregated and treated as one IRA." But the IRS has never applied this *income tax* rule for purposes of the § 72(t) *"additional tax"* and the SOSEPP exception. On the contrary, the IRS said in PLR 9747039 (8/26/97), "If a taxpayer owns more than one IRA, any combination of his or her IRAs may be taken into account in determining the distributions by aggregating the account balances of those IRAs. *The specific IRAs taken into account are part of the method of determining the substantially equal periodic payments....*" (emphasis added). Here are examples:

All IRAs aggregated: In each of PLR 9830042 (4/29/98), 9824047 (3/18/98), and 9545018 (8/16/95), all of the taxpayer's IRAs were aggregated for purposes of computing the SOSEPP. However, the rulings do not say that this aggregation was a *requirement* of the favorable rulings.

Some IRAs aggregated, others excluded: In PLR

9816028 (1/21/98), P had numerous IRAs, seven of which were aggregated to form the basis of his proposed SOSEPP and the rest of which were not to be counted. In PLR 9801050 (10/6/97), P had several IRAs, three of which were aggregated to form the basis of his proposed SOSEPP and the rest of which were not to be counted. The IRS ruled favorably in both cases, requiring only that the series payments be made from the aggregated IRAs and not from the other accounts.

Take payments from one IRA, not aggregated with others: In PLR 9818055 (2/2/98), P was permitted to take a SOSEPP from one of her two IRAs. In PLR 9812038 (12/23/97), P was taking a SOSEPP from one of his three IRAs and wanted to start a second SOSEPP from a new, fourth, IRA, to be created by transfer of funds from one of the other IRAs (not the IRA that was already supporting the first SOSEPP). The IRS permitted this, and the ruling specifically stated more than once that P's IRAs were *not* aggregated. In PLR 9747045 (8/28/97), P's IRS-approved SOSEPP was taken from one of her two rollover IRAs and not the other; the two were not aggregated.

These rulings indicate that P must choose, at the beginning of his SOSEPP, either to aggregate or not to aggregate IRAs for purposes of designing and paying out the series. The SOSEPP can be based on one of several IRAs, on all of P's IRAs on an aggregated basis, or on some IRAs aggregated with others excluded.

The IRAs which are included in the initial design of the SOSEPP must be the sole source of payments in the series. Once the SOSEPP begins, funds should not be transferred *out of* the IRAs that are being used to support the series, except to make payments that are part of the series (or to be transferred to another one of the accounts that were aggregated to determine the series), or *into* any IRA that is part of the support for the series from an IRA or other plan that was not part of the support for the series.

The ability to pick and choose which IRAs will be aggregated in determining the size of the periodic payments gives the client tremendous flexibility:

Example: Rodney, age 56, has several IRAs (his only retirement plans). He wants the largest possible payments for his SOSEPP. He aggregates all his IRA balances, and, with an actuary, constructs the SOSEPP using only his own life expectancy, IRS method three, whichever commonly-used mortality table gives him the shortest life expectancy, and the highest possible "reasonable" interest rate.

Example: Sidney, age 53, has one big IRA. Sidney wants to take small annual payments from his IRA until he reaches age 59½. Even using the lowest possible "reasonable" interest rate, and the joint life expectancy of himself and his beneficiary, it is not possible, using the entire balance of his IRA, to come up with payments as small as he wants. So Sidney divides his IRA into two, one of which is just the right size to support a SOSEPP of the size that Sidney wants.

This tremendous flexibility afforded to IRAs is not unlimited, however. Although P can have two IRAs, and use only one of them to support the SOSEPP, for some reason the IRS absolutely forbids using only *part* of a single IRA to support a series. See PLR 9705033 (11/8/96). Since P can easily get his desired result by dividing one IRA into two, this prohibition is little more than a trap for the unwary.

Multiple plans other than IRAs

The author has found no rulings or other sources dealing with the aggregation or disaggregation of 403(b) arrangements or QRPs for purposes of applying the SOSEPP exception.

Starting a second series concurrently

A taxpayer receiving a SOSEPP from one or more IRAs may initiate a *second* series of equal payments from a different IRA. See, *e.g.*, PLR 9812038 (12/23/97), discussed above, in which P was receiving a SOSEPP from "IRA #1." After that SOSEPP had been under way for a while, he was allowed to begin a second SOSEPP from a different IRA, "IRA #4," that had been created just for the purpose. PLR 9747039 (8/26/97) is another favorable ruling about starting a second SOSEPP from a different IRA.

However, P may not start a second SOSEPP from the same IRA (or plan) that is already supporting the first SOSEPP. Such a second series would constitute an impermissible "modification" of the first series.

Modification of the series prohibited

If P "modifies" his series of payments before he has completed the required series duration (five years or until age 59½, whichever is longer) he is severely punished. His qualification for the SOSEPP exception is retroactively revoked, and his "tax for the 1st taxable year in which such modification occurs shall be increased by an amount, determined under regulations, equal to the tax which (but for paragraph (2)(A)(iv)) would have been imposed, plus interest for the deferral period." § 72(t)(4)(A).

[Note: § 72(t)(4)(B) defines the "deferral period" over which interest must be calculated, but its definition doesn't make much sense. It is: "the period beginning with the taxable year in which (without regard to paragraph (2)(A)(iv)) [which contains the SOSEPP exception] the distribution *would have been includible in gross income* and ending with the taxable year in which the modification" occurs. This shows that even Congress is confused between "penalty-free" (what the § 72(t) exceptions are all about) and "income tax-free" (which § 72(t) has no bearing on), since *any* distribution from the retirement plan "would have been includible" in P's gross income, regardless of whether it qualified under paragraph (2)(A)(iv).]

The only exception to this tough rule is that if the series is modified "by reason of death or disability" there is no penalty. § 72(t)(4)(A). IRS Publication 590 (at page 22) echoes this, saying that a modification does not result in penalty if the "change from an approved distribution method is because of the death or disability of the IRA owner."

It is not clear whether death and disability *automatically* end the requirement of continuing the series, or whether P (or beneficiaries) must somehow demonstrate that *because* of the death or disability the series could not have been continued—for example, by showing that payments were suspended upon P's death because of a lawsuit about who was entitled to the benefits, or that P had to increase his distributions because of his disability.

Period during which modification is prohibited

The beginning date of the no-modification period is the date of the first payment in the series. The ending date is the fifth anniversary of the date of the first payment in the series, or, *if later*, the date on which P attains age 59½. § 72(t)(4)(A). Once this ending date is passed, payments may be freely taken from the plan without penalty (or the series may be suspended—*i.e.*, P can STOP taking payments).

Note that the ending date is not simply the date of the fifth year's payment. The five years ends on the *fifth anniversary of the first payment*. In the case of <u>Arnold v.</u>

Commissioner, 111 T.C. 250 (1998), P, at age 55, took the first of a series of equal annual payments of $44,000 in December 1989. He took the second, third, fourth, and fifth payments in the series in January 1990, 1991, 1992, and 1993, respectively. In September 1993 he turned 59½, and, thinking he had now completed his greater-of-five-years-or-until-age-59½ requirement, since he had taken all five of the annual required payments and was over age 59½, he took another distribution of $6,776 in November 1993 from the same IRA.

The Tax Court, citing legislative history regarding how to calculate the five-year period, held that this $6,776 distribution was an impermissible modification of the SOSEPP because it occurred during the five years beginning on the date of the first distribution. Therefore, P's qualification for the SOSEPP exception was retroactively revoked, and he owed the 10% penalty, plus interest, on all five of his $44,000 distributions.

What changes constitute a modification?

Examples of prohibited modifications of a SOSEPP include:

- Terminating the series (ceasing to take the payments). See PLR 9818055 (2/2/98).
- Taking an extra payment (*i.e.*, a payment that is over and above the payments required as part of the series) from the plan or IRA that is supporting the series (see Arnold v. Commissioner, discussed above).
- Possibly, changing from annual payments to quarterly or monthly payments (or vice versa), even if the total payments for the year add up to the right amount, since there is no authority for the proposition that the size of individual payments in the series does not matter so long

as the annual total is the same each year. So, although the IRS has not explicitly ruled that such a switch would be a "modification," all payments should be equal (or otherwise exactly conform to the SOSEPP that was initially set up) unless a favorable ruling holding otherwise is obtained.

- Changing how the payments in the series are determined. Example:

In PLR 9821056 (2/24/98), P retired at 47 and started a series of equal annual payments from his IRA. These payments were based on his then-life expectancy, existing account balance and projected rate of return. Five years later he wanted to recalculate the rest of the required payments, based on his new life expectancy and account balance and a new projected rate of return which reflected the actual investment experience of the account (which had been much better than originally projected). He sought a ruling that this would not be a "modification" because the change amounted merely to an adjustment to reflect actual experience, and the series was in fact continuing exactly as before. Unfortunately for him, the IRS ruled that "such a proposed change in payments...would be a modification."

Ironically, this taxpayer probably could have designed his series initially to build in the flexibility the IRS did not allow him to add later. For example, in PLR 9531039 (5/10/95) the IRS approved an annuity-method SOSEPP which called for the annual redetermination of the so-called "equal payments" based on P's redetermined life expectancy, account balance and interest rate.

In PLR 199909059 (12/10/98), P, at age 44, started receiving SOSEPP annuity (method three) payments of $176,499 per year from his $2.5 million IRA. Five years later the IRA had grown to $9 million. He switched to a new SOSEPP program, under which the payment amount would be redetermined each year based on a fixed interest rate of 7.2%, the then-current account balance, and his life expectancy reduced by one year each year. The new program was held to be valid as a SOSEPP, but because it was a modification of the old series, he owed the 10% penalty on the four years of payments made under the old program.

What changes are not a modification?

The following changes in a SOSEPP have either been ruled not to be prohibited modifications, or have occurred without negative comment in cases or rulings involving other issues:

- When the paying agent, as part of a change in its computer systems, changed the date of monthly payments in a series to the first day of the month (instead of the last day of the preceding month), the change was ruled to be "ministerial," and not a "modification," even though the change meant that the recipient's income would include one fewer payment in the year of the switch. PLR 9514026 (1/12/95).

- P in PLR 9221052 (2/26/92) was receiving monthly payments from a money purchase pension plan. When that plan terminated in the middle of his SOSEPP, the IRS ruled he could roll over the termination distribution to an IRA and continue paying himself the monthly payments from the IRA.

- In PLR 9739044 (7/1/97), P got divorced after commencing his SOSEPP from IRAs that were community property. The divorce court divided the IRAs equally between the spouses. Both spouses then apparently continued the SOSEPP, with each of them taking (from his or her respective share of the formerly unified IRAs) one half of the required annual distribution. The IRS ruled that, because the division of the IRAs between the spouses was non-taxable under § 408(d)(6), and in view of the "continuous compliance with the requirements of § 72(t)(2)(A)(iv)," there was no modification.

- In the case of annual payments, it apparently does not matter exactly when during the year the payment is taken; in other words it apparently does not have to be on the anniversary of the first payment to avoid having a "modification." For example, in PLR 9747039 (8/26/97), the IRS ruled that P would qualify for the exception "if [he] received at least five annual payments of $510,000 from IRA Y (at least one during each of the years 1997, 1998, 1999, 2000 and 2001) and does not otherwise modify his IRA distribution scheme." See also Arnold v. Commissioner, (discussed above under "*Period during which modification is prohibited*"), where P took his first annual payment in December of 1989 and his second annual payment in January 1990 and the opinion contains no negative comment on this procedure.

How to construct a SOSEPP: software

The following software programs do the calculations necessary to compute SOSEPP payments under IRS Notice 89-25 (among other calculations). For details about how to obtain these programs, see Appendix D. If you are seeking a program *only* for this purpose, the Brentmark "Pension Distributions Calculator" is recommended.

Numbercruncher: One of the 52 estate and financial planning calculations performed by Numbercruncher is "Early distributions" (under "Retirement," "Early"). **Pluses:** Numbercruncher determines the payments required under the "amortization" and "annuity" methods, using single or joint life expectancy and your choice of three life expectancy tables. You determine your own "reasonable interest rate" and supply the age of P and beneficiary and size of the fund. Numbercruncher then gives the annual required payment. Its "help" screen provides some assistance and interpretation. The program is fast and easy to use, like all Numbercruncher features. The printout shows the assumptions used in making the calculations, which is extremely helpful. **Drawbacks:** Numbercruncher does not provide the "minimum distribution" payout method.

Brentmark Pension and Roth IRA Analyzer: Early distribution calculations are one (minor) feature of this program (it is on the "View" menu), but once found it is very easy to use and fast. Pre-59½ distributions are also included in Brentmark's less expensive, handy **"Pension Distributions Calculator."** **Pluses:** Brentmark offers the calculations under all three of the IRS's permitted methods, using single or joint life expectancy; you supply the "reasonable interest rate," ages of P and beneficiary and size of fund. You can choose one of three life expectancy tables; the "help" screen offers interesting information about these mysterious tables. The printout shows the assumptions used in making the calculations, which is extremely helpful. Another thoughtful feature is that the printout shows the annual payout (and estimated remaining fund balance) each year for the required duration of the series (*i.e.*, five years or until age 59½, whichever is longer). **Drawbacks:** The "results" screen shows one method at a time; then you go back to the menu to try a different method and display that. (Numbercruncher shows the results of both its methods together on one page.)

How to construct a SOSEPP: hire an actuary

Although the IRS methods for calculating the equal payments appear easy, and software programs make them appear even easier, consider hiring an actuary to design the series, if the amounts involved are substantial, for several reasons. First, there is the comfort of a professional opinion that the interest rate and life expectancy tables being used are "reasonable." Second, actuarial calculations can easily be bungled by non-actuaries; see, *e.g.*, PLR 9705033 (11/8/96) (penalty imposed because the required payments were improperly calculated by the client's "independent third-party financial advisor"). Even the IRS states that the amortization and annuity methods "generally require professional assistance." IRS Publication 590, page 22.

Finally, an actuary who is familiar with the ins and outs of § 72(t) can take the lead in designing a series that will most precisely achieve the client's goals—goals such as relatively small or large payments, the ability to add another series later, or payments that increase with cost of living or change to reflect investment results.

How professionals are using § 72(t)

The flexibility of the SOSEPP exception offers planning opportunities. The series of payments can help a client under age 59½ achieve financial, investment and estate planning goals.

For example, Bruce J. Temkin, MSPA, EA, author of *The Terrible Truth About Investing*, suggests the following program for an under-age 59½ client who needs a substantial amount of money, for example to start a new business or pay children's college tuition: First, the client refinances his residence. He uses the loan proceeds to cover the immediate financial need. Then he takes from his IRA a SOSEPP (with the size of the payments matched to the mortgage payments) to repay the mortgage. There will be no penalty, and the tax-deductible mortgage interest will reduce the income tax on the IRA distributions.

A financial firm's brochure for financial advisors suggests using familiarity with §72(t) as a marketing technique. An advisor can "use 72(t) to generate sales" by helping clients who have taken early retirement set up a segregated IRA (to support a SOSEPP to pay for living expenses) and meanwhile preserve tax deferral for the rest of the retirement funds in another IRA (presumably invested by the advisor).

People have used pre-age 59½ distribution programs to help finance early retirement, fund an annual exclusion gifting program, fund life insurance premium payments or just achieve a better estate balance when IRA assets constituted a disproportionate share of the estate.

Case Study: Quentin's Semi-Retirement Program

This case study illustrates the planning possibilities of a SOSEPP.

The facts

Quentin, age 56, is cutting back his workload. He is changing his position at his firm from full time managing director to part time employee. He and his wife Frannie plan to take a round-the-world cruise, build their dream house, then settle down and enjoy the good life.

To finance this plan, Quentin figures he needs an annual income of $150,000. Since his profit sharing plan at the firm has $5 million in it, he figures he can afford his proposed agenda—*if* he can get money out of the retirement plan at a reasonable cost.

He knows he has to pay income tax on the plan withdrawals but would like to avoid paying the 10% penalty.

Quentin's options

First, Quentin looks at what would happen if he took money directly out of his company plan and put it in his bank account. *If* he were completely retiring now, he could withdraw from the company plan without penalty, because there is an exception to the 10% penalty for distributions from a QRP upon separation from service at age 55 or later (see *"Distribution after separation from service after age 55,"* below). But this exception is not available to Quentin because he is not terminating his employment; he is just cutting back, not leaving.

The next thing he investigates is the possibility of taking a "series of substantially equal periodic payments" from the company plan. But this avenue, too, is blocked, because this exception is not available for distributions from a QRP unless there has been a "separation from service," and Quentin is not separating from service.

Quentin's solution is to (1) take a partial distribution of his benefits from the company plan, (2) roll the distribution to an IRA (by a "direct rollover"), then (3) use the rollover IRA to support a SOSEPP to him that will satisfy the requirements of § 72(t). He hires an actuary to determine what size fund would be needed to produce equal annual payments of $150,000 over his life expectancy, and generally to help him design the SOSEPP.

Design details of Quentin's SOSEPP

The actuary suggests the following strategy to get Quentin his $150,000 per year:

First, create the *smallest possible* separate rollover IRA

needed, within the "safe harbor" IRS guidelines, to support a $150,000 per year payout to Quentin. It is desirable to use the smallest possible IRA because the less money that is tied up in this IRA (where it must remain untouched for five whole years, except for distributions required for the series), the more money is left in his company plan. Money in the company plan can be withdrawn freely after Quentin reaches age 59½ in three years, without penalty, and without retroactively contaminating the series. Also, if it turns out that Quentin, before reaching age 59½, needs more money than the series is providing, he can always take *another* distribution from the company plan and use it to establish *another* rollover IRA, and use that second IRA to establish a new SOSEPP. In contrast to this, if all or most of his retirement plan money is tied up in the IRA that is supporting the SOSEPP, he will have little or no flexibility to increase his distributions if it turns out that he needs more money in the next five years than he now expects to need.

Note that Quentin does not care whether this particular segregated IRA actually lasts for his entire life expectancy; it only has to last for five years (the minimum no-modification period required, in his case, to avoid retroactive imposition of the 10% penalty).

Now that we know the goal is to get level payments of $150,000 per year, for five years, using the smallest possible rollover IRA, several decisions become easy. First, the IRS's "minimum distribution" method is out; it does not produce the level, predictable payments Quentin is looking for. So the choice narrows down to methods two and three.

Second, as between a joint or a single life expectancy, Quentin should use the single life expectancy; the shorter the payout period, the smaller the fund needed to produce $150,000/year over that payout period.

Third, for the same reason (achieving a shorter payout period) the actuary will use whatever "reasonable mortality table" produces the shortest life expectancy period for Quentin. For example, the actuary will not use a "unisex" mortality table, because a separate male mortality table will show a shorter life expectancy.

Fourth, the actuary will use method three, the annuity method, because that is the only one for which Notice 89-25 blesses the use of any "reasonable mortality table," as opposed to only the IRS mortality tables. Finally, the actuary will use the highest reasonable interest rate he can justify.

Limitations of Quentin's plan

Note that Quentin's program for taking penalty-free early distributions is possible only because his company's profit sharing plan allows in-service withdrawals for employees who have attained age 55. Not all plans allow such withdrawals. If Quentin's plan did not permit any in-service withdrawals there would be no way he could access his retirement plan without quitting his job altogether. This is a reminder that the flexibility of the IRA custom-made to support a SOSEPP is available only to participants who *have* IRAs to begin with, or who can get money from other types of retirement plans into an IRA. An employee all of whose retirement funds are tied up in a company plan may have no way to create a SOSEPP unless he terminates his employment.

The Other Eleven Exceptions to the Penalty

We now turn to the other exceptions to § 72(t)'s penalty. Although these lack the broadly applicable planning possibilities of the SOSEPP, each may be useful in particular situations.

Death benefits

A distribution "made to a beneficiary (or to the estate of the employee) on or after the death of the employee" is exempt from the penalty. § 72(t)(2)(A)(ii). This exception applies to distributions from all types of plans. Thus death benefits may be distributed penalty-free from a QRP, 403(b) arrangement or IRA, regardless of whether the *beneficiary* receiving the benefits is over 59½ and regardless of whether *P* had attained age 59½ at the time of his death.

Despite the unique clarity of this exception, it generates confusion for two reasons:

First, if a surviving spouse rolls over benefits inherited from the deceased spouse to the surviving spouse's *own* IRA, the benefits cease to be "death benefits," and become simply part of the surviving spouse's own retirement account. Thus, distributions from the rollover IRA will once again be subject to the § 72(t) penalty rules if the surviving spouse is under age 59½—even if the deceased spouse was over age 59½ when he died (see "*Drawbacks of spousal rollover*," Chapter 3).

Second, there is another, unrelated, significance to age 59½: A participant must have reached this age in order for a lump sum distribution of his benefits to qualify for five year averaging treatment under § 402(d)(4)(A)(ii). [Five year averaging is repealed after 1999.] For details, see "*Fifth hurdle: participant must be age 59½ or older*," Chapter 2.

Example: Dean dies at age 56, leaving his pension plan to his daughter Carla, age 30. Distributions from the plan to Carla are not subject to the § 72(t) penalty even though neither Dean nor Carla has reached age 59½.

Distributions "attributable" to total disability

A distribution that is "attributable to the employee's being disabled" is not subject to the penalty. § 72(t)(2)(A)(iii). "Disabled" is defined in § 72(m)(7): it means "unable to engage in any substantial gainful activity by reason of any medically determinable physical or mental impairment which can be expected to result in death or to be of long-continued and indefinite duration. An individual shall not be considered to be disabled unless he furnishes proof of the existence thereof [sic] in such form and manner as the Secretary may require."

Reg. § 1.72-17A(f)(1) & (2) (interpreting § 72(m) as it applies to lump sum distributions to self-employed persons) provides the following further elaboration on this definition: "In determining whether an individual's impairment makes him unable to engage in any substantial gainful activity, primary consideration shall be given to the nature and severity of his impairment. Consideration shall also be given to other factors such as the individual's education, training, and work experience. The substantial gainful activity to which section 72(m)(7) refers is the activity, or a comparable activity, in which the individual customarily engaged prior to the arising of the disability or prior to retirement if the individual was retired at the time the disability arose." Although the IRS's own regulation says that the "gainful activity" referred to is the individual's customary activity or a comparable one, IRS Publication 590, at page 22, incorrectly says you must "furnish proof that you cannot do *any* substantial gainful activity because of your physical or mental condition" (emphasis added).

The regulation also lists certain impairments, such as "Damage to the brain or brain abnormality which has resulted in severe loss of judgment, intellect, orientation, or memory," which are said to "ordinarily," but not "in and of themselves," result in the necessary impairment.

Another IRS requirement in Publication 590 is that "A *physician* must determine that your condition can be expected to result in death or to be of long continued and indefinite duration" (emphasis added). This requirement is not waived for those whose religious beliefs prohibit them from hiring physicians; the Tax Court points out that the regulation does not impair the free exercise of religion, it just makes such exercise more expensive in some cases. <u>Fohrmeister v. Comm'r</u>, 73 T.C.Memo 2483, 2486 (1997).

An individual suffering from depression was not "disabled" where he continued his normal occupation (securities trading). <u>Dwyer v. Commissioner</u>, 106 T.C. 337 (1996). Earning a salary and starting an engineering business are both activities that are "inconsistent with the exigencies of the statutory definition of disability." <u>Kovacevic v. Comm'r</u>, 64 TCM 1076 (1992) (another depression case).

What does it mean that the distribution must be "attributable" to the disability? Contrast this wording with § 402(d)/(e)(4)(A) (the definition of "lump sum distribution") (LSD), which gives LSD status to an otherwise-qualifying distribution made "after the employee has become disabled," without any requirement that the distribution be "attributable to" the disability. In Publication 590, the IRS reiterates (at page 22) that the distribution from an IRA must be "because" of the disability to qualify for this exception. Although some professionals assume that any distribution to a totally disabled person is automatically exempt from the penalty, it is possible that the IRS may require P to demonstrate that the distribution was *necessitated* by the disability (*e.g.*, to substitute for employment income lost due to the disability).

Deductible medical expenses

Distributions after 1996 from any type of plan are

penalty-free "to the extent such distributions do not exceed the amount allowable as a deduction under § 213 to the employee for amounts paid during the taxable year for medical care (determined without regard to whether the employee itemizes deductions for such taxable year)." § 72(t)(2)(B). "During the taxable year" presumably means "during the taxable year in which the distribution is received."

This exception may increase P's medical problems by giving him a severe headache. Medical expenses are deductible under § 213 only to the extent such expenses exceed 7.5% of adjusted gross income. § 213(a). But the plan distribution *itself* is includible in gross income and thus decreases the "amount allowable as a deduction."

Example: Cathy's adjusted gross income for the year, before taking any distribution from her IRA, is $100,000. Cathy is 53. She has medical expenses of $10,000. Her medical expenses are deductible to the extent they exceed 7.5% of $100,000 or $7,500, so (again before considering any IRA distribution) she can deduct $2,500 of her medical expenses. She withdraws $2,500 from the IRA to help pay those medical expenses. However, the IRA distribution increases her adjusted gross income to $102,500, thus *decreasing* her permitted medical expense deduction to $2,312.50 ($10,000 of medical expenses minus [$102,500 X 7.5%=$7,687.50]=$2,312.50). So she owes the 10% penalty on $187.50 of the distribution (total penalty $18.75).

To avoid the penalty, while still taking advantage of the ability to withdraw from the plan to pay deductible medical expenses, P must perform a circular calculation, so that the distribution does not exceed [total medical expenses] minus 7.5% of [distribution plus other adjusted gross income]. And of course this assumes that P can determine his adjusted gross income and medical expenses to the penny on or before December 31 of the year in question, since a distribution must be matched with medical expenses incurred in the year of the distribution, not some preceding year.

Separation from service after age 55

A distribution from an employer plan made to an employee "after separation from service after attainment of age 55" is exempt from the penalty. § 72(t)(2)(A)(v). This exception is available for QRPs and 403(b) plans, but not for IRA distributions. § 72(t)(3)(A).

An employee who quits, retires or is fired *before* he reaches age 55 cannot simply wait until age 55 and then take a penalty-free distribution. The exception is available for distributions made "after you separated from service with your employer if the separation occurred during or after the calendar year in which you reached age 55." IRS Publication 575 ("Pension and Annuity Income"; edition for use in preparing 1997 returns) (at page 32). Note that although IRS Publication 575 and Notice 87-13, Q & A 20, both state that the exception applies to separations from service occurring on or after *January 1* of the year the employee reaches age 55, § 72(t) itself limits the exception to distributions made after separations occurring after the actual 55th birthday.

Also, the distribution must occur after the separation from service, not before. Humberson v. Comm'r, 70 TCM 886 (1995). Finally, although § 72(t) (unlike, say, § 402(d)(4)(A)/(e)(4)(D), defining lump sum distributions) does not specifically exclude the self-employed from using this exception, it is not clear what would constitute "separation from service" for a self-employed person.

QDRO distributions

Distributions from a QRP or 403(b) arrangement (but not from an IRA) made to an "alternate payee" under a qualified domestic relations order ("QDRO") (§ 414(p)(1)) are exempt from the early distributions penalty. § 72(t)(2)(C). QDROs, and other special rules dealing with retirement benefits in case of divorce, are beyond the scope of this book.

ESOPs only: certain stock dividends

This book generally does not cover special rules applicable to "employee stock ownership plans" ("ESOPs"). Under § 404(k), a company can take a tax deduction for dividends paid on stock that is held by an ESOP, and the ESOP can pass these dividends out to the plan participants, if various requirements are met. Such dividend payments are not subject to the 10% penalty. § 72(t)(2)(A)(vi).

Health insurance for the unemployed

In years after 1996, an unemployed P can take penalty-free distributions from his IRA (but not from a QRP or 403(b) arrangement) to pay health insurance premiums. § 72(t)(2)(D). Here are the requirements for this exception:

P must have separated from his employment, and, as a result of that separation, must have "received unemployment compensation for 12 consecutive weeks under any Federal or State unemployment compensation law." The distributions must be made during the year "during which such unemployment compensation is paid or the succeeding taxable year." Presumably this phrase does not imply that the 12 consecutive weeks' worth of unemployment compensation must all be received in the same taxable year, but presumably it does mean that the unemployed P does not become eligible until the year the 12 consecutive weeks are completed.

Does this clause mean that the unemployed P can take penalty-free distributions only in one year—*either* the year he completes the 12 weeks of unemployment benefits *or* the following year? Or does it mean that penalty-free distributions may be taken in both years? The IRS has offered no enlightenment.

Editorial observation: If an unemployed person under 59½ withdraws money from his IRA because he has no other source of funds to buy food for his starving children, or to make mortgage payments to stave off foreclosure—too bad. He has to pay the 10% penalty. There is no "hardship" exception as such to the 10% penalty, and poor people have to pay it even if their income is so low overall that the distribution is not subject to any income taxes. But an unemployed person can withdraw money penalty-free to pay his *health insurance premiums* even if he is a millionaire! The Tax Court has held that it is not unconstitutional for Congress to allow penalty exceptions for some hardships and not others, and pointed out that anyone disappointed in Congress's choices has the option of not participating in a retirement plan. Pulliam v. Comm'r, 72 TCM 307 (1996).

The maximum distribution under this exception in any taxable year is the amount paid for "insurance described in § 213(d)(1)(D) [medical and long term care insurance] with respect to the individual and the individual's spouse and dependents." Also, the distribution must be made either while the individual is still unemployed or, if he becomes employed again, less than 60 days after he has been reemployed.

The IRS, in regulations, can permit a self-employed individual to use this exception "if, under Federal or State law, the individual would have received unemployment compensation but for the fact the individual was self-employed." No such regulations have yet been issued.

Expenses of higher education

The 10% penalty will not apply to IRA distributions that do not exceed P's "qualified higher education expenses" for the taxable year of the distribution. This is one of several exceptions added by TAPRA '97. It is not available for distributions from QRPs or 403(b) plans. § 72(t)(2)(E).

The distribution in question must be made, after 1997, to pay for education provided in "academic periods" beginning after 1997; see IRS Notice 97-53 (1997-50 IRB 6) for details. The distribution must be to pay for education furnished to P or his spouse, or to any child or grandchild of either of them. (It's pretty fast work for a taxpayer under age 59½ to have college-age grandchildren.)

This exception borrows certain definitions from § 529(c)(3) (the section allowing various tax breaks to "qualified state tuition programs"), such as for the type of expenses covered ("tuition, fees, books, supplies, and equipment required for the enrollment or attendance of a designated beneficiary at an eligible educational institution") and eligible institutions. The category of "eligible institutions" "includes virtually all accredited public, non-profit, and proprietary post-secondary institutions," according to Notice 97-60, 1997-46 IRB 1, § 4, Q & A 2. Notice 97-60 provides many other details regarding this exception, including the fact that room and board are among the covered expenses if the student is enrolled at least half-time.

To the extent the education expenses in question are paid for by a scholarship, federal education grant, tax-free distribution from an Education IRA (§ 530), tax-free employer-provided educational assistance, or other payment that is excludible from gross income (other than gifts, inheritances, loans or savings), they cannot also be used to support a penalty-free IRA distribution. §§ 72(t)(7)(B), 25A(g)(2); Notice 97-60, § 4, Q & A 1.

Qualified first-time homebuyer

Under § 72(t)(2)(F), beginning after 1997, an individual can withdraw from his or her IRA (but not from a QRP or 403(b) plan) up to $10,000, without paying the 10% penalty, if the distribution is used "before the close of the 120th day after the day on which such payment or distribution is received to pay qualified acquisition costs with respect to a principal residence of a first-time homebuyer who is such individual, the spouse of such individual, or any child, grandchild, or ancestor of such individual or the individual's spouse." § 72(t)(8)(A). For such a small exception, this one is quite complicated. Note the following:

The $10,000 is a lifetime limit. It applies to the person making the withdrawal (the IRA owner), not the person buying the home.

Example: Mom and Dad, both age 54, want to help Junior, age 27, buy his first home. All three of them have IRAs. Mom and Junior each withdraw $10,000 penalty-free from their respective IRAs, and Dad withdraws $5,000 from his IRA penalty-free, to help pay for Junior's new home. (Note that each of them will have to pay *income taxes* on these withdrawals; only the 10% penalty is waived.) The following year, Sis, age 25, wants to buy *her* first home. But Mom and Junior can't dip into their IRAs penalty-free to help her out because they have already used up their $10,000 lifetime limit for such withdrawals. Dad still has $5,000 left that he can withdraw penalty-free to help Sis buy her home; otherwise, Sis is on her own.

"Principal residence" has the same meaning as in § 121 (exclusion of gain on sale of principal residence). § 72(t)(8)(D)(ii). § 121 itself does not contain a definition of "principal residence," but Reg § 1.121-3(a) does, by cross reference to (now-repealed) § 1034 and Reg. § 1.1034-1(c)(3); refer to that regulation if there is doubt as to whether a particular residence is the homebuyer's principal residence.

"Qualified acquisition costs" are the costs of "acquiring, constructing, or reconstructing a residence," including "usual or reasonable settlement, financing, or other closing costs." § 72(t)(8)(C).

A "first-time homebuyer" is not someone who has literally never owned a home before, but just someone who hasn't owned a home in a while. It is a person who has had no "present ownership interest in a principal residence during the 2-year period ending on the date of acquisition of the" residence being financed by the distribution. If the homebuyer is married, both spouses must meet this test. § 72(t)(8)(D).

The "date of acquisition" is the date "a binding contract to acquire" the home is entered into, or "on which construction or reconstruction of such a principal residence is commenced"—but, if there is a "delay or cancellation of the purchase or construction" [what about reconstruction?] and, solely for that reason, the distribution fails to meet the 120-day test, the distribution can be rolled back into the IRA; AND the rollover back into the IRA will be a qualified tax-free rollover, even if it occurs more than 60 days after the distribution, so long as it occurs within 120 days of the distribution, AND the rollover back into the IRA will not count for purposes of the one-rollover-per-year limit of § 408(d)(3)(B). § 72(t)(8)(E). What could be simpler!

Here is another limitation on this exception: under (now-repealed) § 1034, a taxpayer could sell a principal residence and "roll over" the gain on that sale, tax-free, into the purchase of a new principal residence within two years. § 1034(h) provided that the running of the two-year period for reinvestment would be suspended (for up to eight years after the sale of the first residence) so long as P (or his spouse) was on active duty with the Armed Forces of the United States, and § 1034(k) provided that the running of the two-year period would be suspended (for up to four years after the sale of the first residence) for certain taxpayers whose tax home was outside the United States. § 72(t)(8)(D)(II) provides that a taxpayer who is taking advantage of §1034(h) or (k) to extend the two-year reinvestment period cannot at the same time use the "first-time homebuyer" exception.

Finally, to the extent the distribution in question also qualified for one of the *other* exceptions (*e.g.*, a distribution under a QDRO, or to pay deductible medical expenses), it will not count as a "first-time homebuyer" distribution even if it is used to pay expenses that would qualify it for the first-time homebuyer exception. § 72(t)(2)(F).

IRS levy on the account

Generally, even an involuntary distribution is subject to the penalty if received by a participant under age 59½. IRS Notice 87-13, Q-20. However, over the protests of the IRS, the Tax Court has excused *certain* taxpayers from the penalty when their benefits were "distributed" by being seized by the government. See, *e.g.*, Murillo v. Comm'r, 75 T.C. Memo 1564 (1998); this case contains references to earlier cases on point. For distributions after 1999, there is statutory relief for this situation: If the retirement plan is taken by an IRS levy under § 6331, the forced distribution will not be subject to the 10% penalty. § 72(t)(2)(A)(vii).

Return of certain contributions

Certain excess contributions to "cash-or-deferred-arrangement" plans (such as 401(k) plans) may be distributed penalty-free if various requirements are met. See §§ 401(k)(8)(D) and 402(g)(2)(C).

If an IRA contribution for which no deduction has been taken is withdrawn from the account (together with the net earnings on that contribution) before the due date (including extensions) of P's tax return for the year in which the contribution was made, the withdrawal of the contribution is not a taxable distribution (§ 408(d)(4)) and accordingly is also not subject to the penalty. However, "Generally, if an individual is not yet 59½ at the time of the withdrawal, upon withdrawing such amounts the individual will be required to pay the early withdrawal tax under section 72(t) on the earnings (if any) for the year for which the contribution was made." IRS Notice 87-16, 1987-1 C.B. 446 (Q & A 9); Hall v. Comm'r, T.C. Memo 1998-336. IRS Publication 590, at page 22, confirms that any income earned on the contribution that is included in the distribution "may be subject" to the early distributions penalty.

Summary of Planning Principles

1.   Be aware that distributions (even inadvertent and "deemed" distributions) to a participant under age 59½ generally trigger a 10% penalty.

2.   If a client wants to take money from a retirement plan prior to age 59½, refer to this Chapter to determine whether he qualifies for an exception. Note carefully the requirements of any possibly applicable exception (*e.g.*, make sure it is available for the type of plan involved). Do not expect the exceptions to operate in a logical, fair and consistent

manner.

3.   If a client has an IRA (or can create one by rollover from another type of plan), consider the highly flexible "SOSEPP" exception as a possible funding source for gifting programs, life insurance premium payments, tuition bills and other expenditures. Consider hiring an actuary to help design a substantial or creative SOSEPP. In general, create the smallest possible separate IRA to support the desired size of payment, and preserve as much flexibility as possible for future changes in the client's needs.

4.   The penalty does not apply to post-death distributions, but a surviving spouse who rolls over death benefits to her own IRA loses the exemption for death benefits.

Life Insurance, Grandfathers & Other Topics

Life insurance in a retirement plan behaves differently from other retirement plan assets. Planning for a retirement plan that contains life insurance differs accordingly. There are exceptions, in the form of "grandfather rules," to many requirements in the law governing tax treatment of retirement benefits. Proper use of these rules can save money for your clients.

What's in this Chapter

Sections 1, 2, 3 and 4 explain the income, gift and estate tax consequences, to the plan participant (P) and his beneficiaries, of buying and holding life insurance in a **qualified retirement plan** ("QRP"). To enhance understanding, these consequences are contrasted with (a) the tax treatment of non-life insurance plan benefits and (b) the tax treatment of life insurance that is not held in a QRP. The chapter also discusses estate planning considerations involved when dealing with plan-owned life insurance.

This chapter discusses QRP-owned life insurance from the perspective of the individual plan participant (P). Rules that are of concern only at the plan level (such as the limits on how much life insurance can be purchased in a QRP, and ERISA fiduciary investment rules) are beyond the scope of this book. For other sources, see the Bibliography. Similarly, the analysis of insurance products is beyond the scope of this book.

Section 5 discusses three grandfather rules which are exceptions from the minimum distribution rules of § 401(a)(9). Section 6 deals with one other obscure grandfather rule, namely, the continued availability of the estate tax exclusion for retirement benefits of certain individuals. Other grandfather rules are discussed in Chapter 2: the former ability of non-spouse beneficiaries to roll over inherited benefits (see "*Rollovers of inherited benefits*"); and "ten year averaging" and "20% capital gain" income tax treatment for certain lump sum distributions (see "LSD Rewards, Part 2: Special Averaging Treatment").

Although the "grandfather rules" affect relatively few clients, significant tax savings can be achieved for some of those who are eligible for grandfather treatment. Accordingly, it is important to determine what if any grandfathering your client may be entitled to. Use of the "Checklist for Meeting with Client" in Appendix C can assure that you do not overlook grandfather benefits your client may qualify for. The planning principles, if any, for each grandfather rule appear at the end of the discussion of that rule.

Finally, Sections 7 and 8 discuss probate and disability issues respectively.

1. Life Insurance: Income Tax Issues

Income tax consequences during employment

Generally, an employee pays no income tax on his employer's contributions to a retirement plan, or on plan earnings, until these are actually distributed to him. However, if the employer contributions (or plan earnings) are used to purchase *life insurance* on the employee's life, then the employee *does* become currently taxable on part of the retirement plan contributions or earnings.

§ 72(m)(3)(B) and Reg. § 1.72-16(b) govern the tax treatment of life insurance contracts purchased by QRPs when (a) the premium is paid with deductible employer contributions or with plan earnings and (b) the policy proceeds are payable to P or P's beneficiary. The amount "applied to purchase" such life insurance, as determined by IRS regulations, is includible currently in P's gross income (regardless of whether the amount is "vested").

The regulations provide that the amount of "life insurance protection" deemed purchased in any year is the difference between the death benefit payable under the policy and the cash surrender value of the policy at the end of the year. Reg. § 1.72-16(b)(3). Once the "amount of life insurance" is thus determined, the IRS next tells us how much of the employer contribution and plan earnings are deemed to have been "applied to purchase" this life insurance. The IRS has issued the following pronouncements on this subject:

1.   **Term Insurance**. When a QRP buys term insurance on the life of a P, the entire premium is includible in P's gross income. Rev. Rul. 54-52, 1954-1 C.B. 150.

2.   **Other Insurance.** If the policy provides more than "pure" death benefit protection, for example, if it also provides annuity benefits or if it has or will have a cash value, Rev. Rul. 55-747, 1955-2 C.B. 228 provided a table, called "P.S. 58," to be used to calculate the amount includible in P's gross income. This ruling was later modified by Rev. Ruls. 66-110, 1966 C.B. 12, and 67-154, 1967-1 C.B. 11, which provided that the insurer's lowest published rate for one-year term insurance available on an initial issue basis for "all standard risks" could be used if that rate was lower than the "P.S. 58

cost." Generally, the insurer's published term rates are considerably lower than the P.S. 58 Table rates.

Note: in the rest of this chapter, "P.S. 58 cost" is used as shorthand for "the amount P is required to include in gross income because of the plan-held life insurance." In any particular case, this may be the rate from Table P.S. 58 or the insurance company's actual term rates if lower.

The amount of currently taxable income generated by a plan-owned policy rises as the employee gets older because term rates go up with age. This increase may be mitigated by an increase in the cash value, which reduces the "pure death benefit."

The employee must find the cash elsewhere to pay the income tax on the P.S. 58 cost. For example, an employee in the 45% tax bracket (considering federal, FICA, state and local income taxes) must earn $818 of taxable salary to pay the income tax on $1,000 of P.S. 58 cost. For this individual, the tax on $1,000 of P.S. 58 cost is $450. He must earn $818 of taxable salary in order to have, after income taxes, the $450 of cash he needs to pay the income tax on the P.S. 58 cost. This income tax obligation continues even if the employer stops paying premiums on the policy. This may happen if the policy becomes "self-financing," so the premiums are paid through policy dividends. If the only source of value in the policy is employer contributions and plan earnings, the annual P.S. 58 cost would continue to constitute gross income to the employee.

The amount included in P's gross income over the years on account of the P.S. 58 cost is considered his "investment in the contract" and in effect becomes his "basis" in the policy. P is entitled to recover this basis tax-free, but only if the policy itself is distributed to him. Reg. § 1.72-16(b)(4). If the policy lapses, or is surrendered for its cash surrender value (CSV) at the plan level, P's "basis" disappears and cannot be offset against other plan distributions. In other words, the payment of income taxes over the years on the P.S. 58 cost generates a "basis" that may or may not be recouped later.

On the other hand, since the "P.S. 58 cost" is supposed to represent the annual cost of pure insurance protection, it is surprising the IRS allows it to be used as "basis" for any purpose; it is really an expense. An "owner employee" does not get to treat even the P.S. 58 cost as an investment in the contract. Reg. § 1.72-16(b)(4).

Income tax issues at retirement: the rollout

At retirement, P will typically face some thorny issues regarding the life insurance policy.

A life insurance policy cannot be rolled over to an IRA. § 408(a)(3). Also, with some possible exceptions (see "*Certain profit sharing plans*," below), the IRS requires that policies be either converted to cash or distributed to P at retirement. This is one of the constellation of plan qualification requirements known as the "incidental benefit rule." See Rev. Rul. 54-51, 1954-1 C.B. 147, as modified by Rev. Ruls. 57-213, 1957-1 C.B. 157, and 60-84, 1960-1 C.B. 159. So, at retirement, if P wants to keep the policy in force, P must either take the policy out of the plan as a distribution, or buy the policy from the plan, or terminate the policy.

Distributing the policy to P

If the policy is distributed to P, P must include in gross income the "fair market value" of the policy. Reg. § 1.402(a)-1(a)(1)(iii). The IRS has stated that the fair market value of a life insurance policy is its CSV *unless* "the total policy reserves [established by the insurer to cover the death benefit, advance premium payments, etc.] represent a much more accurate approximation of the fair market value of the policy." If the policy's reserves substantially exceed the policy's CSV, the reserves represent a much "more accurate approximation of the fair market value of the policy," and P is required to include the amount of the policy reserves, not the CSV, in gross income. Notice 89-25, Q&A 10, 1989-1 C.B. 662.

This is hardly a bright line test. How much larger than the CSV must the reserves be before the reserves are deemed to "substantially exceed" the CSV? In the Notice's example, the reserves were 3.8 times greater than, and were held to "substantially exceed," the CSV. It appears that, if the policy is to be distributed *or sold* to P, the following steps are required:

1.   Determine the policy's CSV.

2.   Obtain from the insurer a statement of the value of all policy reserves as of the proposed date of distribution of the policy.

3.   If (2) "substantially exceeds" (1), use (2) as the policy's value.

4.   If (2) does not "substantially exceed" (1), use (1) as the policy's value.

5.   If (2) exceeds (1), but it is unclear whether (2) "*substantially*" exceeds (1), obtain an IRS ruling regarding which figure to use.

In determining his taxable income from distribution of the policy, P is entitled to offset, against the "fair market value" of the policy, the amounts includible in his gross income over the years on account of the policy (P.S. 58 cost), which are considered to be "premiums or other consideration paid" by P.

Reg. § 1.72-16(b)(4).

A discrepancy between the CSV and the "policy value" may create problems at the *plan* level, possibly affecting the plan's qualification, according to Notice 89-25. Those issues are beyond the scope of this book.

P buys policy from plan

If the policy is distributed to P at retirement, then all further opportunity to defer income taxes on the amount represented by the policy value (and on the potential future earnings on that amount) is lost. For this reason, many retiring participants look at the possibility of purchasing the policy from the plan. Although this requires P to come up with some cash from other sources, it does allow him to continue deferring income tax on the policy value. P will own the policy (which he can transfer to an irrevocable trust, if he wants to remove the proceeds from his gross estate); and the plan will own cash, which can then be distributed to P and rolled over to an IRA for maximum continued deferral.

Buying the policy from the plan creates an ERISA problem. ERISA § 406(a) prohibits the sale of plan assets to a "party in interest." The definition of "parties in interest" includes categories one would expect, such as plan fiduciaries, the employer, and officers, directors and 10% owners of the employer. It also includes, surprisingly, any *employee* of the employer. ERISA, § 3(14). Thus, as an initial proposition, the sale of a life insurance policy from the plan to the insured employee is a "prohibited transaction."

The Department of Labor has issued a "Prohibited Transaction Class Exemption" (PTE 92-6, 2/12/92; reproduced at CCH <u>Pension Plan Guide</u>, Vol. 5, ¶ 16,637) which exempts such sales if certain requirements are met. Thus, if the desired approach is to have P buy the policy from the plan, there are two ways that this might be accomplished:

     1.   Comply with PTE 92-6; or,

     2.   If P does not have any connection with the employer or the plan except as an employee, it might be worth exploring the possibility that the sale is not a "prohibited transaction" once P retires and ceases to be an employee. Consult an ERISA specialist before embarking on this course.

     To comply with PTE 92-6 when the insured employee is buying the policy from the plan, the following two requirements must be met:

     1.   The contract would, but for the sale, be surrendered by the plan. This requirement is not a problem, if P is retiring, for the type of QRP that is *required* to sell or surrender the policy at that point (see "*Income tax issues at retirement: the rollout*," above).

     2.   The price must be "at least" the CSV.

     To comply with PTE 92-6 *and* avoid any income tax inclusion to P, the price should be the *greater* of:

     (a)   The cash surrender value; or

     (b)   The amount P would be required to include in gross income if the policy were simply distributed to him (see "*Distributing the policy to P*," above).

     If using (a), note that P is not allowed to offset his "basis" in the contract against the purchase price, because PTE 92-6 sets the CSV (with no offset) as the *minimum* purchase price to avoid a prohibited transaction. The price under (b) would be used if the policy reserves "substantially exceed" the CSV *and* the value of the policy reserves, minus P's basis, exceeds the CSV.

Note also that the rollout problem may not wait until the client is age 65. It could crop up earlier if the client is laid off, chooses early retirement or becomes disabled. Some of these situations will be made even more difficult by the forced unraveling of the insurance-retirement plan marriage.

In contrast, if the employee buys his insurance *outside* of the retirement plan to begin with, these issues at retirement (which one insurance agent has described as "the enormous gift and income tax consequences associated with a rollout to an insurance trust") simply do not arise. *All* retirement benefits can be cleanly rolled over to an IRA and taken out when the employee feels like it (subject to the minimum distribution rules); and the cash value build-up of the insurance policy is not subject to income tax at retirement or death or any other time.

Certain profit sharing plans

Even if P is retiring, it may be possible that these unpleasant choices can be postponed *if* the plan is a profit sharing plan *and* the policy was purchased with money held in the plan for more than two years, because this type of money is not subject to the "incidental benefit rule." Rev. Rul. 60-83, 1960-1 C.B. 157. Under this circumstance, it may be possible for P to leave the policy in the plan along with his other benefits and withdraw it later (subject to the minimum distribution rules). Of course, the annual taxable income to him from the existence of the policy in the plan will continue.

The ability to keep the policy in the plan does not exist even for a profit sharing plan in the case of many small businesses, where the retirement plan is often terminated altogether when the owner retires. This would typically be true, for example, in the case of a small medical practice. If the plan is terminated, then the retiring business owner or doctor must either pay income tax on the value of the policy, cash it in at the plan level (terminating coverage), or buy it back from the plan with after-tax dollars accumulated outside the plan.

Income tax consequences to beneficiaries

Life insurance proceeds paid out of a QRP to a beneficiary are includible in gross income to the extent of the policy's CSV immediately prior to death. § 72(m)(3)(C) dictates that, in the case of a life insurance policy purchased by a retirement plan, the distribution of the CSV is treated as a "payment under such plan," rather than as a (tax-exempt) distribution of life insurance proceeds. Thus, to the extent of the CSV immediately before P's death, life insurance proceeds are treated the same as all other retirement plan distributions, which are normally subject to income tax when paid out to the beneficiaries after P's death.

Despite the fact that P might have been taxable on *more* than the CSV if the policy had been distributed to him during life (see "*Distributing the policy to P*," above), the regulations clearly state that only the CSV is taxable to the beneficiaries after P's death. Also, the beneficiaries are entitled to offset the amount of P's "basis" in the policy (*i.e.*, the amount included in P's gross income over the years on account of the P.S. 58 cost) against the amount otherwise includible in their gross income. See Reg. § 1.72-16(c)(3), Ex. 1.

This treatment of plan-owned life insurance compares unfavorably with the treatment of insurance policies purchased outside of retirement plans, proceeds of which are received by the beneficiaries 100% income-tax-free. § 101(a).

2. Life Insurance: Estate Tax Issues

For the estate tax-conscious client, an important consideration in buying life insurance is to keep the insurance out of the insured's estate and his spouse's estate, to increase the value of the benefits for their children. If the policy is purchased *outside* the retirement plan, it is easy to accomplish this goal. The parent creates an irrevocable trust for the benefit of the spouse and children; and the trustee buys the policy. The policy proceeds are never part of either spouse's estate.

The life insurance subtrust

If the policy is bought through a retirement plan, on the other hand, it is not clear how, if at all, the proceeds can be kept out of P's estate.

Generally, the estate tax includability of retirement plan benefits is governed by § 2039. However, § 2042, not § 2039, governs life insurance even if the insurance is held inside a retirement plan. § 2039(a). Life insurance is subject to estate tax if the insured owns any "incident of ownership." § 2042. To keep plan-held life insurance out of the insured participant's estate, therefore, it would be necessary to deprive P of such "incidents of ownership" as the power to name the beneficiary of the policy, the power to surrender or borrow against the policy, and a reversionary interest (worth 5% or more) in the policy. § 2042(2).

Some practitioners believe this goal can be accomplished by establishing a "subtrust," which is defined as "an irrevocable life insurance trust slotted within the trust otherwise used to fund the pension or profit sharing plan" (definition from "The Qualified Plan as an Estate Planning Tool," by Andrew J. Fair, Esq., published by Guardian Life Insurance Company of America, New York, NY, 1995) (Pub. No. 2449).

The merits of the subtrust have been debated in numerous articles. See the Bibliography. Some writers conclude that the subtrust "works" to keep policy proceeds out of the estate, without disqualifying the underlying retirement plan. Other writers state that either the existence of the "subtrust" disqualifies the plan, or, if the plan *is* qualified, it is impossible for P not to have estate-taxable "incidents of ownership" in the policy.

It remains to be seen whether the subtrust device works as a way of keeping the policy proceeds out of the estate. To date, there is no published ruling or case upholding (or denying) the estate tax exclusion for life insurance held in a retirement plan "subtrust." A loss on the estate tax issue would result in a tax of 40%-60% of the amount of the policy proceeds.

Furthermore, even if the subtrust concept "works" to keep the death benefit out of the gross estate if P dies prior to retirement, new problems arise once P reaches retirement. If he then either buys the policy out of the plan or receives it as a distribution (see *"Income tax issues at retirement: the rollout,"* above), P is right back in the position of owning the policy. He will then have to contribute it to an irrevocable trust, and survive for three more years after the transfer, in order to get it out of his estate again. § 2035.

Can the three-year rule be avoided at rollout time?

As discussed above, the normal course is for the retirement plan to sell or distribute the policy to P at retirement. P may wish at that point to transfer the policy to his children or to an irrevocable trust to get the proceeds out of his estate. Since gifting the policy would not remove the proceeds from P's estate until three years have elapsed (§ 2035), practitioners look for an alternative way to get the policy into the hands of the beneficiaries without the three year waiting period.

Since the plan cannot distribute benefits to anyone other than P during P's lifetime, the only way out is for the plan to *sell* the policy to the intended beneficiaries, or else distribute or sell the policy to P, and have P sell it to the beneficiaries. Such sales raise several issues.

The first problem is the "transfer for value" rule of § 101(a)(2). Life insurance proceeds are taxable income to a recipient who acquired the policy in a "transfer for value," unless an exception applies. The purchase of the policy from P, or from the plan, by P's children (or a trust for their benefit) would be a "transfer for value," causing the eventual death benefit to be taxable income instead of tax exempt income. However, the transfer for value rule does not apply if the policy is bought by the insured, a partner of the insured or a partnership in which the insured is a partner. Thus, the sale could be made to a partnership in which P and his children are the partners, to avoid the "transfer for value" problem.

The next question is, whether life insurance owned by a partnership in which P is a partner is in or out of P's gross estate. As a partner, does P have "incidents of ownership" in a policy owned by the partnership? A number of cases and IRS rulings have held that a partner does not have "incidents of ownership" in a policy on his life held by the partnership. It should be noted that these cases and rulings apparently involved arms' length, business partnerships, not family partnerships formed solely for the purchase of life insurance. Nevertheless, this is a promising route to explore when buying an insurance policy from a retirement plan. A discussion of partnership-owned life insurance is beyond the scope of this book.

Another alternative which has been suggested by a prominent estate planning attorney is for P to sell the policy, for fair market value, to a "defective **grantor trust**," *i.e.*, a trust all of which is deemed to be "owned" by P under the "grantor trust rules" of §§ 671-677. The theory is that a transaction between

P and his grantor trust is not treated as a sale (and therefore there is no transfer for value) because P and the trust are regarded as "one taxpayer" for income tax purposes. The trust could be structured so it would not be included in P's estate. Exploration of this idea is also beyond the scope of this book.

The third problem is the prohibited transaction rules of ERISA, discussed above. The Department of Labor's class exemption, PTE 92-6, exempts the sale of a life insurance policy by the plan to the insured participant or his beneficiaries, if various requirements are met. If the sale is to someone *other than* P, and would be a prohibited transaction if not specially exempted, the following requirements must be met, in addition to those discussed elsewhere:

1.   The buyer must be a "relative" of the insured participant. "Relative" means either a relative as defined in § 3(15) of ERISA or IRC § 4975(e)(6) (spouse, ancestor, lineal descendant or spouse of a lineal descendant), or a sibling.

2.   The buyer must be the beneficiary of the policy.

3.   The policy must first be offered for sale to P, who must give a written refusal to purchase, and must consent to the proposed sale to the beneficiary.

Note that the PTE's definition of "relative" does not include partnerships or trusts. If the strategy is to sell the policy from the plan directly to a partnership of P and P's children, the plan's ERISA counsel will have to determine whether (a) the transaction is a "prohibited transaction" and (b) if it is, whether the transaction is exempt under PTE 92-6. These issues can be avoided by having the plan sell or distribute the policy to P, and having P make the sale to the partnership or trust.

A final problem is, how the partnership (or trust) is

going to get the money to buy the policy.

Second-to-die insurance

Buying a second-to-die ("joint and survivor life") policy inside a retirement plan raises additional problems. Trying to minimize estate taxes on a second-to-die insurance policy (insuring the lives of P and S) owned by a QRP involves considerable complexity.

If the policy is purchased *outside* the plan, the only legal paperwork required to avoid estate and gift tax is one irrevocable trust to buy the policy, plus "Crummey" notices. If the policy is bought *inside* a retirement plan, on the other hand, one widely distributed booklet recommends the following steps to reduce (not eliminate) estate tax:

1.   Draft an irrevocable trust to receive policy from plan if P dies before S.

2.   The irrevocable trust buys a single life insurance policy on P so trust can pay income and estate taxes due on the policy at P's death.

3.   P executes a special beneficiary designation, leaving the second-to-die policy to the irrevocable trust, with waiver of QPSA (see Chapter 3) by S, and containing a presumption of S's survivorship, in case of common accident, as to the policy.

4.   If S dies before P, then:

A.   The second-to-die policy must be distributed to or purchased by P; if purchased, comply with DOL PTE 92-6;

B.   P transfers the second-to-die policy to an irrevocable trust, which removes policy from his estate *if he lives more than three years;*

C.   The irrevocable trust buys additional insurance on P to pay estate taxes if P dies within three years.

D.   To avoid estate taxes altogether if S dies first, skip steps A-C, and instead of P buying the policy from the plan, a family partnership of P and his children buys the policy.

5.   Buy a single life policy on S to finance step 4A or step 4D (as the case may be).

6.   If P retires, the policy is purchased from the plan by a family partnership of P, S, and the children. No mention of how this purchase is financed.

This scheme involves one trust, either three or four separate life insurance policies, and possibly a family partnership. An additional complexity with employer-provided second-to-die insurance is that there are no IRS rulings or regulations indicating how to calculate the amount to be included in P's gross income for this form of coverage ("Table P.S. 58" deals only with single life policies).

3. Life Insurance: Miscellaneous

Reasons to buy life insurance inside the plan

There can be good reasons to buy life insurance inside a retirement plan. For example, this approach can be attractive if:

1.   The client is rated or uninsurable, and wants to buy insurance, and there is a policy available through the plan which the client can purchase without evidence of insurability.

2.   The purchase of insurance can increase permitted contributions to a defined benefit plan.

3.   The client needs insurance but has no money to pay for it outside the retirement plan. In this case, however, it is still advisable to look at the possibility of taking some money out of the plan to buy the insurance. Unless there is some reason the client cannot conveniently get money out of the plan (unacceptable level of tax on plan distributions; creditor or marital problems; plan doesn't permit it), the purchase of insurance outside the plan may be more tax-effective.

Miscellaneous

Borrowing against the policy at the plan level may cause the plan to be subject to income tax on "unrelated business taxable income." See PLR 7918095 (1/31/79).

The "P.S. 58 cost" that the employee must report each year on his income tax return is not considered a "distribution" to the employee for purposes of the 10% penalty on premature distributions (see Chapter 9). IRS Notice 89-25.

Does the "P.S. 58 cost" income that the employee pays taxes on every year count towards the minimum distributions required under § 401(a)(9)? Nothing in the proposed regulations says that it does.

4. Life Insurance: Summary of Planning Principles

1.   If it is possible under the plan to designate a

different death beneficiary for the life insurance policy proceeds, on the one hand, and any other plan death benefits, on the other, determine how much of the life insurance proceeds would be subject to income tax if the client died today, *i.e.*, the cash surrender value (CSV) of the policy. If the CSV is relatively small, and the client has insufficient other assets to fully fund a credit shelter trust, consider naming the credit shelter trust as beneficiary of the plan-held policy. Since most of the proceeds would be income tax-free, the usual drawbacks of funding a credit shelter trust with plan benefits (see Chapter 2, and the *Allen Able* case study) would be minimized. The rest of the benefits, being fully income-taxable, could be left to the surviving spouse, who could roll them over to an IRA and continue to defer income taxes. See Form 3.1, Appendix B.

2.   Is it possible to further fine-tune the beneficiary designation for the life insurance policy, to the extent of directing that the income-taxable portion (pre-death CSV, minus P's investment in the contract) will be paid to S, and the "pure death benefit" portion and return of basis would pass to, say, the credit shelter trust? It is not clear that such a beneficiary designation would be effective, as far as the IRS is concerned, to allocate the income-taxable portion to one beneficiary and the income-tax-free portion to the other. Although the author has found no IRS pronouncement on the subject one way or the other, the IRS might require the taxable and tax-free parts of the policy proceeds to be allocated among the recipients in proportion to what each receives from the contract.

3.   If a substantial portion of the life insurance proceeds will constitute taxable income to the beneficiary, consider making the life insurance proceeds payable to S, who can then roll over the taxable portion. § 402(c)(2), (c)(9).

4.   In general, it is better to buy life insurance outside the retirement plan if estate taxes are a consideration. While the "subtrust" scheme may offer a chance of keeping plan-owned insurance out of P's estate, it is at best an unproven technique. *Definite* estate tax exclusion can be easily obtained for insurance owned outside the plan. With estate tax rates at 40%-60%, this factor will weigh heavily, especially for older and wealthier participants.

5.   If the client is not insurable at standard rates, investigate the availability of group insurance through his retirement plan (and elsewhere).

6.   If life insurance is owned by the client's retirement plan, investigate the "subtrust" as a way of keeping the policy proceeds out of the gross estate.

7.   When the time comes to remove the policy from the plan, investigate ways to get/keep the policy out of the client's gross estate without triggering the "three year rule" of § 2035, while avoiding a "transfer for value" or "prohibited transaction."

5. Minimum Distribution Rule Grandfathers

Chapter 1 describes the "minimum distribution rules" of § 401(a)(9) as they are today, in 1999. Today's rules have evolved through a number of mutations over the years. At several stages of this evolution, "grandfather" exceptions were created, so that today some individuals have benefits that are wholly or partly exempt from the rules. The three types of benefits grandfathered from the minimum distribution rules are: benefits covered by a TEFRA "242(b) designation"; benefits of unretired, born-before-6/30/17, non-5% owners; and pre-1987

403(b) plan account balances.

History of § 401(a)(9)

Prior to TEFRA '82, the minimum distribution rules applied only to Keogh plans and only to lifetime distributions. All benefits had to be distributed not later than the taxable year (a) in which P reached age 70½, or, (b) "in the case of an employee other than an owner employee... in which he retires," if later; or, beginning in that year, over the life or life expectancy of the employee (or employee and his spouse).

TEFRA significantly expanded the minimum distribution rules. For plan years beginning after 1983, § 401(a)(9) would apply to all "QRPs," corporate as well as Keogh. Effective for 1984 and later years, all benefits were required to be distributed not later than the year in which P attained age 70½, or, "in the case of an employee other than a key employee who is a participant in a top heavy plan, in which he retires," whichever was later (or, beginning in such year, over the life or life expectancy of the employee or employee and spouse). TEFRA '82, § 242(a).

TEFRA also added the *after-death* minimum distribution requirement. After 1983, all QRPs would have to provide that, if any employee died before his entire interest had been distributed, the balance would "be distributed within five years after his death (or the death of his surviving spouse)." An exception provided that, if distributions had already commenced, over a permitted term certain (such as the life expectancy of the employee and spouse), the balance of the employee's interest could continue to be paid out over the rest of the term certain. TEFRA '82, § 242(a). TEFRA included a grandfather exception for this substantial extension of the minimum distribution rules. See "*TEFRA 242(b) designations*," below.

§ 401(a)(9) was amended again by the Tax Reform Act

of 1984, § 521(a). For the first time, the use of a life expectancy payout was extended to any "designated beneficiary," not just the spouse, for both retirement and death benefits.

TRA '84 added the requirement that, in the case of death benefits, if distribution had begun in accordance with the lifetime minimum distribution rules, and the employee died before his entire interest had been distributed, "the remaining portion of such interest will be distributed at least as rapidly as under the method of distributions being used... as of the date of his death." Finally, TRA '84 added the special rule that a surviving spouse beneficiary would not have to begin taking out death benefits until the year the employee would have reached age 70½, and the concept that the life expectancy of an employee and spouse could be redetermined annually.

As amended by TRA '84, § 401(a)(9) retained the concept that distributions would have to begin in the year in which the employee attained age 70½, or in the year of retirement whichever was later, except for *certain* employees. Certain employees would have to begin withdrawals at age 70½, and would not have the option of delaying distributions until actual retirement. However, TRA '84 slightly changed the definition of these "certain employees." The restricted participants under TRA '84 were "5% owners" rather than "key employees." § 416(i)(1)(A)(iii).

The changes made by TRA '84 were regarded as "cleaning up" the changes made by TEFRA '82. Accordingly, TRA '84 said that these amendments were to take effect "as if" included in TEFRA, and the TEFRA grandfather rule was continued. Accordingly, the TRA '84 changes would not apply to "distributions under a designation (before January 1, 1984) by any employee in accordance with a designation described in section 242(b)(2) of [TEFRA] (as in effect before the amendments made by this Act)." TRA '84, § 521(d)(2)-5.

The Tax Reform Act of 1986 brought more fine tuning.

The minimum distribution rules were extended for the first time to 403(b) plans; and the exception permitting non-key or non-5% owner employees to postpone distributions until actual retirement was eliminated (only to be brought back again in slightly modified format by the Taxpayer Relief Act of 1997; see "The Required Beginning Date: When It Is," Chapter 1). Each of these changes created a new batch of "grandfathers."

TEFRA 242(b) designations

The famous TEFRA § 242(b)(2) provides that a plan will not be disqualified "by reason of distributions under a designation (before January 1, 1984) by any employee of a method of distribution...

> "A.   which does not meet the requirements of [§ 401(a)(9)], but
> "B.   which would not have disqualified such [plan] under [401(a)(9)] as in effect before the amendment" made by TEFRA.

TEFRA affected many people. First, it affected all plan participants by adding the new minimum distribution requirement for death benefits. Second, it affected *corporate* QRP participants because it created stringent and specific minimum distribution requirements, where before there had been only the vague "incidental death benefit rule" (see discussion of 403(b) plans, below). Finally, it affected "key employees" in "top heavy plans" a little more than it affected non-key employees because, under the new rule, they would have to start taking minimum distributions in the year they reached 70½ whether they had retired or not.

As a result, there was a flurry of activity among sophisticated plan participants trying to make a "designation" by

December 31, 1983 that would enable them to continue to use the older, more liberal rules. The benefits of a participant who made a proper and timely "designation" would not be subject to the new minimum distribution rules.

Theoretically, participants with "242(b) designations" can postpone distributions until retirement, and their death benefits are not subject to the "five year rule" or the "at least as rapidly" rule. Unfortunately, TEFRA 242(b) designations have not proved as useful as originally expected for several reasons:

(a)		The requirements for a valid "designation" (as set forth in IRS Notice 83-23, 1983-2 C.B. 418, 11/15/83) are quite restrictive: "The designation must, in and of itself, provide sufficient information to fix the timing, and the formula for the definite determination, of plan payments. The designation must be complete and not allow further choice." P. 419. This does not mean the designation may not be amendable or revocable. Rather, the designation must be self-executing, requiring no further actions or designations by P to determine the size and date of distributions. Many purported TEFRA 242(b) designations do not meet this test.

(b)		Also, a participant generally cannot carry over a 242(b) designation from one plan to another. For example, by rolling over corporate plan benefits protected by a 242(b) designation into an IRA, P loses the 242(b) protection. However, grandfather protection is not lost if benefits are moved to another plan without any election on the part of P—e.g., as a result of a plan merger—IF the transferee plan accounts for such benefits separately. Prop. Reg. § 1.401(a)(9)-1, J-2, J-3.

(c)		TEFRA 242(b) designations generally attempted to defer distributions for as long as possible. This turned out to be counterproductive, because an unrealistically long proposed deferral made it more likely that an individual grandfathered from the minimum distribution rules by a 242(b) election would want to make withdrawals sooner than his "designation" indicates. However, "any change in the designation will be considered to be a revocation of the designation." Notice 83-23, p. 420 (next to last sentence).

(d)   If the 242(b) designation is revoked or modified in any way, drastic results ensue. In effect the grandfathered status is revoked retroactively, and P is required to take "make-up distributions"—withdraw from the plan all the prior years' distributions he had skipped. Prop. Reg. § 1.401(a)(9)-1, J-4.

Thus, participants relying on TEFRA 242(b) designations live in a perilous state. The longer they defer their distributions, the larger becomes the "make-up" distribution which will be required if they ever change their minds.

The hardworking aged non-5% owners

A person who attained age 70½ before January 1, 1988 (*i.e.* was born on or before June 30, 1917), and who was not a 5% owner (see § 416(i)) at any time during a plan year ending during or after the calendar year in which he reached age 66½, is entitled to defer commencement of distributions until actual retirement. See § 1121(d)(3)-(5) of TRA '86, as amended by TAMRA '88, and Prop. Reg. § 1.401(a)(9)-1, B-2(b). These non-5% owners, would now (as of 1999) be at least 82 years old and since they are still working I refer to them as HANOs (Hardworking Aged Non-5% Owners).

These individuals are not subject to the same hazardous conditions as those relying on TEFRA 242(b) designations. The HANO can take money out of his plan any time he wants to without thereby losing his grandfathered status and without triggering any requirement of make-up distributions; and he can make or modify elections regarding the form of distribution of his benefits with no adverse effect on his protected status.

However, the effects of indefinitely postponing all distributions until retirement at some ancient age are not all benign. The plan balance grows larger and larger if it is not depleted by withdrawals; and the period over which it will have to be withdrawn will be much shorter, once the employee actually does retire, because his life expectancy will be that much shorter.

Pre-1987 403(b) plan balances grandfathered...

At one time, 403(b) plans were exempt from most of the minimum distribution rules. The Tax Reform Act of 1986 made these plans subject to the minimum distribution rules on the same basis as other plans. TRA '86 § 1852(a)(3)(A) added § 403(b)(10), which provides that, "under regulations prescribed by the Secretary," a 403(b) plan will lose its tax-favored qualities "unless requirements similar to" § 401(a)(9) and the incidental death benefit requirements of § 401(a) are met. This amendment was to apply "as if" included in the Tax Reform Act of 1984 (see § 1881 of TRA '86), because it was considered a technical correction of TRA '84.

Prop. Reg. § 1.403(b)-2 (7/27/87) governs these distributions. The regulation says that § 403(b) annuities and 403(b)(7) mutual fund custodial accounts (described collectively as "403(b) contracts") will be treated the same as individual retirement annuities under § 408(b) and individual retirement accounts under § 408(a), respectively, and accordingly the minimum distribution rules will be the same as for IRAs under Prop. Reg. § 1.408-8. However, certain *plan participants* and *plan balances* are "grandfathered":

(a)   Transition rule for older participants still working

There is a "transition rule" for 403(b) *plan participants* who turned age 70½ before 1988. These participants do not have to commence withdrawals from *any* part of their 403(b) plans until April 1 of the year following the year in which they retire. Notice 88-39, 1988-1 C.B. 525. These participants are in the same situation as the "hardworking aged non-5% owners" discussed in the previous section.

(b)   Grandfathering of pre-'87 balance

The grandfathering for certain *plan balances* is available regardless of P's age. The *amount* that is grandfathered is the account balance on December 31, 1986, *provided* that the plan sponsor/custodian keeps records that enable it "to identify the pre-'87 account balance and subsequent changes as set forth in" the regulations. (These regulations pertain to whether withdrawals made over the years from the 403(a) or (b) arrangement come out of the pre-'87 or post-'86 account balance). "If the issuer does not keep such records, the entire account balance" is subject to the full panoply of minimum distribution rules.

...But still subject to the MDIB rule

Even though pre-'87 balances are not subject to the so-called "minimum distribution rules" of § 401(a)(9) of the Code, they are still subject to the "incidental death benefit" rule, which pre-dated the 1986 tax act.

Thus, any 403(b) plan, if the custodian keeps proper records, contains two portions: the December 31, 1986 account balance (as reduced by subsequent distributions); and the post-'86 account balance, which consists of post-'86 contributions, earnings on post-'86 contributions, and earnings on pre-'87 contributions (minus distributions therefrom). Theoretically, these two different portions are subject to two different sets of distribution rules: The post-'86 balance is subject to all the minimum distribution rules of § 401(a)(9) and to the "minimum distribution incidental benefit" (MDIB) rule, which is the modern version of the "incidental death benefit" rule. The pre-'87 account balance is subject only to the "incidental death benefit" rule.

The earlier (1996) edition of this book contained a lengthy discussion of exactly what rules governed the pre-1987 account balance of a participant's 403(b) plan, and the planning implications of this grandfather rule. Since 1996, however, the possible significance of this grandfather rule has diminished considerably, for several reasons:

1.   Until retirement, a 403(b) participant is not required to make any withdrawals from his grandfathered (pre-'87) balance. However, with enactment of the Taxpayer Relief Act of 1997, *any* employee who is not a 5% owner of the sponsoring employer can postpone required distributions until retirement. Since 403(b) plans are by definition maintained by not-for-profit employers (which are not "owned" by anyone) it appears that 403(b) plan participants should be entitled to postpone distributions until actual retirement as to *all* of their 403(b) plan balances, regardless of whether they qualify for the pre-1987 grandfather rule.

2.   The pre-1987 grandfather amount is a frozen, fixed-dollar amount; investment earnings and gains do not increase the grandfathered balance (though distributions in excess of required distributions decrease it). With the passage of time, additional contributions to the plan, and investment growth, the pre-1987 balance becomes a smaller and smaller

percentage of the overall plan balance. This makes it less of a concern in P's planning.

What special rules still apply to the pre-1987 balance?

The special rules applicable to the pre-1987 balance, not available to the post-1986 balance are:

1.   Once a participant has retired, he should be able to postpone distributions on his pre-1987 balance until age 75 (see PLRs 7825010, 7913129 (12/29/78), and 9345044 (8/16/93); Reg. § 1.401-1(b)(1)(i); and Krass, Stephan J., Esq., *The Pension Answer Book* (10th ed., Panel Publishers 1995), Q29:40, p. 29-44). For the post-1986 balance, age 70½ is the trigger age for post-retirement required distributions.

2.   When required distributions begin, the post-1986 balance is subject to the regular minimum distribution rules of § 401(a)(9), whereas the pre-1987 balance can be distributed in accordance with the pre-1987 "incidental death benefit rule." This rule was nowhere near as specific and stringent as today's minimum distribution rules. All the old rule required when distributions commenced was that, if any form of installment or annuity payout were elected, the actuarial value of P's expected lifetime distributions had to be at least 50% of the total value of the benefits; *i.e.*, the expected death benefits had to be less than 50% of the total value. Rev. Ruls. 72-241 and 72-240, 1972-1 C.B. 108. For the possibility that even this 50% requirement may not apply if P's spouse is the beneficiary, or if the payout period is limited to the lives/life expectancies of P and spouse, see Rev. Rul. 72-240, previously cited, and PLR 7825010.

3.   Also, unlike today's rules, the old rule had no application after the death of P. Thus, if a 403(b) participant

dies before the required beginning date applicable to his pre-1987 balance, theoretically the pre-1987 balance does not have to be distributed at any particular time to the beneficiaries. There is no five year rule and no requirement that the beneficiary take distributions over the beneficiary's life expectancy.

6. The Federal Estate Tax Exclusion Lives!

Once upon a time IRC § 2039 provided an unlimited federal estate tax exclusion for most kinds of retirement benefits. Then the exclusion was limited to $100,000 by TEFRA '82 and repealed by TRA '84. However a grandfather clause was included in TRA '84 for both laws; and then the Tax Reform Act of 1986 made major substantive retroactive amendments to these grandfather clauses. The retroactive TRA '86 changes made it substantially easier to qualify for the exclusion than it was under the "original" grandfather provision in TRA '84.

However, the TRA '86 amendments are so obscure that they are not even mentioned in widely used estate tax reporting services. The casual researcher may find only the strict TRA '84 grandfather rules (as embodied in IRS Temp. Reg. § 20.2039-1T, 1/29/86) under which only participants who were "in pay status" and had "irrevocably elected a form of benefits" by 1982 or 1984 still qualified for the exclusion. But TRA '86 simply *repealed* those two requirements and substituted others. Thus Temp. Reg. § 20.2039-1T is nugatory.

The best explanation of this incredible tangle appears in PLR 9221030 (2/21/92). The current requirements for a decedent's estate to be eligible for a total (or $100,000) estate tax exclusion, as stated by the IRS in this ruling, are:

1.   A decedent who separated from service before 1983, and died after 1984, without having changed the "form of benefit" before his death, will be entitled to 100% exclusion of

the benefit. A change of beneficiary is fine; it is a change of the *form of payment* of benefit that triggers loss of the exclusion.

    2.   If the decedent separated from service after 1982 but prior to 1985, and did not change the form of benefit between the time of separation from service and the time of death, the estate is still entitled to the exclusion but it is limited to $100,000.

    Both of these exclusions under the retroactive amended grandfather clause are available *regardless* of whether the election of form of benefits was irrevocable, and *regardless* of whether the benefits were "in pay status" on December 31, 1984 or any other particular date.

    Under the ruling in question, P retired in 1979, selected a form of benefit and designated a beneficiary. He had the right to change the form of benefit but never did. The plan administrator made some minor administrative changes in the method to be used for calculating certain joint and survivor benefits, but this was not deemed to be a change of form of benefit by P. P also changed his beneficiary a couple of times, but never changed the form of benefit. The IRS held that P's estate was entitled to a 100% exclusion of the benefits from the gross estate.

7. Probate Issues

    In some states, "custodial" IRAs and 403(b) accounts are treated as probate assets subject to the requirements applicable to wills, so that the mere filing of a designation of beneficiary form, lacking the formalities of a will, is not sufficient to pass the asset to the beneficiary. In Massachusetts, this is not a problem because M. G. L. ch. 167D, § 30, gives effect to the designation of a beneficiary under IRAs and other retirement plans, if proper under the plan, "notwithstanding any purported testamentary disposition allowed by statute, by operation of law or otherwise to the contrary."

8. Planning for Disability

Designating a beneficiary for disability benefits

Retirement plan documents should (but may not) permit the participant to direct the payment of lifetime benefits (disability and retirement) to his revocable living trust.

§ 401(a)(13) prohibits "assignment" of QRP benefits. Regulations provide that a voluntary, revocable assignment is not an "assignment" for purposes of § 401(a)(13). § 72(p)(1)(B) treats all "assignments" of plan benefits as loans from the plan, apparently taxable as distributions, and neither § 72(p) nor regulations thereunder suggests an exception for a voluntary revocable assignment of benefits. However, an "assignment" to a revocable trust should not be treated as an assignment for purposes of § 72(p) or § 401(a)(13) because P and his revocable trust are essentially treated as "one person" for income tax purposes under the **grantor trust rules** (§§ 671-677).

Power of attorney

The client's power of attorney should at a minimum enable the power holder to receive benefit checks and endorse them. It can go further and give the holder the power to make elections as to the form and timing of benefits (subject to the rights of client's spouse) but this would necessarily involve the power holder in making choices between the client and the beneficiary of death benefits under the plan. Giving the power to designate a beneficiary of plan death benefits gives even greater responsibility to the power holder. See form 5 in Appendix B.

11

Case Studies

The Ables: Funding a Credit Shelter Trust

One of the most common problems presented in estate planning is that of the married couple whose combined estate is large enough to be subject to estate taxes, but who cannot adopt a **credit shelter** estate plan unless retirement benefits are used to fund the credit shelter share of one or both spouses.

The facts

Allen and Alice Able are both age 66. Both are retired. They are living on Social Security, Allen's pension from Big Corp. and investment income. Their assets are:

Ables	Husband	Wife
House		300,000
Mutual Funds		350,000
Life Insurance	50,000	
IRA	600,000	
Subtotals	650,000	650,000
Total family assets for estate planning purposes: $1.3 million		

Allen's Big Corp. pension is not listed as an asset for estate planning purposes because it ends on the death of the surviving spouse. Therefore it will not be subject to estate taxes and it not an asset the Ables can pass to their daughter Jane.

For now, Allen and Alice do not need to withdraw from the IRA for their living expenses. They would like to preserve the IRA and let it continue to build up as long as possible, with the goal of leaving it to their child. Allen Able wants to take advantage of the tax saving ideas he has read about in several books on estate planning. He states his goals as follows:

1.   Allen's primary goal is to provide for Alice Able's financial security, support and comfort.

2.   He also wants to take advantage of his federal estate tax exemption (credit shelter), so that neither spouse's estate will exceed the $650,000 limit (applicable to deaths in 1999), and the Ables' child will have no estate taxes to pay.

3.   Finally, Allen wants to maximize the income tax deferral potential of his IRA by causing it eventually to be paid out to the Ables' child over her life expectancy.

The bad news for Allen is: the estate plan can achieve any two of his goals, but cannot achieve all three.

Scenario 1: Name daughter Jane as beneficiary

Allen can best achieve his *tax saving* goals by naming his daughter, Jane, as beneficiary of his IRA.

Naming Jane minimizes *estate taxes* because, when he dies, the benefits will not be subject to estate tax in his estate (because the total passing to the child will be less than the credit shelter amount). The benefits are also out of *Alice's* estate because they pass directly to the daughter at Allen's death.

Naming his daughter also minimizes *income taxes*, both during Allen's life and after his death. During his life, when Allen reaches his required beginning date (RBD), if Jane is named as his designated beneficiary (DB), Allen can withdraw from the plan over the joint life expectancy of himself and Jane (as limited by the MDIB rule). The first year's required payment under the MDIB rule would be only 1/26.2th of the account balance. In contrast, if Allen names wife Alice (or a trust of which she is the oldest beneficiary) as his DB, their joint life expectancy at Allen's RBD will be 20.6 years, and Allen will be forced to make withdrawals more quickly.

Clearly, naming the child as his DB is the most tax effective course for Allen. Unfortunately, this choice utterly fails to achieve Allen's primary goal—to provide for Alice.

Scenario 2: Name wife Alice as beneficiary

The best way to achieve the goal of *providing for Alice* is to name her personally as the DB.

If she survives Allen, she can roll the benefits over to an IRA in her own name, then withdraw as much as she wants or needs to every year. She will be required to withdraw something each year from her rollover IRA once she reaches her RBD; assuming she names daughter Jane as her DB, her minimum required distributions will be calculated based on the joint life expectancy of herself and the child, as limited by the MDIB rule. When she dies, the remaining balance will be distributed to Jane over the remainder of Jane's life expectancy. Thus if Alice survives Allen, the deferral period for the benefits will be shorter than if Jane had been named *directly* as Allen's DB, but is still fairly generous.

If Alice dies before Allen and before Allen's RBD, Jane will be considered Allen's DB and the results will be the same as under scenario 1.

But what if Allen reaches his RBD, and names Alice as his DB, and then Alice dies before Allen? Then all possibility of deferring income taxation of these benefits over the life expectancy of daughter Jane is lost. The payout of the benefits will have to be completed over no longer than the joint life expectancy of Allen and Alice.

Thus, under scenario 2, the family gets the following result:

- Best financial protection for Alice.
- Income tax deferral will be less favorable than scenario 1; it will be "not bad" if Alice survives Allen but very limited if Alice predeceases Allen after his RBD.
- The estate tax result is terrible. The entire IRA will be included in Alice's estate. Adding this to her existing assets of $650,000 will generate a big estate tax bill.

Scenario 3: Name a credit shelter trust as beneficiary

Another approach is to name a **credit shelter trust** as beneficiary. This would achieve the estate tax goal, since the trust would keep the benefits out of Alice's taxable estate.

The estate tax savings from establishing a credit shelter trust with Allen's IRA will not be as great as they would be if Allen had non-"income in respect of a decedent" (Chapter 2) assets with which to fund his credit shelter trust. If we assume that the $600,000 in the IRA will eventually be drawn down by the trust at an income tax cost of about 40%, or $240,000, the net that is truly being preserved from estate taxes is only $360,000 (the after-tax value of the IRA). Based on a 50% estate tax rate, this produces estate tax savings of only $180,000. If Allen had a $600,000 non-IRD asset with which to fund his credit shelter trust, the estate tax savings (again assuming a 50% estate tax rate) would be $300,000.

Alice can be the life beneficiary of the credit shelter trust; thus the retirement benefits will be available for her if she needs them, and the goal of "protecting Alice's financial security" *appears* to be achieved. However, her financial security is not as well protected as it would be if the benefits were paid to her personally, because of the negative income tax effects of this form of disposition, namely:

1. **High trust tax rates.** To the extent benefits are paid to the credit shelter trust as principal, they will be taxed at the trust's income tax rate, which is probably going to be higher than Alice's. After Allen's death, Alice will be in the 31% marginal federal income tax bracket, even if she withdraws $35,000 a year or so from Allen's IRA. The trust will be in the 36% or 39.6% bracket for annual income over $6,200/$8,450. As a human being, Alice will not hit the top bracket unless she has more than $283,150 of taxable income, which she is not likely ever to have.

2. **Distributions during spouse's life will be based on a single rather than a joint life expectancy.** Benefits will have to be distributed over Alice's single life expectancy, since she is the oldest beneficiary of the trust. This will produce a much more rapid distribution of the benefits than would be required if the benefits were payable to Alice personally. If Alice received the benefits personally, rolled them over to an IRA, and named daughter Jane as her DB, she wouldn't have to take any distributions at all until she reached age 70½, and she could then withdraw over the joint life expectancy of herself and Jane (subject to the MDIB rule).

The faster-required withdrawals and higher income tax rate will mean less money available for Alice during her life than if benefits were paid to her personally.

The income tax drawbacks of the credit shelter trust continue after Alice's death. Because benefits paid to a trust of which she is the oldest beneficiary must be paid out over only her life expectancy (at *best*; this assumes the "trust rules" of

Chapter 6 are complied with) there is no deferral possible beyond Alice's life expectancy (currently 19.2 years) (or beyond the end of Alice's life, if the trust elects to recalculate her life expectancy). By contrast, with a rollover IRA established by Alice and payable to daughter Jane as DB, after Alice's death the payout could be made to Jane over Jane's life expectancy.

The solution chosen

    Despite the loss of estate tax savings, Allen decides that the best way to achieve his primary objective of providing for Alice's financial security is to name her directly as beneficiary of the IRA. That way, she can take advantage of the spousal rollover, defer all distributions until she reaches age 70½, and then take out the benefits gradually using the MDIB rule. The Ables take the following steps to implement their estate plan:

    1. They divide their non-retirement plan assets equally between them, so that, regardless of which spouse dies first, *some* assets will go into the estate tax-saving credit shelter trust of the first spouse to die. Following this rearrangement, their assets look like this:

	Allen	Alice
House	$150,000	$150,000
Mutual Funds	150,000	200,000
Life Insurance	50,000	
IRA	600,000	
Totals	950,000	350,000

    2. Although Allen wishes to name Alice directly as his primary beneficiary, he also wants to preserve the option for

her to disclaim some of the benefits so they would after all pass to the credit shelter trust. She might choose to disclaim if, for example, her financial situation or the tax laws, at the time of Allen's death, had changed so that having the IRA pass to the credit shelter trust would no longer have a negative effect on her financial security. See Form 3.6, Appendix B.

3.   The final step taken to minimize taxes is to structure the revocable trust with retirement benefits in mind, in case Alice disclaims the benefits into it: The trust uses a **fractional** formula to divide assets between the marital and credit shelter shares (not a **pecuniary** formula; see *"Planning pitfall: assignment of the right-to-receive IRD,"* Chapter 2), and the marital share is distributable outright to Alice—it is not a "QTIP" (see *"Rollover when S inherits benefits through an estate or trust,"* Chapter 3). See Form 3.2(B). The credit shelter trust is drafted so as not to require the trustee to withdraw all income from the IRA each year, if that would be more than the minimum required distribution. And finally, the trust is drafted to comply with the IRS's "trust rules" in the proposed regulations.

Ken Koslow: A Second Marriage: Retirement Benefits and the QTIP Trust

The facts

Ken Koslow is a 62-year-old executive, with two children by his first marriage, ages 36 and 33. His second wife, Karen, is also an executive; she is 54.

His plan is to leave his life insurance to his children, the jointly-owned house to his wife, and all of his retirement benefits to a QTIP trust. The trust would pay income to Karen for life and on her death the balance would pass to his children.

Ken's assets consist of:

House - joint with spouse	$ 450,000
Qualified plan	1,200,000
IRA	600,000
Non-plan investments	500,000
Life Insurance	500,000
Total	$3,250,000

The problem with this proposal is that paying his retirement benefits to a marital trust has many disadvantages, namely:

1.   **Distributions start immediately instead of being deferred until spouse reaches age 70½.** When the beneficiary is a QTIP trust, the minimum distribution rules will require that distribution of the benefits begin in the calendar year after Ken's death (or, possibly, at the latest, the year Ken would have reached age 70½; see *"When is a trust for the spouse the same as the spouse?"* Chapter 6). When benefits are left *outright* to the surviving spouse, she can roll them over to an IRA and then defer the commencement of distributions until *she* reaches age 70½. Karen Koslow is an executive who already has a high income. She will probably have no need for money from Ken's retirement plans until her own retirement eleven or more years from now. Thus, commencing distributions immediately following Ken's death wastes a deferral opportunity.

2.   **Distributions during spouse's life will be based on a single rather than a joint life expectancy.** This is the same drawback that occurs when benefits are left to a credit shelter trust of which the spouse is the oldest beneficiary; see the *Allen Able* case study.

3.   **Marital deduction requires distribution of all income annually, even if that exceeds the "minimum required distribution."** The marital deduction rules require that all income of the IRA be distributed annually to Karen, or at least that she have the right to demand that all income be distributed to her annually. The distinction, discussed at *"Income requirement: general power trusts,"* Chapter 3, between "distributing all income to the spouse" and "giving the spouse the right to require distribution of all income" makes no difference in the Koslow case, or any other "second marriage" situation, since the surviving spouse in such a situation could be expected to exercise the demand right. Thus, the marital deduction requirements do not allow even as much income tax deferral as the minimum distribution rules permit. This accelerated distribution is wasteful because Karen does not need or want this additional income for current spending. Possibly this drawback can be overcome by having Karen roll over distributions of income to the extent they exceed the MRD; see *"Mandatory income distributions,"* Chapter 3.

4.   **Loss of the ability to distribute benefits over the life expectancy of Ken's children.** If benefits were paid directly to Ken's children as beneficiaries, they could use their own life expectancy(ies) to measure MRDs of those benefits under the minimum distribution rules. When the benefits are paid to a trust of which they are only the remainder beneficiaries, however, the benefits have to come out based solely on Karen's life expectancy. The ability to use the long life expectancy of the children to measure MRDs is forever lost.

5.   **Benefits will be subject to higher income taxes.** The QTIP trust will be in the highest bracket for distributions of "principal" from Ken's retirement plans; see the *Allen Able* case study. Ken's children are not in the highest tax

bracket; but the only way to take advantage of that is to make some benefits payable directly to them, rather than to a trust. Thus, paying benefits to a trust results in their being taxed at a higher rate than if they were paid to family members.

6.   **Children probably have a long wait for a little money.** Karen is only 18 years older than Ken's oldest child. Thus it is quite likely that Ken's children themselves will be "old" before they see anything from the marital trust. Karen's life expectancy is currently about 30 years under the IRS tables. Since the IRS tables do not reflect recent advances in longevity, and are "unisex" (so they do not reflect Karen's above-average life expectancy as female), they understate the average life expectancy of a female Karen's age. Thus the children can expect, based on average life expectancy, to wait at least 30 years before they get any benefits from their father's retirement plan; and at the end of this time they will get 60% of the original value. In the meantime Karen and the children are left competing with each other regarding the investment policies of the trust.

The solution

Using software, we project that the eventual value of the benefits to the family under this scenario (leaving all benefits to a QTIP trust) is $5,526,000 after 30 years. (Assumptions are discussed in more detail below.) Of this amount, assuming Karen dies in 30 years, $1,087,000 would pass to the children (being the then-remaining principal of the marital trust) and $4,439,000 would be held by Karen's estate (representing the accumulated distributions to her from the marital trust). There would be no dollars left inside the retirement plans.

This proposed scenario was compared with "Scenario 2," under which there would be no QTIP trust. The $1.2 million of QRP benefits would be made payable to Karen personally, and the $600,000 IRA would be payable directly to Ken's children. Ken would make sure his life insurance and investments outside the plan were sufficient to pay the estate taxes on the benefits passing to the children.

This scenario has many advantages over the QTIP scenario. Each beneficiary would have total control of his or her own share of the benefits, without having to compete for the attention of the trustee of the QTIP trust. The children could use their long life expectancies to measure MRDs of their benefits.

Karen could roll over her share of the benefits to an IRA in her own name and defer the commencement of distributions until she reached age 70½. She would name her nieces as her DBs on the rollover IRA. Her oldest niece is 30 years younger than Karen, so Karen will be able to measure her MRDs using the MDIB rule.

No benefits would be subject to the high income tax bracket of a trust. The children would not have to be left wishing that Karen would die young. Karen would not have to feel the children are looking over her shoulder with regard to the investments of the marital trust.

Another advantage of this approach has to do with the practicalities of plan distribution options. QRPs very often do not permit an installment payout to any beneficiary other than a surviving spouse. Thus, if QRP benefits are made payable to a marital trust, the plan may not permit the trust to draw those benefits out over the life expectancy of the oldest trust beneficiary. If the benefits are payable to Karen personally, by contrast, she can roll them to an IRA which has whatever payout distribution options she wants.

Furthermore, most QRPs are subject to "REA" (Chapter 3), meaning that the benefits cannot be distributed to someone other than the spouse without her consent. By making the QRP benefits payable to Karen personally, Ken avoids the need for obtaining her consent, which would be required to make the benefits payable to a QTIP trust or some other beneficiary. Since REA does not apply to IRAs, Ken can make the IRA payable to his children without Karen's consent (subject to any requirements of state law or prenuptial agreements they may have signed).

Last but definitely not least: both Karen and the children would end up with *substantially more dollars* in their pockets, as the following pages demonstrate.

Assumptions

The following projections assume that all investments earn 7% pre-tax, whether inside or outside a retirement plan, and that all plan distributions, net of income taxes, are accumulated rather than spent. The results compare values of the accumulated funds at the end of 30 years.

Scenario 1: All benefits ($1.8 million) left to a QTIP trust.

This *trust* distributes all of its income annually to Karen Koslow as required by the marital deduction rules. Each *plan* distributes to the *trust*, each year, the *greater* of the income for that year or the MRD required for that year based on the life expectancy of Karen Koslow (29.5 years). The trust then distributes the *income* portion of the distribution to Karen personally; *principal* distributions (*i.e.* the minimum distribution amount, to the extent it exceeds the income distribution) are retained in the trust fund as principal. It is assumed that the trust and Karen are both in the 39.6% bracket at all times (even though Karen's bracket might possibly drop after her eventual retirement). After 30 years here are the results:

Amount held in a retirement plan in Karen's name: $0.

Amount held in Karen's name personally (accumulated income distributions from the QTIP trust): $4,439,000.

Amount held in the QTIP trust (passing to children): $1,087,200 (gross of $1,800,000 paid to marital trust, minus 39.6% tax)

Total value to family: $5,526,000

Assuming Karen were to die at this point, the QTIP trust would pass to the children (actually, it would be subject to estate tax on Karen's death; however, for purposes of illustration, these scenarios assume that all estate taxes on both spouses' estates are paid by some other source of funds).

Scenario 2: QRP benefits paid to Karen, IRA to children.

Here are the assumptions used in Scenario 2:
One of Ken's children will probably be in the 31% bracket; the other would probably be in the 36% bracket. To compromise these differences, an overall tax rate of 33.5% on the children's benefits is used. The trust and Karen are always in the 39.6% bracket (even though Karen's bracket might drop after her eventual retirement).

The IRAs would be distributed gradually to the children over the 46.4-year life expectancy of the oldest child. This would call for very small minimum distributions especially in the early years, but each child's income from this source would gradually increase. By the time the children reach their 60's, *each* would be receiving distributions of $40,000 per year (and growing) from the IRA fund. It would be a major source of retirement funding for them.

Karen would take the plans payable to her as a lump sum and roll them over to her own IRA. She would then defer all distributions until her age 70½, when she would name her nieces as her beneficiary and start withdrawing benefits over the life expectancy of herself and the oldest niece, under the MDIB rule.

Under this scenario here is what each beneficiary would have in 30 years: The children's accumulated personal funds (outside the IRA) would be, for both children together, $1,419,000, consisting of the accumulated after-tax MRDs from the inherited IRA. In addition, they would have $1.509 million *still inside* the IRA, to be distributed to them over the next 17 years. Contrast this with their having $1,087,000 outside of an IRA and *nothing* inside a retirement plan under Scenario 1. Increase in value to children: $1,841,000.

Karen would have, in 30 years, accumulated $2.771 million *outside* of her rollover IRA from the accumulated MRDs, and would still have $4.164 million *inside* her rollover IRA. Thus her combined value would be $6.935 million, vs. $4.439 million under Scenario 1. Increase to Karen: $2,496,000.

Note: under Scenario 2 a substantial portion of Karen's and the children's money would still be inside an IRA and would not yet have been taxed, whereas under Scenario 1 all of the money would be after-tax. But, under Scenario 2, even if Karen totally liquidated her IRA 30 years from now (as opposed to continuing to distribute it gradually to herself over 15.3 more years), her after-tax value would be $5.286 million, which is still $847,000 *more* than under Scenario 1.)

Summary: If all benefits are left to a QTIP trust, all beneficiaries are *substantially worse off* than if some benefits are left to Karen outright and some to the children outright.

	Scenario 1: Benefits to Marital Trust	Scenario 2: QRP to Karen; IRA to Children	Increase:
Karen holds:			
In IRA	-0-	4,164,000	
Outside IRA	4,439,000	2,771,000	
Total	4,439,000	6,935,000	2,496,000
Children Hold:			
In IRA	-0-	1,509,000	
Outside IRA	1,087,000	1,419,000	
Total:	1,087,000	2,928,000	1,841,000
Total Value to Family:	5,526,000	9,863,000	4,337,000

Bill and Lenore Stoltz: Choices at Age 70½

The facts

Bill and Lenore Stoltz both reached age 70½ in 1998. Bill has two IRAs, one worth $3,245,591 as of December 31, 1997, and the other worth $135,000. Lenore has an IRA worth $185,000 as of December 31, 1997. They seek advice regarding the minimum distributions they must now start to take.

Lenore Stoltz: leaving small IRA direct to children

For Mrs. Stoltz, we recommended leaving her IRA to her children rather than to Mr. Stoltz, for both estate tax and income tax reasons:

Memorandum to Lenore Stoltz explaining minimum distributions and our recommendations

1.   <u>Introduction</u>

As you know, because you reached age 70½ in 1998 your "required beginning date" is April 1, 1999. By that date you must begin withdrawing from your IRA. As we have discussed, *how much* you are required to withdraw depends on who is named as beneficiary to inherit your IRA when you die.

2.   <u>Children to be Named as Beneficiaries</u>

We have recommended you name your children for the following reasons.

First, any assets that you leave outright to Bill will increase his estate. His estate is already large enough to be subject to federal estate tax. To minimize estate taxes, you have decided that you want to leave the "federal estate tax exemption amount" (currently $650,000) either to your children directly or to a "credit shelter trust" which would benefit Bill for life but not be included in his estate on his death.

For reasons we discussed, however, the IRA is not a good asset to leave to a credit shelter trust. Also, Bill doesn't need the funds from your IRA because he has a very substantial IRA of his own. Your assets even including this IRA do not add up to $650,000. Therefore, for *estate tax reasons*, it is desirable to leave the IRA to your children.

For *income tax reasons* also, leaving your IRA direct to your children is a good choice. Naming the children as your "designated beneficiaries" produces the smallest possible "minimum required distributions" during your life and after your demise. By naming your children as your beneficiaries, you are entitled to calculate your minimum distributions based on the joint life expectancy of yourself and your oldest child.

Actually, there is a limit on this, because letting you use the true joint life expectancy of yourself and your oldest child would be "too good a deal." So, during your lifetime, the IRS tables pretend that your oldest child is only 10 years younger than you! This means your distributions will be calculated based on the joint life expectancy of yourself and someone who is initially age 60. This artificial limitation is called the "MDIB rule." But that still gives you an initial payout period of 26.2 years; that is longer than the joint life expectancy of you and Bill (20.2 years) and longer than your single life expectancy (16 years).

After your death, your children will be able to withdraw the balance of the benefits over whatever is left of the *actual* joint life expectancy of yourself and your oldest child. The artificial limit called the MDIB rule goes away at that point.

3.   Method of Determining Life Expectancy

Another election you must make irrevocably before the "required beginning date" is what method to use to determine your life expectancy: "fixed term" or "redetermine annually." For reasons we discussed, we recommend you use the fixed term method.

4.   1998 Minimum Distribution

You have only one IRA. The custodian is First River

Bank. The December 31, 1997 account balance statement from the custodian shows the market value of the securities in this account on that date as $185,000.

Based on the joint life expectancy of yourself and your oldest child and the "MDIB rule," the 1998 required distribution is $7,061.

Note that your IRA *cannot* be combined with Bill's IRAs for purposes of computing the minimum distributions to either of you. Your IRA stands on its own; it has its own separate beneficiary and minimum distribution requirement. So each year a distribution will have to be taken out of your IRA and paid to you, and also a distribution each year will have to be taken out of one or more of Bill's IRAs and paid to him.

5.   Income Tax on 1998 Distribution

A final question would be, whether any of the contributions to your account were non-deductible. If any of these contributions were made with after-tax dollars, that would reduce, slightly, the amount you have to pay tax on. IRS Form 8606 attached to your most recent income tax return should show the amount of after-tax dollars contributed to your IRA.

Bill Stoltz: choice of life expectancy method

With Bill Stoltz, we had a more difficult decision regarding how to determine life expectancies, since he was naming his spouse rather than his children as beneficiary. We also confronted practical problems regarding a difficult-to-value asset, and the problem of multiple IRAs.

Memo to William Stoltz explaining minimum distributions and our recommendation

Re: Minimum Required Distributions from your IRAs

Importance of designated beneficiary

As you know, because you turned 70½ in 1998, you are required to start taking distributions from your IRAs. The first year for which a distribution is required is 1998, the year you turned 70½. For this year only, you are entitled, if you wish, to postpone the distribution until next year, provided you take it by April 1, 1999.

For 1999 and later years, the minimum distribution must be taken by December 31 each year, so, if you postpone the 1998 distribution until early 1999, you create some bunching of income in 1999 because there would then be two distributions required that year.

As to how much the minimum distribution is each year, that all depends on certain choices which you make *now*. Specifically, your choice of a "designated beneficiary" and "method of determining life expectancy" will dictate the amount of required distributions for all future years.

Currently you have named Mrs. Stoltz as your designated beneficiary on both of your IRAs. That is because you want her to receive the account when you die, so that is who you should name.

Because you have named your wife as beneficiary, you are entitled to calculate your "minimum required distributions" based on the joint life expectancy of yourself and Mrs. Stoltz. Note that it is *extremely important* not to change your primary beneficiary in any way that would upset the ability to use the joint life expectancy method for determining distributions, because that is generally the most favorable method. If you were to change the primary beneficiary, even temporarily, to (say) "my estate," that would have the effect of permanently accelerating the distributions, according to the IRS.

Choice of method of determining life expectancy

The second factor which goes into determining your minimum required distributions is a little more complicated. It is the choice of method for determining life expectancy. The required distribution for each year is determined by dividing [the IRA balance as of the preceding year end] by [the applicable life expectancy]. Your and Lenore's joint life expectancy as of 1998 (according to the IRS tables) is 20.2 years.

There are three alternative methods for computing your life expectancy in future years—and you have to choose *one* now.

One method is the "fixed term method." Under this method, you would start with the 20.2 years that you initially have, and then just deduct one year each year. By 20 years from now the entire account would have been distributed. The advantage of this method is total predictability: Regardless which spouse dies when, the distributions can be spread over 20 years, whether paid to you, your wife or your children, as the case may be. The disadvantage of this method is that, once you reach your 80's the distributions begin to become enormous and the IRA is rapidly depleted by distributions after that time.

The second method is called "recalculation." Under this method, rather than just using a fixed term that diminishes by one every year, your joint life expectancy would be "re-determined" or "recalculated" every year based on your new attained ages. Since actuarial life expectancy does not decline by one full year every year, the advantage of this method is that it stretches out the distribution of the IRA for potentially as long as 40 years—if you live that long. So if you knew that you and

Mrs. Stoltz were both going to live to be 110, this would be the most favorable method.

Unfortunately, the drawback of recalculation is that, once death actually occurs, the life expectancy that is being recalculated disappears. For example, if Mrs. Stoltz predeceased you, you would no longer be able to use her life expectancy jointly with your own to measure your distributions. From then on, your distributions would have to measured by your life expectancy only, so distributions would suddenly accelerate to you at that point.

Furthermore, if you also died, your children would have to withdraw the entire IRA within one year. Needless to say, in the event of a common accident causing a premature demise, this would create a tremendous tax burden, dumping the entire IRA into the taxable income of the children all in one year. (Under the fixed term method, if you and Lenore both died, the children could continue to withdraw the IRA over the balance of the fixed term—in other words they wouldn't have to cash it out all at once, they could continue to draw it down over the balance of the 20 year period.)

There is a third method, which I would recommend that you use, that avoids the worst problems of both of the other methods. This third method is called the "split method." Under this method, *your* life expectancy is recalculated and your *beneficiary's* life expectancy (*i.e.*, Mrs. Stoltz's life expectancy) is not recalculated. While it sounds complicated, it really involves no more calculations than the other two because the computer does all the calculations automatically anyway. (I have enclosed printouts showing the distribution patterns under all of the methods).

Here is why I recommend the split method. If you could tell me exactly how long each spouse is going to live, and which spouse would die first, then I would know which method of distribution is going to produce the most income tax deferral for you and your family. If you both live a really long time, recalculation is best. If you both die prematurely in a common accident, the fixed term method would be the best. But since we do not know which scenario will occur and who will die when, the split method gives you a "not bad" result under all possible scenarios, to wit:

If you, Bill, live into your 90's—you will not "outlive" your IRA. Because your life expectancy is being recalculated, you will get the benefit of stretching out the payments over that long life.

If you die prematurely, but Lenore survives you—she can roll over the IRA into a new IRA in her own name, naming the children as her beneficiaries, and getting a fresh start on minimum distributions.

Finally, if both of you die in a common accident prematurely, the children would at least be guaranteed the original period of Lenore's life expectancy over which to take out distributions from the IRA (*i.e.*, until approximately 2014, 16 years from now).

Assuming you agree with the choice of the split method, I have prepared forms for you to send to the First River Bank making clear that you want to elect this method with respect to the IRA at that institution. However, you should send us a copy of the Bank's IRA Account Agreement form so I can review it and make sure that this method is permitted. If you give me the name of the person you deal with there I can call them and get the forms myself.

Hard to value asset held by the IRA

We will need to file the same forms with, and see the Account Agreements for, the Basic Inn Securities IRA, unless you decide to close out that IRA as part of your 1998 distribution, as discussed in the following paragraph.

Your 1998 required distribution (no matter which "method" you elect; the first year's distribution is the same under all methods) is $167,356. I note that you have already taken out $140,000 this year, so you need to take out the rest of this required distribution by April 1, 1999 (or by December 31, 1998 if you want it taxed in 1998).

However, there is one problem. In calculating the minimum distribution, you are required to use the fair market value of the IRA assets as of December 31, 1997. One of the assets held in the Basic Inn Securities IRA is 10 Units of the Howdy Limited Partnership. Although The IRA custodian is supposed to be filing a form with the IRS every year that tells the fair market value of this IRA, it appears they have just been using the capital account (currently $17,450) as the value, rather than actually appraising the Units every year.

Because of the difficulty of valuing this partnership interest, and because of the substantial penalties that could be incurred if it is not valued correctly for purposes of calculating your minimum required distributions, I would suggest that you consider distributing the Howdy partnership interest out from the IRA to yourself in 1998 as part of the 1998 minimum distribution. Since this partnership seems to be generating losses anyway, I don't see any tax advantage to holding it in the IRA. Getting it out of the IRA would simplify, and reduce the risks of, calculating your minimum IRA distributions.

Taking distributions from multiple IRAs

Here is another fine point: each year, you have to calculate the minimum required distribution separately for *each* IRA that you have, based on the fair market value of that IRA, the designated beneficiary of that IRA, and the method of determining life expectancies chosen for that IRA. But then, having calculated the minimum distribution required for each account, you don't actually have to *take* the minimum distribution separately from each account. You just take the total number and you can take that combined distribution from any one or more of the accounts.

Thus, for example, you could take your total 1998 required distribution entirely out of the First River Bank IRA if you wish; or distribute out to yourself all the Howdy Partnership units and treat that distribution as part of the minimum distribution from the combined accounts; whichever you wish.

For purposes of simplification, you might consider terminating the small IRA at Basic Inn Securities and distributing it to yourself in 1998 or early 1999 as part of your required distributions for those years, just to simplify things. Then you will not have to calculate required distributions for two accounts every year.

Margaret Mandel: Young and Single with Changing Assets and Intentions

Margaret Mandel is age 50 and single and has no children. Her assets are:

House (no mortgage)	200,000
Rollover IRA	150,000
TIAA-CREF 403(b)	300,000
Various IRAs and annuities	100,000
Cash and securities	50,000
Total	800,000

Her retirement plans are growing, through both earnings and additional employer contributions.

Her estate planning objectives are: to provide for the care of her parents (now in their 80's) if she predeceases them; to provide for the college education of her niece and nephew (now 10 and 6); and to leave what's left after fulfilling those objectives to the Shore Country Day School (a charity).

If we knew that Margaret were going to die *today*, her estate plan could be arranged to obtain maximum tax efficiency. Depending on the projected needs of the individual beneficiaries, the following ideas would be tested:

1.   Leave some or all retirement benefits to a charitable remainder trust (CRT) for the life of Margaret's parents. The CRT would receive the benefits income tax-free, Mom and Dad would get the income for life, and the estate would get a nice estate tax deduction for the value of the remainder. But Margaret is a little hesitant on this because she wants her parents to have as much as they need, and not be limited to the CRT income stream.

2.   Leave some retirement benefits to the niece and nephew to take advantage of their low income tax brackets and long life expectancies for maximum deferral with minimum tax. The trouble with this is that Margaret doesn't want the niece and nephew (they're too young) or their parents (too irresponsible) to control the money—it must be used *solely* for education, and that result can be obtained only with a trust. Also, since the money is to be used for college or graduate school before they are 25, a life expectancy payout continuing until they reach age 80 doesn't match the need.

It became apparent that working through the tangle of competing tax and non-tax considerations to achieve a "perfect" tax plan was not worth the expense in terms of professional fees, especially considering the following factors:

1.   Margaret's parents, now age 85, are highly unlikely to be still living 15 years from now.

2.   In 15 years, the niece and nephew will be through with school, so this need will also cease to exist.

3.   In 15 years, Margaret will be 65. Being a now healthy, highly educated, non-smoking female, she is highly likely to still be living in 15 years.

4.   A "perfect" tax-targeted estate plan is likely to be expensive in terms of legal fees, involving not only the usual will and trust but also a careful review of numerous retirement plan provisions and coordinated drafting of multiple retirement plan beneficiary designations. This expense and trouble is highly likely to be completely wasted in view of factors 1, 2 and 3.

The solution: It was decided to structure the estate plan this way: Margaret adopts a revocable living trust. The provisions of the trust at her death provide *exactly* what she wants to provide for her parents, niece and nephew and residuary charity, not restricted by limitations that would have to be imposed to assure such things as a charitable estate tax deduction or a long-term payout of retirement benefits. Her will and retirement plan beneficiary designation forms simply pour all assets and benefits into the above trust at Margaret's death.

If Margaret dies before her parents die (highly unlikely) and before her niece and nephew finish school (highly unlikely) the above structure will not minimize taxes. There will be no charitable estate tax deduction (because of the non-qualifying split interest) and relatively high income taxes on the retirement benefits (no long term deferral and no attempt to steer the benefits to a low bracket beneficiary). To cover these extra tax costs, Margaret buys a 15-year term life insurance policy for a few hundred dollars a year. The total insurance cost is the same as or less than the legal fees Margaret would have to incur to get a perfect tax-minimized plan, but does not necessitate the compromises in her true objectives that she would have to accept to get a tax-minimized plan.

Mr. & Mrs. Fallon: Pension Millionaires: Planning after the RBD Charitable Giving; Generation Skipping

All calculations in this case study were done using Numbercruncher™ software (see Appendix D).

The facts

Fred Fallon is age 73. He and his wife Felicia have $8 million in total assets: $3 million in Fred's IRA and another $5 million of liquid investments and residential real estate divided equally between them. In addition, Fred receives a pension of $180,000 a year from his former company (there is no survivor benefit under this pension); and Felicia receives $200,000 a year from a trust established by her grandparents; income from this trust will be paid to the Fallons' children after Felicia's death.

The Fallons have two children, ages 46 and 44, and several grandchildren. The children are well provided for already. The Fallons are interested in using their **generation skipping** exemption by leaving part of Fred's IRA to a trust that could take advantage of the grandchildren's long life expectancies. They have some interest in charitable giving, especially if it can be done with little "cost" to the family beneficiaries.

Fred is withdrawing MRDs from his $3 million IRA over the joint life expectancy of Fred and Felicia, with both life expectancies recalculated annually. Because Fred is past his RBD, and both life expectancies are being recalculated annually, the options for distribution of the account on Fred's death are quite different depending on which spouse dies first.

If Fred dies first, and Felicia survives him long enough

to roll over the IRA, there is every possibility of keeping at least part of this IRA alive for 60 years. Felicia could roll over $1 million of Fred's IRA into an IRA in her own name payable to the grandchildren, and the other $2 million to an IRA in her name payable to the children. (In either case, a trust for the children or grandchildren could be substituted for the children or grandchildren individually with no ill effects.)

She would then take payouts from the IRAs over the joint life expectancy of herself and the children or grandchildren (subject to the "MDIB Rule"). Then, upon her demise, the payout schedule would revert to being based on the *actual* joint life expectancy of herself and the beneficiaries (children or grandchildren). In the case of the grandchildren, that actual life expectancy is in the range of 60 years, which gives incredible tax-deferred compounding possibilities for that IRA.

If Felicia *predeceases* Fred, on the other hand, payout options become severely limited. Because both life expectancies are being recalculated, as each spouse dies, his or her life expectancy goes to zero. Thus, after Felicia's death, Fred would be limited to using his own single life expectancy to measure payouts; and upon his demise, all benefits would have to be distributed by the end of the year after the year of his death. There would be no advantage to leaving *any* IRA benefits to the grandchildren in that case, since there would be no possibility of using their long life expectancies to measure MRDs, and part of the **GST** exemption would simply be wasted paying income taxes on the accelerated distribution.

Choices which became irrevocable on Fred's RBD

Fred did not seek knowledgeable advice about his minimum distributions prior to his RBD. He now realizes that Felicia will not need all of his IRA, and it would have made the IRA "more valuable" to make part of it payable to the grandchildren; this would have permitted greater income tax deferral both during Fred's life and after his death.

But because Fred is past his RBD, it is too late to change to a new designated beneficiary (DB) with a longer life expectancy. To be more precise, Fred can change the beneficiary of his IRA, that is to say he can change the beneficiary from Felicia to the grandchildren, and they will then inherit it. But making that change now, after his RBD, would not be effective to lengthen the payout period for distributions. See Chapter 1.

On Fred's RBD, his DB was Felicia (and still is). Thus, the "slowest" he can withdraw benefits from his IRA is over the joint life expectancy of himself and Felicia.

Another decision which became irrevocable on the RBD was the decision to recalculate the life expectancies of Fred and Felicia annually. See Chapter 1.

There is only one escape hatch: If Fred dies first, Felicia can roll over the IRA to her own IRA (or elect to treat Fred's IRA as her own) and start a whole new payout period based on the LE of herself and a new DB. See Chapter 3. Thus, this rollover (or election) by Felicia at Fred's death is crucial to obtaining a long term payout.

How do we assure Felicia "rolls over" Fred's IRA?

If Fred dies before Felicia, all of the benefits are paid to her as Fred's beneficiary. She then rolls them over to her own IRA. However, it is very important that she do this *as soon as possible* after Fred's death. If they die simultaneously, or if Felicia dies shortly after Fred before doing the rollover, her executor probably cannot do the rollover for her.

Is there any way to assure that the payout period desired on Felicia's death is attainable, even if Felicia dies simultaneously with or shortly after Fred? The only hope for accomplishing this would be for Fred's IRA to be treated as

Felicia's own IRA *immediately* upon the death of Fred, with a beneficiary designation by Felicia, naming the children or grandchildren, that would immediately kick in in that case.

In order to have the best shot at getting this treatment the Fallons could take the following steps:

(1)   Add to Fred's IRA a provision that in case of simultaneous death Felicia is presumed to survive Fred.

(2)   Include a provision that if Felicia survives Fred, or if she is deemed to survive Fred, she elects to treat the IRA as her own IRA, names the children or grandchildren as her DB, and elects to have benefits distributed according to the result that would be desired in that case (discussed below).

(3)   Finally, have this beneficiary designation co-signed by Felicia *now* (even though Fred is still living).

There is no guarantee whatsoever that the IRS will recognize Felicia's election to treat Fred's IRA as her own IRA if she makes this election before Fred has even died. Accordingly, it is still vital, if Fred predeceases, for Felicia actually to do the rollover as soon as possible after Fred's death. But if she doesn't get around to it, having her sign this "pre-death election" may *possibly* succeed. It is worth trying. See Form 4.1 in Appendix B.

Felicia's beneficiary designation for rollover IRA

After Fred's demise, and once Felicia has transferred the IRA into her own IRA, the clients would like the IRA, if possible, to be paid out at Felicia's demise to a trust for their grandchildren. The trust would be able to withdraw the money from the IRA over the life expectancy of the oldest grandchild, which should be in excess of 60 years.

The problem is the limit on what can be left to grandchildren, under the GST tax. Each individual can leave up to $1 million (plus COLA) in the form of a GST free of this tax; but amounts over that would be subject to the GST tax. The GST tax is equal to the highest estate tax rate, currently 55%.

Thus the Fallons are looking at the following disposition of the IRA on Felicia's demise: $1 million to a generation skipping trust for the grandchildren, designed to take advantage of Felicia's $1 million GST exemption and the grandchildren's ability to defer distributions from the IRA over their long life expectancy; and the balance to the Fallons' children. However, there are further complications:

Need to divide the IRA before Fred's death

When more than one person is named as beneficiary of a retirement benefit, the life expectancy of the oldest individual in the group will be treated as the measuring life. Thus, for example, if Felicia had an IRA, and she named a grandchildren's trust as partial beneficiary and the children as partial beneficiary, the *children* are the oldest members of the entire group. The oldest child's life expectancy would have to be used as the measuring life for all payouts, *even the payouts to the grandchildren's trust*. Thus, if the Fallons want the grandchildren's trust to receive its share over the life expectancy of the *grandchildren*, Felicia must make the grandchildren's trust the sole beneficiary of her rollover IRA.

So in order for the desired distribution of Felicia's rollover IRA to be attained at Felicia's demise, of $1 million to the grandchildren's trust and the rest to the children, the IRA would have to be divided up into two separate IRAs, one of approximately $1 million and the other with all of the rest of the money. To increase the likelihood that this occurs even if Felicia dies simultaneously with Fred, the division into two separate IRAs would have to occur before *Fred's* death.

Accordingly, the Fallons take the following steps:

(a)   Fred's IRA is divided into two totally separate IRAs now. One account would contain approximately $1 million. The other would contain all the rest of the money.

(b)   Felicia would continue to be the DB on each of these new IRAs. Both IRAs would contain the elaborate provisions described above whereby, in case of simultaneous death, Felicia is deemed to survive Fred, and she elects to treat the IRA as her own. See form 4.1 in Appendix B.

(c)   For the $1 million earmarked "generation skipping" IRA, the beneficiary designation would be as described in the next subsection. It is anticipated that Felicia's $1 million GST exemption would be allocated to this IRA.

(d)   On the "children's" IRA, the children would be named as Felicia's DBs.

Beneficiary designation for the "grandchildren" IRA

Since Fred's IRA is still growing with investment income, and going up and down as Fred takes out MRDs each year, what happens if the IRA earmarked for the grandchildren is worth *more* than the GST exemption at the relevant time (Felicia's death)? The answer is, the excess over the exemption amount should *also* be paid to the grandchildren's trust but with the trust being required to keep such excess segregated from the exempt amount; or alternatively, and more simply, the excess could simply be distributed outright to the grandchildren. That excess over the GST exemption amount will be subject to GST tax but there is no avoiding that. If some beneficiary *other* than the grandchildren (or their trust) is named as the beneficiary of the excess, the Fallons would be right back where they started, having multiple beneficiaries for that IRA. If the "excess" beneficiaries have a shorter life expectancy than the grandchildren, the *entire IRA* would be subject to minimum distribution rules based on the life expectancy of some person older than the grandchildren.

Is it desirable to use the GST exemption on retirement benefits?

There are mixed views among estate planners on this subject. One school of thought emphasizes that retirement benefits are subject to income taxes. Therefore, when the grandchildren inherit $1 million of retirement benefits they will realize only $600,000 to $700,000, ultimately, from this asset, not the full $1 million. Leaving them some *other* asset worth $1 million, on which the client had already paid the income taxes, would make better use of the GST exemption.

The other school of thought holds that retirement benefits are the *best* assets to leave to grandchildren, because of the amazing power of income tax deferral that can be achieved using the grandchildren's long life expectancy.

If Felicia predeceases Fred

If Felicia does not survive Fred and "cleanse" the IRA by means of a spousal rollover, no further deferral through the IRA is possible. In this case, the grandchildren are "out" as beneficiaries, and we compare two other possible scenarios. The first is simply making the benefits payable to the children. They cash out the IRA totally within one year after Fred's death, pay the income taxes on it, and invest what's left. The calculations show that after 44 years (which is the average joint and survivor life expectancy for two people age 46 and 44) the ultimate net value to family of this scenario is $11,083,390.

The other alternative is to have the benefits distributed to a **charitable remainder trust** ("CRT"). The advantage of this is that the CRT pays no income tax on the distribution it receives. All the benefits still have to be distributed within a year after Fred's death, but the distribution can occur without any income tax. The children would then receive, for life, the income from the *entire* $3 million IRA fund, not just from what is left of it after income taxes. On the death of the surviving child, the remainder would go to charity.

In addition to eliminating any income taxes on the distribution, this approach produces a small estate tax deduction for the value of the charitable remainder. The calculations show that, after 44 years, the accumulated value of the estate tax savings, and the accumulated value of distributions from the CRUT, total $12,195,566—more than $1 million more, in terms of value to the children, than simply distributing the IRA to them outright on Fred's death.

These numbers suggest that, if Felicia predeceased Fred, leaving the benefits to a CRT does not "penalize" the children substantially or at all. (See the "Limitations of these Projections," below, to see as to why we can't *categorically* say that this method of distribution doesn't penalize the children at all.) The bottom line here is that, if Fred has any charitable inclinations, then this would definitely be an appealing approach to funding his charitable gifts. Even if he has no charitable inclinations, and his sole goal is to maximize benefits to his family, use of the CRT as *contingent* beneficiary might actually achieve that result.

Calculations; explanation to client

MEMORANDUM

TO:	Mr. & Mrs. Fred Fallon
FROM:	Your attorney, Bernie
DATE:	December 1, 1998
RE:	Payout Scenarios for IRA if Fred survives

I.   Facts and assumptions used

Fred and Felicia Fallon are age 73 and 71 respectively. Felicia dies, then Fred dies two days later, both in December 1999. Under the "minimum distribution rules" of the Internal Revenue Code section 401(a)(9), because both life expectancies were being "recalculated," all benefits must be distributed from the IRA by the end of the year following Fred's death, in other words by December 31, 2000.

Fred's other assets total $5 million, so his total estate is $8 million. All estate taxes are paid out of the non-IRA assets. The state death tax on his estate is exactly equal to the maximum credit for state death taxes allowed against his federal estate taxes. The two Fallon children are in the 39.6% tax bracket for all income. All the family's investments earn 6% income, fully taxable.

Two scenarios are compared. First, what do the children receive, after paying estate taxes and income taxes, if the IRA benefits are simply distributed to them outright in 1999? Then, in contrast to that, what do they receive if the IRA benefits are instead distributed to a 6% charitable remainder unitrust ("CRUT") which lasts until the death of the survivor of them?

Without CRUT: After paying income taxes on the $3 million

IRA distribution, the children are left with $2,314,286 to invest. This produces annual income of $138,857 ($83,870 after income taxes).

With CRUT: With the entire $3,000,000 paid to a 6% CRUT, the children have an annual income of $180,000 from the CRUT, plus a cash side fund of $172,936 representing the estate tax savings from the charitable deduction, which produces an additional $10,376 of income. Total income stream is therefore $190,376 per year (vs. $138,857 per year with no CRUT), or $114,987 per year after tax (vs. $83,870 with no CRUT).

The children's average joint and last survivor life expectancy is 44 years. At the end of 44 years, if all after-tax income is accumulated, the children will have $1.1 million more under the CRUT plan than if the entire IRA had simply been left to them outright. Detailed calculations follow:

II.   Calculations

Step 1: Calculate federal estate tax on the IRA for purposes of the § 691(c) ("IRD") income tax deduction:

A.   <u>Federal estate tax with IRA:</u>

Taxable estate, with IRA	$8,000,000
Federal estate tax:	$3,065,550

B.   <u>Federal estate tax, without IRA:</u>

Taxable estate, without IRA	$5,000,000
Federal estate tax	$1,797,150

3.   <u>Difference (federal estate tax on the IRA):</u> $1,268,400

Step 2: Calculate income tax on the IRA if it is paid outright to children:

Gross IRA distribution:	$3,000,000
Less: § 691(c) deduction for federal estate taxes paid on the IRA (see Step 1)	-1,268,400
Taxable income	$1,731,600
Times 39.6%	x .396
Income tax on IRA	$ 685,714

Net to children to invest:	
Gross distribution	$3,000,000
Less income tax	- 685,714
Net children have to invest	$2,314,286

Annual income on this at 6%:	$ 138,857

Annual income after 39.6% income tax:	$ 83,870

Step 3: Calculate charitable deduction

$3 million 6% Unitrust for 2 lives ages 46 and 44 using "§ 7520" rate of 6.20%; deduction is: $ 314,430

Step 4: Estate tax savings from charitable deduction

A.   Estate taxes with no charitable deduction (Step 1A):

Federal	$3,065,550
State	$ 773,200
Total estate tax	$3,838,750

B.   Estate tax with charitable deduction:

Gross estate:	$8,000,000
Less: charitable deduction (Step 3)	- 314,430
Taxable estate	$7,685,570

Estate tax:	
Federal	$2,935,376
State	$ 730,438
Total	$3,665,814

C.   Difference

"A" minus "B" is:	$ 172,936

Step 5: Future Values

A.   Average Joint Life Expectancy is 44 years

B.   Future Value of no-CRUT plan:

Annual after-tax income (step 2) is	$ 83,870
Accumulated value of after-tax annual income of $83,870 for 44 years (at 6% minus income tax):	$8,769,104
Plus principal (see step 2)	$2,314,286
Total	$11,083,390

C.   Future Value of CRUT plan:

Income stream:	
CRUT income: 6% x 3,000,000	$ 180,000

Income on estate taxes saved:

6% x $172,936=	$	10,376
Total (gross annual income)	$	190,373
Less: 39.6% income tax	$	- 75,389
Net annual income	$	114,987

Accumulated value of annual income of $114,985 for 44 years:	$12,022,630
Plus principal of saved estate tax	$ 172,936
Total value	$ 12,195,566

D.   <u>**Difference (the CRUT advantage):**</u> $ 1,112,176

E.   <u>**Present value of "D":**</u>

Discounted to present value at 3.624%
(the after tax value of 6%): $ 232,230

III.   <u>Limitations on Projections</u>

The calculations assume a 6% rate of income, year in and year out, on all investments. Actual investment return might be less or more than 6% in any particular year. Investments can also decline in value.

Furthermore, the calculations assume that the entire 6% consists of interest and dividends taxable as ordinary income. In actuality, it is probable that at least some of the investments *outside* the retirement plans would be invested for capital gain and that part of the return would therefore be capital gain. Capital gain is not taxed currently, but only when the asset is sold; and when it is sold, the tax rate on capital gain is lower than on other kinds of income.

The projections assume a 39.6% tax rate for all individuals and trusts. It is possible that some individuals would be in a lower bracket. A higher bracket could apply if state income taxes are figured in; and federal rates will probably change over the period of the projections.

The CRT scenario assumes that at least one child lives for 44 years. If both of them die before the 44 years are up, the entire trust at that point moves to the charity and they stop receiving any distributions. Thus, in case of premature death, the value of this scenario could be *lower* than the value of the scenario it's being compared with. The children can overcome this risk by buying decreasing term insurance on their lives; or, Fred could simply decide that this risk is not of concern to him.

The CRT scenario assumes a 6% payout rate to the children and that the trust earns exactly 6% each year.

The scenarios assume that there is a separate fund, outside the IRAs, of $3,838,700. This would be the amount needed at the death of the surviving spouse (if both deaths occurred right now) to pay the estate taxes if all the benefits are paid to the family. If the benefits are paid to a CRT, the estate taxes would be reduced, so some of this fund would be available for the family, rather than going to pay estate taxes, and that has been figured into the value of the CRT scenario.

Both these scenarios assume that Mr. and Mrs. Fallon die in 1999. The only purpose of these scenarios is to help determine who should be designated as the *contingent* beneficiary for Fred's IRA. Actually it is more likely that the spouses will live another decade or more than that they will both die now. If they both live for many years more, the IRA may be diminished to such an extent through required distributions that it may no longer make much difference who is named as the beneficiary.

Appendix A

Tables

1. <u>MDIB Rule Divisor Table</u>. See "Naming a Non-Spouse DB: the MDIB Rule," Ch. 1. From IRS Publication 590.

Table for Determining Applicable Divisor for MDIB (Minimum Distribution Incidental Benefit)			
Age	Applicable divisor	Age	Applicable divisor
70	26.2	93	8.8
71	25.3	94	8.3
72	24.4	95	7.8
73	23.5	96	7.3
74	22.7	97	6.9
75	21.8	98	6.5
76	20.9	99	6.1
77	20.1	100	5.7
78	19.2	101	5.3
79	18.4	102	5.0
80	17.6	103	4.7
81	16.8	104	4.4
82	16.0	105	4.1
83	15.3	106	3.8
84	14.5	107	3.6
85	13.8	108	3.3
86	13.1	109	3.1
87	12.4	110	2.8
88	11.8	111	2.6
89	11.1	112	2.4
90	10.5	113	2.2
91	9.9	114	2.0
92	9.4	115 and older	1.8

2.   Tax on Various 1999 Lump Sum Distributions
      (Chart prepared by Ed Slott, CPA)

If Your 1999 Lump Sum Distribution is:	10 Year Averaging Tax Is:	5 Year Averaging Tax Is:
$100,000	14,471	15,000
150,000	24,570	25,263
200,000	36,922	39,263
250,000	50,770	53,263
275,000	58,270	60,263
300,000	66,330	67,263
318,833	72,733	72,733
350,000	83,602	82,395
375,000	93,102	90,145
400,000	102,602	97,895
450,000	122,682	113,395
500,000	143,682	128,895
550,000	164,682	144,395
600,000	187,368	159,895
650,000	211,368	175,395
700,000	235,368	193,333
750,000	259,368	211,333
800,000	283,368	229,333
850,000	307,368	247,333
900,000	332,210	265,333
1,000,000	382,210	301,333

Charts 2 and 3 are reproduced from the July 1999 issue of the highly recommended newsletter, **Ed Slott's IRA Advisor**, with permission of the newsletter's author and publisher, Ed Slott, CPA. For subscription information or reprint permission, call 1-800-663-1340, or visit his website at **www.irahelp.com**.

3. <u>Single Life Expectancy - Table V (ages 5-34)</u>

Age	Life Expectancy	Age	Life Expectancy
5	76.6	20	61.9
6	75.6	21	60.9
7	74.7	22	59.9
8	73.7	23	59.0
9	72.7	24	58.0
10	71.7	25	57.0
11	70.7	26	56.0
12	69.7	27	55.1
13	68.8	28	54.1
14	67.8	29	53.1
15	66.8	30	52.2
16	65.8	31	51.2
17	64.8	32	50.2
18	63.9	33	49.2
19	62.9	34	48.3

4. IRS "Table V": Single life expectancy (ages 35-110).
    From IRS Publication 590.

Age	Divisor	Age	Divisor
35	47.3	73	13.9
36	46.4	74	13.2
37	45.4	75	12.5
38	44.4	76	11.9
39	43.5	77	11.2
40	42.5	78	10.6
41	41.5	79	10.0
42	40.6	80	9.5
43	39.6	81	8.9
44	38.7	82	8.4
45	37.7	83	7.9
46	36.8	84	7.4
47	35.9	85	6.9
48	34.9	86	6.5
49	34.0	87	6.1
50	33.1	88	5.7
51	32.2	89	5.3
52	31.3	90	5.0
53	30.4	91	4.7
54	29.5	92	4.4
55	28.6	93	4.1
56	27.7	94	3.9
57	26.8	95	3.7
58	25.9	96	3.4
59	25.0	97	3.2
60	24.2	98	3.0
61	23.3	99	2.8
62	22.5	100	2.7
63	21.6	101	2.5
64	20.8	102	2.3
65	20.0	103	2.1
66	19.2	104	1.9
67	18.4	105	1.8
68	17.6	106	1.6
69	16.8	107	1.4
70	16.0	108	1.3
71	15.3	109	1.1
72	14.6	110	1.0

5. IRS "Table VI": Joint Life and Last Survivor Expectancy: Participant is Age 70 (or 71), Beneficiary is Age 35-74. From "Table II," IRS Publication 590.

AGES	70	71
35	47.5	47.5
36	46.6	46.6
37	45.7	45.6
38	44.7	44.7
39	43.8	43.8
40	42.9	42.8
41	41.9	41.9
42	41.0	41.0
43	40.1	40.1
44	39.2	39.1
45	38.3	38.2
46	37.4	37.3
47	36.5	36.5
48	35.7	35.6
49	34.8	34.7
50	34.0	33.9
51	33.1	33.0
52	32.3	32.2
53	31.5	31.4
54	30.7	30.5

AGES	70	71
55	29.9	29.7
56	29.1	29.0
57	28.4	28.2
58	27.6	27.5
59	26.9	26.7
60	26.2	26.0
61	25.6	25.3
62	24.9	24.7
63	24.3	24.0
64	23.7	23.4
65	23.1	22.8
66	22.5	22.2
67	22.0	21.7
68	21.5	21.2
69	21.1	20.7
70	20.6	20.2
71	20.2	19.8
72	19.8	19.4
73	19.4	19.0
74	19.1	18.6

Appendix B
Forms

Table of Contents

4.   Other Beneficiary Designation Forms

5.   Power of Attorney for Retirement Benefits

6.   Election Regarding Form of Benefits and Method of Determining Life Expectancy at Age 70½

Introduction; Drafting Checklist

This Appendix contains forms which the author has used in particular situations to achieve the dispositive and tax goals of particular clients. These forms can be used to provide ideas, or a starting point, for drafting forms for your clients and *their* particular situations.

In drafting forms to dispose of retirement benefits, keep in mind the following points:

1.   Impress on the client that the "Designation of Beneficiary Form" is just as important a legal document as a will or trust. Often, more of the client's assets are controlled by this form than by his will. An improperly drafted (or missing) beneficiary designation form could cost the client's estate and family thousands of dollars in taxes, lost deferral opportunities and increased settlement costs.

2.   Read the applicable sections of the "Account Agreement" establishing the client's IRA or Roth IRA, to make sure the beneficiary designation and payout method the client desires are permitted. In a case involving a qualified retirement plan (QRP) and a substantial benefit, try to read the actual plan document especially if the proposed disposition is in any way complex. In the case of a smaller benefit and/or a simple disposition, it may be sufficient to rely on the "Summary Plan Description" or the description of available benefit payout options in the employer-provided beneficiary designation form.

3.   There are certain issues in the disposition of death benefits which are quite likely to arise, yet may not be covered at all in the IRA agreement or QRP documents. You should cover these in the beneficiary designation form:

A.   Who chooses the form of death benefits, the client-participant or the beneficiary? In the forms in this Appendix, the beneficiary chooses the form of death benefit (see ¶ 3 .01 in the Master Beneficiary Designation forms, 2.1 and 2.2).

B.   On the death of the participant ("P"), the primary beneficiary is entitled to the benefits. If the beneficiary does not withdraw them immediately, what happens to benefits that are still in the IRA (or plan) when the *primary beneficiary* dies? Will those remaining benefits then go to the person P originally named as *contingent* beneficiary? Will they pass to a new beneficiary designated by the primary beneficiary? Do they now belong to the primary beneficiary's estate, so they pass under his or her will? See *"Estate planning for the beneficiary who inherits an IRA,"* Chapter 1. The Master Beneficiary Designation Forms in this Appendix (see ¶ 3.02, Forms 2.1 and 2.2) specify that the beneficiary can name his or her own beneficiary, and also dictate where the benefits go if the beneficiary doesn't get around to naming a beneficiary. If the spouse is named as primary beneficiary, and you use a successor beneficiary provision such as ¶ 3.02, you may wish to use also the "Preservation of Marital Deduction" provision (¶ 3.07 in the Master Beneficiary Designation forms); see *"Other marital deduction issues,"* Chapter 3.

C.   In the case of an IRA (or Roth IRA), can the beneficiary transfer the benefits to another IRA (or Roth IRA) still in the name of the decedent? (See ¶ 3.10 of the IRA/Roth IRA Master Beneficiary Designation form, 2.1.)

4.   Consider whether you wish to alter the applicable presumptions in case of simultaneous death. See "Simultaneous Death Clauses," Chapter 3.

5.   If the disposition is intended to qualify for the marital deduction, include language to that effect. See ¶ 3.07 in the Master Beneficiary Designation forms (2.1 and 2.2); and several others, including Form 7.4; and "Marital Deduction for Benefits Payable to QTIP Trust," Chapter 3.

6.   Consider the extent to which you need to define any terms such as "issue *per stirpes*," or "income"; and/or specify which state's law shall be used to interpret terms you use in the form. It is highly likely that the QRP or IRA (or Roth IRA) agreement specifies that the law of the sponsor's state of incorporation will be used. Since that may well not be the state in which your client lives (or dies), there is a potential for problems if the disposition depends on a definition which varies from state to state. Although you cannot change the governing law of the "plan," a statement that the language of the beneficiary designation will be interpreted according to the laws of a particular state should be accepted in the sense that it will lead to the correct determination of the client's intent. See ¶ 3.04 in the Master Beneficiary Designation forms.

7.   Follow the required formalities of execution. Most IRAs are, in essence, simply custodial accounts. As such, they may be considered "probate" assets of P's estate. Some states do not recognize a disposition of certain forms of retirement benefits unless executed with the formalities of a will. See "Probate Issues," Chapter 10.

8.   The choice of a contingent beneficiary should not be overlooked. For example:

        A.   If benefits are being made payable to a trust, to take advantage of the client's unified credit while providing life benefits for the surviving spouse, consider naming the trust as primary beneficiary only if the spouse survives. Consider naming the children directly as contingent beneficiaries if the spouse does not survive, to avoid the complications of running benefits through a trust (see Form 3.5A).

B.   For a client who has not yet reached his RBD, remember that the "contingent beneficiary" will become the "designated beneficiary" if the original primary beneficiary happens to die before P (and before P's RBD).

C.   Consider whether different contingent beneficiaries should be named depending on whether the primary beneficiary actually dies before P, or merely disclaims the benefits (see Form 3.6).

Red flag reminder!

9.   Whenever a trust is named as beneficiary, you must comply with the IRS's "trust rules" (Chapter 6) or lose the benefits of the life expectancy payout (see Chapter 1). Use the Trust Review Questionnaire in Appendix C to test compliance, and be sure to file the required documentation (see Forms 8.1 through 8.4). Some beneficiary designation forms in this Appendix in which benefits are left to a trust describe the trust as "the [TRUST NAME] Trust, a copy of which is attached hereto." The phrase "a copy of which is attached hereto" is intended merely to identify the trust which is named as beneficiary, and does NOT in and of itself satisfy the "documentation requirement." You could choose to identify the trust by other means (*e.g.*, "under agreement dated 1/1/98") instead of attaching a copy of the trust to the beneficiary designation form. No matter how you choose to identify the trust which is named as beneficiary, you ALSO must comply with the documentation requirement; see Chapter 6 and Forms 8.1 through 8.4.

10.   If P dies before his RBD, and his beneficiary is his spouse, or a trust of which the spouse is the oldest beneficiary, it is advisable to specify that the spouse's life expectancy will not be recalculated annually (unless the beneficiary or P affirmatively elects otherwise prior to the first required distribution). If this is not specified, it is possible that a plan rule (or IRS rule) would create a presumption that the spouse's LE is to be redetermined annually, which could have disastrous effects if the spouse dies prematurely. This issue does not arise if P dies on or after his RBD, because P's elections at the RBD will also govern upon his later death. See ¶ 3.06 in the Master Beneficiary Designation forms (2.1 and 2.2).

1.   SIMPLE BENEFICIARY DESIGNATION FORM

Who might use this form: The simple beneficiary designation form may be suitable for a client who wants to leave benefits outright to his spouse if living, otherwise to his children equally (and issue of deceased children). This form is included primarily for use with retirement plans that are of relatively small value. If the benefit is of substantial value, either absolutely or relative to the rest of the client's estate, it would be advisable to use the longer Master Beneficiary Designation forms (2.1 and 2.2) which cover more issues.

1.1   Simple Beneficiary Designation Form: Spouse, Then Children (or their Issue)

DESIGNATION OF BENEFICIARY

TO: [Name of IRA or Roth IRA Provider or Plan Administrator]

FROM: [Name of Participant]

RE: [IRA or Roth IRA No._____] or [or Name of Plan]

1.   I hereby designate as my beneficiary, my spouse, [SPOUSE NAME], whose date of birth is [SPOUSE BIRTHDATE], to receive all benefits payable under the above [account] [plan] in the event of my death.

2.   If my spouse does not survive me, I designate as my beneficiaries, in equal shares, such of my children as shall survive me; provided, that if any of my children does not survive me, but leaves issue surviving me, such issue shall take the share such deceased child would have taken if living, by right of representation.

My children are:

Name	Date of Birth	Social Security Number

3.   Any benefits becoming distributable to a person under the age of twenty-one (21) years shall be distributed to such person's surviving parent, if any, otherwise to my oldest then living child, as custodian for such person under the Uniform Transfers to Minors Act. Such custodian shall be entitled to act for the minor in all respects with regard to the benefits.

4.   Each beneficiary may choose the form and timing of distribution of his or her benefits, subject to limits imposed by the [plan] [Account Agreement] and applicable law.

5.   Unless I or the beneficiary has duly made a different

election prior to the date of payment of the first "minimum required distribution" (under § 401(a)(9) of the Internal Revenue Code), the life expectancy of my spouse shall not be redetermined annually.

Signed this _____ day of _____, _____.

_____
Signature of Participant

2. MASTER BENEFICIARY DESIGNATION FORMS: MORE COMPLEX PROVISIONS

Who should use these forms: These Master Beneficiary Designation forms are meant to be used with all beneficiary designation forms provided in Sections 3 and 4 of this Appendix. Form 2.1 is meant to be used with IRAs (traditional and Roth). Form 2.2 is for QRPs. Although most of the subject matter in these forms is not dealt with at all in most IRA agreements and QRP documents, it is desirable nevertheless to make sure the IRA agreement or plan document does not contradict anything contained in these forms before using them.

Other notes: Drafters will not use all of these provisions in every beneficiary designation form. ¶ 3.03 can be omitted if no minors can possibly become beneficiaries (for example, if the beneficiary is a trust). ¶ 3.06 and ¶ 3.07 can be omitted if P is not naming his spouse as beneficiary or contingent beneficiary. ¶ 3.06 can be omitted if the participant is past his RBD. For discussion of the reason behind ¶ 3.07, see *"Other marital deduction issues,"* Chapter 3. These provisions, like all forms, should be modified as necessary for individual clients. Also, note that a particular IRA provider or QRP administrator may not be willing to accept some of these provisions.

2.1   Master Beneficiary Designation Form: Traditional or Roth IRA

DESIGNATION OF BENEFICIARY

TO: _____

       Name of Custodian or Trustee of the Account

FROM: _____

       Name of Participant

RE: Account No. _____

I.   Definitions

The following words, when used in this form and capitalized, shall have the meaning indicated in this Section.

"Account" means the "Individual Retirement Account," "Individual Retirement Trust," "Roth Individual Retirement Account" or "Roth Individual Retirement Trust" referred to above, which is established and maintained under § 408 or § 408A of the Code.

"Administrator" means the IRA custodian or trustee named above, and its successors in that office.

"Agreement" means the account agreement between the Administrator and the undersigned establishing the Account.

"Beneficiary" means any person or entity entitled to ownership of all or part of the Account as a result of my death (or as a result of the death of another Beneficiary), whether such person or entity is a Primary, Contingent or Successor Beneficiary.

"Code" means the Internal Revenue Code of 1986, as

---

amended; reference to any section of the Code includes applicable successor provisions of the law as well as duly issued regulations thereunder.

"Contingent Beneficiary" means the person(s) I have designated in this form to receive the Death Benefit if my Primary Beneficiary does not survive me (or disclaims the benefits).

"Death Benefit" means all amounts payable under the Account on account of my death.

The "Minimum Distribution Amount" is, in each year, the minimum amount required by the Code to be distributed from the Account in such year.

"Primary Beneficiary" means the person or persons I have designated in this form to receive the Death Benefit in the event of my death.

"Successor Beneficiary" means a person entitled to receive the balance of another Beneficiary's benefits if such other Beneficiary dies before distribution of all of his or her share of the Death Benefit.

II.   Designation of Beneficiary

[Here insert the chosen designation of beneficiary provision, from Section 3 or 4 of this Appendix B, or elsewhere.]

III.   Other Provisions

3.01   Form of Benefit Payments after my Death. After my death, there must be distributed, in each calendar year, at least the Minimum Distribution Amount for such year; provided, that this sentence shall not be deemed to limit any Beneficiary's right to use the alternative method of compliance described in

IRS Notice 88-38. Except as may be otherwise specifically provided herein, or in the Agreement, or by applicable law, each Beneficiary shall be entitled to elect the form and timing of distribution of benefits payable to him or her.

3.02   Death of Individual Beneficiary. No person shall have the discretion, after my death, to change my Beneficiary(ies). The Death Benefit shall be payable to the Primary (or Contingent) Beneficiary specified herein, whichever is applicable. However if an individual Primary or Contingent Beneficiary, having survived me, becomes entitled to ownership of all or part of the Account, but later dies prior to the complete distribution of such Beneficiary's share of the Account to him or her, the remaining balance of such Beneficiary's share of the Account shall belong to a Successor Beneficiary, who shall be:

(i)   such person or persons as such Beneficiary shall have indicated by written notice to the Administrator; or, if such Beneficiary shall have failed to give such written notice, or to the extent such written notice does not make effective disposition of all of such Beneficiary's share of the Account,

(ii)   such Beneficiary's issue surviving such Beneficiary, by right of representation; or, in default of such issue,

(iii)   my issue surviving such Beneficiary, by right of representation, or, in default of such issue,

(iv)   such Beneficiary's estate.

3.03   Payments to Minors. If any Beneficiary becomes entitled to ownership of any part of the Account at a time when he or she is under the age of twenty-one (21) years, such ownership shall instead be vested in the name of such Beneficiary's surviving parent, if any, otherwise in the name of my oldest then living child if any, otherwise in the name of some other person selected by my Executor, as custodian for such Beneficiary under the Uniform Transfers to Minors Act of the state of my domicile at death, and such custodian shall have the power to act for such Beneficiary in all respects with regard to the Account.

3.04 <u>Governing Law</u>. The interpretation of this beneficiary designation form shall be governed by the law of the State of _____.

3.05 <u>Multiple Beneficiaries</u>. If there are multiple Beneficiaries entitled to ownership of the Account simultaneously, they shall be entitled, by joint written instructions to the Administrator, to have the Account divided into separate accounts corresponding to each Beneficiary's separate interest in the Account, as of or at any time after my death, to the maximum extent such division is permitted by law (without causing a deemed distribution of the Account). Following such division the separate accounts shall be maintained as if each were an Account in my name payable solely to the applicable Beneficiary. Following such division, no Beneficiary shall have any further interest in or claim to any Account other than the separate Account representing his or her interest.

3.06 <u>Determination of Spouse's Life Expectancy</u>. Unless I or the Beneficiary has duly made a different election prior to the date of payment of the first Minimum Distribution Amount, the life expectancy of my spouse shall not be redetermined annually.

3.07 <u>Preservation of marital deduction</u>. If my spouse

survives me, this paragraph shall apply to any portion (or all) of the Account as to which my spouse is the Beneficiary or as to which my spouse becomes the Beneficiary by virtue of the death of (or a disclaimer by) a prior Beneficiary. My spouse, as such Beneficiary, shall have the right, exercisable solely by my spouse, annually or more frequently (in my spouse's discretion), to require distribution to my spouse of all income of the Account, and also shall have the power, exercisable by my spouse alone and in all events, at any time or times and from time to time, to appoint all of the principal of the Account (including undistributed income) to my spouse. Rights given to my spouse under this paragraph shall be in addition to and not in limitation of any rights given to my spouse by law, by the Agreement or by other provisions hereof.

3.08   Instructions   of   attorney   or   personal representative. I direct the Administrator to comply with all instructions issued to it on my behalf by my duly appointed legal guardian, conservator or other personal representative, and/or, whether or not such a representative has been appointed, by my agent acting under a power of attorney executed by me which grants the authority the agent seeks to exercise.

3.09   Allowing Beneficiary to Appoint Investment Manager. The Beneficiary may designate an Investment Manager for the Account (or, if the Account has been divided pursuant to the preceding provisions hereof, such Beneficiary's share of the Account). Upon receipt of written authorization from the Beneficiary, and until receiving notice that such authorization is revoked, the Administrator shall comply with investment instructions of the Investment Manager in accordance with the Beneficiary's authorization.

3.10 <u>Transferring Account</u>. The Beneficiary shall have the right to have the Account (or, if the Account has been divided pursuant to the preceding provisions hereof, such Beneficiary's share of the Account) transferred to a different individual retirement account or trust, of the same type ("traditional" or "Roth") as the Account, still in my name, with the same or a different custodian or trustee, if at the applicable time such transfer is permitted by law without causing a deemed distribution of the Account.

Signed this _____ day of _____, ____.

_____
Signature of Participant

Receipt of the above beneficiary designation form is hereby acknowledged this ___ day of _____, _____.

_____
Name of Custodian or Trustee

By:_____
Title

2.2 Master Beneficiary Designation Form: Qualified Retirement Plan

WARNING: spousal consent required if anyone other than spouse is named as beneficiary! See "REA '84 and Spousal Consent," Chapter 3.

DESIGNATION OF BENEFICIARY

TO: _____

Name of Trustee or Plan Administrator

FROM: _____

Name of Participant

RE: _____

Name of Retirement Plan

I.   Definitions

The following words, when used in this form and capitalized, shall have the meaning indicated in this Section.

"Administrator" means the Plan Administrator or Trustee named above, and its successors in such office.

"Beneficiary" means any person entitled to receive benefits under the Plan as a result of my death (or as a result of the death of another Beneficiary).

"Code" means the Internal Revenue Code of 1986, as amended; reference to any section of the Code includes applicable successor provisions of the law as well as duly issued regulations thereunder.

"Contingent Beneficiary" means the person(s) I have designated in this form to receive the Death Benefit if my Primary Beneficiary does not survive me (or disclaims the benefits).

"Death Benefit" means all benefits payable under the Plan on account of my death.

The "Minimum Distribution Amount" is, in each year, the minimum amount of my benefits under the Plan that is required to be distributed for such year from the Plan under § 401(a)(9) of the Code.

"Plan" means the qualified retirement plan or other retirement arrangement described at the beginning of this form.

"Primary Beneficiary" means the person designated in this form to receive benefits under the Plan on account of my death.

"Successor Beneficiary" means a person entitled to receive the balance of another Beneficiary's benefits if such other Beneficiary dies before distribution of all of his or her share of the Death Benefit.

II.   Designation of Beneficiary

[Here insert the chosen designation of beneficiary provision, from Section 3 or 4 of this Appendix B, or elsewhere.]

III.   Other Provisions

3.01   Form of Benefit Payments After My Death. Except as may be otherwise specifically provided herein, in the Plan, or by applicable law, each Beneficiary shall be entitled to elect the form and timing of distribution of any benefits payable to such Beneficiary, provided that there must be distributed, in each calendar year, at least the Minimum Distribution Amount.

3.02   Death of Beneficiary. No person shall have the discretion, after my death, to change my Beneficiary(ies). The Death Benefit shall be payable to the Primary (or Contingent) Beneficiary specified herein, whichever is applicable. However if an individual Primary or Contingent Beneficiary, having survived me, becomes entitled to benefits under the Plan, but later dies prior to the complete distribution of such benefits to him or her, such deceased Beneficiary's remaining benefits shall be payable to a Successor Beneficiary, who shall be:

     (a)   such person or persons as such Beneficiary shall have indicated by written notice to the Administrator; or, if such Beneficiary failed to give such written notice, or to the extent such written notice does not make effective disposition of all of such Beneficiary's benefits under the Plan, then

     (b)   such Beneficiary's issue surviving such Beneficiary, by right of representation; or, in default of such issue,

     (c)   my issue surviving such Beneficiary, by right of representation, or, in default of such issue,

     (d)   such Beneficiary's estate.

     3.03   <u>Payments to Minors.</u> If any Beneficiary becomes entitled to benefits under the Plan at a time when he or she is under the age of twenty-one (21) years, such benefits shall be instead payable to such Beneficiary's surviving parent, if any, otherwise to my oldest then living child, if any, otherwise to some other person selected by my Executor, as custodian for such Beneficiary under the Uniform Transfers to Minors Act, and such custodian shall have the power to act for such Beneficiary in all respects with regard to the benefits to which such Beneficiary is entitled.

     3.04   <u>Governing Law</u>. The interpretation of this beneficiary designation form shall be governed by the law of the State of _____.

     3.05   <u>Multiple Beneficiaries</u>. If there are multiple Beneficiaries who are simultaneously entitled to the Death Benefit, they shall be entitled, by joint written instructions to the Administrator, to have the Death Benefit divided into separate accounts corresponding to each Beneficiary's separate interest in the Death Benefit, as of or at any time after my death, to the maximum extent such division is permitted by law (without causing a deemed distribution of the Death Benefit). Following such division, the separate accounts shall be maintained as if each were a Death Benefit payable solely to the applicable Beneficiary, and no Beneficiary shall have any further interest in or claim to any part of the Death Benefit other than the separate account representing his or her interest.

3.06 <u>Determination of Spouse's Life Expectancy</u>. Unless I or the Beneficiary has duly made a different election prior to the date of payment of the first Minimum Distribution Amount, the life expectancy of my spouse shall not be redetermined annually.

3.07 <u>Preservation of marital deduction</u>. If my spouse survives me, this paragraph shall apply to any portion (or all) of the Death Benefit as to which my spouse is the Beneficiary or as to which my spouse becomes the Beneficiary by virtue of the death of (or a disclaimer by) a prior Beneficiary. My spouse, as such Beneficiary, shall have the right, exercisable solely by my spouse, annually or more frequently (in my spouse's discretion), to require distribution to my spouse of all income of the Death Benefit, and also shall have the power, exercisable by my spouse alone and in all events, at any time or times and from time to time, to appoint all of the principal of the Death Benefit (including undistributed income) to my spouse. Rights given to my spouse under this paragraph shall be in addition to and not in limitation of any rights given to my spouse by law, by the Plan or by other provisions hereof.

3.08 <u>Instructions of attorney or personal representative</u>. I direct the Administrator to comply with all instructions issued to it on my behalf by my duly appointed legal guardian, conservator or other personal representative, and/or, whether or not such a representative has been appointed, by my agent acting under a power of attorney executed by me which grants the authority the agent seeks to exercise.

    3.09   <u>Allowing Beneficiary to Appoint Investment Manager</u>. The Beneficiary may designate an Investment Manager for the Death Benefit (or, if the Death Benefit has been divided pursuant to the preceding provisions hereof, such Beneficiary's share of the Death Benefit). Upon receipt of written authorization from the Beneficiary, and until receiving notice that such authorization is revoked, the Administrator shall comply with investment instructions of the Investment Manager in accordance with the Beneficiary's authorization.

    Signed this _____ day of _____, _____.

_____
Signature of Participant

    Receipt of the above beneficiary designation form is hereby acknowledged this ____ day of _____, _____.

_____
Name of Plan Administrator or Trustee

By:_____
Title

3.   SEVEN WAYS TO LEAVE BENEFITS TO THE MARITAL AND/OR CREDIT SHELTER SHARE

Each of the following forms is a beneficiary designation designed to leave benefits to a marital or **credit shelter** share, or to split benefits between a marital and credit shelter share. These can be inserted into "Part II" of the appropriate "Master Beneficiary Designation Form" (Form 2.1 for a traditional or Roth IRA, Form 2.2 for a QRP) in the preceding section of this Appendix. Related provisions to be included in the client's trust instrument, when applicable, follow the beneficiary designation form.

3.1 Life Insurance Proceeds Payable to Credit Shelter Trust, All Other Benefits to Spouse

Who would consider using this form: Any client who holds life insurance inside his qualified retirement plan, and wants the insurance proceeds payable to a trust (*e.g.,* to "fill up" a credit shelter trust), but wants the surviving spouse to be able to roll over the non-insurance portion of the benefits.

Warning: A client whose plan-held insurance is held in a "subtrust" (see Chapter 10) cannot designate the beneficiary for the policy.

3.1 Beneficiary Designation Form

II. <u>Designation of Beneficiary</u>   A. <u>Primary Beneficiary</u> If my spouse, [SPOUSE NAME], survives me, the Death Benefit shall be distributed to the following Primary Beneficiaries:

1.   Any amount payable under any contract of life insurance on my life shall be paid to [TRUSTEE NAME], as Trustee of the [TRUST NAME] Trust, under Agreement of Trust dated [TRUST DATE], a copy of which is attached hereto.

2.   The balance of the Death Benefit shall be paid to my spouse.

   B.   Contingent Beneficiary

   If my spouse does not survive me (or to the extent my spouse disclaims any benefits otherwise distributable to my spouse under section A above), I direct that 100% of the Death Benefit (or the amount disclaimed as the case may be) shall be paid to [TRUSTEE NAME], as Trustee of the "Family Trust" of the said [TRUST NAME] Trust.

3.2   Benefits Payable to "Pourover" Trust, Under Which Assets Are Divided Between a Marital Share (Paid to Spouse Outright) and a Credit Shelter Trust by a Fractional Formula. Benefits Are Allocated to Marital Share

   Who would consider using this form: Client who expects to need to use some or all of his retirement benefits to "fill up" a credit shelter trust, and wants any benefits not needed for that purpose paid to the spouse outright so she can roll them over.

   Drawbacks of this form: Under this form and the related trust provision, the trustee is required to fund the marital share with retirement benefits to the maximum extent possible, and then is required to distribute the marital share outright to the spouse on her request. This approach is based on IRS private letter rulings, permitting the surviving spouse to roll over benefits which pass to her through a trust, if she has the unfettered right to withdraw the benefits. See Chapter 3. Since this IRS policy has so far appeared only in private letter rulings, there is no guarantee the IRS will continue to recognize such rollovers, although it appears *likely* (and correct under the Code) that such rollovers will be allowed.

Other notes: This form names only the trust as beneficiary, regardless of whether the spouse survives. If the entire trust is to be distributed to P's issue outright on the death of the surviving spouse, consider naming the trust as primary beneficiary only if the spouse survives, and naming the issue directly as beneficiaries if the spouse does not survive. See form 3.5 for an example of this approach.

3.2(A) Beneficiary Designation Form

II.   Designation of Beneficiary

         A.   Primary Beneficiary

         I hereby designate as my Primary Beneficiary, to receive 100% of the Death Benefit in case of my death, [TRUSTEE NAME] (hereinafter "my Trustee"), as Trustee of the [TRUST NAME] Trust, under Agreement of Trust dated [TRUST DATE], a copy of which is attached hereto.

         B.   Distribution of Benefits to Spouse

         My Trustee is directed under the said Agreement of Trust to allocate the Death Benefit, pursuant to a formula, between my spouse and the "Family Trust" established under said Agreement of Trust. My Trustee is further directed under said Agreement of Trust, if so requested by my spouse, to cause the part of the Death Benefit so allocated to my spouse to be (i) distributed outright to my spouse or (ii) transferred directly to an "individual retirement account" in my spouse's name. Accordingly, if the Administrator is so instructed by my Trustee, the Administrator shall, with respect to the amount indicated by my Trustee, (i) distribute such amount outright to my spouse or (ii) transfer such amount directly to an "individual retirement account" in my spouse's name.

3.2(B) Related Trust Provisions

___.   Payments After My Death

Upon my death, the Trustee shall hold and administer all property of the Trust, including any amounts received or receivable then or later as a result of my death or otherwise, as follows:

.01   If my spouse does not survive me, the Trustee shall designate all of such property as the "Family Trust," to be held and administered as provided in Article ___.

.02   If my spouse survives me, the Trustee shall divide the said property into two separate shares, to be designated respectively the Marital Share and the Family Trust. The two separate shares shall be funded pursuant to the following formula. If application of the formula results in assets being allocated to only one of the shares instead of both, the Trustee shall fund only such one.

.03   The Trustee shall allocate to the Marital Share a portion of the Remaining Trust Property determined by multiplying the Remaining Trust Property by a fraction. The numerator of the fraction shall be: the smallest amount necessary, if allowed as a marital deduction, to eliminate the federal estate tax otherwise payable by reason of my death; reduced by the value of all other items included in my estate which qualify for the federal estate tax marital deduction and which pass or have passed to my spouse otherwise than under this provision. The denominator of the fraction is the value of the Remaining Trust Property. For purposes of this formula:

(i)   It shall be assumed with respect to property not passing under this trust that my Executor will elect to treat as "qualified terminable interest property" all property eligible for such treatment.

(ii)   The "values" of assets shall be their values as finally determined for purposes of the federal estate tax on my estate.

(iii)   The "Remaining Trust Property" means all property of this trust that is included in my federal gross estate, reduced by the amount of any debts, expenses of administration, specific and pecuniary bequests and death taxes payable out of such property.

(iv)   The federal estate tax credit for state death taxes shall be taken into account only to the extent its use does not increase the state death taxes otherwise payable on my estate.

.04   All property not allocated to the Marital Share pursuant to the preceding formula shall be designated as the Family Trust, and administered as provided in Article __.

.05   In selecting which assets shall be used to fund which share, the Trustee shall, to the maximum extent possible, allocate tax-favored retirement plans to the Marital Share and assets other than tax-favored retirement plans to the Family Trust. A "tax-favored retirement plan" means an individual retirement account (within the meaning of § 408 of the Code), Roth individual retirement account (within the meaning of §

408A of the Code), qualified retirement plan (within the meaning of § 401(a) of the Code), "tax-sheltered annuity" (described in § 403(b) of the Code) and similar plans, accounts and arrangements.

.06   The Marital Share shall be distributed to my spouse, outright and free of trusts. To the extent that all or part of any tax-favored retirement plan is allocated to the Marital Share pursuant to the foregoing provisions, the Trustee may (and shall, if requested to do so by my spouse) cause such plan (or part thereof) to be paid directly from such plan to my spouse as beneficiary, or transferred (if so requested by my spouse) directly from such plan into an individual retirement account in my spouse's name, without the intervening step of transferring it to this Trust.

3.3   All Benefits Payable to a "Pourover" Trust, Under Which Assets are Divided Between a QTIP Marital Trust and a Credit Shelter Trust by a Fractional Formula; Drafter May Choose to Specify Allocation of Benefits to Marital Trust or Credit Shelter Trust

Who should consider this form: A client who does not want any benefits paid to the spouse outright and whose pourover trust will be allocated between a "marital trust" and a "credit shelter trust" by a fractional formula. The related trust provisions contain two alternatives regarding funding these shares: one version requires benefits to be allocated to the marital share to the extent possible; the other requires benefits to be allocated to the credit shelter share to the extent possible. A third option is to omit both versions of paragraph .06 and allow the trustee to choose which assets to use to fund which share.

Drawbacks of this form: No spousal rollover is possible under this form.

3.3(A) Beneficiary Designation Form

II.   Designation of Beneficiary

A.   Primary Beneficiary

I hereby designate as my Primary Beneficiary, to receive 100% of the Death Benefit, [TRUSTEE NAME] (hereinafter "my Trustee"), as trustee of the [TRUST NAME] Trust, under Agreement of Trust dated [TRUST DATE], a copy of which is attached hereto.

B.   Division of Benefit

Under the terms of said Agreement of Trust, my Trustee is directed, if my spouse survives me, to divide the assets of said Trust into two separate trusts, to be designated the "Marital Trust" and the "Family Trust." If so instructed by my Trustee, the Administrator shall divide the Death Benefit into two separate accounts, both still in my name, one payable solely to the Marital Trust as Beneficiary and the other payable solely to the Family Trust as Beneficiary; or, in accordance with such instructions, shall designate the entire Death Benefit as payable to one of said trusts. The Administrator shall have no responsibility to determine the correctness of my Trustee's instructions regarding such allocation, and shall have no liability whatsoever to any person for complying with my Trustee's said instructions. The beneficiaries of the Marital Trust and Family Trust shall look solely to my Trustee for enforcement of their rights under the said Trusts.

C.   Benefits Payable to Marital Trust

With regard to any portion of the Death Benefit so allocated to the Marital Trust, there must be distributed to the Marital Trust in each year, beginning with the year of my death, from the Marital Trust's portion of the Death Benefit, at least the net income of the Marital Trust's portion of the Death Benefit for such year accrued after my death. My Trustee, and not the Administrator, shall have sole responsibility for determination of the amount of such income, and directing the distribution of such income to the Marital Trust.

3.3(B) Related Trust Provisions

___.   <u>Payments Upon My Death</u>

Upon my death, the Trustee shall hold and administer all property of the Trust, including any amounts received or receivable then or later as a result of my death or otherwise, as follows:

[here, copy sections .01 through .04 from form 3.2(B), but change "Marital Share" to "Marital Trust", and add:]

.05   The Marital Trust shall be held and administered as provided in Article ___.

[Use one or the other of the following optional funding provisions, or neither, **but not both**]

[optional funding provision: alternative 1].

.06   Any death benefit under any "qualified retirement plan," individual retirement account, Roth IRA or similar tax-favored retirement arrangement that is payable to this Trust shall be allocated to the Marital Trust to the maximum extent possible within the limits of the preceding formula.

[optional funding provision: alternative 2].

.06   Any death benefit under any "qualified retirement plan," individual retirement account, Roth IRA or similar tax-favored retirement arrangement that is payable to this Trust shall be allocated to the Family Trust to the maximum extent possible within the limits of the preceding formula.

[here insert form 7.4, or otherwise take steps to qualify for marital deduction; see Chapter 3.]

3.4   Benefits Payable to a Marital Trust Which Is Part of a "Pourover" Trust with a Pecuniary Marital Formula

Who should consider using this form: A client who wants to use a pecuniary marital formula for his marital/credit shelter share division because it is easier to administer; who wants his retirement benefits paid to a marital trust, and not outright to his spouse; and whose retirement benefits will probably not be needed to fund the credit shelter share. By making the benefits payable directly to the Marital Trust, the client avoids having any kind of formula applied to the benefits, avoids the complexity of transferring the retirement benefits from a "funding" trust into a Marital or Family Trust, and avoids having to use a fractional formula for any assets.

The preferred simplicity of administration which comes from using a pecuniary formula does not have to be sacrificed just because part of the trust will consist of retirement benefits.

Under this form, the retirement benefits do not go through the pecuniary funding formula—the benefits bypass the formula and go straight into the Marital Trust.

Drawbacks: If the retirement benefits turn out to be a greater amount than is required to eliminate estate taxes, then this form would overfund the marital share. That problem can be solved easily post mortem by a fractional QTIP election, or, less easily, by a disclaimer by the marital trust. Also, no spousal rollover is possible under this form.

3.4(A) Beneficiary Designation Form

II.   Designation of Beneficiary

    A.   Primary Beneficiary

    I hereby designate as my Primary Beneficiary, to receive 100% of the Death Benefit, [TRUSTEE NAME], as trustee of the [MARITAL TRUST NAME] Marital Trust, established under Agreement of Trust dated [TRUST DATE], a copy of which is attached hereto.

    B.   Form of Distribution of Benefits

    After my death, there shall be distributed to the Beneficiary, in each year, so long as my spouse is living, whichever of the following amounts is the greatest:

        (a)   the net income of the Death Benefit for such year;

        (b)   the Minimum Distribution Amount for such year; or

---

    (c)   such amount as the Beneficiary shall direct by written instructions to the Administrator.

    The Beneficiary, and not the Administrator, shall have sole responsibility for determining the amounts under subparagraphs (a), (b) and (c).

3.4(B) Related Trust Provisions

__.   <u>Payments After My Death</u>

    Upon my death, the Trustee shall hold and administer all property of the Trust, including any amounts received or receivable then or later as a result of my death or otherwise, as follows:

    .01   If my spouse does not survive me, the Trustee shall designate all such property as the "Family Trust" to be held and administered as provided in Article ___.

    .02   If my spouse survives me, the Trustee shall divide the said property into two separate trust funds, to be designated the Marital Trust and the Family Trust, pursuant to the following formula. If application of the formula results in assets being allocated to only one of the trusts instead of both, the Trustee shall fund only such one.

    (a)   The Trustee shall allocate to the Marital Trust all benefits payable under any "qualified retirement plan," "individual retirement account" (other than Roth IRAs), or similar retirement plan, annuity or arrangement, as well as any assets which are payable by the terms of my will, beneficiary designation form or otherwise directly to the Marital Trust.

(b)   The Trustee shall allocate to the Marital Trust such additional amount, if any, as is necessary to bring the total value of the Marital Trust up to the Optimum Federal Marital Amount. This gift to the Marital Trust shall be funded only with assets or the proceeds of assets which qualify for the federal estate tax marital deduction.

(c)   The Marital Trust shall be held and administered as provided in Article ____

(d)   The "Optimum Federal Marital Amount" means the smallest amount which, if it passed to my spouse in a manner qualifying for the federal estate tax marital deduction, would eliminate the federal estate tax on my estate (or minimize such tax, if it is not possible to eliminate it), reduced by the value of any property passing to my spouse otherwise than under this trust to the extent such property qualifies for the federal estate tax marital deduction (or would so qualify if my Executor so elected). In computing the Optimum Federal Marital Amount, the federal estate tax credit for state death taxes shall be taken into account only to the extent its use does not increase the state death taxes otherwise payable on my estate.

(e)   All property not allocated to the Marital Trust pursuant to the preceding formula (or, if no property is allocable to the Marital Trust pursuant to preceding formula, then all property of the Trust) shall be designated as the Family Trust, to be held and administered as provided in Article ____.

[here insert form 7.4, or otherwise take steps to qualify for marital deduction; see Chapter 3.]

3.5   Benefits Payable to "One Big QTIP" Trust if Spouse Survives; Trustee Has Authority to Divide the Trust; Issue are Contingent Beneficiaries

Who would use this form: The client who wants all income of his benefits paid to his spouse for life, but wants principal remaining at the spouse's death to pass to beneficiaries selected by client. This form leaves all the benefits to "one big QTIP trust," with the trustee having discretion to either make a fractional QTIP election, or divide the trust into two separate trusts at the client's death, with the QTIP election being made for only one of them, whichever seems best at the time. P's issue are named directly as contingent beneficiaries if spouse does not survive P.

Drawbacks: See discussion in the *Koslow* case study.

Warning: The trust form 3.5(B) allows the trustee to divide the trust into two or more separate trusts. Such a discretionary division of a trust will not be recognized for purposes of allocating the decedent's **generation skipping** (GST) tax exemption unless GST regulations are complied with.

3.5(A) Beneficiary Designation Form

II.   Designation of Beneficiary

A.   Primary Beneficiary

I hereby designate as my primary Beneficiary, to receive 100% of the Death Benefit, if my spouse survives me, [TRUSTEE NAME], as Trustee of the [TRUST NAME] Trust under Agreement of Trust dated [TRUST DATE], a copy of which is attached hereto. The beneficiary of said trust, within the meaning of the Proposed Treasury Regulations, is my spouse, [SPOUSE NAME].

B.   Form of Distribution of Benefits

After my death, there shall be distributed to the Beneficiary, in each year, so long as my spouse is living, whichever of the following amounts is the greatest:

      (a)   the net income of the Death Benefit for such year;

      (b)   the Minimum Distribution Amount for such year; or

      (c)   such amount as the Beneficiary shall direct by written instructions to the Administrator.

The Beneficiary, and not the Administrator, shall have sole responsibility for complying with these instructions as to the Form of Distribution of Benefits.

      C.   <u>Contingent Beneficiary</u>

I hereby designate as my Contingent Beneficiary, to receive 100% of the Death Benefit if my spouse does not survive me, my issue surviving me, by right of representation.

3.5(B) Related Trust Provisions

      ___.   <u>Payments After My Death</u>

Upon my death, the Trustee shall hold and administer all property of the Trust, including any amounts received or receivable then or later as a result of my death or otherwise, as follows:

      .01   If my spouse does not survive me, the Trustee shall designate all of such property as the "Family Trust," to be held and administered as provided in Article __.

.02   If my spouse survives me, the Trustee shall pay to my spouse the net income from the date of my death, at least quarter annually, for life.

.03   If this Trust is the beneficiary of death benefits under any "individual retirement account," "Roth IRA," "qualified retirement plan," or similar tax-favored retirement arrangement or annuity (the "Plan") the Trustee must withdraw from the Plan, in each calendar year, and deposit in this trust fund, at least whichever of the following amounts is the greater:

(a)   the Plan's net income for such year; or

(b)   the "minimum distribution amount" which is required to be withdrawn from such Plan under § 401(a)(9) of the Code or other Code provisions or applicable law.

This paragraph .03 shall not be deemed to limit the Trustee's power and right to withdraw from the Plan in any year more than the greater of the said two amounts.

.04   Upon the death of my spouse, the principal, as it may then exist, shall be held, administered and distributed as provided for property of the Family Trust under Article __.

.__   Division of the Trust

The Trustee in its discretion may divide the trust into two or more separate shares, each such separate share to be administered as a separate trust on all the same terms provided herein for the undivided trust fund. I anticipate that the Trustee will exercise its discretion under this Article for reasons of administrative convenience, or in order to recognize different characteristics the separate shares or trusts will have for purposes of certain taxes.

3.6   Benefits Payable to Spouse, "Disclaimable" to Credit Shelter Trust; Different Contingent Beneficiary Specified Depending on Whether Spouse Actually Predeceases or Merely Disclaims

Who would consider using this form: A client who does not have sufficient non-retirement plan assets to fully fund a credit shelter trust, but wants nevertheless to leave the benefits to his spouse and allow the spouse to make the ultimate decision whether to (a) keep the benefits and roll them over to an IRA or (b) disclaim some or all of the benefits and allow them to flow to the credit shelter trust. See, *e.g.,* the *Able* case study.

Drawbacks: See Chapter 8.

3.6   Beneficiary Designation Form

II.   Designation of Beneficiary

    A.   Primary Beneficiary

I hereby designate as my Primary Beneficiary, to receive 100% of the Death Benefit, my spouse, [SPOUSE NAME], if my spouse survives me.

    B.   Contingent Beneficiary in Case of Disclaimer

If my spouse survives me, but disclaims the Death Benefit (or part of it), I hereby designate as my Contingent Beneficiary, to receive the part of the Death Benefit so disclaimed, [TRUSTEE NAME], as Trustee of the [TRUST

NAME] Trust, under agreement dated [TRUST DATE], a copy of which is attached hereto.

C. Contingent Beneficiary in Case of Death

If my spouse does not survive me, I hereby designate as my Contingent Beneficiary, to receive 100% of the Death Benefit, my issue surviving me, by right of representation.

3.7 Benefits Payable to Credit Shelter Trust, "Disclaimable" to Spouse

Who would consider using this form: A client who does not have sufficient non-retirement assets to fund a credit shelter trust, and expects to use his retirement benefits for that purpose, but wants to leave the door open for a spousal rollover because he thinks that (a) there might possibly be sufficient other assets to fund the credit shelter trust by the time he dies so the retirement benefits won't be needed after all or (b) even if there are not sufficient other assets to fund the credit shelter trust when he dies the rollover might appear at that time likely to produce a better overall tax and financial picture for his beneficiaries. This client does not want to make the benefits payable to the spouse and "disclaimable" to the credit shelter trust because (a) he doesn't believe the spouse is capable of handling the decision, or can be relied upon to make the right decision or (b) only the children, not the spouse, are beneficiaries of the credit shelter trust and he does not want to risk having them be stuck with using the spouse's life expectancy if she disclaims (see Chapter 8).

Drawbacks of using this form: Do not use this form without first thoroughly investigating applicable state law on disclaimers by fiduciaries.

3.7(A) Beneficiary Designation Form

II.   Designation of Beneficiary

     A.   Primary Beneficiary

     I hereby designate as my Primary Beneficiary, to receive 100% of the Death Benefit [TRUSTEE NAME] (hereinafter "my Trustee"), as Trustee of the [TRUST NAME] Trust, under Agreement of Trust dated [TRUST DATE], a copy of which is attached hereto.

     B.   Alternative Primary Beneficiary

     If and to the extent that my Trustee disclaims any of the Death Benefit, I name as my Primary Beneficiary, for the portion so disclaimed, my spouse, [SPOUSE NAME], if my spouse survives me.

3.7(B) Related Trust Provisions

     .__   Disclaimers by Trustee

     .01   The Trustee shall have the power and authority, without the approval of any court, and without the consent of any beneficiary, to disclaim (refuse to accept) any property or interest in property that is payable to the trust by gift, devise, inheritance, bequest or otherwise, if the Trustee, in its discretion, determines that such disclaimer is in the best interest of beneficiaries of this Trust or will otherwise help achieve the objectives of this Trust.

     .02   In exercising its discretion under this Article, the

> Trustee shall be entitled to presume that any benefit conferred on an individual is likewise a benefit to the descendants of that individual, unless the trustee has been presented with clear and convincing evidence to the contrary, and shall bear in mind my objective of minimizing taxes for my family as a whole.

4.   OTHER BENEFICIARY DESIGNATION FORMS

4.1   Designating Spouse as Primary Beneficiary of IRA with Presumption Spouse Survives, and Election by Spouse to Treat the IRA as Her Own If She Survives Participant

Who might consider this form: A participant who is past his RBD, and who wants to take all possible steps to allow his spouse, if she survives him, to elect to treat the IRA as her own IRA and name a new DB. See the *Fallon* case study.

Drawbacks of this form: It is not yet known whether the IRS will recognize a spousal election executed prior to the original participant's death, or a presumption of survivorship in case of simultaneous death.

4.1(A) Designation of Beneficiary by Participant

> II.   Designation of Beneficiary
>
>   A.   Primary Beneficiary
>
>   I hereby designate as my Primary Beneficiary my spouse, [SPOUSE NAME], if my spouse survives me. If my said spouse and I die simultaneously or under such circumstances that it is difficult to determine which of us survived the other, my spouse shall be deemed to have survived me.

B. Contingent Beneficiary

I hereby designate as my Contingent Beneficiary, if my said spouse does not survive me, [TRUSTEE NAME], as Trustee of the [TRUST NAME] Charitable Remainder Trust, under Agreement of Trust dated [TRUST DATE].

4.1(B) Election and Designation of Beneficiary by Spouse

---

1. I, [SPOUSE NAME], spouse of the above named participant, hereby elect, in the event that I survive or am deemed to have survived my said spouse, to treat the Account as my own individual retirement arrangement. Accordingly, if I survive my said spouse, or am deemed to have survived my said spouse, I hereby designate as my Primary Beneficiary, to receive 100% of the Account in the event of my death, my issue surviving me, by right of representation.

2. I elect, as the form of payment of benefits to me, installments commencing no later than my required beginning date, over the joint life expectancy of myself and my oldest Beneficiary who is living on my required beginning date, subject to the requirements of the incidental benefit rule. My life expectancy shall not be recalculated annually.

Signed this _____ day of _____, ____.

_____
[SPOUSE NAME]

4.2 Designating Spouse as Primary Beneficiary; Children as Contingent Beneficiaries.

This is simply a designation of spouse if living otherwise children (or their issue), suitable for use with the Master Beneficiary Designation forms.

II.   Designation of Beneficiary

    A.   Primary Beneficiary

I hereby designate as my Primary Beneficiary, to receive 100% of the Death Benefit, my spouse, [SPOUSE NAME], if my spouse survives me.

    B.   Contingent Beneficiary

If my spouse does not survive me, I hereby designate as my Contingent Beneficiary, to receive 100% of the Death Benefit, my children surviving me, in equal shares; provided, that if any child of mine does not survive me, but leaves issue surviving me, such issue shall take the share such deceased child would have taken if living, by right of representation.

4.3 Designating Children (Or Their Issue) as Beneficiaries.

This is a designation of living children (and issue of deceased children) as the primary beneficiaries, suitable for use with the Master Beneficiary Designation forms.

II.   Designation of Beneficiary

> I hereby designate as my Primary Beneficiary, to receive 100% of the Death Benefit, my children surviving me, in equal shares; provided, that if any child of mine does not survive me, but leaves issue surviving me, such issue shall take the share such deceased child would have taken if living, by right of representation.

5.   POWER OF ATTORNEY FOR RETIREMENT BENEFITS

Add this clause to the client's existing power of attorney or create this as a separate power of attorney:

> My Agent shall have the power to establish one or more "individual retirement accounts" or other retirement plans or arrangements in my name.
>
> In connection with any pension, profit sharing or stock bonus plan, individual retirement arrangement, Roth IRA, § 403(b) annuity or account, § 457 plan, or any other retirement plan, arrangement or annuity in which I am a participant or of which I am a beneficiary (whether established by my Agent or otherwise) (each of which is hereinafter referred to as "such Plan"), my Agent shall have the following powers, in addition to all other applicable powers granted by this instrument:
>
> 1.   To make contributions (including "rollover" contributions) or cause contributions to be made to such Plan with my funds or otherwise on my behalf.
>
> 2.   To receive and endorse checks or other distributions to me from such Plan, or to arrange for the direct deposit of the same in any account in my name or in the name of [name of client's revocable living trust].
>
> 3.   To elect a form of payment of benefits from such

Plan, to withdraw benefits from such Plan, to make contributions to such Plan and to make, exercise, waive or consent to any and all elections and/or options that I may have regarding the contributions to, investments or administration, of, or distribution or form of benefits under, such Plan.

      4.   To designate one or more beneficiaries or contingent beneficiaries for any benefits payable under such Plan on account of my death, and to change any such prior designation of beneficiary made by me or by my Agent; provided, however, that my Agent shall have no power to designate my Agent directly or indirectly as a beneficiary or contingent beneficiary to receive a greater share or proportion of any such benefits than my Agent would have otherwise received unless such change is consented to by all other beneficiaries who would have received the benefits but for the proposed change. This limitation shall not apply to any designation of my Agent as beneficiary in a fiduciary capacity, with no beneficial interest.

6. ELECTION REGARDING FORM OF BENEFITS AND METHOD OF DETERMINING LIFE EXPECTANCY AT AGE 70½

6.1 Individual Retirement Account

Note: This form can be adapted for use with a QRP. It is not required for a Roth IRA.

To: _____

     Name of Trustee or Custodian

From: _____

     Name of Participant

Re: Individual Retirement Account No._____

Participant's Required Beginning Date: _____

A. Recital; Method of Determining Life Expectancy

I am the owner of the above-entitled individual retirement account. Under § 401(a)(9) of the Internal Revenue Code, I am required to withdraw benefits from the account, beginning no later than my "Required Beginning Date," in installments over the joint life expectancy of myself and my Designated Beneficiary. Under Proposed Treasury Regulations, I am required to elect irrevocably the method of determining my "life expectancy," and (if my Designated Beneficiary is my spouse) the life expectancy of my Designated Beneficiary. I hereby elect as follows:

My life expectancy:

_____ shall be redetermined annually

_____ shall not be redetermined annually ("term certain" or "fixed term" method).

If my Designated Beneficiary is my spouse, the life expectancy of my Designated Beneficiary:

_____ not applicable; spouse is not designated beneficiary

_____ shall be redetermined annually

_____ shall not be redetermined annually ("term certain" or "fixed term" method).

B. Form of Benefit Payments During My Lifetime

I elect as the form of payment of my benefits the following. There shall be distributed to me, in each calendar year, beginning with the year in which I reach age 70½, the Minimum Distribution Amount, except as follows:

1.   I reserve the right to request and receive, at any time, distribution of any amount greater than the Minimum Distribution Amount.

2.   The Minimum Distribution Amount for the year in which I reach age 70½ may be paid in January, February or March of the following year.

3.   I reserve the right to use the alternative method to satisfy the requirements for minimum distributions specified in IRS Notice 88-38, 1988-1 C.B. 524.

C.   Definition of Minimum Distribution Amount

In each calendar year, beginning with the year I reach age 70½, the Minimum Distribution Amount shall be the minimum amount required to be distributed for such year under § 401(a)(9) of the Code (and regulations thereunder) based on my election to take my benefits in annual installments over the joint life expectancy of myself and my Designated Beneficiary.

Signed this ___ day of _____, _____.

_____
Signature of Participant

Receipt   of   the   above   election   form   is   hereby

acknowledged this ___ day of _____, _____.

_____
Name of Custodian or Trustee

By:_____
Authorized Representative

7.   TRUST PROVISIONS DEALING WITH RETIREMENT BENEFITS

7.1   Trust Administration During Donor's Life, Including Irrevocability Provision

The purpose of including this language in a revocable trust is to assure the trust is a "grantor trust" as to the participant and to make it clear to any plan administrator that the "*Third rule*" (irrevocability; see Chapter 6) is complied with. This form is not suitable for a testamentary trust.

___. Administration During my Life

.01   The Trustee shall distribute to me such amounts of the principal or income of the trust (including all thereof) as I may request from time to time, or (if I am legally incapacitated) as my guardian, conservator or other legal representative may request on my behalf.

.02   I reserve the right to amend or revoke this trust by one or more written and acknowledged instruments delivered to the Trustee during my lifetime. This trust shall become irrevocable at my death.

7.2 Insulating Retirement Assets From Estate Claims and Charitable Gifts

> Notwithstanding any other provision hereof, and except as provided in this paragraph, the Trustee may not distribute to or for the benefit of my estate, any charity or any other non-individual beneficiary any benefits payable to this trust under any qualified retirement plan, individual retirement account or other retirement arrangement subject to the "minimum distribution rules" of § 401(a)(9) of the Code, or other comparable provisions of law. It is my intent that all such retirement benefits be distributed to or held for only individual beneficiaries, within the meaning of § 401(a)(9) and applicable regulations. This paragraph shall not apply to any charitable bequest which is specifically directed to be funded with retirement benefits by other provisions of this instrument.

7.3 Excluding Older Adopted "Issue"

> Notwithstanding any other provision hereof or of state law, the class of my (or any other person's) "issue" shall not include an individual who is my (or such person's) "issue" by virtue of legal adoption if such individual (i) was so adopted after my Required Beginning Date or my death, whichever occurs first and (ii) is older than the oldest beneficiary of this trust who was a living member of said class on the earlier of said dates. My "Required Beginning Date," for purposes of this paragraph, means April 1 of the year following the year in which I reach age 70½, or, if later, the date on which this trust is first named as a beneficiary of any retirement plan, benefit or arrangement subject to the "minimum distribution rules" of § 401(a)(9) of the Code.

7.4 Marital Deduction Savings Language

If any marital trust created by this instrument becomes the beneficiary of death benefits under any "individual retirement account," "Roth IRA," "qualified retirement plan," or similar tax-deferred retirement arrangement or annuity (the "Plan") the Trustee must withdraw from the Marital Trust's share of the Plan, each year, at least whichever of the following amounts is the greater:

A.   the net income of the Marital Trust's share of such Plan for such year; or

B.   the "minimum distribution amount" which is required to be withdrawn from such share under § 401(a)(9) of the Code or other comparable Code provisions or applicable law.

This paragraph shall not be deemed to limit the Trustee's power and right to withdraw from the Marital Trust's share of the Plan in any year more than the greatest of the said amounts.

8.   FORMS TO COMPLY WITH THE DOCUMENTATION REQUIREMENT OF IRS "TRUST RULES" WHEN TRUST IS NAMED AS BENEFICIARY OF RETIREMENT BENEFITS

8.1   Documentation Requirement for Trust Named as Beneficiary of Retirement Benefits: Death Before the RBD: If Copy of Trust Is Given to the Plan:

See "*Fourth Rule: documentation requirement (death before RBD)*," Chapter 6. By the end of the ninth month beginning after the death of P, the trustee of the trust that is named as beneficiary must send a copy of the trust (or the alternative "certification"; see Form 8.2) to the plan administrator. Although there is no requirement that any particular form accompany the copy of the trust, here is a suggested form of cover letter:

"To the Plan Administrator:

"Enclosed herewith is a copy of the actual trust document for the trust, of which the undersigned is the trustee, that is named as a beneficiary of [NAME OF DECEASED PARTICIPANT] under the [NAME OF RETIREMENT PLAN] as of the employee's [participant's] date of death.

"Signed: _____
(Signature of trustee)"

8.2 Form to Comply with Documentation Requirement for Trust Named as Beneficiary of Benefits: Death Before the RBD: If Copy of Trust Is NOT Given to the Plan:

See "*Fourth Rule: documentation requirement (death before RBD),*" Chapter 6. By the end of the ninth month beginning after the death of P, if the trustee does not send a copy of the trust itself to the plan administrator (see Form 8.1), the <u>trustee of the trust that is named as beneficiary</u> must send the plan administrator the following certification:

"To the Plan Administrator:

"The late [NAME OF DECEASED PARTICIPANT] named the [NAME OF TRUST] ("the Trust"), established under instrument of trust dated [DATE OF TRUST], of which the undersigned is the trustee, as beneficiary of his/her death benefits under the [NAME OF RETIREMENT PLAN] ("the

Plan"). In accordance with Proposed Treasury Regulation § 1.401(a)(9)-1, D-7:

"(i) I hereby certify that the following is a complete list of all beneficiaries of the Trust with respect to the trust's interest in the Plan (including contingent and remainderman beneficiaries, with a description of the conditions on their entitlement):

[The following is this author's interpretation of what the IRS is looking for when it requires "a complete list of all beneficiaries of the Trust"; this is not an official form. The following assumes a trust for the life benefit of participant's spouse, with remainder to participant's issue who are living at the death of the spouse; it assumes there are such issue living at the participant's death, and that no person has the power to vary the identity or relative shares of the beneficiaries.]

"**Current beneficiary(ies)**: The participant's spouse, [NAME OF SPOUSE], who is entitled to all income of the trust for life, plus principal distributions if needed for medical expenses or support. If at any time during the spouse's life there is no child of the participant (and no issue of a deceased child of the participant) living, the trust terminates and is distributed to the spouse outright and free of trusts.

"**Remainder beneficiary(ies)** (entitled to benefits upon the death of the participant's spouse, if they survive the spouse): The participant's children in equal shares, with issue of any deceased child to take the share such deceased child would have taken had he/she survived the participant's spouse; these beneficiaries take the trust property outright and free of trust on the death of the spouse. The names, addresses, Social Security numbers and dates of birth of the participant's currently living children are: [INSERT].

"**Contingent beneficiary(ies)**: If at any time neither the participant's spouse nor any issue of the participant is living, and there is still money in this trust, the trust terminates and is distributed to the [NAME OF CONTINGENT BENEFICIARY].

"(ii) I certify that to the best of my knowledge: the above list is correct and complete; and that, within the meaning of Prop. Reg. § 1.401(a)(9)-1, D-5A, paragraphs (b)(1), (2) and (3), the trust is valid under applicable state law, all beneficiaries of the trust are identifiable and the trust was and is irrevocable by its terms, all as of the participant's date of death.

"(iii) I agree to provide to you a copy of the Trust instrument upon demand.

"Signed:_____
              (Signature of trustee)"

8.3 Form to Comply with Documentation Requirement for Trust Named as Beneficiary of Retirement Benefits: at or after the RBD: If Copy of Trust Is Given to the Plan:

See "*Fourth Rule, continued: documentation requirement (at RBD)*," Chapter 6. The participant must send a copy of the trust (or the alternative certification; see Form 8.4) to the plan administrator, ON OR BEFORE the RBD (or when the trust is first named as beneficiary, if that occurs after the RBD); and, IN ADDITION, must promise to send the plan administrator copies of any future trust amendments. (This form is not required for

Roth IRAs (see Chapter 5), which have no RBD.) Although there is no official form, here is a suggested form of cover letter:

"To the Plan Administrator:

"I enclose herewith a copy of the trust instrument establishing the trust which I have named [or am now naming] as beneficiary of my death benefit under the [NAME OF RETIREMENT PLAN] ("the Plan"). I hereby agree that if the said trust instrument is amended at any time in the future, I will provide a copy of each such amendment to you within a reasonable time.

"Signed:_____
                    (Signature of participant)

Note: Although not so specified in the proposed regulation, it would seem that the participant should not have to promise to provide copies of future amendments if the trust is in fact irrevocable as of the RBD (or on or before the date the trust is named as beneficiary, if that occurs later than the RBD).

8.4 Form to Comply with Documentation Requirement for Trust Named as Beneficiary of Retirement Benefits: at the RBD: If Copy of Trust Is Not Given to the Plan:

See "*Fourth Rule, continued: documentation requirement (at RBD)*," Chapter 6. If the participant does not send the plan administrator a copy of the actual trust instrument (along with the participant's agreement to provide copies of future amendments) (see Form 8.3), the <u>participant</u> must send the following alternative certification to the plan administrator, ON OR BEFORE the RBD (or when the trust is first named as beneficiary, if that occurs after the RBD). (This form is not required for Roth IRAs (see Chapter 5), which have no RBD.)

"To the Plan Administrator:

"I am naming the [NAME OF TRUST] ("the Trust"), established under instrument of trust dated [DATE OF TRUST] as beneficiary of death benefits under the [NAME OF RETIREMENT PLAN] ("the Plan") (see separate beneficiary designation form filed herewith). In accordance with Proposed Treasury Regulation § 1.401(a)(9)-1, D-7:

"(i) I hereby certify that the following is a complete list of all beneficiaries of the Trust with respect to the Trust's interest in the Plan (including contingent and remainderman beneficiaries with a description of the conditions on their entitlement):

[The following is this author's interpretation of what the IRS is looking for when it requires "a complete list of all beneficiaries of the Trust"; this is not an official form. The following example assumes a trust for the life benefit of the participant's spouse, with remainder to the participant's issue who are living at the death of the survivor of the participant and his spouse; it assumes there are such issue living at the participant's RBD, and that no person has the power to vary the identity or relative shares of the beneficiaries.]

"**Current beneficiary(ies)** (entitled to benefits immediately upon my death if he/she survives me): My spouse, who is entitled to all income of the trust for life, plus principal distributions if needed for medical expenses or support. If at any time after my death and during my spouse's life there is no child of mine (and no issue of a deceased child of mine) living, the trust terminates and is distributed to my spouse outright and free of trusts. My spouse's name, date of birth, address and Social Security number are [INSERT].

"Remainder beneficiary(ies) (entitled to benefits upon the death of the survivor of myself and my spouse, if they survive my spouse and me): My children in equal shares, with issue of any deceased child to take the share such deceased child would have taken had he/she survived my spouse and me. These beneficiaries take the trust property outright and free of trust on the death of the survivor of my spouse and me, or upon attaining the age of 25 years if later. The names, addresses, Social Security numbers and dates of birth of my now-living children are: [INSERT]

"Contingent beneficiary(ies): If at any time after my death neither my spouse nor any issue of mine is living, the trust terminates and is distributed to [NAME OF CONTINGENT BENEFICIARY].

"(ii) I certify that to the best of my knowledge: the above list is correct and complete; and that, within the meaning of Prop. Reg. § 1.401(a)(9)-1, D-5A, paragraphs (b)(1), (2) and (3), the trust is valid under applicable state law, all beneficiaries of the trust are identifiable and the trust will be irrevocable by its terms as of my death.

"(iii) I agree to provide you with corrected certifications to the extent that any amendment to the trust changes any information hereby or hereafter certified.

"(iv) I agree to provide to you a copy of the Trust instrument upon demand.

"Signed: _____

(Signature of participant)"

Appendix C
Checklists

1. Checklist For Meeting With Client

Here is a list of information the planner needs to gather, when meeting with a client, regarding that client's retirement benefits. This checklist will help determine what options are available for taking (or deferring) distributions from the client's various plans. The information provided here will establish the minimums the client must withdraw (to avoid penalties) and the maximum period of tax deferral available.

I.   Client Information

A.   Client: Name: _____
      Date of Birth: _____
      Current Age: _____
      Year the client turns 70½: _____
      Age on birthday in the "70½ year": _____
      IRA required beginning date: April 1, _____
(This is the RBD for the client's traditional IRAs; Roth IRAs have no "RBD." For possible delayed RBD for certain QRPs and/or grandfathered benefits, see subsequent questions.)

B.   Spouse: Name: _____
      Date of Birth: _____
      Current Age: _____
      Age on birthday that occurs
      in client's "70½ year": _____

C.   Names and birthdates of children (or other intended beneficiaries):

II.   Plan Information: Qualified Retirement Plans (QRPs)

For EACH qualified plan, obtain the following information:

A.   Name of plan: _____

B.   Sponsoring employer: _____

C.   Does client own less than 5% of the sponsoring employer? (If "yes," then client's "required beginning date" for this plan may be delayed until April 1 following the year of his retirement; see Chapter 1). _____

D.   Type: _____ Profit sharing
            _____ ESOP
            _____ 401(k)
            _____ Plain old profit sharing
       _____ Pension
            _____ Money purchase
            _____ Defined benefit
       _____ Stock bonus
       _____ Other: _____
       _____ Type of plan not determined

E.   Value of benefits as of _____: $_____

After-tax contributions or other "basis" or "investment in the contract" included in above, if any: $_____

F.   If the plan holds any life insurance on the client (see Chapter 10), complete the following:

       Insurance company name: _____
       Policy No.: _____

Face amount of policy: $_____

Cash Value: $_____

G. If the plan contains any employer stock, what is:
    (i)   the total current value of the stock $_____
    (ii)   the plan's cost basis in that stock $_____
    (iii) the net unrealized appreciation [(i) - (ii)] $_____

The NUA may receive favorable tax treatment if benefits are taken as a lump sum distribution, or if some of the stock was purchased with employee contributions; see Chapter 2.

H. "Five year averaging" eligibility:

1. If answer to any of the following is "NO," the client is not currently eligible for 5YFA treatment (see Chapter 2):

(a) Is client over 59½? _____

(b) Has client been a participant in the plan for five or more full calendar years prior to current year? _____

(c) Is it true that client has elected 5YFA treatment for no other plan in any other taxable year? _____

(d) Is it true that client has taken no distributions from any of the aggregated plans (see next question) since the most recent to occur of the following events: reaching age 59½; separation from service (common law employees only); disability (self-employeds)? _____

(e) Is the distribution occurring before January 1, 2000?

2. All employer plans of the same type must be aggregated to

determine whether there has been a distribution of the employee's entire balance. List here plans which must be aggregated:

3.   Was client born before 1936? _____ If yes, client is potentially eligible for 10YFA as well as 5YFA.

4.   Was client a participant in this plan before 1974? _____ If no, skip this question. If yes, determine:

(a) _____   Calendar <u>years</u> prior to 1974 during any part of which the client was an active participant in this plan (a whole number)

(b) _____   Calendar <u>months</u> after 1974 during any part of which client was an active participant

(c) _____   Portion eligible for 20% cap gains treatment: $c = $ (a) divided by (a + b/12)

III. <u>Plan Information: "Traditional" Individual Retirement Accounts</u>

Has client made any non-deductible contributions to traditional IRAs? If so, write the amount here: $_____ and attach most recent copy of IRS form 8606.

Complete the following for EACH traditional IRA:

A.   Name of account: _____

B.   _____ Custodian or _____ Trustee:
        _____

C.   Account No.: _____

D.   Participants other than surviving spouses: What type of contributions does this account contain?

_____   Rollover contribution from a qualified plan only
_____   Non-rollover contributions (up to $2,000/year)
_____   Both types

E.   IRA balance as of _____ : $_____

IV.   Plan Information: Roth IRAs (see Chapter 5):

Answer A, B and C if the client has any Roth IRA:

A.   Did the client "convert" all or part of any traditional IRA to a Roth IRA (not counting conversions that were "recharacterized" and therefore deemed not to have occurred), prior to attaining age 59½? (If "yes," withdrawals from a Roth IRA within five years of that conversion may subject the client to a 10% penalty.) ____

B.   If before 2001: did the client convert a traditional IRA to a Roth IRA in 1998 and elect to spread the resulting income tax over 4 years? (If "yes," withdrawals from a Roth IRA before 1/1/2001 may accelerate the taxation of the conversion.) ____

C.   If after 2002: Have five years elapsed since January 1 of the first year in which the client opened any type of Roth IRA (not counting conversions or other Roth IRA contributions that were recharacterized and therefore deemed not to have occurred)? ____

Complete D, E, F and G for EACH Roth IRA the client has:

D.   Name of account: _____

E.   _____ Custodian or _____ Trustee:

_____

F.   Account No.: _____

G.   Roth IRA balance as of _____: $_____

V.   Plan Information: 403(b) Plans

For each 403(b) plan the client participates in:

A.   Name of account: _____

B.   Name of _____ Custodian or _____ Trustee:

_____

C.   Account No.: _____

D.   This annuity (or mutual fund custodial account) is funded
by:

_____   Employer contributions other than salary
reduction
_____   Salary reduction agreement

E.   Plan value as of _____: $_____

F.   If the client has a separately accounted-for pre-1987
balance in this plan, the client may be eligible for a deferred
RBD (see Chapter 10); in this case, complete the following:

(i)   Remaining 12/31/86 balance: $_____
(ii)   Do the funds in this annuity (or account) represent only funds accumulated in the service of the client's current employer? _____

VI. Permitted Forms of Benefits: Complete for all Plans

A.   Benefit forms offered: death prior to RBD (cross out or skip if client is past RBD).

_____ Lump sum
          If yes: Is this option permitted for spouse?_____
          For other individual beneficiaries? _____
          For trusts? _____

_____ Installments over life expectancy of beneficiary
          If yes: Is this option permitted for spouse? _____
          For other individual beneficiaries? _____
          For trusts? _____

_____ Other installment options (describe):

_____ Annuity options (describe):

B.   Benefit forms offered at RBD [not applicable to Roth IRAs]:
          _____ Lump sum (suitable for rollover)

          _____ Installments payments over:
                    _____ LE of participant?
                    _____ Joint LE of participant and spouse?
                    _____ Joint LE of participant and other individual?
                    _____ Joint LE of P and trust beneficiary?

C. If installments over life expectancy are permitted, is redetermination of life expectancy:

_____ Mandatory

_____ Not permitted

_____ Participant can choose

D. Documents needed from client (check if received):
Plan description or account agreement _____
Current beneficiary designation _____

VII. "Grandfathering" information (Chapter 10)

A. TEFRA 242(b) designation

1. Did the client file a designation, before January 1, 1984, regarding the timing of distribution of his plan benefits? _____ If yes, obtain a copy of the election(s) filed, and determine:

2. Did election meet requirements of Notice 83-22? _____

3. Has client done anything which would invalidate the election? _____

4. What "catch-up" required minimum distributions would be required if the election were revoked today? $_____

B. TRA '86 § 1121(d)(d)-(5), as amended by TAMRA

1. Was the client born after 6/30/17? _____

2. Is the client a 5% owner of the employer (plan sponsor), or has client ever been a 5% owner at any time during a plan year ending on or after the calendar year (19_) in which he/she reached age 66½? _____

3.   Is the client retired? _____

If the answer to ALL THREE of these questions is "NO" then the client is grandfathered from the minimum distribution rules until actual retirement.

C.   Estate tax exclusion

1.   Did client "separate from service" prior to 1983? _____
      After 1982 but prior to 1985? _____

2.   Has client changed the "form of benefit payments" since separating from service? _____

If the answer to either part of #1 is "yes" and if the answer to #2 is "no," client's benefits are eligible for total or partial federal estate tax exclusion.

VIII. If client is already past his/her RBD (not applicable to Roth IRAs):

For each plan and IRA:

A.   Determine RBD.

B.   Obtain: Copy of beneficiary designation in effect on the RBD. If there have been any changes since the RBD (*e.g.*, benefits transferred from a plan to an IRA, or from one IRA to another; or beneficiary designation changes); obtain, in addition, copies of all beneficiary designations in effect since the RBD.

C.   Based on the beneficiary designation and plan terms in effect on the RBD, what method of determination of life expectancy was irrevocably elected then?

Client's life expectancy: _____   Redetermined annually
                               _____   Not redetermined
                                                 (term certain)

Spouse's life expectancy
(if spouse was DB):   _____   Redetermined annually
                               _____   Not redetermined
                                                 (term certain)

D.   Determine whether required minimum distributions have
been taken. Make this determination separately for (i) each
qualified plan, (ii) all 403(b) plans collectively and (iii) all
traditional IRAs collectively.

2. Rollover Checklist

This checklist presents factors to consider when deciding
whether to take money out of a "qualified retirement plan"
(QRP) (such as a Keogh, money purchase, profit sharing,
defined benefit or 401(k) plan) and "roll it over" to a traditional
IRA. This checklist does *not* cover the technical requirements
for a valid rollover (such as the 60-day time limit, or the limit on
the number of rollovers within one year). Rather, the purpose of
this checklist is to help the planner and client have confidence
that all relevant factors have been considered before money is
taken out of a qualified plan and transferred to an IRA.

This checklist does not apply to Roth IRA conversions.

For most retirees, taking money out of an employer-
sponsored retirement plan, and rolling over the distribution to an
IRA, is an attractive way to increase their investment control,
and the distribution flexibility, of their retirement benefits.
However, the move from QRP to IRA (or, in the case of a
surviving spouse dealing with inherited benefits, the change
from a plan in the decedent's name to an IRA in the spouse's
name) should not be made without a careful review of many

factors, great and small, which may affect the desirability of such a step. It is unfortunate when benefits are transferred for one particular good reason (such as the ability to self-direct investments), and it is later discovered that, due to other factors not considered, the change has been disadvantageous.

The planning factors to be considered differ depending on whether the client is a—

- **PE**: Participating employee who earned the benefits in his plan, but does not own the employer business or control the administration of the plan.

- **SS**: Surviving spouse, dealing with a plan benefit or IRA inherited from a deceased spouse.

- **SBO**: Small business owner, for whom the question is not solely whether to transfer the benefits to another type of plan but whether to terminate the qualified plan altogether. This checklist addresses only the issues facing the SBO whose plan covers no other employees. A plan which covers other employees besides the SBO involves many additional factors not considered here.

The checklist assumes that the participant is not losing any vesting or accrual of benefits by transferring out of the qualified plan, or has decided to forego available further vesting and accrual; and does not address whether there should be a termination of employment at a particular time.

Not all subjects mentioned in the checklist are discussed in the text. When a checklist item is discussed at greater length in the text, a cross-reference is provided.

1.   Consider the loss of the ability to receive a "lump sum distribution" (LSD).

PE, SS, SBO: A distribution of all benefits from a qualified plan within one taxable year may qualify for special treatment as a LSD under § 402. See Chapter 2. IRA distributions are never eligible for LSD treatment. Once benefits come out of a qualified plan and go into an IRA, this favorable treatment is lost—although if the rollover IRA is kept separate from other IRAs, the favorable treatment can in some cases be restored later by rolling back to another qualified plan (see 4(A), below).

2.   Consider the other advantages of a qualified plan that you may be giving up:

In addition to the special LSD treatment available for some qualified plan distributions, qualified plans offer certain features that IRAs do not. (Sometimes these advantages can be restored by rolling back to a qualified plan; see 4(A), below.)

A. **Creditor protection**. PE, SS, SBO: Both qualified plans and IRAs can offer some protection from creditors, and neither is completely invulnerable. Generally speaking, however, qualified plans are more protected than IRAs.

B. **Loans**. PE, SBO: Qualified plans often permit plan participants to take loans from the plan. IRAs cannot do this.

C. **Investment alternatives**. SBO: IRAs cannot invest in "collectibles." Also, due to the requirement of having an institutional trustee or custodian, IRAs are effectively limited to investing in assets the institution is willing to hold—which may not include partnerships, venture investments or other non-publicly traded or offbeat investments you would like to hold.

PE, SS: A large, employer-run plan may offer professional investment management superior to, and cheaper than, what you can provide through a self-directed IRA.

D. **Choice of trustee.** SBO: Although you can be trustee of your own business's plan, you cannot be trustee or custodian of your IRA. However, except for the issue of investment alternatives (C, above), this is rarely a significant factor, since a "self-directed IRA" can be easily obtained with no trustee's fee and a nominal custodial fee.

E. **Life Insurance.** PE, SBO: An IRA cannot hold life insurance. Thus, any existing policies must be canceled, distributed or purchased from the qualified plan before the plan benefits are "rolled" to an IRA. See Chapter 10. Cancellation may involve loss of needed benefits. Distribution requires payment of income tax on the policy's value, and loss of the potential for further income tax deferral on this value. Purchase of the policy for its cash value may be costly. On the bright side, distribution or purchase of the policy allows the participant to transfer the policy to an irrevocable trust, removing it from his taxable estate, which may be better for the family in the long run than leaving it in the plan indefinitely.

F. **Distribution Options**. PE, SS, SBO: A QRP may offer annuity alternatives that are effectively subsidized by the plan. For example, the plan's "joint and survivor annuity" option may offer a married couple who are in good health a better value than the supposedly "equal value" lump sum distribution. Alternatively, actuarial factors (especially changing interest rates) may radically change the amount of your "lump sum distribution" from a defined benefit pension plan over a few months. If the plan offers subsidized annuities, and there are substantial dollars involved, consider hiring a professional actuary to evaluate the alternatives offered by the plan before opting for a lump sum.

G. **State tax issues.** PE, SS, SBO: Certain states exempt from income tax all pensions paid by defined benefit plans; this exemption would cease to apply to benefits that had been rolled over to an IRA. It is essential to review the tax laws of the taxpayer's state of domicile (and of the state taxpayer plans to retire in) before changing the status of retirement benefits.

H. **Contribution limits.** SBO: The maximum IRA contribution of $2,000/year (or 15% of income, maximum $22,500, for a SEP-IRA) is less than the maximum qualified plan contribution, which is 25% of income, maximum $30,000 (or, potentially, much more for a defined benefit plan).

I. **After tax contributions**. PE, SBO: An employee's after-tax contributions to a plan cannot be rolled over to an IRA. Thus, terminating participation in the plan will require distribution of the after-tax contribution account and loss of further tax deferral on the earnings from this amount.

J. **TEFRA 242(b) election**. Rolling from a qualified plan to an IRA automatically terminates any TEFRA 242(b) election in effect for the plan. Such termination causes acceleration of any previously postponed required "minimum distributions." See Chapter 10.

K. **Distributions before age 59½.** PE, SBO: Generally, distributions before reaching age 59½ are subject to a 10% penalty. See Chapter 9. There are various exceptions, and the exceptions applicable to QRPs differ from those available for IRAs. By transferring benefits to an IRA, you may lose the exceptions you would have qualified for had the money remained in the QRP (or, alternatively, you may become eligible for more helpful exceptions).

L. **Distributions before age 59½.** SS: See *"Drawbacks of spousal rollover,"* Chapter 3.

M. **Loss of federal estate tax exclusion for grandfathered individuals**. An employee who separated from service prior to 1985 and has not since changed the form of distribution of his benefits may be entitled to have all or part of his remaining benefits excluded from his federal gross estate. See Chapter 10. This favorable tax treatment will be lost for benefits rolled to an IRA.

3. **Consider the advantages an IRA has over a QRP.**

A. **Investment alternatives**. PE, SS: The self-directed IRA offers more control of, and alternatives for, investment than the typical employer plan. This feature is attractive if you have the knowledge, skill and time to manage your own investments or to select and supervise an investment manager. This is not a factor for the SBO who can control his own plan's investments in much the same manner as an IRA.

B. **Administrative costs.** SBO: An IRA does not have to file the annual form 5500, and in general has minimal to non-existent administrative expenses, compared to a QRP.

C. **Distribution options.** PE: To achieve maximum income tax deferral, the most desirable distribution option is usually (at the RBD), "installments over the joint life expectancy of the participant and designated beneficiary (DB)" or (in case of death prior to the RBD) "installments over the life expectancy of the DB." See Chapter 1. These options are often not offered at all by employer-maintained plans, or, if offered, are limited to only certain beneficiaries such as the spouse. Most self-directed IRAs offered by mutual funds, brokerage firms and banks provide all distribution options permitted by the tax laws.

D. **Distribution options.** SBO: Although the SBO can draft his plan to provide every conceivable desired distribution option, as a practical matter, once the SBO dies or retires, the "employer" ceases to exist. Continuation of the plan may require expensive legal maneuvering or be legally impossible. Since surviving beneficiaries (with the sole exception of the spouse) cannot roll over inherited plan benefits to an IRA, it may be wise to get the plan terminated, and the benefits transferred to an IRA which has the desired distribution options, before death.

E. **Distribution options.** SS: By rolling over the deceased spouse's benefits to an IRA in her own name, the SS can generally achieve maximum income tax deferral by naming her own DB. Then, upon her subsequent death (or attaining age 70½) the benefits can be distributed over the DB's life expectancy (or the joint life expectancy of the SS and DB). See Chapter 1. In contrast, if the SS leaves the benefits in the decedent's plan, then the benefits will have to be distributed over the remaining joint life expectancy of the deceased spouse and the SS (if the deceased spouse died after his RBD) or (if the deceased spouse died before his RBD) over only the SS's life expectancy (or, if the decedent died before the end of the year in which he would have reached age 70½, and the SS *also* dies before that time, see Chapter 3).

F. **State tax law issues.** PE, SS, SBO: See 2(G) above.

G. **Freedom from REA requirements**. PE, SBO: The spouse of a qualified plan participant has an automatic legal right under the Retirement Equity Act of 1984 to receive part of the participant's death benefits and (in the case of a pension plan) retirement benefits. See Chapters 3 and 4. These rights can be eliminated by transferring the benefits to an IRA (since IRAs are not subject to REA) although, in the case of all pension plans and some profit sharing plans, the distribution of a lump sum to the participant will require the spouse's consent.

4. **What IRA will you put the distribution into?**

A. SBO, PE: If the distribution is coming from a qualified plan, it can eventually be returned to a qualified plan, and regain some or all of the advantages of qualified plan benefits listed at 1 and 2 above, if the distribution is kept in a separate "rollover" IRA, and is not commingled with other ("contributory") IRAs. This option is not available for a SS.

B. PE, SS, SBO: If you are past your RBD when you receive the distribution, do not roll it into an IRA without first making sure that the beneficiary designation of the IRA is what you want it to be. Since you are past your RBD, you must withdraw the benefits over the joint life expectancy of yourself and your designated beneficiary (DB). A SS can create a new IRA to receive the new distribution, with a new DB, and use the joint life expectancy of the SS and new DB to measure distributions. SBOs and PEs who receive an eligible rollover distribution after the RBD for the distributing plan will have already established a maximum payout period for the benefits, but could inadvertently shorten it by rolling the benefits to an IRA with the "wrong" DB. See Chapters 1 and 3.

5. **Other things to remember.**

A. If you cannot decide what to do, and want to think

about it for a while, do NOT in the meantime take a partial distribution from the qualified plan to pay for living expenses (*e.g.*) while you consider the question of what to do with the rest of the benefits. A partial distribution may permanently end eligibility for favorable LSD treatment later. See Chapter 2.

B. When the time comes to take the distribution, do it as a "direct rollover" from the plan trustee directly to the IRA, rather than as a distribution followed by a rollover. A distribution will be subject to the 20% withholding tax even though it is going to be entirely rolled over.

3. Trust Review Questionnaire

The purpose of this questionnaire is to help the person who is reviewing or drafting a trust agreement determine whether the trust complies with the "trust rules" of the IRS's proposed minimum distribution regulations ($\S$ 1.401(a)(9)-1), so that the participant (P) who names such trust as beneficiary of his retirement benefits will be deemed to have a "designated beneficiary" (DB). Section references refer to that proposed Treasury regulation.

Apply these questions to the trust. If the benefits are required by the terms of the trust and/or beneficiary designation to be paid only to one (or more) particular share(s) of the trust, apply these questions only to that (or those) share(s). Explanations of the questions are found in the cross referenced sections of this book.

The relevant date for applying these questions is (except as otherwise noted) P's required beginning date (RBD), or (if he dies before that date) the date of death. If the trust is not named as beneficiary until after the RBD, the test is applied as of the date the trust is named as beneficiary; however, the ability to use the trust beneficiary's life expectancy to measure required distributions in that case (even if the trust passes this test with flying colors) may be limited by P's choices of beneficiary made at and since the RBD.

The explanations include some suggestions for "cleanup mode" (the client has already died or passed his RBD, and this trust was P's beneficiary on the critical date). If you are in "planning mode" (you are reviewing the trust BEFORE the date of death, and BEFORE the RBD, or BEFORE the trust has been named as beneficiary), you can correct any problems by amending the trust or changing to a different beneficiary prior to the date of death (or RBD).

Start at the beginning, with Question one. Then proceed to where your answer directs you. Do NOT answer all questions; answer only those which you are directed to answer by your answers to previous questions. Some answers may lead you into THE GRAY AREA, where this author cannot guarantee that your trust "passes," but on the other hand it might be just fine.

1. Is the trust valid under applicable state law, or will it be valid under applicable state law once it is funded?
If yes, go to Question 2.
If no, go to ANSWER A.

See "*First Rule: trust must be valid under state law*," Chapter 6.

2. Is the trust irrevocable, or will it become irrevocable upon P's death?
If yes, go to Question 3.
If no, go to ANSWER A.

See "*The new requirement as to irrevocability*," Chapter 6.

3. If P is past his RBD, did he provide the required documentation to the plan administrator on or before the RBD (or on or before the date the trust was named as his beneficiary, if that occurred after the RBD)?

If not applicable, go to Question 4.

If yes, go to Question 6.

If no, but the "plan" is an IRA, go to THE GRAY AREA.

Otherwise, go to ANSWER A.

Explanation: See *"Fourth Rule, continued: documentation requirement (at RBD),"* Chapter 6.

4. If P died before his RBD, did (or will) the trustee of the trust that is named as beneficiary provide the required documentation to the plan administrator by the end of the ninth month beginning after the date of death?

If not applicable, [because P is still living and has not reached his RBD] go to Question 6.

If yes, go to Question 5.

If no, but the "plan" is an IRA, go to THE GRAY AREA.

Otherwise, go to ANSWER A.

Explanation: See *"Fourth Rule: documentation requirement (death before RBD),"* Chapter 6.

5. If P died before his RBD, was the first distribution paid out from the retirement plan to the trust (or will it be paid out) by the end of the calendar year following the year in which death occurred?

If yes, go to Question 6.

If no, go to Bonus Question #1.

Explanation: See *"Distributions must commence by year after death,"* Chapter 1.

6. All individual beneficiaries, part 1: "The estate" as beneficiary of the trust: Does the trust contain a provision allowing or requiring the trustee to pay trust assets to P's estate or to pay P's debts, administration expenses, funeral expenses, estate taxes and/or bequests to non-individual beneficiaries under P's will, and is it possible under the trust that retirement benefits could be used by the trustee for these payments?

If no, go to Question 7.

If yes, go to THE GRAY AREA.

Explanation: See *"Paying estate expenses, taxes, etc. from the trust,"* Chapter 6.

7. All individual beneficiaries, part 2: Is the trust a "100% grantor trust" with respect to an individual beneficiary under Code § 678?

If yes, go to Answer B.

If no, go to Question 8.

Explanation: See *"The 100% Grantor Trust,"* Chapter 6.

8. All individual beneficiaries, part 3: Is the trust a "conduit trust" as to one or more individual beneficiaries?

If yes, go to Answer B.

If no, go to Question 9.

Explanation: See *"The MRD Conduit Trust,"* Chapter 6.

9. All individual beneficiaries, part 4: If all present and potential future beneficiaries of the trust who are living on the applicable date (and later-born siblings of such now-living beneficiaries) live until their life expectancy (under IRS tables), will the trust assets all *necessarily* be distributed to individuals?

If definitely yes, go to Question 10.

If probably yes depending on the future fertility of the said individuals, go to THE GRAY AREA.

Otherwise (*i.e.* "No"), go to Answer A.

Explanation: See generally "Who Are the Beneficiaries of a Trust?" and in particular *"Disregarding certain contingent beneficiaries,"* Chapter 6.

    10.   **Is it possible to identify with certainty the oldest person who could ever possibly be a beneficiary of this trust?**

If "definitely yes," go to Question 11.

If one or more older beneficiaries could be added later, *but* any such future-older-added-beneficiary could share in the trust only if a prior, currently-existing individual beneficiary dies before his or her life expectancy, go to Question 11.

Otherwise (*i.e.*, one or more older beneficiaries could be added later, and you cannot prove that any such future-older-added beneficiary could share in the trust ONLY if a prior, currently existing individual beneficiary dies before his or her life expectancy), go to ANSWER A.

Explanation: see *"Second Rule: beneficiaries must be identifiable,"* Chapter 6.

    11.   **Does any person have a power of appointment over the benefits the exercise of which is not limited to a narrow clearly defined group?**

If definitely no, go to Answer B.

If yes, but such power will affect the ownership or enjoyment of the benefits only after the death of a prior beneficiary, AND if such prior beneficiary lives to his or her life expectancy the power will not affect the ownership or enjoyment of the benefits at all, go to Answer B.

Otherwise, go to THE GRAY AREA.

Explanation: See "*Effect of powers of appointment,*" Chapter 6.

BONUS QUESTIONS. Do not answer any of these questions unless you have been specifically directed to answer such question by your answer to another question!

Bonus Question #1: Is the surviving spouse the *sole* beneficiary of the trust?
>   If definitely yes, go to Bonus Question #2.
>   If definitely no, go to ANSWER A.
>   If maybe, go to the GRAY AREA.

Explanation: See "*When is a trust for the spouse the same as the spouse?*, Chapter 6.
Definitely yes: The surviving spouse is *definitely* the "sole beneficiary" of the trust if either: (a) she is treated as the sole owner of all of the trust's income and principal under § 678, which would be the case if she has the unlimited right to withdraw all principal and income of the trust ("100% grantor trust") (see Question 7); or (b) distributions will be made from the plan to the trust over a period not exceeding the surviving spouse's life expectancy *and* all distributions made from the plan during her life will be distributed outright to her from the trust ("conduit trust") (see Question 8).
Definitely no: If there are other beneficiaries of the trust who may receive distributions from the trust during the surviving spouse's lifetime, the answer is "definitely no."
Maybe: If there are no other beneficiaries during the surviving spouse's lifetime, and the surviving spouse is the oldest trust beneficiary, and she will receive all income of the trust, but does not have the absolute right to receive all plan distributions made

during her lifetime, go to the GRAY AREA.

Bonus Question #2: Was the first distribution paid out from the retirement plan or IRA to the trust (or will it be paid out) by the end of the calendar year in which P would have reached age 70½?

If yes, go back to (regular) Question 6.
If no, go to ANSWER A.

Explanation: See *"When MRDs must start if P dies before his RBD,"* Chapter 3.

THE GRAY AREA

These are unresolved questions regarding the IRS's treatment of retirement benefits payable to trusts. If your trust is in THE GRAY AREA, it cannot be given an automatic "clean bill of health" as is, but that does not necessarily mean you must go to ANSWER A because: in most of these matters the IRS has not spoken clearly; or, if the IRS has spoken clearly, the IRS might change its mind or be held wrong in court. Issues that land you in THE GRAY AREA are:

Questions 3 and 4: Who is plan administrator of an IRA: See *"To whom is documentation provided?"* Chapter 6. **Cleanup mode:** If the required documentation was not provided to the IRA custodian or trustee, consider taking the position that P was the "plan administrator" of his own IRA, and therefore the documentation requirement was met (because P had a copy of his own trust). If you take this position, either get a ruling on your situation, or prepare for possible IRS challenge, and proceed to Question 5. If not willing to take this position, then capitulate and go to ANSWER A.

Question 6: Trust paying debts, expenses and taxes of estate: See *"Fifth Rule: all trust beneficiaries must be* *individuals*," and the three subsections that follow it, Chapter 6. **Cleanup mode:** Either get a ruling on your situation, or prepare for possible IRS challenge, or capitulate and go to ANSWER A. If you are not capitulating, proceed to Question 7.

Question 9: Trust does not clearly vest in currently living individuals even if they live to their life expectancy: If the trust will be paid to individuals only *if* currently living individuals produce issue, but there are non-individual beneficiaries who will take in case of default of issue, it is not clear whether the trust passes the "all beneficiaries are individuals" test. See "*Disregarding certain contingent beneficiaries*," Chapter 6. **Cleanup mode:** If you are confident that your trust is payable to designated beneficiaries based on a "reasonable interpretation of the statute and proposed regulations," you could answer "yes" (consider applying for an IRS ruling to back you up) and proceed to Question 10; or capitulate and go to ANSWER A.

Question 11: See "*Sixth Rule: no changing beneficiaries after P's death*" and "*Effect of powers of appointment*," Chapter 6.

Bonus Questions 1 and 2: See "*When is a trust for the spouse the same as the spouse?*" Chapter 6. **Cleanup mode:** if you fit within the favorable IRS rulings, consider whether you want to rely on them as a "reasonable interpretation of the statute" and answer yes to Bonus Question 1; or (alternatively) capitulate and go to ANSWER A.

ANSWERS. When you arrive here, you have reached the end of the quiz. Your answer is:

ANSWER A: Bad news: this trust "flunks" the minimum distribution trust rules of the IRS's proposed regulations. If benefits are payable to this trust, P has "no DB." If P is still alive and has not yet reached his RBD, you can correct the problem by amending the trust or changing to a different beneficiary prior to the date of death (or RBD). If P is already deceased or past his RBD, then see, for the consequences of having "no DB," *"The five year rule and its exceptions," "What happens at the RBD,"* or (if the trust is first being named as beneficiary after P's RBD) *"Changing DBs after the RBD,"* Chapter 1. However, the IRS's proposed regulations do not have the force of law; before concluding that there is no hope, see *"Legal status of proposed regulations,"* Chapter 1. See also, for the possibility of fixing the problem after P's death before the RBD, *"Cleanup strategies: death before RBD."*

ANSWER B: Congratulations! Your trust passes the test. Remember, however, that if P has not yet died or reached his RBD, continued qualification will depend on providing required documentation to the "plan administrator" before the RBD (or by the end of the ninth month after the date of death in case of death before the RBD) (see Questions 3 and 4); and that any amendment of the trust will necessitate another pass through this checklist (as well as providing a copy of the amendment to the plan administrator, if P is past his RBD). For the results of passing this test, see *"Effects of complying with (or flunking) the trust rules,"* Chapter 6.

Appendix D

Software

There are several software programs designed to assist professionals in evaluating retirement distribution options. Unfortunately, there was not time to evaluate the newest versions of the major programs before publication of this edition of *Life and Death Planning for Retirement Benefits*. Watch the Ataxplan Publications website **www.ataxplan.com** and <u>Choate's Notes</u> newsletter for future reviews of these programs. This Appendix describes the programs available and tells how to obtain more information. For review of the pre-59½ analysis features of some of these programs, see Chapter 9.

Brentmark Software: Pension & Roth IRA Analyzer (v. 5.10). $449. Includes 6 months' free maintenance. 60 days returnable for full refund. Brentmark has updated and renamed its excellent "Pension and Excise Tax Planner" software to enable planners and their clients to analyze proposed plan distribution strategies from QRPs, IRAs and Roth IRAs (comparing up to 4 scenarios simultaneously), including income tax, estate tax and spousal rollover aspects, and determine whether it is worthwhile to convert a traditional IRA to a Roth IRA, as well as making numerous other useful determinations regarding retirement plan distributions, such as pre-59½ distributions (see review in Chapter 9), impact of life insurance and annual exclusion gifting. The new version promises to produce client-friendly and customizable reports. Brentmark also offers two "mini" programs, "Pension Distributions Calculator" (v. 4.0, $149), for quick minimum distribution projections, and "Roth Optimizer." Brentmark Software, Inc., 3505 Lake Lynda Drive #212, Orlando FL 32817-8327; 1-800-879-6665 or 407-679-6555; or visit **www.brentmark.com** for a downloadable demo.

Ocaso Software Company: 2nd ½ (v. 1.0). $700. A newcomer, "2nd ½" is nevertheless the product of a veteran in the distribution-planning software wars, Kit Mueller, who left his prior firm to co-found Ocaso. This product, which is just shipping its first disks as this book goes to press, ambitiously seeks to "do it all" in distribution planning with (paraphrasing from the brochure) user-friendly menu driven interface, distributions to insurance trusts, charity, CRT or CLT, multi-generation IRA rollover analysis, lump sum distribution of employer securities, and "stunning and understandable client presentations." Info at **www.ocaso.net**, or: Ocaso Software Company, 322 NW Fifth Ave Suite 207, Portland OR 97209; (503) 248-4746 or (877) 622-7600.

R Planner v. 2.0. $330. Another excellent (though less comprehensive) software product to help professionals evaluate Roth conversions and minimum distribution alternatives. Easy to learn and use; good for quick analysis with client-understandable reports. The website **www.rplanner.com** provides a downloadable trial copy of this product, or call (941) 598-3730 for more information.

Numbercruncher. $349. This is not a retirement distributions analysis product, but it does pre-59½ distribution calculations (see review in Chapter 9) as well has 51 estate planning calculations. Indispensable tool for estate planners. Leimberg & LeClair Inc., PO Box 1332, Bryn Mawr, PA 19010, (610) 527-5216. Spectacular website **www.leimberg.com**.

TigerTables. $199. Not a retirement distribution analyzer, but an excellent, easy-to-use source of estate planning computations such as QPRT, CRUT, GRAT, etc. Developed by estate planning expert Larry Katzenstein, Esq., who says the IRS estate audit staff use this product. Visit **www.tigertables.com**.

Bibliography

<u>Estate Planning</u> is a magazine published by Warren Gorham & Lamont, 31 St. James Ave., Boston, MA 02116.

"TMP" refers to the "Tax Management Portfolio" series published by the Bureau of National Affairs, Inc., 1231 25th St., N.W., Washington, D.C. 20037.

"CCH" stands for Commerce Clearing House, Inc., 4025 W. Peterson Ave., Chicago, IL 60646-6085.

<u>ACTEC Notes</u> magazine is published by the American College of Trust and Estate Counsel, 3415 South Sepulveda Boulevard, Los Angeles, CA 90034, (310) 398-1888.

Introduction: Books and Other Resources on Retirement Plans and Estate Planning Generally

Stephen J. Krass, *The Pension Answer Book*, 1999 edition (Panel Publishers, (800) 638-8437, $136). Far and away the best handy desktop reference work on pension topics I have encountered. Mainly deals with "employer" issues such as the design, funding and qualification of retirement plans, but several chapters have material on distributions.

A Professional's Guide to the IRA Distribution Rules, by Seymour Goldberg, CPA, MBA, JD (300 pages, softbound, Foundation for Accounting Education, 4th ed. 1998). The new edition of the distribution book that started it all. In 500+ questions and answers, the author guides the reader through the tax rules applicable to IRA distributions: pre-59½, inherited IRAs, minimum distributions, excess distributions, etc. May be purchased for $39.95 + $3 shipping by calling (800) 537-3635.

By the same author, *Pension Distributions: Planning Strategies, Cases and Rulings* (2d ed., 300 pages; $59.50 plus $4 shipping; call (800) 877-4522). Covers many subjects discussed in this book and in addition provides: sample letters to clients; information about IRS audits and plan loans.

Estate and Gift Tax Issues for Employee Benefit Plans, by Louis A. Mezzullo, Esq. (TMP 378, 1996) and *An Estate Planner's Guide to Qualified Retirement Plan Benefits* by the same author (American Bar Assoc., Section of Real Property, Probate and Trust Law, 1992) are excellent overviews of the subject. The former also covers subjects not covered in this book, including descriptions of the different types of retirement plans, non-qualified deferred compensation plans, REA rights, QDROs, and gift and estate tax issues.

For treatment of annuities, non-qualified plans, withholding rules, rollover details and many other distribution topics not covered in depth (or at all) in this book, I highly recommend *Retirement Benefits Tax Guide*, 2d ed. (in one volume) by Thomas F. Rutherford, J.D. (CCH, (800) 248-3248, $189).

For 403(b) plans in general and TIAA-CREF plans in particular, the unsurpassed resource is two articles by Irving Schloss, Esq., and Deborah Abildsoe, Esq., both published in Tax Management <u>Estates, Gifts and Trusts Journal</u>, "A Roadmap through TIAA-CREF" (Vol. 22, p. 151, July-August 1997) and "Off the Map: More on TIAA-CREF and Paradoxes of Retirement Planning" (Vol. 23 No. 3, p. 107, May-June 1998). These authors are publishing a book on this topic through Oxford Press; when available it will be announced on the Ataxplan website, www.ataxplan.com, or call Ms. Abildsoe at (203) 453-9075.

Chapter 2:   Income Tax Matters

For more about IRD, see Alan S. Acker, *Income in Respect of a Decedent*, TMP 862.

For discussion of withholding rules applicable to plan distributions, and more discussion of lump sum distributions, see Frederick J. Benjamin, Jr., Esq., *Qualified Plans: Taxation of Distributions*, TMP 370-2d (1992).

For lump sum distributions see also *Taxation of Distributions from Qualified Plans*, by Diane Bennett *et al.*, Warren, Gorham & Lamont, ch. 5.1.

For further information on cases defining "separation from service," and determining whether a distribution is "on account of" such a separation, a good place to start is the 1999 CCH *Standard Federal Tax Reporter*, ¶ 18,217A.082.

For fiduciary income tax, see *Federal Income Taxation of Estates, Trusts and Beneficiaries*, by Howard Zaritsky, Esq., et al. (Warren, Gorham & Lamont), and *Preparing Fiduciary Income Tax Returns*, by Jeremiah W. Doyle IV, Esq., <u>et al.</u> MCLE, 10 Winter Place, Boston, MA 02108, 1997.

Chapter 3:   Marital Matters

For more information on spousal waivers under REA, see Lynn Wintriss, Esq. "Practice Tips: Waiver of Rights Under the Retirement Equity Act and Premarital Agreements," 19 <u>ACTEC Notes</u>, no. 2, Fall 1993.

For an excellent discussion of the spousal consent requirements of REA, see Alson R. Martin, P.A., "Income and Estate Planning for Individuals with Qualified Retirement Plans and IRAs," in <u>How to Determine the Capital Necessary to Retire</u>, seminar materials published by ALI-ABA, 4025 Chestnut Street, Philadelphia, PA   19104-3099, 10/28/93, pages 107 to 114.

Chapter 4:   Retirement Benefits and the Non-Citizen Spouse

For requirements of the marital deduction when the surviving spouse is not a U.S. citizen, see CCH *Federal Estate and Gift Tax Reporter*, ¶ 7650 *et seq.*

Chapter 5:   Roth IRAs

Mervin M. Wilf, Esq., "The Roth IRA: A New Estate Planning Opportunity," in <u>Estate Planner's Alert</u>, October 1997, page 11 (Research Institute of America), and "Innovative Estate Planning Strategies Using Roth IRAs," <u>Estate Planning</u> March/April 1998 (Vol. 25, No. 3) page 99.

Michael J. Jones, CPA, "Roth IRA Gifts May Terminate Income Tax Benefits," <u>Tax Notes</u>, 6/1/98, p. 1156,

For a discussion of the hidden pitfalls built into the assumptions used in financial and tax planning software, see *The*

Terrible Truth About Investing by Bruce J. Temkin (Fairfield Press, 1998; 1-888-820-5958; $24.95 plus shipping), p. 223.

A thorough treatment of Roth IRAs in layman's language, complete with economic analysis and financial projections (both generally and to illustrate specific case studies) is the *Roth IRA Book: An Investor's Guide*, by Gobind Daryanani, Ph. D. (Digiqual Inc., Bernardsville, NJ, 1998; $34.95). Call toll-free 1 (877) Roth911, or visit www.rothirabook.com.

Chapter 7:   Charitable Giving with Retirement Benefits

The Harvard Manual on Tax Aspects of Charitable Giving, by the late David M. Donaldson, Esq., and Carolyn M. Osteen, Esq. (Seventh edition, 1992) is a magnificent summary of sophisticated charitable giving techniques, replete with citations. When using it, keep in mind that it was written from the point of view of counsel for the charitable donee. Wait for the new edition (written by Carolyn M. Osteen), due out in the fall of 1999. The *Manual* can be obtained, for a donation ($60 for the 1992 edition) by calling The Harvard University Office of Planned Giving, Cambridge, MA 02138.

Conrad Teitell, Esq., is one of the country's top experts in the tax law of charitable giving, and fortunately for the rest of us he is also a prolific author and superb public speaker. For a complete catalogue of his books, newsletters and amazing seminars, call (800) 243-9122

Zoe M. Hicks, Esq., "Charitable Remainder Trust may be more Advantageous than a Qualified Plan," Estate Planning (5-6/90, p. 158). This is not about estate planning for plan benefits, but rather about using a CRUT *instead of* a qualified plan as an accumulation/payout vehicle for retirement.

Jonathan G. Blattmachr, Esq., "Income in Respect of a Decedent," 12 Probate Notes 47 (1986). This excellent article discusses numerous strategies for reducing taxes on retirement benefits and other IRD, including charitable dispositions.

Roger L. Shumaker, Esq., and Michael G. Riley, Esq., "Strategies for Transferring Retirement Plan Death Benefits to

Charity," 19 ACTEC Notes, no. 3, p. 162 (1993), and follow-up comments published in 20 ACTEC Notes, p. 22 (1994). Compares the economic effects of various ways of funding a $1 million charitable gift from a $4 million estate, including the use of retirement benefits.

Louis A. Mezzullo, Esq., "Using an IRA for Charitable Giving," March/April 1995 Probate & Property, the Journal of the ABA Section of Real Property, Probate and Trust Law, p. 41.

Chapter 8:   Disclaimers

See, generally, on disclaimers, the CCH *Federal Estate and Gift Tax Reporter;* or the RIA *Federal Tax Coordinator 2d;* or Mary Moers Wenig, Esq., *Disclaimers* (TMP 848, 1992).

Chapter 9:   Pre-Age 59½ Distributions

Toolson, Richard B., "Structuring Substantially Equal Payments to Avoid the Premature Withdrawal Penalty," Journal of Taxation, Nov 1990, page 276.

The "applicable federal rates" published monthly by the IRS can be obtained from the website **www.tigertables.com**; for readers who can afford a subscription, from the Daily Tax Report published by BNA; and from the Leimberg & LeClair (phone (610) 525-6957) "FaxNet Newsletter" which provides these rates (along with other interest rates and indicators) to subscribers by fax monthly.

Chapter 10:   Life Insurance, Grandfathers and Other

For an excellent discussion of life insurance in the retirement plan, see Beverly R. Budin, Esq., *Life Insurance*, TMP 826.

Another work on this subject is the *Life Insurance Answer Book: For Qualified Plans and Estate Planning*, 2d ed., edited by Gary S. Lesser, Esq., and Lawrence C. Starr, CLU etc., with 30 contributing authors (a Panel Publication of Aspen

Publishers, (800) 638-8437, 1999).

For more on life insurance in qualified plans, see CCH *Pension Plan Guide*, Vol. 1A, ¶ 3808 *et seq.* ¶ 4540 discusses "prohibited transactions."

Regarding "subtrusts," see: "The Qualified Plan as an Estate Planning Tool," by Andrew J. Fair, Esq., booklet distributed by Guardian Life Insurance Co. Of America, 201 Park Ave. South, New York, NY 10003; "Estate Tax on Life Insurance Held in Qualified Plans," by Mervin M. Wilf, Esq., in Retirement Plan Trio seminar 6/22/95, materials published by ALI-ABA, 4025 Chestnut St., Philadelphia, PA 19104-3099 (Publ. No. Q239); "IRS opens the way toward favorable estate and income tax treatment of plan distributions," by Kenneth C. Eliasberg, Esq., Estate Planning (7/83, p. 208); "Subtrusts and Reversionary Interests: A Review of Current Options," by I. Meyer Pincus, L.L.B., Journal of the American Society of CLU & ChFC (9/92, p. 64); "Excluding Qualified Plan Insured Incidental Death Benefits from the Participant's Gross Estate; Minority and Non-Stockholders," by Jonathan Davis, Esq., The Estates, Gifts and Trusts Journal (9-10/83, p.4); "Excluding Defined Benefit Plan Insured Death Benefits from the Gross Estate -- Sole and Majority Shareholders," by Jonathan Davis, Esq., Tax Management Compensation Planning Journal (5/84, p. 123).

Creditors' rights:

For an excellent discussion of the status of retirement benefits as against claims of creditors, see Alson R. Martin, P.A., "Income and Estate Planning for Individuals with Qualified Retirement Plans and IRAs," in How to Determine the Capital Necessary to Retire, seminar materials published by ALI-ABA, 4025 Chestnut Street, Philadelphia, PA 19104-3099, 10/28/93, pages 116 to 122.

Glossary

This book assumes the reader is familiar with estate planning concepts and general retirement plan terminology. This Glossary provides brief definitions of terms in these specialized fields to accommodate readers who do not have expertise in both fields. Terms that are an integral part of estate and tax planning for retirement benefits (such as "rollover" and "IRD") are defined in the text dealing with that topic, not here.

Bypass Trust. See "Credit Shelter Trust."

Charitable Remainder Trust. A trust which lasts for either a term of years or the life or lives of specified individuals. The term (or life) beneficiary(ies) are individuals and the remainder beneficiary is one or more charities. In this book, "charitable remainder trust" (CRT) means a charitable remainder annuity trust (under which the non-charitable beneficiary receives a fixed dollar amount every year) or charitable remainder unitrust (under which the non-charitable beneficiary receives a fixed percentage of the value of the trust's assets each year) which complies with § 664. A CRT pays no income tax (although the non-charitable beneficiary may be subject to income tax on distributions from the trust). The person who funds the trust receives either an estate tax deduction (if the transfer occurs at death) or an income and gift tax deduction (for lifetime transfers) for the value of the charitable remainder interest. For more information, see the Bibliography under Chapter 7.

Credit shelter trust. The Code allows each person a tax credit which may be applied to gift or estate taxes otherwise due on transfers by that person. To the extent the credit is not used for lifetime transfers, it is available to shelter the person's estate from estate taxes. Because it may be applied to either gift or estate taxes, it is referred to as a "unified" credit.

The maximum credit allowed for deaths or gifts in 1999 is equal to the estate tax on a taxable estate of $650,000. Therefore, the effect of the credit is that each person can transfer up to $650,000 free of gift or estate taxes to his children, or any other beneficiary who is not the person's spouse or a charity. (*Unlimited* amounts may be transferred tax-free to the spouse or charity.) The credit amount/exemption equivalent is scheduled to increase gradually over the years so that, for deaths in 2006 and later, the exemption is $1 million.

Basic tax-oriented estate planning for a husband and wife involves making sure that each spouse takes full advantage of the federal estate tax exemption, most commonly by making sure that the first spouse to die leaves the exemption amount either to the children or grandchildren directly, or to a trust for their ultimate benefit. The surviving spouse may be a beneficiary of this trust, but does not have sufficient control over it to make it includible in his or her estate. Thus, this trust escapes estate tax at both deaths: it is not taxed in the first spouse's estate because it was sheltered by the decedent's unified credit; it is not taxed in the surviving spouse's estate because he or she does not own it. Because such a trust is "sheltered" by the first spouse's unified credit, this type of trust is called a "credit shelter trust." It is also called a "bypass trust" because it "bypasses" the surviving spouse's taxable estate and goes (eventually) to a younger generation tax-free.

403(b) plans. These retirement plans are available only to tax-exempt employers. These plans are similar to qualified plans (QRP) in that the employee is not taxed currently on the plan contributions or earnings, but is taxed only as distributions are made to him. One difference is that the plan assets will be solely in the name of the employee, like an IRA. Another difference is that 403(b) money can be invested in only two types of investments: annuity contracts purchased by the employer and issued in the name of the employee; and "regulated investment companies" (mutual funds) held by a bank (or other approved institution) as custodian for the employee.

The main differences between 403(b) plans and other plans from a tax planning perspective are that a 403(b) plan distribution is never eligible for treatment as a "lump sum distribution" under § 402 (see Chapter 2) and the minimum distribution rules apply slightly differently. See "*Pre-1987 403(b) plan balances grandfathered...*," Chapter 10.

Fractional bequest. A bequest or gift expressed as a fraction or percentage of a fund. A typical fractional bequest: "I bequeath my estate in equal shares to my children surviving me." A fractional bequest may be in the form of a formula, for example: "The Trustee shall pay to the Marital Trust a portion of the trust property determined by multiplying the value of the trust (as of my date of death) by a fraction, the numerator of which is the smallest amount necessary (if left to my spouse) to eliminate the estate tax on my estate, and the denominator of which is the total value of the trust." See forms in Appendix B for samples.

Generation Skipping Transfer (GST) Tax. The estate tax applies to all assets transferred by a decedent at death. The decedent's estate pays estate taxes, and then distributes whatever is left to the beneficiaries of the estate—typically the decedent's children. In the normal course of events, the children themselves die some decades later and the same assets are taxed *again* before being passed along to the children's own children.

To avoid having assets be subject to estate taxes in every generation, a grandparent might leave assets directly to grandchildren (to "skip" the estate taxes at the child's generation level), or to a trust which would benefit the children's generation for their lifetimes but not be included in the children's estates. Such "generation skipping trusts" are an important and valid way to reduce the estate tax burden on a family. The generation skipping transfer (GST) tax (Chapter 13 of the Internal Revenue Code) allows each person to transfer up to $1 million (adjusted for cost of living increases after 1998) in the form of "generation skipping transfers," but imposes a 55% tax on generation skipping transfers that exceed that limit.

Grantor Trust. Generally speaking, a trust is a separate taxpayer. It files its own tax returns and pays income tax on its income at special trust rates. (The only exception is that income distributed to the beneficiaries of the trust will normally be taxed at the beneficiary's rate rather than the trust's rate.)

However, in certain cases, the Code ignores the trust as a taxable entity and treats the income and deductions as belonging directly to the "grantor" (the person who contributed the money to the trust). The most common example is a "revocable living trust," under which the grantor can take the assets back any time he wants to. The Code just ignores the trust during the grantor's life and treats its income and deductions as belonging directly to the grantor. There are many less obvious examples, and quite a number of complicated rules under §§ 671-677, under which part or all of a trust's income may be taxable directly to the grantor (or, under § 678, to the beneficiary). If an individual is treated as the owner of all of a trust's assets under these rules, transactions between the trust and the deemed owner are ignored for tax purposes because in effect they are regarded as "one taxpayer."

Keogh plan. Also called "H.R. 10 plans," these are simply QRPs adopted by self-employed persons. The name "Keogh plan" (which never appears in the Code) comes from the Congressman who sponsored legislation allowing the self-employed to have retirement plans. At one time, the Code made numerous distinctions between Keogh plans which covered "owner-employees" (sole proprietors and 10% partners) and QRPs adopted by corporations (or other QRPs which covered only "common-law employees"). While TEFRA '82 ended most differences, a few distinctions still remain, particularly in the areas of plan loans (not covered in this book) and lump sum distributions (see Chapter 2).

Marital deduction. An unlimited estate tax deduction is allowed for property left by the decedent to his surviving spouse. § 2056. To qualify for this "marital deduction," the property must be left to the spouse either outright or in certain particular forms of trust, one of which is called a "QTIP" trust. See Chapters 3 and 4.

Pecuniary bequest. A bequest or gift of a specific sum of money, for example: "I bequeath $10,000 to my son." A pecuniary gift may be in the form of a formula which produces a specific dollar amount, such as: "The Trustee shall pay to the

Marital Trust an amount of money or other property equal in value to the smallest amount necessary, if taken as a marital deduction, to eliminate the federal estate tax on my estate." This is in contrast to a fractional bequest (*q.v.*).

Power of appointment. A power given by one person (the original transferor) to another person (the power holder) to decide who will receive property. Example: A trust which provides that Wife will receive the income of the trust during her life, and at her death the principal will be distributed among Husband's issue "as Wife shall appoint by her will." Wife has a power of appointment over the principal. In this book, "power of appointment" refers to a power exercisable by a beneficiary (*i.e.*, in a non-fiduciary capacity). See also "**spray power**."

QTIP. A "qualified terminable interest property" trust is a special kind of trust that qualifies for the marital deduction. See Chapter 3.

Qualified Retirement Plan (QRP). A retirement plan which meets the requirements of § 401(a), and is sponsored by an employer. Types of QRPs include Keogh, 401(k), ESOP, profit sharing, defined benefit, target benefit, money purchase and stock bonus plans.

Specific bequest. A bequest of a specific item of property, for example "I leave my Honda Civic automobile to my father" or "I give and bequeath to my spouse any IRA or other retirement benefits payable to my estate."

Spray power. This is not an official term, but is used to describe a trustee's power to "spray" (or "sprinkle") income and/or principal of a trust among a class of beneficiaries. Example: "The Trustee shall pay the income and principal of the trust to my children for their health, education and welfare, in such amounts and proportions as the Trustee deems advisable." This is a type of "power of appointment."

INDEX

ORDER FORM
Save your book! Photocopy this form....

FORMS ON DISK

Now, all the forms in *Life and Death Planning for Retirement Benefits* plus several more that didn't fit into the book, are available ready to plug into your word processor and use in your practice. The checklist for meeting with clients, all beneficiary designation and election forms and related trust provisions, plus a "MRD conduit trust" are included, in 8.5 x 11 page size. Provided for your convenience to save typing, meant to be used in conjunction with the book, so no instructions are included. Format: WordPerfect 8.0 and Word 97, 3.5" disk.

Price: $39.95 (includes shipping and handling). Please add $2.00 Mass. sales tax for Mass. delivery.

Yes, please send me "Forms on Disk."	$ 39.95
For Mass. delivery, add $2.00 Mass. sales tax	$_____
TOTAL	$_____

Photocopy this order form, fill out the copy, and mail it to:

Ataxplan Publications
P.O. Box 1093-W
Boston, MA 02103-1093

Name: _____
Company name:_____
Address:_____
City: _____ State: _____ Zip: _____-_____
Telephone: (___) _____

Payment:
□ Check
□ Credit card: □ Visa □ Mastercard
Card number: _____
Name on card: _____Exp. date_____/__

Signature (required for credit card orders):

_____

Order Form
Save your book! Photocopy this form....

Life and Death Planning for Retirement Benefits

✳   Fax order: (419) 281-6883   @   Web orders: **www.ataxplan.com**

☎   Telephone orders: Call Toll Free: 1(800) 247-6553. Have your
       AMEX, Discover, VISA or MasterCard ready.

✉   Mail orders: Send check payable to "Book Masters" to:
                    BookMasters, Inc.
                    30 Amberwood Parkway
                    Ashland, OH 44805

**Please send me ____ copies of Life and Death Planning for
Retirement Benefits (3rd ed. 1999) at $89.95, plus $7.00 shipping,
each.** I understand that I may return any books for a full refund for any
reason, within 90 days.

Name: _____
Company name:_____
Address:_____
City: _____ State: _____ Zip: _____ - _____
Telephone: (___) _____

Sales tax:
Please add 5% sales tax for books shipped to a Massachusetts address.
Please add required sales tax for books shipped to an Ohio address.

Shipping: $7 charge is for UPS ground. For overnight service, inquire.

Payment:
□ Check payable to "BookMasters"
Credit card: □ Visa, □ Mastercard, □ AMEX, □ Discover
Card number: _____
Name on card: _____Exp. date_____/__

Signature (required for credit card orders):

_____

Call *toll free* and order now

IRA **Post-Death** Distributions

This chart covers two pages. Read each row across from left to right.

Beneficiary	Death *Before* Required Beginning Date
Non-Individual 1) Estate 2) Charity 3) Non-qualified trust	**"Five Year Rule"** Beneficiary must withdraw account balance at any time or times prior to Dec. 31 of 5th year after year of owner's death.
Non-Spouse Individual 1) Child(ren) 2) Grandchild(ren) 3) Other individual(s) 4) Qualified trust	1) **Five year rule** (see above). **OR** 2) Over **life expectancy** of oldest beneficiary; first distribution <u>must</u> be made by Dec. 31 of the year following the year of owner's death.
Spouse Individually [For extent, if any, to which a trust for the benefit of spouse can qualify for special spousal rules, see *"When is a trust for the spouse the same as the spouse?"* Chapter 6.]	1) **Five year rule** (see above); **or** 2) Over **life expectancy** of spouse beginning no later than 12/31 of the year owner would have turned 70½ (or, if later, year after owner's death); **or** 3) **Rollover** to spouse's own IRA

Notes: in general see Chapter 1 and (for spouse) Chapter 3

1. For requirements of a qualified trust see Chapter 6.
2. Required Beginning Date is April 1 of year following year account owner turns 70½ (not for Roth IRAs; see Chapter 5).
3. LE = Life expectancy. For meaning of "adjusted joint life expectancy," see *"P and S: 'split' or 'hybrid' method,"* Chapter 1.